RIGHTS OF LIGHT

THE MODERN LAW

RIGHTS OF LIGHT
THE MODERN LAW

Stephen Bickford-Smith BA(Oxon), FCIArb
Barrister and Chartered Arbitrator,
A Master of the Bench of the Inner Temple
4 Breams Buildings, London

and

Andrew Francis MA(Oxon)
Barrister of Lincoln's Inn
11 New Square, London

with

Elizabeth de Burgh Sidley BA, FRICS
Chartered Surveyor
Drivers Jonas, London

JORDANS
2000

Published by
Jordan Publishing Limited
21 St Thomas Street
Bristol BS1 6JS

British Library Cataloguing-in-Publication Data
A catalogue record for this book is available from the British Library.

ISBN 0 85308 487 4

Typeset by Mendip Communications Ltd, Frome, Somerset
Printed in Great Britain by MPG Books Ltd, Bodmin, Cornwall

Acknowledgements

Our thanks are due to: Roger J Smith, Fellow and Tutor in Law of Magdalen College, Oxford, who read and commented on those parts of the text dealing with the general law; Daniel Kolinsky, BA(Hons), Barrister of the Inner Temple for major contributions to the text of Chapter 15; Martin West of Jordans for his patience and encouragement; Mrs Janet Steel for typing the majority of the text; Matthew Craske who produced the drawings in Chapter 12; and the editorial staff at Jordans for thorough and painstaking proofreading and uncomplaining incorporation of 'Second Thoughts', which we often produced in manuscript.

In addition, we have to thank our respective spouses for the forbearance they have shown while this book was dominating the authors' lives.

As practising lawyers, we frequently seek informally the views of colleagues in our respective chambers, which have been generously given, and we would like to thank them collectively. We would also acknowledge the great debt we owe to those in the surveying profession who practise in the area of rights of light, and whose roles as advisers, negotiators, and experts have been, and continue to be, crucial.

STEPHEN BICKFORD-SMITH
ANDREW FRANCIS
February 2000

Foreword

I am pleased to be invited to write a foreword to this new work on rights of light. It promises to become the standard practitioners' handbook on this important subject. As the authors point out in their preface, it is a subject which can have a profound impact on the development potential of land. They point to the fact that there may be no physical evidence of the existence of such rights other than the presence of windows in buildings which receive light over other land. Rights to light may be acquired by 20 years' user without any requirement of registration, and qualify as 'overriding interests'. Such considerations make it of the first importance that lawyers advising their clients on potential developments should be fully aware of the principles involved.

The book offers a comprehensive treatment of the subject. It covers the definition and extent of rights to light, their acquisition, their extinguishment, and their regulation by deed. There is also an extensive treatment of litigation relating to rights to light, brought fully up to date to take into account the Woolf reforms. The section on the measurement and valuation of light contains a clear exposition of the difficult technical issues. I particularly welcome the practical approach to explaining the interaction of rights to light with planning law. Finally, the conveyancing issues arising in relation to rights to light are fully examined.

In its Seventh Programme, approved in 1999, the Law Commission announced a new project for the examination of easements and analogous rights, with a view to their reform and rationalisation. This will be a major undertaking, and it is unlikely that it will yield legislative change for some years. In the meantime, the practitioner could have no better guide than this book. It will also provide a valuable starting point for our own work on this aspect of the law of easements. I strongly commend it to the legal world.

ROBERT CARNWATH
The Law Commission
21 January 2000

Preface

The purpose of this book is to give a full account of the modern law relating to rights to light. The authors believe that this has not been attempted since the appearance in 1911 of the now long-forgotten *Treatise upon the Law of Light* by R. Nicholson Combe.

For many reasons, the time is right for a book dedicated solely to rights to light. At a time when the pace of economic and social change is accelerating and the world is increasingly seen as a single market-place, redevelopment of the built environment is becoming more necessary and more time-constrained to accommodate the exigencies of business and residential occupiers and their financial backers. Rights to light issues often arise in the redevelopment context. The raison d'être of rights to light is to protect the light received through windows in existing buildings from unreasonable interference by new buildings.

At this point, two peculiarities of rights to light as easements are important. First, there may be no physical evidence of their existence other than the presence of windows in buildings which receive light over other land. This is in contrast, for example, to a right of way, where it would normally be possible to discern the existence of the way both from its physical presence and from its use. Secondly, rights to light (like other easements) can be acquired in various ways. But rights to light, unlike other rights, can come into existence through 20 years' actual user, whether or not as of right, unless they are exercised by written permission. Such rights are, for land registration purposes, overriding interests, and hence are valid whether or not they are registered on the titles of dominant and servient owners.

For developers, the emergence of claims for rights to light over their land in favour of nearby buildings can, indeed, come as an unwelcome surprise, particularly if the project is already under way. There are, therefore, sound practical reasons for lawyers concerned with conveyancing and development to be aware of the problems of rights to light; this alone justifies a book dedicated to the subject.

A further reason for a fresh look at the law in this area is that it is in a state of constant development and change. Rights to light are affected directly by few Acts of Parliament: they form part of that body of the common law going back for many hundreds of years which recognises, as legal interests in land, not only complete ownership and leases but a diverse collection of other rights. This apparent antiquity, however, can be deceptive. The interface between the right to light and other areas of the law, often of more recent origin, raises important issues. For example, the relationship between rights to light and the law relating to town and country planning poses interesting riddles for lawyers and planners. Light obstruction notices, under the Rights of Light Act 1959, can involve judicial review issues. The remedies available to a person whose rights to light have allegedly been infringed involve issues on the grant of equitable remedies by way of injunctions and damages, which depend heavily on recent and ongoing developments in other legal contexts.

There is, therefore, a need to synthesise a number of diverse elements to cover the area satisfactorily. This we have sought to do.

Practitioners will be well aware that, both in negotiations and legal proceedings, issues of valuation of loss of light are of great importance. Detailed treatment of them is, therefore, essential and so a chapter on valuation has been contributed by a chartered surveyor with experience of both the legal and valuation issues which arise.

It is perhaps reasonable to ask whether rights to light ought to continue to exist, or at least be capable of being acquired (as at present) by prescription. There are two objections to the present law, neither of which is wholly unjustified. The first is that it skews the law too far in favour of the owners and occupiers of existing buildings, a kind of common law 'nimbyism'. A narrower objection is that by allowing rights to light to be acquired by 20 years' user, without any requirement of registration at the Land Registry, since they qualify as 'overriding interests', both the uncertainty of titles and difficulty of developing sites in urban areas are unnecessarily increased.

As to the latter point, the Law Commission and the Land Registry have recently reviewed the land registration system. The results of their investigations have been published in a document whose grandiose title *Land Registration for the Twenty-First Century* (Law Com 254) belies the thoroughness of its analysis of the existing land registration system. However, whilst its authors acknowledge the criticism of the existing system that easements acquired by prescription (as overriding interests) may be undiscoverable from searching the registering title, they reject significant changes to the present system in this regard, although there are suggestions governing the extinguishment of easements, and for registration of those which are expressly granted or contracted to be granted. It seems, therefore, that the present law can safely be regarded as unlikely to be changed soon.

By contrast, in other countries where common law applies, more radical solutions have been adopted. In the USA, there is no general recognition of a right to light in State law or Federal law. The courts there have taken the view that rights to light and air ought not to be recognised because they would inhibit building and expansion, although, in practice, light and views may be protected in various ways. For instance, the written grant of an easement of light may be recognised or local statute may restrict buildings in various ways, and where an area of land is sub-divided, or forms part of a planned unit development, there may be covenants, conditions and restrictions ('CC and Rs') embodied in a document which is issued to each owner providing for restrictions on the use of their properties. In practice, light issues relating to the construction of major buildings in down-town locations are governed by local ordinances which include provisions for protecting light received by existing buildings.

In New Zealand and Australia, the law has been changed by statute to restrict the acquisition of rights to light. In New Zealand, Part IX of the Property Law Act 1952 prohibits the acquisition of a right to light or air except as provided by that Act. The only rights to light or air which are recognised are those made by deed (or in appropriate statutory form), and which are duly registered within 12 months from the date of execution by the grantor, and which limit and define accurately 'the area or parcel of land on, to, or over which the uninterrupted access of light or air, or light and air, is intended to be provided for'. This system, which has been in force in various forms since 1894, addresses the twin problems of unreasonable restriction on development which may result from prescriptive rights to light and uncertainty as to the existence of such rights.

Likewise, in Australia the creation of easements of light arising by way of prescription has been abolished by legislation, and thus such rights can be acquired only by express or implied grant. Generally, local statutory provisions require that the existence of easements be registered in relation to the dominant and servient land. New South Wales requires that land benefited and burdened be identified in the instrument creating the easement if it is to be enforceable against an owner of the burdened land other than the original party to the arrangement.

Further, in some States in Australia, jurisdiction is conferred on the relevant Supreme Court, upon the application of any person interested in the land, to modify, or extinguish easements on certain specified grounds. These grounds include:

(a) where the easement ought to be deemed obsolete, or its continued existence would impede the reasonable use of the servient land without securing a practical benefit to the persons entitled to the easement;
(b) where those entitled to the easement have agreed to the easement being wholly or partly extinguished, or may reasonably be considered to have abandoned the easement wholly or partly; and
(c) where the extinguishment would not substantially injure those entitled to the easement.

The provisions find an echo in those of s 84 of the (English) Law of Property Act 1925 relating to the variation and discharge of restrictive covenants, although, once again, there is no equivalent provision in English law.

Possibly, the time may have arisen for some fresh thought to be given as to whether some changes are needed to the English law on rights to light to meet modern needs and avoid the uncertainty and expensive disputes which are endemic in the law as it stands at present.

A more fundamental issue may be whether rights to light serve any useful purpose at a time when the development of land is so closely controlled by town and country planning legislation. Given, or so the argument runs, that planning is carried out in the public interest by democratically elected local bodies, what need is there of private rights which may conflict with the public interest? The authors would not accept this suggestion: those who are closely involved in planning law are conscious that its practical application does not always live up to its aspirations in terms of securing a consistent pattern of decision-making. More fundamentally, it is precisely because planning law operates in the *public* interest that there needs to be independent protection of *private* rights. These rights should not be expropriated by stealth, and any such attempt could raise issues under the Human Rights Act 1998.

The appearance of a Consultation Paper from the Department of the Environment, Transport and the Regions on the problems posed by high hedges and their detrimental effects on light to buildings and gardens, suggests that the law relating to rights to light may be on the move, although any new legislation seems some way off. The Consultation Paper is covered in Chapter 2.

We have endeavoured to state the law as at 1 February 2000, save where it has been possible to incorporate late material at proof stage.

STEPHEN BICKFORD-SMITH
ANDREW FRANCIS
February 2000

Contents

Table of Cases

References are to paragraph numbers.

Table of Statutes

References are to paragraph numbers.

Table of Statutory Instruments

References are to paragraph numbers.

Town and Country Planning (Use Classes) Order 1988, SI 1988/764 13.4

Town and Country Planning (General Permitted Development) Order 1995, SI 1995/418 13.4

Sch 2, Part 2 7.8

Town and Country Planning (General Development Procedure) Order 1995, SI 1995/419

Art 8 13.19

Table of Abbreviations

BRE	Building Research Establishment
CCR	County Court Rules 1981
CPR	Civil Procedure Rules 1998
DoE	Department of the Environment, Transport and the Regions
ECHR	European Court of Human Rights
EFZ	equivalent first zone
Lord Cairns' Act	Chancery Amendment Act 1858
LPA	local planning authority
LRA 1925	Land Registration Act 1925
LRR 1925	Land Registration Rules 1925
the 1832 Act	Prescription Act 1832
the 1959 Act	Rights of Light Act 1959
the 1998 Act	Human Rights Act 1998
the Commission	European Commission of Human Rights
the Secretary of State	the Secretary of State for the Environment, Transport and the Regions
PPGs	Planning Policy Guidance notes
RSC	Rules of the Supreme Court 1965
UDP	Unitary Development Plan
YP	Years' Purchase

Chapter 1
The Property Law Context

EASEMENTS IN PROPERTY LAW

1.1 Rights to light are an example of those rights known to the law as easements. An easement is defined in *Halsbury's Laws of England*[1] as:

> '. . . a right annexed to land to utilise other land of different ownership in a particular manner (not involving the taking of any part of the natural produce of that land or any part of its soil) or to prevent the owner of the other land from utilising his land in a particular manner.'

An easement has been said judicially to be 'a familiar creature of English land law'.[2]

1.2 This definition applies to an easement of light as to others. One point of importance should, however, be stressed at the outset. A right to light can exist *only* in favour of *defined apertures* in *buildings*. There is no right recognised by law to receive light falling on unbuilt land. This distinguishes rights to light from many other easements such as, for example, rights of way, which can exist for the benefit of land whether or not it is built on.

> 'The principle . . . I conceive to be that, until defined and confined, there is . . . as in light . . . in its natural state, no subject matter capable of being the subject of a lawful grant, nor from the very nature of the thing can there be any definite occupation or enjoyment'.[3]

The reason for the rule is that an easement is a property right which must be sufficiently definite to be capable of being the subject of a grant, and

> 'Although the general access of light from the heavens to the earth is indefinite, the light which enters a building by a particular aperture does and may pass over the adjoining land in a course which, though not visibly defined is really certain and, in that sense, definite'.[4]

1.3 The essential idea behind the concept of a right to light, as with other easements, is a *right over land belonging to another*, falling short of full ownership or possession. In Roman (and Scots) law the analogous concept is that of the servitude, a burden of land in favour of another. From the Roman law derive the English expressions *dominant owner* (from *dominus* = Lord, Master), the person entitled to exercise the easement and *servient owner* (from *servus* = slave, servant), the owner of the land which is subject to the easement. The land benefiting from the easement is generally called the *dominant tenement*

---

1 4th edn vol 14 para 1.
2 Per Hoffmann LJ in *Willies-Williams v National Trust* (1993) 65 P&CR 359 at 361, CA.
3 *Dalton v Angus* (1881) 6 App Cas 740 at 759 per Beld J. See Chapter 2 at **2.3**.
4 Ibid at 794 per Lord Selborne LC.

(tenement being an old word for a parcel of land) and the land subject to the easement the *servient tenement*.

1.4 The theoretical legal basis of easements (including that of light) is based on legal concepts of considerable antiquity whose relevance it is sometimes tempting to question. However, issues relating to the existence, creation, and transmission of rights to light do frequently turn on general concepts of real property law. No apology, therefore, is made for the following brief summary of the relevant salient features of the area.

1.5 Easements are a species of what the law terms 'incorporeal hereditaments'. In *Re Christmas*,[1] Cotton LJ, citing Blackstone's classic *Commentaries on the Law of England*, defined an incorporeal hereditament in the following words:

> 'a right issuing out of a thing corporate, whether real or personal, or concerning or annexed to, or exercisable within, the same. It is not the thing corporate itself, which may consist in lands, houses, jewels, or the like; but something collateral thereto, as a rent issuing out of these lands or houses, or an office relating to those jewels.'

In another passage, Blackstone then said:

> 'Their existence is merely in idea and abstracted contemplation; though their effects and profits may be frequently objects of our bodily senses.'

1.6 The term 'hereditament' (from late Latin *haereditas* = inheritance) refers to property which devolved to the heirs at law of the owner, ie real property as opposed to personal property which could be disposed of by will. For present purposes, it may be equated to an interest in land.

1.7 Incorporeal hereditaments are, in law, contrasted with 'corporeal' hereditaments; medieval lawyers drew a distinction between interests in land giving rights to full possession which were said to be 'corporeal' and other such interests. Ownership of a 'corporeal' hereditament gave control over the *corpus* (body) of the land. An incorporeal hereditament gave lesser, intangible, rights over land. Modern technology would use the term 'proprietary interest' to describe a corporeal hereditament.[2]

1.8 Incorporeal hereditaments include both easements and profits. Easements are traditionally divided between positive and negative. Positive easements are those which entitle the dominant owner either to do some act on the servient land, such as exercise a right of way over it, or an act elsewhere than on the servient land, but which affects its enjoyment, for example to carry on activities which would otherwise amount to a nuisance.[3] Negative easements require the servient owner to abstain from certain activities or uses on his land. A right of light is a negative easement, since it obliges the servient owner to restrain from

---

1 (1886) 33 ChD 332.

2 For a recent case on the distinction between corporeal and incorporeal rights, see *Brackenbank Lodge Ltd v Peart and Others* (1993) 67 P&CR 249, CA (concerned with whether stint holdings were corporeal or incorporeal hereditaments).

3 *Sturges v Bridgman* (1879) 11 ChD 852.

erecting buildings on his land which obstruct the light received by the dominant tenement.

1.9 The category of rights over land which are capable in law of constituting easements is wide, and still growing and adapting to changes in economic and social conditions affecting land use.[1] However, as will be seen below this does not mean that the incidents of established types of easements will be extended by the courts simply because it is reasonable or desirable to do so. Further, the courts have declined to recognise certain proposed species of easement on various grounds, either because they lack precedent or because they are insufficiently clear or too widely restrictive of the servient owners' rights to be accepted:

> 'Incidents of a novel kind cannot be devised, and attached to property, at the fancy or caprice of any owner.'[2]

1.10 A right to light, like other easements, is said to be an 'appurtenant' incorporeal hereditament. This means simply that, however created, it is annexed to land. One cannot enjoy a right to light *in gross*, except as an incident of ownership of an interest in the land to which the right to light belongs.[3]

1.11 Although easements are of ancient origin, the importance of such matters as rights to light and rights of way to modern property transactions is obvious. Rights to light remain essentially an area of judge-made law. No statutory definition of a 'right to light' exists, and it is therefore necessary to consider the decided cases to establish the nature, extent, and limitation of such rights. Recognition of the fact that easements are interests in land is provided by the Law of Property Act 1925 and the Land Registration Act 1925. By s 205(1)(ix) of the Law of Property Act 1925, 'land' is defined as including easements. By s 1(2)(a) of the same Act, as an interest in land, an easement is required to be:

> 'for an interest equivalent to an estate in fee simple absolute in possession or a term of years absolute.'

The Land Registration Act 1925, s 3(xi) defines land in terms which includes easements. By s 187(1) of the Law of Property Act 1925:

> 'Where an easement, right or privilege for a legal estate is created, it shall enure for the benefit of the land to which it is intended to be annexed.'

The effect of this is that, once a legal easement is created, it attaches to the dominant land even if the actual interest benefiting from the easement at any time is equitable only.[4]

---

1 In *London & Blenheim Estates v Ladbroke Retail Parks Ltd* [1993] 1 All ER 307, a right to park vehicles was recognised as an easement. The issue was not considered on appeal (see [1993] 4 All ER 157, CA).

2 See *Ackroyd v Smith* (1850) 10 CB 164 at 188 per Cresswell J citing Lord Bingham CJ in *Keppell v Bailey* (1834) 2 My&K 517 at 535.

3 *Rangeley v Midland Railway Co* (1868) LR 3 Ch App 306 at 310–311; *King v David Allen & Sons Billposting Ltd* [1916] 2 AC 54; *London & Blenheim Estates Ltd v Ladbroke Retail Parks Ltd* [1993] 4 All ER 157; see also **1.7**.

4 See Barnsley 'Equitable Easements – Sixty Years On' (1999) 115 LQR 84.

1.12 The express grant of a legal easement requires and can be effected only by deed.[1] In the case of registered land, when both dominant and servient titles are registered, an easement takes effect in equity only until registered.[2] Where the servient title alone is registered, the existence of the easement requires protection by entry of a notice against the servient title. A legal easement passes on transfer of the land to which it is appurtenant, without any express words, and irrespective of the provisions of s 62 of the Law of Property Act 1925.[3] A legal easement cannot be overreached, and does not require registration under the Land Charges Act 1972. In the case of registered land, a legal easement of light is an 'overriding interest' by virtue of s 70(1)(a) of the Land Registration Act 1925.[4]

1.13 A legal estate is not capable of existing or being created in an undivided share of land.[5] However, s 187(2) of the Law of Property Act 1925 provides that:

> 'Nothing in the Act affects the right of a person to acquire, hold or exercise an easement ... over or in relation to land for a legal estate in common with any other person, or the power of creating or carrying such an easement.'

There is therefore no problem about several different dominant tenements, or the union of separate interests in the dominant tenement, enjoying and being granted legal easements of light over the same servient tenement.

1.14 Easements which do not satisfy the requirements of legal easements will take effect in equity only. Such easements differ from legal easements principally in the extent to which they affect third parties. Equity would not grant equitable remedies to enforce easements which did not enjoy legal title, except against those who acquired their land with notice of the equitable rights, and whose conscience was thereby affected. An example of an equitable easement is one granted otherwise than by deed.[6] The term 'equitable easement' is, however, not entirely clear, as the Law of Property Act 1925 and the Land Registration Act 1925 are not consistent in their terminology. The expression was not in current use as a term of art when those Acts came into force. The primary meaning seems to be an equitable right to a legal easement.[7]

1.15 In the case of unregistered land, the term 'equitable easement' has been interpreted (for the purpose of determining whether such an easement is void for non-registration) as limited to interests which prior to 1 January 1926 could have been created or conveyed at law, but after that date take effect only in equity.[8] Equitable easements created after 1925 are void against a purchaser for money or

1 Law of Property Act 1925, s 52(1).
2 Land Registration Act 1925, ss 19(2) and 22(2).
3 See *Godwin v Schweppes Ltd* [1902] 1 Ch 926. For creation of rights of light under s 62 of the Law of Property Act 1925, see Chapter 5 at **5.21**.
4 See, generally, Chapter 14.
5 Law of Property Act 1925, s 1(6); Land Registration Act 1925, s 3(viii), (ix).
6 *McManus v Cooke* (1887) 35 ChD 681.
7 See Barnsley 'Equitable Easements – Sixty Years On' 115 LQR 89.
8 See Ruoff and Roper *Registered Conveyancing* (Sweet & Maxwell, 1997) at para 6.06. *Ives (ER) Investments Ltd v High* [1967] 1 All ER 504, CA at 508C–F.

money's worth unless registered as a land charge before completion.[1] This is so even if the purchaser has actual notice.[2] When title to the land is registered, s 70 of the Land Registration Act 1925 excludes from the actual definition of overriding interests (which includes legal easements)[3] 'equitable easements required to be protected by notice on the register'.[4] However, in *Celsteel Ltd v Alton House Holdings Ltd*,[5] it was held that such an easement constitutes a right 'enjoyed [with land] ... which adversely affects registered land', and was by r 258 of the Land Registration Rules 1925 an overriding interest. The basis of the decision is that in the case of registered land the clear intention of the Land Registration Act 1925 is that equitable easements should be protected either by entry on the register or as overriding interests.[6] This decision was followed by the Court of Appeal decision in *Thatcher v Douglas*.[7] It has attracted some criticism as creating effectively different interests in registered land and unregistered land, and as not reading the relevant rule in the context of its statutory antecedents.[8] However, the position seems well established. It follows that whenever an easement is expressly granted or reserved, it will be unnecessary to protect it by registration, even though it is a registered disposition, provided that it is openly exercised and enjoyed with the land to which it is appurtenant.[9]

1.16 In many situations, the grant of an easement may arise by implication, for example under the rule in *Wheeldon v Burrows*,[10] or by virtue of s 62 of the Law of Property Act 1925.[11] By the Land Registration Rules 1925, r 258,[12] 'rights, privileges, and appurtenances appertaining or reputed to appertain to land or demised, occupied, or enjoyed therewith or reputed or known as part or parcel of or appurtenant thereto, which adversely affect registered land, are overriding interests'. Thus such rights do not require registration. This provision extends to validating equitable easements which could otherwise be void for non-registration. Thus in *Celsteel Ltd v Alton House Holdings Ltd*,[13] it was held that a right of way granted by a lease which should have been, but had not been, registered was an overriding interest. In the case of easements acquired by

---

1 Land Charges Act 1972, s 4(6).
2 Law of Property Act 1925, s 199(1)(i); *Midland Bank Trust Co Ltd v Green* [1981] 1 All ER 153, HL.
3 See **1.12**.
4 See Land Registration Act 1925, s 70(1)(a), set out at Appendix 1.
5 [1985] 2 All ER 562 reversed on other grounds not material to this point, see [1986] 1 All ER 608, CA.
6 See Ruoff and Roper *Registered Conveyancing* (Sweet & Maxwell, 1997) at para 6–07.
7 (1996) 146 NLJ 282.
8 See Creed 'Equitable Easements and the Pitiless Purchaser' *The Conveyancer* (1999) at p 6.
9 See Law Commission Report No 254 *Land Registration for the 21st Century*, paras 5.9, 5.24. The Law Commission provisionally recommends that all easements should be overriding interests except where they have been expressly granted or arise from a contract to grant such a right expressly, and that the Land Registration Rules 1925 be revoked.
10 (1879) 12 ChD 31.
11 See Chapter 5 at **5.8–5.21**.
12 See Appendix 2.
13 [1985] 2 All ER 562. See also **1.15**.

prescription,[1] these may be acquired in favour of registered land in the same way as if the land were not registered.[2] Until such a right has been declared by a court to exist, it cannot be said to amount to more than a simple claim. Once established, however, it should be mentioned in the title documents and (in the case of registered land) noted against the title of the servient tenement.[3] A procedure also exists under which the Land Registry may note the existence of a prescriptive easement against the servient title without a court hearing, if its existence can be demonstrated to the Land Registry.[4]

THE ESSENTIALS OF EASEMENTS

1.17 We have seen that rights to light are a species of negative easement, appurtenant to the dominant tenement over the servient tenement. The courts have evolved a number of tests for establishing whether the rights claimed in a particular case contain the necessary ingredients of an easement.

1.18 There are four requirements to be satisfied before an easement (including a right to light) can be shown to exist. These are the following:

(1) there must be a dominant and a servient tenement;
(2) the easement must accommodate the dominant tenement;
(3) the dominant and servient tenements must be in separate ownership;
(4) the easement must be capable of forming the subject-matter of a grant.

Each requirement will now be considered in detail.

1. There must be a dominant and a servient tenement

1.19 The first requirement means that there must be separate pieces of land which respectively benefit from the easement and over which the easement is enjoyed. It is not therefore possible for the same piece of land both to enjoy and be burdened by the same easement, although it is of course possible, and indeed not uncommon, for two separate parcels of land each to enjoy easements over the other. For example, two houses may share a driveway one half of which lies within the curtilage of each property, each property enjoying an easement of way over the half belonging to the other.

2. The easement must accommodate the dominant tenement

1.20 Turning to the second requirement, easements are rights appurtenant to land, and hence cannot exist unless they benefit a particular area of land. It is, therefore, not possible to create an easement recognised by the law in gross, ie as a freestanding right, not appurtenant to land. For example, it would not be

1 See Chapter 6.
2 Land Registration Act 1925, s 75(5); Land Registration Rules 1925, r 250(1).
3 Land Registration Rules 1925, r 302.
4 Ibid, r 250.

possible to create an easement of light, nor a right of way, which did not benefit any particular land (where there is no servient tenement). It is therefore said that:

> 'It is trite law that there could be no easement in gross'.[1]

1.21 This principle is illustrated by *London and Blenheim Estates v Ladbroke Retail Parks Ltd*,[2] a case concerning the purported grant of a right to park vehicles. In that case a transfer of land to the plaintiff contained the grant of an easement entitling the plaintiff to park on certain land retained by the transferor. The transfer further provided that if the plaintiff purchased other land and gave notice to the transferor within 5 years of the original transfer, such other land would (provided the plaintiff was the owner of the originally transferred land at the date of the notice) also benefit from the same easement. The plaintiff purchased additional land. The transferor then sold the retained land (the servient tenement), and it subsequently vested in the defendants. Subsequent to the sale of the servient land by the transferor, the plaintiff gave notice under the terms of the original transfer to it that the other land it had purchased subsequent to the original transfer should benefit from the easement of parking on the land retained by the transferor. The plaintiff sought to establish that it had an enforceable easement against the defendants. The claim was rejected on the ground that at the date of the original transfer to the plaintiff there was no identified dominant tenement (apart from the original land transferred to the plaintiff), and, therefore, the terms of the original transfer did not create an enforceable option to create an easement. Since the servient land had been disposed of by the transferor before the dominant tenement had been created, the terms of the original transfer had not created an enforceable option. The court rejected a further argument that an easement was created when the plaintiff gave notice of acquisition of the further land, on the ground that by the time such notice was given the grantor had disposed of the servient land.

1.22 Although an easement must benefit the dominant tenement, the dominant and servient tenements need not be contiguous. In the case of rights to light, frequently the dominant and servient tenements are separated by land belonging to a third party, or a public or private road. The importance of the requirement is that the easement must directly benefit the dominant tenement. So, for example, if in the case of a right to light the dominant tenement in fact receives no light over the servient tenement the purported creation of an easement in favour of the dominant tenement will be invalid. There must be some connection between the existence of the easement and normal enjoyment of the dominant tenement.[3]

---

1 See *London and Blenheim Estates Ltd v Ladbroke Retail Parks Ltd* [1993] 4 All ER 157 at 162h per Peter Gibson LJ, citing *Rangeley v Midland Railway Co* (1868) LR 3 Ch App 306 at 310–311; see also **1.10**. See further *Voice v Bell* [1993] 68 P&CR 441.

2 [1993] 4 All ER 157, CA.

3 *Re Ellenborough Park* [1956] Ch 131 at 153.

3. The dominant and servient tenements must be in separate ownership

1.23 As to the third requirement, it is well established that an easement cannot exist in circumstances where the same person both owns and occupies the 'dominant' and 'servient' tenements, on the ground that no person can have a right against himself.[1]

1.24 However, where the owner of a piece of land disposes of part of it and retains the remainder himself, or disposes of the whole to different owners by simultaneous or near-simultaneous conveyances, rights to light may arise by implication of law, or under s 62 of the Law of Property Act 1925, in favour of the purchaser of a piece of land having buildings on it, against the vendor. Thus if a vendor owns land with buildings on it, and divides the land into two plots, A and B, and sells plot A, on which there are buildings with windows receiving light across plot B, the purchaser may acquire a right to light in favour of these windows.

1.25 Acquisition in this way may also occur under the rule in *Wheeldon v Burrows*,[2] whose application to rights to light is well established.[3] All these methods of acquiring rights to light are reviewed in Chapter 5.

1.26 It should, of course, be noted that a right to light cannot arise in this way unless either the vendor retains the land *over which* the windows receive light or disposes of his entire land simultaneously. Thus, if in the example above the vendor sells plot B before plot A, the windows on plot A's buildings will enjoy no right to light over plot B. The position where simultaneous dispositions of both plots take place is considered in Chapter 3.

1.27 It is sometimes said that although a person has no easement over his own land, there can exist quasi-easements. If, whilst plots A and B are owned by the common owner in the above example, the buildings on plot A actually enjoy light through the windows of the buildings on plot A over plot B (albeit that plots A and B have not yet been conceived of or marked out) this enjoyment is capable of ripening into a true easement when plot A is laid out and sold.

1.28 It can sometimes be difficult to distinguish between quasi-easements and the enjoyment by a landowner of the totality of his land arising simply from the fact that he owns and has access to all of it, which does not create rights when part is sold off. If, for example, a vendor sells part of his garden, in which he was accustomed to walk for recreation, the purchaser will obviously not have the right to wander round the part retained by the vendor. There must be some actual

---

1 *Metropolitan Railway Co v Fowler* (1892) 1 QB 165; *Attorney General of Southern Nigeria v John Holt & Co (Liverpool) Ltd* [1915] AC 599 at 617–618, PC. But note the effect of occupation by tenants, see Chapter 6 at **6.30**.

2 (1879) 12 ChD 31. See Chapter 5 at **5.10–5.20**.

3 *Swansborough v Coventry* (1832) 9 Bing 305; *Leech v Schweder* (1874) 9 Ch App 463 per Mellish LJ at 472.

enjoyment of the part subsequently sold off, to which the quasi-easement relates.[1]

1.29 Thus in the case of rights to light, if in the example given at **1.24** the windows in the buildings on plot A had been at the time of sale permanently bricked up, or obscured by a high hedge or wall from plot B, no quasi-easement would exist, and hence no easement of light could arise on sale.

1.30 Where a building is occupied by a tenant of the owner, there is an important difference between an easement of light and other easements, by virtue of s 3 of the Prescription Act 1832.[2] In cases other than rights to light, a tenant of a landowner cannot by long-use enjoyment acquire an easement against his own landlord or another tenant of his landlord, since the law considers the occupation of the tenant to be that of the landlord.[3] It is a principle of common-law prescription that the user must be by or on behalf of the owner of a fee simple interest in land against another fee simple owner.[4] However, this rule does *not* apply to the acquisition of easements of light. Section 3 of the Prescription Act 1832 provides for the acquisition of a right to light by 20 years' *actual* enjoyment. It follows from this that a tenant can acquire an easement of light by prescription against both his landlord and another tenant of the same landlord.

1.31 This constitutes an important exception to the general rule that easements cannot be acquired except where the dominant and servient tenements are owned and occupied by different persons.[5] Leases frequently make provision to avoid the consequence.[6]

4. The easement must be capable of forming the subject matter of a grant

1.32 The fourth requirement derives from the fact that the basis of the law of easements is a grant by one landowner to another of a recognised right over land capable of substituting as a legal estate.[7] Some doubt was expressed in the past as to whether a right to light, being a negative easement,[8] can properly be regarded as the subject of a grant. In *Birmingham Dudley and District Banking Co v Ross*,[9] Lindley LJ regarded a right to light as more in the nature of a restrictive covenant.[10] However, the position now seems to be well established that a right

---

1 *Long v Gowlett* [1923] 2 Ch 177; *Sovmots Investments Ltd v Secretary of State for the Environment* [1979] AC 144; *Payne v Inwood* (1997) 74 P&CR 42.

2 See Appendix 1.

3 *Kilgour v Gaddes* [1904] 1 KB 457.

4 *Simmons v Dobson* [1991] 4 All ER 25, CA.

5 See *Frewen v Philipps* (1861) 11 CBNS 449; *Mitchell v Cantrill* [1887] 37 ChD 56; *Morgan v Fear* [1907] AC 425; *Mallam v Rose* [1915] 2 Ch 222. See Chapter 6 at **6.17**.

6 See Chapter 7 at **7.4–7.6**.

7 See **1.11**.

8 See **1.36**.

9 (1888) 38 ChD 295.

10 Cf *Hall v Litchfield Brewery Co* (1880) 49 LJ Ch 665 per Fry J.

to light does satisfy this requirement. This was expressly recognised by Lord Selborne LC in *Dalton v Angus*.[1]

OTHER CATEGORISATIONS OF EASEMENTS

1.33 Easements are divided into *continuous* and *non-continuous* easements depending on whether the easement confers a right to do something of a continuous and constant nature. A non-continuous easement is one where enjoyment is of its nature only possible from time to time, by a series of acts. Easements of light come into the category of continuous easements, as do easements of the right to receive water through a water course, and (perhaps anomalously) a right of way if exercised over a formed road.[2]

1.34 The distinction was at one time of importance in conveyancing, since upon severance of tenements easements used as a necessity, or in their nature continuous, would pass by implication of law without any words of grant, but easements which were discontinuous did not pass unless the owner by appropriate language showed an intention that they should pass.[3] However, the importance of the distinction has been lessened by s 62 of the Law of Property Act 1925.[4]

1.35 It remains of importance to the question whether an easement may be acquired under the rule in *Wheeldon v Burrows*,[5] but since it is well established that an easement of light can be so acquired the point is not generally relevant to rights to light. It is possible to conceive of circumstances where a claimed easement of light might fail to be 'continuous', for example in the case of a temporary window aperture formed in a building or the intermittent use of a doorway for admission of light.[6] In *Harris v De Pinna*,[7] for example, the Court of Appeal rejected a claim for a right to light to an open-sided timber shed on the ground that:

> 'it will not do in order to establish a right, to show that though at some time light did not come in through a particular access, at other times it did, and that sometimes it came in through one and sometimes through another opening, which was there in the structure of the building, which would admit light.'[8]

---

1 (1881) 6 App Cas 740 at 794.
2 *Watts v Kelson* (1870) LR 6 Ch App 166 at 174 per Mellish LJ. See also *Brown v Alabaster* (1887) 37 ChD 490.
3 *Polden v Bastard* (1865) LR 1 QB 156 at 161 per Erle CJ.
4 Considered in Chapter 5 at **5.21**. See also Appendix 1.
5 (1879) 12 ChD 31.
6 See, further, Chapter 4 at **4.13**.
7 (1886) 33 ChD 238.
8 Per Cotton LJ at p 257.

The position as regards which apertures in buildings may enjoy rights to light, and how the enjoyment of light may be inferred to have been abandoned, are considered elsewhere in this book.[1]

1.36 A further division of easements is into *positive* and *negative* easements. As has been seen, an easement must be capable of being the subject-matter of a grant.[2] The right to do any positive act (unless illegal or contrary to public policy) can be granted. There is no reason why such a grant may not by implication allow the grantee to damage the servient land. For example, the grant of a right to mine under land may allow the grantee to let down the surface.[3] On the other hand, negative rights (in strict analysis immunities) are not a concept the law regards as often capable of being granted. Considered from the point of view of whether it can be granted, a right to light is conceptually different. For what the servient owner is granting in effect is not a positive right, but an immunity against further actions by him on his own land. Hence, in many cases, it has been suggested that a right to light, being such a negative easement, cannot derive from a grant, actual or notional.[4] On the other hand, there are many authoritative pronouncements to the contrary, the most authoritative being that of Lord Selborne in the House of Lords in *Dalton v Angus*,[5] where he said:

> 'Some of the learned judges [ie those who were summoned to give their opinion] appear to think otherwise, and to doubt whether it could be the subject of grant. For that doubt I am unable to perceive any sufficient foundation. Littledale J., in *Moore v Rawson*, spoke of the right to *light* as being properly the subject, not of grant, but of covenant. If he had said (which he did not), that a right to light could not be granted, in the sense of the word "grant" necessary for prescription, I should have doubted the correctness of the opinion, notwithstanding the great learning of that eminent Judge . . . the light which enters a building by particular apertures does and must pass over the adjoining land in a course which, though not visibly defined, is really certain and, in that sense, definite. Why should it be impossible for the owner of the adjoining land to grant a right of unobstructed passage over it for that light in that course?'

1.37 The issue is, in any event, of less practical importance since s 3 of the Prescription Act 1832 came into force.[6] This enables a prescriptive right to light to be established by 20 years' actual user. Formerly, to establish an easement by prescription, it was necessary to establish either common law prescription, involving (at least in theory) use from 1189 or prescription under the doctrine of lost modern grant, including a (fictional) grant of the right in question. Under the regime, the question of whether or not a right to light was capable of being the

---

1 See Chapter 4.

2 See **1.18**.

3 *Rowbotham v Wilson* (1860) 8 HLC 348.

4 *Moore v Rawson* (1824) 3 B&C 332; *Rowbotham v Wilson* (1860) 8 HLC 348; *Scott v Pape* (1886) 31 ChD 554 per Bowen LJ at 571; *Birmingham, Dudley and District Banking Co v Ross* (1888) 38 ChD 295; *Hall v Lichfield Brewery Co* (1880) 49 LJ Ch 565.

5 (1881) 6 App Cas 760 at 794. For other cases to the same effect, see *Booth v Alcock* (1873) 8 Ch App 663; *Leech v Schweder* (1874) 9 Ch App 463; *Philips v Low* [1892] 1 Ch 47.

6 See Appendix 1.

subject of a grant was vital to attempts to establish prescription rights.[1] The law should now, in any event, be regarded in favour of the view that a right to light, though negative in character, is capable of being the subject of a grant as a negative easement.

---

1 For common law prescription and lost modern grant as ways of acquiring rights to light, see Chapter 6.

Chapter 2

Rights to Light Defined and Contrasted

THE RIGHT DEFINED

2.1 A right to light is one which carries with it the entitlement to receive sufficient natural illumination from the sky through defined apertures in a building to enable use of the interior areas receiving light through such apertures for ordinary purposes to which the building is or may normally be expected to be put.

2.2 Three points should be made at this stage:

(1) the right can only be enjoyed in respect of a building. Questions as to what constitutes a building for these purposes and, where it is under construction, when the building is first taken to be sufficiently complete to give rise to enjoyment of such a rights are considered in Chapter 4;

(2) the right can only be enjoyed in respect of defined apertures in a building intended to admit light. Questions as to what apertures are sufficient are also considered in Chapter 4. Where a building is demolished, so destroying the defined apertures, whether the right to light previously received through these apertures is lost depends on matters examined in Chapter 8;

(3) the right is limited in respect to the intensity of illumination to which the claimant owner is entitled. The test is whether, after any obstruction, there is still enough light received for ordinary purposes. As Farwell J said in *Higgins v Betts*:[1]

> 'The dominant owner was never entitled either by prescription or under the Act [ie the Prescription Act 1832] to all the lights that came through his windows. It was not enough to show that some light had been taken, but the question always was whether so much had been taken as to cause a nuisance . . .'

The appropriate standard is considered in Chapter 3.

THE LIMITS OF PROTECTION

2.3 Rights to light do not, therefore, concern all the possible amenities which may be conceived to be enjoyed by the absence of other buildings in proximity to one's own windows. There are at least nine situations in which the law relating to light offers the dominant owner no protection.

---

1 [1905] 2 Ch 210.

(1) As has been already noted, there is no right to receive natural light falling on land which has no buildings on it.[1] The reason for this is that such a right is too indefinite to form the subject of a grant.

(2) To an extent, a corollary of the foregoing, the protection afforded is in respect not of particular building(s) but in respect of defined apertures in buildings designed for the receipt of light. Doorways intended to be closed by opaque doors are, therefore, excluded.[2]

(3) The law relating to rights to light does not protect the right to a particular view. Thus it cannot be invoked by reason of a building being erected which deprives a window of a pleasant prospect, or even of a direct view of the sky, if light is not interfered with to an actionable extent.

> 'But . . . for prospect, which is a matter only of delight and not of necessity, no action lies for stopping thereof, and yet it is a great commendation of a house if it has a long and large prospect . . . But the law does not give an action for such things of delight.'[3]

The same principle prevents a claim being made of a right to *be viewed*, for example so that commercial premises or a billboard may attract customers.[4] However, where the act causing the interference with the view is a public nuisance, any special damage sustained by an individual as a result may, subject to issues of foreseeability, be actionable.[5] Views may be protected by restrictive covenants or by planning law.[6]

(4) Just as the view out cannot be guaranteed, neither can the absence of the view in. The law does not protect from prying eyes. Thus in *Browne v Flower*,[7] a landlord let a flat on three floors of a mansion block to Mrs Lightbody. Subsequently, a flat on the ground floor was let to the plaintiffs. Both flats had windows overlooking a communal garden. Subtenants of Mrs Lightbody's flat, with the landlord's consent, erected an open-work iron staircase leading from the garden to the first floor, between the windows of two of the bedrooms in the plaintiffs' flat, seriously affecting their privacy. The plaintiffs' claim against the landlord based on breach of an implied covenant for quiet enjoyment in their lease, and derogation from grant, to have the staircase removed, failed, on the ground that the staircase did not impair the user of the flat for the purposes for which it was demised. The

---

1 *Robert v Macord* (1832) 1 Mood & R 230; *Potts v Smith* (1868) LR 6 Eq 311; *Dalton v Angus* (1881) 6 App Cas 740; *Harris v De Pinna* (1886) 33 ChD 238. See Chapter 1 at **1.2** and **2.16**.

2 *Levet v Gas Light & Coke Co* [1919] 1 Ch 24.

3 *Bland v Moseley* Trinity 29 G/12 cited in *Aldred's* case (1616) 9 Co Rep 57(6); *Dalton v Angus* (1881) 6 App Cas 740 at 824; *Browne v Flower* [1911] 1 Ch 219, 225; *Phipps v Pears* [1965] QB 76 at 83 per Lord Denning MR.

4 *Butt v Imperial Gas Co* (1866) 2 Ch App 158.

5 *Campbell v Paddington Corporation* [1911] 1 KB 869.

6 For restrictive covenants generally, see Francis: *Restrictive Covenants and Freehold Land: A Practitioner's Guide* (Sweet & Maxwell, 1999); see also **2.6–2.12**. For planning law, see Chapter 14.

7 [1911] 1 Ch 219.

actual decision does not deal directly with the question of a possible easement enjoyed by a freeholder as opposed to the implied obligation of a landlord. But Parker J said at p225:

> 'In as much as our law does not recognise any easement or prospect of privacy, and (as I have already held) the Plaintiffs' light is not interfered with, it is difficult to find any easement which can have been interfered with by the erection of the staircase in question.'

This has not been questioned as a correct statement of the law, and is supported by the earlier case of *Chandler v Thomson*.[1] It seems consistent with principle, and with the well-established rule that it is not unlawful to open windows overlooking neighbouring land which may in due course acquire rights to light.[2] Further, a right to protection from overlooking would, like a right to a view, inhibit development of land to an unacceptably great extent.

(5) The law recognises no right to air percolating generally over land. Thus in *Harris v De Pinna*[3] it was held that there was no right in favour of the owners of a timber yard in which timber was stacked for drying in open-sided sheds, to a flow of air from neighbouring land. The position is thus analogous to that of light, which can only be the subject of an easement if received through a defined aperture. However, it seems that where air is received through a defined aperture it may form the subject of an easement.[4] For example, in *Gale v Abbott*[5] an injunction was granted to restrain the erection of a skylight over a yard which would interfere with air received to the plaintiff's window. Thus the same obstruction may interfere with both easements.

(6) The law recognises no right to uninterrupted television reception as an easement.[6] Presumably, the same applies to radio, telephone, and data transmission by airwaves.[7]

(7) The law recognises no easement to prevent building by a neighbour which would interfere with the visibility of one's own premises to others; such visibility may benefit commercial premises by, for example, attracting passing trade or by providing a suitable surface for advertisements.[8]

---

1 (1811) 3 Camp 81, 170 ER 1313.

2 *Dalton v Angus* (1881) 6 App Cas 740 at 797 per Lord Selborne LC.

3 (1886) 33 ChD 238. See also Chapter 4 at **4.11**.

4 *Gale v Abbott* (1862) 8 Jur NS 987; *Dent v Auction Mart Co* (1866) LR 2 Eq 238; *Bass v Gregory* (1870) 25 QBD 481; *Aldin v Latimer Clark, Muirhead & Co* [1894] 2 Ch 437, 446; *Chastey v Ackland* [1895] 2 Ch 389; *Cable v Bryant* [1908] 1 Ch 259. Dicta to the contrary of Littledale J in *Moore v Rawson* (1824) 3 B & C 332 are probably to be regarded as relating to the natural passage of air over land – see *Dalton v Angus* (1881) 6 App Cas 740 at 797 per Lord Selborne LC. For a case where an easement of ventilation was held to exist, see *Wong v Beaumont Property Trust* [1964] 2 All ER 119, CA.

5 (1862) 8 Jur NS 987.

6 *Hunter v Canary Wharf Ltd* [1997] 2 AC 655, HL. See Chapter 10 at **10.4**.

7 Cf *Bridlington Relay Ltd v Yorkshire Electricity Board* [1965] Ch 436.

8 *Butt v Imperial Gas Co* (1866) 2 Ch App 158.

(8) There is no right to receive direct solar radiation for energy purposes.[1] It seems, therefore, that protection of solar panels used for heating, for example, swimming pools, from obstructions to sunlight cannot be demanded.

(9) English law does not prohibit erection of the 'spite fence'. Statutes in some states of the United States create a presumption that a fence over a certain height, where the height gives no practical benefit, is built to annoy a neighbour and is a nuisance. Heights above which the presumption applies vary from state to state.[2] In England, complaints have arisen with regard to the height of hedges of Leyland Cypress trees planted on boundaries. No private law rights exist in England to enable the adjoining owner to have unreasonably high fences or hedges reduced in height, unless they interfere with rights to light or otherwise constitute a nuisance or trespass.

LICENCES AND OTHER ARRANGEMENTS

2.4 An easement, creating an interest in land, may be distinguished from a personal licence not having this effect.[3] Unlike an easement, a licence cannot (generally) be taken advantage of by a successor in title of the licensee. Further, a licence (unlike an easement) is subject to revocation by the licensor.

2.5 A licence to open or maintain a window will not, therefore, ripen into an easement, will not benefit successors of the licensee, and is precarious. Indeed, the device of a written licence for such purposes is frequently used to prevent the acquisition of a light under s 3 of the Prescription Act 1832, as discussed in Chapter 7.

THE RIGHT TO LIGHT CONTRASTED WITH OTHER RIGHTS

Restrictive covenants

2.6 Restrictive covenants affecting freehold land are used to create a kind of private planning law, in a particular area. The efficacy of such covenants was considered by the leading case of *Tulk v Moxhay*,[4] which related to Leicester Square in London. It was held that a covenant taken on conveyance of land not to build on the land conveyed was enforceable against successors of the purchasers

---

1 Although, in some circumstances, the standard of light for a particular building to which the dominant owner is entitled may be such as to imply sunlight to some extent. See Chapter 3 at **3.14–3.21**.

2 See, eg, Massachusetts General Laws App 49.21 California Civil Code 841-4.

3 *IDC Group Ltd v Clark* [1992] 2 EGLR 184. Cf *Britel Developments (Thatcham) Ltd v Nightfreight (Great Britain) Ltd* [1998] 4 All ER 432.

4 (1848) 2 Ph 774.

who had notice of the covenant, by those who retained the land for the benefit of which the covenant was taken.

2.7 The doctrine applies only to restrictive covenants, not positive obligations.[1] As in the case of easements, there must be a dominant tenement, though this need not be a separate plot of land. A different estate in the same land is sufficient.[2] The covenant must benefit the dominant tenement directly.[3] For the benefit of the covenant to 'run with' the dominant land (ie be enforceable by successors in title of the original covenantee who from time to time own the dominant land) it must be either annexed to it,[4] assigned, or the covenant must have arisen as part of a building scheme.[5] By comparison with the right to light, the law relating to restrictive covenants is in some respects wider and in others narrower in the protection afforded.

2.8 First, whilst the law of easements is of universal application (except where excluded by agreement) restrictive covenants must be specifically imposed on land. There are no implied restrictive covenants.

2.9 Secondly, restrictive covenants, like easements, require in effect a dominant and a servient tenement, though the terminology used is that of the 'benefited' and 'burdened' land. But, unlike easements, they also require the benefit of the covenant to be attached to the dominant tenement, whereas in the case of a right to light the easement attaches to the land automatically.

2.10 Thirdly, restrictive covenants if created after 31 December 1925 require protection by registration as land charges to be enforceable against successors of the covenantor.[6] This is not the case in relation to easements, apart from equitable easements.[7]

2.11 Fourthly, restrictive covenants, unlike easements, are capable of protecting views and general visual amenities. Indeed, this is one of their principal purposes.

2.12 Finally, however, restrictive covenants which are obsolete are potentially subject to modification by the Lands Tribunal under s 84 of the Law of Property Act 1925. A review of the principles of the legislation lies outside the scope of this book. Rights to light and other easements are not subject to this jurisdiction, which also applies to covenants imposed in certain long leases.[8]

---

1 *Rhone v Stephens* [1994] 2 AC 310.

2 *Hall v Ewen* (1887) 37 ChD 74.

3 *Rogers v Hosegood* [1900] 2 Ch 388.

4 See Law of Property Act 1925, s 78; *Federated Homes Ltd v Mill Lodge Properties Ltd* [1980] 1 WLR 594; *Roake v Chadha* [1984] 1 WLR 40.

5 *Elliston v Reacher* [1908] 2 Ch 374, 665, CA.

6 Land Charges Act 1972, s 2(5); Land Registration Act 1925, ss 2, 50(1). In the case of covenants entered into prior to 1926, the equitable doctrine of notice continues to apply – Law of Property Act 1925, s 2(5).

7 See Chapter 1 at **1.15** and Chapter 14.

8 Law of Property Act 1925, s 84(12).

LEASES

2.13 Covenants in leases may impose restrictions on lessee or lessor which may have the effect of preserving light to windows on the demised premises or premises of the lessor. One particular feature of the law relating to rights to light is that a lessee may, under s 3 of the Prescription Act 1832, acquire a right to light over his lessor's premises. Hence, leases frequently contain provisions negating the acquisition of such right.[1] By contrast, a right to light cannot be acquired under the doctrine of Lost Modern Grant[2] against a freeholder where the property in question is the subject of a lease.

2.14 Subject to these points, a lessee acquires by virtue of s 62 of the Law of Property Act 1925 all quasi-easements actually enjoyed therewith, including all rights over the lessor's land which, immediately before the demise, were actually used and enjoyed whether as of right or by possession, with the demised premises. These will include a right to light, where the demised premises contains windows overlooking adjoining land of the lessor.[3]

2.15 Thus a lessee may effectively acquire a right to light as part of his lease. Such a right, however, expires with his lease, and arises (save where it is acquired by prescription) by virtue of the lease itself. Rights to light in general, however, exist in favour of and against freehold owners between whom there is no legal relationship.

2.16 In December 1999, the Department of the Environment, Transport and the Regions published a Consultation Paper[4] seeking views on the problem of hedges which obstruct light to buildings and gardens. The specific problem which has arisen is that caused by the fast growing species of conifer, *X Cupressocyparis leylandii* (Leyland Cypress), commonly known as 'leylandii'.[5]

2.17 The Consultation Paper considers whether the existing law of light should be extended so that an easement of light could be granted or acquired over land generally rather than just in relation to buildings.[6] There would be a restriction of such a general right to gardens or residential land. However, as the Paper recognises, the scope of such legislative change could not be retrospective, and would be costly and difficult to enforce. Even interference with light would not be easy to prove on an open site where the offending hedge might have little effect on the general level of light and notwithstanding the hedge's ability to cast a dark shadow over all or part of the complainant's land.

---

1 *Morgan v Fear* [1907] AC 425; *Haynes v King* [1893] 3 Ch 439; *Foster v Lyons & Co* [1927] 1 Ch 219; *Hapgood v J.H. Martin & Son Ltd* (1934) 152 LT 72; *Willoughby v Eckstein (No 2)* [1937] 1 Ch 167; and see Chapter 7 at **7.4–7.5**.

2 See Chapter 6 at **6.2**.

3 *Wheeldon v Burrows* (1879) 12 ChD 31; *Allen v Taylor* (1880) 16 ChD 355.

4 'High Hedges'.

5 The scale of the problem is shown at Part 3 of the Paper, where it is suggested that there may be as many as 17,000 problem hedges in England and Wales.

6 Ibid at para 5.17.

2.18 Whilst the Consultation Paper covers a range of options, and is not designed to do more than seek comments, the solution which the Department appears (with qualification) to favour is a system whereby those suffering from the effects of 'high hedges' (tentatively defined as those unduly interfering with the enjoyment or amenity of property or those hedges not in compliance with certain height and location restrictions) may lodge a formal complaint with their local authority. That authority will be empowered to hear both sides to the complaint and direct remedial action. Some form of appeal system will be needed and various routes are proposed, for example, to the magistrates' court, or to the Planning Inspectorate.[1]

2.19 At the time of writing, it is clear that legislation to deal with the problem of high hedges may be some way off. However, the Paper demonstrates how the major limits to the existing law of light, namely its restrictions to light to buildings, is proving a grave disadvantage in residential areas of England and Wales where 'problem hedges' (if not then features on land) are interfering with the use and enjoyment of open spaces such as gardens. Beyond the proposals for reform contained in the joint Law Commission and Land Registry Paper,[2] nothing is currently proposed which seeks to deal with the inherent complexity of the law of easements, and in particular the law of light.

1 See Part 6 of the Paper.

2 *Land Registration for the 21st Century* (Law Commission No 254 (1998)). See Chapter 14 at **14.20**.

Chapter 3
Extent of Rights to Light

TEST OF SUFFICIENCY

Generally

3.1 As has already been noted,[1] no easement of light may be acquired in respect of land which has not been built on. The right exists in favour of defined apertures to buildings intended to admit light.

3.2 Once a right to light to a window in a building has been acquired (either by act of the parties or prescription) the *extent* of the dominant owner's right has been described as follows:

> '... generally speaking an owner of ancient lights is entitled to sufficient light according to the ordinary notions of mankind for the comfortable use and enjoyment of his house as a dwellinghouse, if it is a dwellinghouse, or for the beneficial use and occupation of the house if it is a warehouse, a shop or other place of business. The expressions "the ordinary notions of mankind", "comfortable use and enjoyment", and "beneficial use and occupation" introduce elements of uncertainty; but similar uncertainty has always existed and exists still in all cases of nuisance, and in this country an obstruction of light has commonly been regarded as a nuisance, although the right to light has been regarded as a peculiar kind of easement.'[2]

In more modern idiom in *Allen v Greenwood*[3] Buckley LJ said as follows:

> 'The authority which must now be regarded as the leading case on this topic is undoubtedly the decision of the House of Lords in *Colls v Home and Colonial Stores Ltd* from which I think the following formulation of the principle can be distilled: the amount of light to which a dominant owner is entitled under a prescriptive claim is sufficient light, according to ordinary notions, for the comfortable or beneficial use of the building in question, again according to ordinary notions, for such purposes as would constitute normal uses of a building of its particular character. If the building be a dwellinghouse, the measure must be related to reasonable standards of comfort as a dwellinghouse. If it be a warehouse, a shop or a factory, the measure must be related to reasonable standards of comfort or beneficial use (for comfort may not be the most appropriate test in the case of such a building) as a warehouse, a shop or a factory as the case may be. These may very probably differ from the standards which would apply to a dwellinghouse. If the building be a greenhouse, the measure must in my opinion be related to its reasonably satisfactory use as a greenhouse.'

---

1 See Chapter 1.
2 Per Lord Lindley in *Colls v Home & Colonial Stores Ltd* [1904] AC 179.
3 [1979] 1 All ER 819, CA.

3.3 There were cases prior to *Colls*, which suggested the possibility of two other standards. The first of these looked at the amount of light necessary to the use made of the dominant building at the time the right to light was acquired. So in *Martin v Goble*[1] premises had acquired a prescriptive right to light at a time when they were used as a malt-house. Subsequently, the use of the premises was changed to that of a dwelling-house. The jury was directed that 'the house was entitled to the degree of light necessary for a malt-house, not a dwelling-house. Thus converting it from one to the other could not affect the rights of the owners of the adjoining ground'. The other standard was the actual amount of light received, rather than the amount necessary for ordinary purposes. Hence, on this basis, any effect on the light would be actionable, even if the room remained sufficiently well lit for ordinary purposes.[2] The rationale of the first standard was the unfairness of allowing the dominant owner to increase the burden on the servient owner by changing the use of the dominant building to one acquiring more light. The proponents of the second standard, however, stressed the unfairness of allowing the servient owner to interfere with the present or future rights which the dominant owner enjoyed from the quality of light he actually received. Many judicial disagreements resulted. The cases relating to these alterations must now be read as no longer representing the law insofar as it is inconsistent with *Colls*, and which establishes that the correct approach is to apply a uniform standard to the amount of light to which the dominant building is entitled.

3.4 The test, accordingly, as to whether an actionable nuisance by interference with light has been caused, is not by reference to the amount of light originally received through the aperture before the obstruction complained of, but whether the amount of light received after the obstruction is in place will enable the building (or that portion of it which receives light through the aperture) to continue to be enjoyed for ordinary purposes. The locality in which the dominant tenement is situated is probably of no effect in determining whether the standard is maintained:

> 'The human eye requires as much light for comfortable reading or sewing in Darlington Street, Wolverhampton, as in Mayfair.'[3]

Relevance of actual and prospective layout and uses of affected areas

3.5 In establishing whether sufficient light continues to be received, it is necessary to have regard not only to the existing layout and purposes for which

---

1 *Martin v Goble* (1808) 1 Camp 320, 120 GR 971. See also *Lanfranchi v Mackensie* (1867) LR 4 Eq 427. *Martin v Goble* was dissented from in *Moore v Hall* (1878) 3 QBD 178, and considered overruled in *Dicker v Popham* (1890) 63 LT 379. In *Colls v Home and Colonial Stores Ltd* [1904] AC 179, Lord Davey (at 202) treated it as a case which involved alteration of the substance as opposed to the quality of the dominant tenement. The report of *Martin v Goble* does not suggest, however, that internal alterations had been carried out.

2 *Moore v Hall* (1878) 3 QBD 178 (*Martin v Goble* was dissented from).

3 *Horton's Estate Ltd v James Beattie Ltd* [1927] 1 Ch 75 at 78.

the building is used, but also foreseeable future changes in internal arrangements and uses.

3.6 This is illustrated by *Carr-Saunders v Dick McNeil Associates.*[1] In that case, the issue concerned the interference with light to the second floor of the plaintiff's building, which received light from four windows at the front and two at the rear. The front of the second floor had at one time been separately occupied by a lessee who used it as an office but the plaintiff, having obtained possession of the separately occupied part, used the whole floor initially as an open plan area for living accommodation. Subsequently he converted the floor into six consulting rooms, with two rooms at the rear and four at the front, the rooms at the rear each incorporating one of the rear facing windows. The defendant subsequently obstructed the light to the rear facing windows, resulting in the consulting rooms in question suffering a significant loss of light. The defendant argued that the obstruction of light was not actionable since, had the plaintiff kept the whole of the second floor laid out in open plan, there would have been no significant effect by virtue of the interference with the light received to the rear windows on the light enjoyed by the second floor as a whole. The defendant argued that it was not open to a dominant owner by an act on his part to increase the burden on the servient tenement, and accordingly the internal partition works carried out by the plaintiff to form the separate consulting rooms should be disregarded in determining whether an actionable interference had occurred.

3.7 The court rejected this argument for three reasons: first, since the case was one of a prescriptive right to light under s 3 of the Prescription Act 1832, the issue was not one of whether there was an easement of access of light to a particular room in a building, but to the building as a whole, so that the extent of the right was not necessarily to be measured by the internal arrangements of the building. Secondly, the issue in a case of nuisance was whether there was disturbance of the dominant owner in the comfortable enjoyment, not of a particular room, but of his property. Thirdly, the dominant owner's right to light was not measured by the particular use to which the dominant tenement had been put in the past:

> 'The extent of the dominant owner's right is neither increased nor diminished by the actual use to which the dominant owner has chosen to put his premises or any of the rooms in them: for he is entitled to such access of light as will leave his premises adequately lit for all ordinary purposes for which they may reasonably be expected to be used. The court must, therefore, take account not only of the present use, but also of other potential uses to which the dominant owner may reasonably be expected to put the premises in the future.'[2]

3.8 The same principle had earlier been applied in *Colls v Home and Colonial Stores Limited*,[3] where Lord Davey said:[4]

---

1 [1986] 2 All ER 888.
2 Per Millett J at [1986] 2 All ER 888 at 894c–d.
3 [1904] AC 179.
4 Ibid at 202–204.

> 'The easement is for access of light to the building, and if the building retains its substantial identity, or if the ancient lights retain their substantial identity, it does not seem to me to depend on the use which is made of the chambers in it, or to be varied by any alteration which may be made in the internal structure of it.'

He went on to say:

> 'According to both principle and authority, I am of opinion that the owner of the dominant tenement is entitled to the uninterrupted access through his ancient windows of a quantity of light, the measure of which is what is required for the ordinary purposes of inhabitancy or business of the tenement according to the ordinary notions of mankind, and that the question for what purpose he has thought fit to use that light, or the mode in which he finds it convenient to arrange the internal structure of his tenement, does not affect the question.'[1]

3.9 A corollary of this principle is that the court will consider not only present use of a particular room, but also possible future uses. For example, if a room lighted by a window enjoying a right to light is used as a scullery, an obstruction which reduces the light received by the window below the acceptable standard is actionable despite the fact that ordinary notions of mankind do not require sculleries to be well lit.[2]

3.10 As is clear from *Carr-Saunders v Dick McNeil Associates*,[3] internal partitioning which results in the creation of small rooms in a previously open plan area which are more significantly affected by an obstruction to light than the previous open plan area would have been does not affect the plaintiff's right to complain. It is also clear that not only actual sub-division but any future foreseeable sub-division must be taken into account. Presumably, the converse also applies, so that if it is possible that a small room might be thrown into a larger area, once again this would not affect the claimant's position. Although normally the creation of an open plan area might be expected to result in better light, this might not necessarily be the case, where the existing room is small and no part of it is far from the window in question. Throwing the existing room into a larger area can result in the area so formed being more sensitive to loss of light from the existing window, if no additional windows are available to light the enlarged area. This is because the light received by the parts of the newly formed space furthest from the existing window will be less well lit.

3.11 What future arrangements of the claimant's building's internal space are reasonably foreseeable is, presumably, a question of fact. Relevant matters, it is submitted, would include:

(1) the structural possibilities of the building;
(2) economic considerations, such as the cost of doing the work set against the likely benefit in terms of creation of lettable space;

---

1 *Colls v Home & Colonial Stores Limited* [1904] AC 179 at 202–204.
2 *Price v Hilditch* [1930] 1 Ch 500 at 507–508 per Maugham J.
3 [1986] 2 All ER 888.

(3) whether before the work is done there is a need to obtain possession of the relevant area, and the prospects of this being achieved;
(4) whether third party consents, such as from a landlord or holder of the benefit of a restrictive covenant are required, and the prospects of such consents being obtained;
(5) where applicable, the need for planning or listed building consent and the prospects of this being obtained.

Relevance of impact of loss of light on particular locations within the affected area

3.12 A further matter of relevance in deciding whether sufficient light remains in any case is the location where loss has occurred. Loss in areas whose utility is marginal, or which are inherently unlikely to be used for purposes with high amenity value will be given less weight than loss of an area where there is a greater reasonable expectation of good natural light. So in *Smyth v Dublin Theatre Co Limited*[1] Meredith J said:

> '... no inconvenience is felt by reason of the fact that portions of the room are in comparative darkness, provided the room as a whole is fairly well lit and a reasonable area near the window enjoys a sufficiency of direct light. If a plaintiff is unreasonable if he complains of defective lighting in corners of the room where adequate light is not to be expected and is generally comparatively useless ... is he to be considered unreasonable if he complains of defective light a few feet from the window, though such light is well above the expert's standard for a room as a whole, if near the window is a place where better light may be expected to be found?
>
> ... and interpreting the term "ordinary light" in a common sense manner I hold that a plaintiff is not claiming more than ordinary light simply because he claims a reasonable amount of direct light where he may expect to find it in a room laterally lighted ... If that much latitude is not given to the expression "ordinary light" the flexibility of the legal principle stressed in *Colls v Home & Colonial Stores* ([1904] AC 179, [1904–7] All ER Rep 5) is lost, and a rigid standard set up by experts is introduced.'

3.13 These remarks were cited with approval by Millett J in *Carr-Saunders v Dick McNeil Associates Limited.*[2] In *Deakins v Hookings,*[3] Judge Cooke said:

> '(i) In a room that is already ill-lit every bit of light is precious.
> (ii) Save in an extreme case it would be difficult to say that once a living room (contrast a store) fell below 50/50 that the light left was adequate.
> (iii) In considering whether a room where more than 50% remained well-lit regard should be had to the use to be made of the remainder and how bad, *vis-à-vis* that use, the remaining light was.
> (iv) The test is not merely a statistical one; test (ii) provides a pretty irreductible minimum.'

1 [1936] IR 692 at 703, 705–706.
2 [1986] 2 All ER 888 at 893B.
3 [1994] 1 EGLR 190 at 193A–B.

Right to extraordinary light

3.14 The extent of light acquired may depend on the type of building. In *Allen v Greenwood*,[1] it was held that in the case of a right to light acquired by prescription, the extent of light acquired under s 3 of the Prescription Act 1832 was to be measured according to the nature of the building and the purposes for which it was normally used. In that case, the dominant building was a greenhouse, and it was held that the extent of light acquired by prescription was the right to that degree of light and the benefits of light including the rays of the sun required to grow plants in the greenhouse, and not just the amount of light required for illumination.

3.15 An alternative basis for the decision in *Allen v Greenwood* was that a right to an exceptional quantity of light could be acquired by prescription provided it had been enjoyed for the full prescriptive period to the knowledge of the servient owner. Thus, in some cases, at any rate where the light is acquired by prescription, there may be a right to an extraordinary quantity of light where there is the requisite degree of knowledge on the servient owner's part.

3.16 The principle that the amount of light to which the dominant owner is entitled may depend on the nature of the building and the purpose for which it is normally used has certain corollaries.

(1) As was accepted in *Allen v Greenwood*, it does not necessarily follow that simply because a building is used as a greenhouse the dominant owner will have the right to such degree of light and warmth as is necessary for every conceivable use to which a greenhouse can be put. It seems that the extent of light to which the dominant owner is entitled would not be such as to enable him to use the greenhouse for 'exotic purposes'.[2] The growing of tomatoes and pot plants may be protected, but the growing of exotic orchids or plants whose natural habitat is tropical rain forest or western American desert may not.

(2) It seems to be the case that where the building is a swimming pool, the dominant owner has no right to expect to receive the sun's rays on his bare skin. As Goff LJ said in *Allen v Greenwood*:[3]

> '... the defendants say that ... the only complaint the plaintiffs can have is loss of heat or radiant properties, and they postulate the example of a swimming pool, part of which is fortuitously warmed by sunlight coming through a south window. They say, and I have no doubt rightly, that the owners could have no cause of action against one who, whilst leaving fully adequate light for the complete enjoyment of the swimming pool, so shaded the sun as to deprive it of this chance warmth.'[4]

---

1 [1979] 2 All ER 819, CA.

2 *Allen v Greenwood* [1979] 2 All ER 819 at 825F–G.

3 [1979] 1 All ER 819 at 827D.

4 Presumably, the reference is to an indoor swimming pool whose position in this respect is analogous to that of a greenhouse. It is doubtful whether an *outside* pool could constitute a 'building' capable of acquiring rights to light – see Chapter 4 at **4.4** and **4.11**.

3.17 It would seem to follow from the principles, first, that regard must be had to actual and potential foreseeable uses of the building in question, and, secondly, that the present use of the building is not to be regarded as fixing the extent of light required, that where the nature of a building is such as to require an extraordinary quantity of light, and the right to such light has been acquired, it is irrelevant that the present use of the building is not such as to require that quantity of light. For example, a greenhouse used for storage purposes, or simply derelict, will nonetheless be entitled to an extraordinary quantity of light within the above definition.

3.18 The dominant owner cannot, self-evidently, increase the burden on the servient owner by enlarging his windows (although the enlarged windows may ultimately acquire prescriptive rights to light). However, he is entitled to receive light to the full extent of the aperture, no account being taken of frames or glazing bars.[1] Equally, he cannot, by reducing the size of his windows, increase the burden on the servient owner. Thus if the dominant owner reduces the size of his window, and the servient owner erects a building which obstructs the light, the dominant owner has no claim if (taking into account the obstruction) sufficient light would have continued to be received through the window if its size had not been reduced.[2]

3.19 A further way in which a claimant may be able to establish a right to an extraordinary quantity of light is by virtue of an express or implied grant. In the case of an express grant, the extent of the rights granted will depend on the words used, construed in the factual matrix in which the transaction is set.[3] The words of a grant will be construed against the grantor in case of ambiguity.[4]

3.20 Where the premises in question are let, the lessor is under an implied obligation not to derogate from his grant.[5] This principle operates to prevent the lessor from acting in a way which interferes with the lessee's use of the premises for some particular purpose for which they were let. Acts which may be prevented include those interfering with the light needed for the activity which at the time of the lease it was contemplated the lessee would carry on at the premises. So in *Herz v The Union Bank of London*,[6] the plaintiff was a diamond merchant, who held certain premises under a lease. His business depended on his being able to assess accurately the condition and value ('quality and water') of jewels; this activity required an extraordinary quantity of light. The defendants, owners of adjacent property, proposed to erect buildings which would interfere with the plaintiff's light, but not to an extent which could be actionable ordinarily. However, before the case came on the defendants became the plaintiff's landlord by purchasing the premises he occupied, subject to his lease,

---

1 *Turner v Spooner* (1861) 1 Drew and Sm 467 62 ER 457.

2 *Ankerson v Connelly* [1906] 2 Ch 544; [1907] 1 Ch 678; see also Chapter 8 at **8.52**.

3 *Investors Compensation Scheme v West Bromwich Building Society* [1998] 1 All ER 98, HL.

4 See, eg, *Savill Brothers v Bethell* [1902] 2 Ch 523.

5 See, generally, *Hill and Redman's Law of Landlord and Tenant* (Butterworths) vol 1 paras [6884]–[6900].

6 (1859) 2 Giff 686, 66 ER 287.

which described him as a diamond merchant. The court granted the plaintiff an injunction, the Vice-Chancellor saying:

> 'But it is said that this is an ancient light in a dwelling-house: and an authority has been cited to shew that the Defendants are entitled to obscure or diminish the light to such an extent as would not interfere with the enjoyment of a mere dwelling-house. The case referred to certainly supports the proposition that, where the character of a building is altered to that which requires a greater quantity of light, the owner of adjoining land has a right to erect any obstruction which would not obstruct the light to an extent sufficient to injure it in its former state of enjoyment before the alteration. The principle of that decision is that no man is entitled by any act of his own suddenly to impose a new restriction on his neighbour; but the application of that principle was to a case where no right of personal enjoyment was interfered with, and where the Plaintiff did not even state who was in possession, but merely complained of an injury to his inheritance, and not to himself.
>
> The present case is of a different kind; the Defendants are the owners of the reversion, and the Plaintiff is described in the lease as a diamond merchant.
>
> There seems to be no sound principle on which, where the demise of the house is to a person known to sustain such a character as that any diminution of the light would disturb his enjoyment in that character, the reversioner can be allowed to withdraw or obstruct anything necessary to his enjoyment of the demised property in that character.'

3.21 Similarly, in *Frederick Betts Ltd v Pickfords Ltd*,[1] a lessor was held to have derogated from his grant when he converted what ought to have been an outside wall into a party wall under the London Building Act 1894 so that the lessee was obliged to block up his windows in the wall.

THE TEST OF WHETHER THERE HAS BEEN AN ACTIONABLE INTERFERENCE WITH LIGHT

Generally

3.22 Whether there has been an actionable interference is a question of fact, and at least in the past some judges regretted the growing tendency to seek to answer the question by reference to measurements and scientific evidence:

> 'I have had quite a considerable body of evidence on both sides, two experts for the plaintiff and two for the defendant, one or two lay witnesses for the plaintiff, and, I think, some six or seven witnesses of a lay character on behalf of the defendant. On one side it is alleged that the injury to the plaintiff's two rooms has been very serious, and on the other side it is denied that there has been any injury at all. I confess that for my part I would prefer, in cases of this kind where the injury is not, as it so often is, hypothetical, to deal with the matter very largely as depending upon the actual evidence of ordinary members of the public who have used the rooms before and

1 [1906] 2 Ch 87.

after the alleged obstruction, and who could give positive evidence as to the injury, if any, which they have suffered.'[1]

3.23 This indicates the approach classically adopted by the court, which has, however (as the judge in the case himself recognised), been supplanted if not wholly superseded by expert evidence. In practice, however, the evidence of lay witnesses as to the effect of the loss of light remains of importance for a number of reasons.

(1) As will be seen below, the court's approach to the scientific tests generally adopted is that they do not lay down absolute rules as to what is or is not an actionable interference. There is what might be termed a band (in percentage terms) of loss of light which may or may not, depending on the circumstances, be actionable. In this borderline area the impact on witnesses, particularly the owner and occupier of the dominant tenement, may be important. As Judge Cooke said in *Deakins v Hookings*:[2]

> 'But it is not merely a question of statistics. The plaintiff's evidence makes it obvious to me that there is an appreciable drop in the comfortable occupation of the room going beyond the comparatively slight drop that the expert evidence alone would suggest. Whilst the expert evidence alone would be enough to say that there was an actionable interference but a slight one, the plaintiff's evidence goes to show that it is real and deleterious in terms of beneficial occupation and goes beyond the merely slight.'

(2) It is of course possible that there may be divergence between the experts called for the respective parties: in such cases the importance of lay evidence is obvious.

(3) When the court has to decide what relief ought to be granted the lay evidence may be of importance, both in deciding whether to grant an injunction or to leave the plaintiff to his remedy in damages, and, if the remedy is to be in damages, in assessing the level of such damages. On the first point, Lord Lindley said in *Colls v Home & Colonial Stores Limited*:[3]

> '... the good sense of judges and juries may be relied upon for adequately protecting rights to light on the one hand and freedom from unnecessary burdens on the other ...'

Relevant matters will include the extent of the infringement, the effect on the plaintiff, and whether the effect of an injunction would be oppressive, which may involve comparison between the plaintiff's loss and the defendant's position if an injunction is granted.[4] It is clear that the convenience of the parties is a relevant matter. In *Price v Hilditch*,[5] for example, an injunction was refused because the inconvenience to the

1 Per Maugham J in *Price v Hilditch* [1930] 1 Ch 500 at 504.
2 [1994] 1 EGLR 190.
3 [1904] AC 179 at 213.
4 See Chapter 11 at **11.72–11.129** for full consideration of the factors influencing the grant or refusal of an injunction.
5 [1930] 1 Ch 500.

plaintiff of the interference with light to a room which was used as a scullery was minor.

3.24 As already noted, the test is whether the light left is sufficient for ordinary purposes. The geographical location of the premises, and the character of the neighbourhood in which they are situated are not relevant considerations.[1] In practice, the test which is used most commonly involves ascertaining whether at least half the room affected continues to receive an adequate quantity of light after the obstruction is in place. This is sometimes termed the '50/50' rule. However, as will be seen, it is somewhat misleading as it is not a rule of law and is not applied inflexibly. As has already been seen, the 'amenity' impact of the loss of light is important. Further, the rising expectations and the emergence of various other tests, of sufficiency of daylight, including a British Standard,[2] suggest that broader criteria should now be applied.

3.25 The starting point is to evaluate the extent of the light lost. For these purposes, specialist surveyors have evolved the 'Waldram' method of measurement. This method is based on the theory that a certain level of illumination is adequate for normal purposes. The unit of measurement is the 'lumen', itself based on measurement of the amount of light obtainable from the dome of the sky, excluding direct sunlight, during daytime. One lumen per square foot is equivalent to 0.2 per cent sky factor. This is the accepted test for sufficiency of light.[3]

3.26 Accordingly, the Waldram method involves preparation of plans of each room or other area affected, showing the area that falls within the 0.2 per cent sky factor contour lines before and after the obstruction is (or will be) in place. From calculations of the difference between the areas 'before' and 'after' it is possible to ascertain the extent of the area where after the obstruction is in place the light is no longer adequate. A full description of the Waldram method of measurement is given in Chapter 9.

3.27 The Waldram method is well established, but the courts have declined to apply it slavishly. There was at one time thought to be a '50/50' rule, under which provided at least 50 per cent of the room remained well lit (in the sense of falling within the 0.2 per cent sky factor) after the obstruction no actionable interference had occurred. It is now, however, clear that this is not the case.

3.28 In *Carr-Saunders v Dick McNeil Associates*,[4] Millett J referred to the consensus of experts based on daylight contour plans by which a room might be regarded as adequately lit for all ordinary purposes if 50 per cent or more of its area receives not less than 1 lumen per square foot at table level. The judge said:

---

1 *Horton's Estate Limited v James Beattie Limited* [1927] 1 Ch 75. See also **3.4**.

2 See Chapter 13 at **13.8**.

3 See, generally, Chapter 12.

4 [1986] 2 All ER 888.

> 'The 50/50 rule is not in my judgment to be applied without any regard to the shape and size of the room or the disposition of the light within the room to which it is applied. The justification of the 50/50 rule is that an owner is unreasonable if he complains that the corners or other parts of the room where good light is not expected are poorly lit, if the room as a whole remains well lit.'

3.29 In *Ough v King*,[1] the Court of Appeal upheld the decision of the judge who had found there was an actionable interference even though more than half the room was well lit after the obstruction of light. It was held that the judge was entitled to have regard to the locality and the higher standards expected of comfort as years go by. Lord Denning MR said:[2]

> 'I would not myself be prepared to regard the figures 50/50 rule of Mr Waldram as a universal rule. In some cases a higher standard may be reasonably required.'

3.30 In *Deakins v Hookings*,[3] Judge Cooke likewise said that the 50/50 rule was not a rigid test, and that in some cases a higher standard might be appropriate having regard to changing expectations. He described the rule as 'a bare minimum' in the case of living rooms, and went on to say that regard should be had to the use to be made of that part of the room which was not well lit and how bad, vis-à-vis that use, the remaining light was.

3.31 It is also necessary to consider the position where the room was one where even before the obstruction less than 50 per cent was adequately lit. In such circumstances, obviously the obstruction will not reduce the area of room well lit to below 50 per cent. In this situation, the better view seems to be that this factor does not prevent the dominant owner complaining of an actionable injury. It is not for the servient owner to tell the dominant owner how he should construct his premises; further, if the dominant owner installs new larger windows in response to an obstruction, to maintain his light, the new apertures will not themselves (until the prescriptive period has elapsed) enjoy rights to light.[4] On the other hand, a *dictum* of Lord Robertson in *Colls v Home and Colonial Stores Ltd*[5] suggests that the dominant owner has to suffer the consequences of 'making one window where there should be five to give proper light, and living 20 years in this cave'. It is suggested that this reasoning would not now be followed (particularly given the modern need to obtain planning permission and listed building consent) at least in relation to parts of the dominant building which are of importance to its enjoyment. This view seems consistent with the decision in *Litchfield-Speer v Queen Anne's Gate Syndicate Ltd (No 2)*, discussed below. Irish cases support the proposition that where premises are badly lit a small interference may be treated by the court as more serious than where they are well

---

1 [1967] 1 WLR 1547.
2 Ibid at 1553B.
3 [1994] 1 EGLR 190.
4 See *Dent v Auction Mart Co* (1866) LR 2 Eq 238. See, generally, Hudson: *Light for Inadequate Windows* 48 Conv (NS) 408.
5 [1904] AC 179 at 181.

lit.[1] Against this, in *Litchfield-Speer v Queen Anne's Gate Syndicate Limited (No 2)*,[2] an injunction was refused in respect of an interference with light in a kitchen which was already poorly lighted. It is submitted that where rooms or other areas are already ill lit, any reduction in the well-lit area is proportionately more serious than in the case of a room where more than 50 per cent is well lit prior to the obstruction, and that the Irish cases, although of only persuasive authority, should be followed.

3.32 There was formerly thought to be a rule that if no obstruction projected above a line subtending an angle of 45° drawn from the base of the window in question no obstruction was established,[3] but this is not the case.[4] Equally, there may be no claim even if the obstruction extends considerably beyond the 45° line.[5]

3.33 In the *Colls* case, it was suggested by Lord Lindley that it was:

> 'a fair working rule to consider that no substantial injury is done ... where an angle of 45° is left ... especially if there is good light from other directions as well.'[6]

The burden on a servient tenement cannot be increased by a voluntary action of the owner of the dominant tenement. Thus, in *Smith v Evangelisation Society*,[7] an action was started to restrain interference with light to a window in a room also lighted, at the beginning of the period of 20 years before the action was brought, by skylights. During that period, they had been blocked up. They were not ancient lights, but could only have been obstructed by the dominant owner himself. The court treated the skylights as reinstated, and declined to disregard the vertical light which the skylights would afford, even though it was established that for some purposes use of the vertical light would be unsatisfactory.

3.34 It is unclear whether a church or other building with stained glass windows is entitled to greater protection than a building with clear windows.[8] But it seems on principle that it ought to be, by analogy with the position of greenhouses.[9] There is some support for this view in *Attorney-General v Queen Anne Garden & Mansions Co*,[10] in which it was held that an unconsecrated memorial chapel could acquire, under s 3 of the Prescription Act 1832, a right to the light necessary not only for conducting services and confirmation classes but also for the designed illumination of the stained glass windows and mosaics.

---

1 *O'Connor v Walsh* (1908) 42 ILTR 20; *McGrath v Munster & Leinster Bank* [1959] IR 313.
2 [1919] 1 Ch 407.
3 *Hackett v Baiss* (1875) LR 20 Eq 494.
4 *Colls v Home & Colonial Stores Limited* [1904] AC 179 at 210.
5 *Charles Semon & Co v Bradford Corporation* [1922] 2 Ch 737.
6 [1904] AC 179 at 210.
7 [1933] Ch 515.
8 *Newham v Lawson* (1971) 115 Sol Jo 446, 22 P&CR 852.
9 See **3.14–3.17**.
10 (1889) 60 LT 759.

Whether this would also apply to an ordinary building constructed with tinted windows is an open question. On the one hand, the nature of the building is not such as to require a special quantity of light. On the other hand, the use of tinted windows may be important for comfort and privacy of the occupants or in terms of the aesthetic appearance of the building. In practical terms, replacement of the existing glazing by clear glazing may be expensive or impractical for some reason. It is suggested that where a building is originally constructed with tinted glazing this may affect the quantity of light to which the owner is entitled, by prescription.

RELEVANCE OF LIGHT FROM OTHER SOURCES

3.35 The general rule is that where a building has windows on more than one side, all of which are entitled to protection as ancient lights (ie they have prescriptive rights to light), the owners of the land on each side of the building can build only to such a height as, if a building of like height were erected on the other side, would not deprive the room of so much light as to cause a nuisance.[1]

3.36 The possibility of supplementing light by artificial light must, clearly, be disregarded in establishing whether a nuisance has been committed by an obstruction. It may, however, be relevant on such matters as the extent of relief to be granted, and in particular whether an injunction rather than damages should be granted.

3.37 Where an issue arises as to whether the dominant tenement has lost light to an actionable extent, account may be taken of light received through apertures which have not been the subject of an obstruction, including skylights.[2] However, where the other apertures enjoy no right to light, by prescription or grant, it appears that the light received through them ought to be ignored.[3]

3.38 The effect of obstructions to the dominant owner's light on the servient tenement must be considered globally, so that if the owner of the servient tenement raises one part of his building, but lowers another, the effect of the lowering must be balanced against the raising in deciding whether an actionable interference has occurred.[4]

3.39 In deciding whether an actionable interference has occurred, the court will not take account of the benefit received by the dominant tenement from light-reflecting surfaces. The principle is clear, where the light-reflecting surfaces (eg glazed tiles) are on the land of the servient owner, the rationale of the rule is that the dominant owner has no power to compel the servient owner to maintain

---

1 *Sheffield Masonic Hall Co Limited v Sheffield Corporation* [1932] 2 Ch 17.

2 *Smith v Evangelisation Society (Incorporated) Trust* [1933] Ch 515.

3 *Colls v Home & Colonial Stores Ltd* [1904] AC 179 at 211 per Lord Lindley; *Kine v Jolly* [1905] 1 Ch 480 at 493 per Vaughan-Williams LJ and at 497 per Romer LJ; [1907] AC 7 per Lord Atkinson.

4 *Davies v Marrable* [1913] 2 Ch 421.

the tiles in position or clean them. Such obligations, even if undertaken by the servient owner would constitute positive covenants which would not be capable of running with the land.[1] It follows that efforts by those infringing rights to light to mitigate or avoid liability by offering to place reflective surfaces on the sides of their buildings nearest the plaintiff's premises will not succeed:

> '... it is quite preposterous to say, "let us damage you, provided we apply such and such a remedy".'[2]

3.40 There seems little doubt that the same principle would apply even were the tortfeasor to offer to install a reflecting surface on the plaintiff's land, so that the plaintiff could himself gain access to it for repair and maintenance. The position would still remain that damage had been caused to the plaintiff's land by the obstruction to light, and there seems no reason why the plaintiff should be obliged to consent to have his premises altered so as to mitigate the liability of the defendant.

INADEQUATE WINDOWS

3.41 The principle appears to be that where, owing to the relevant part of the plaintiff's building receiving light through a small window, it is particularly susceptible to any diminution in the light to that window, the court will be more vigilant to protect the plaintiff's rights than if the size of the windows renders the effect of a given obstruction correspondingly smaller.[3]

---

1 *Rhone v Stephens* [1994] AC 310.
2 *Dent v Auction Mart Co* (1866) LR 2 Eq 238 at 251–252.
3 See **3.31**. For the position where the dominant owner himself reduces the size of his windows, see **3.18**.

Chapter 4

Buildings and Structures capable of enjoying Rights to Light

GENERAL

4.1 As has already been stated in Chapter 1, no right to light can exist in favour of land which has no buildings on it. Further, a right can arise only in respect of light received through defined apertures in such buildings, intended for the purposes of admission of light. This is undoubtedly the position at common law. Section 3 of the Prescription Act 1832, which provides for the acquisition of a right to light based on 20 years' actual enjoyment[1] provides that:

> 'When the access and use of light to and for *any dwellinghouse, workshop, or other building* shall have been actually enjoyed therewith for the full period of 20 years without interruption, the right thereto shall be deemed absolute and indefeasible...'

Thus the position under the 1832 Act is, broadly, the same as at common law, although the particular words of the statute fall to be considered in relation to any claim under its provisions.

4.2 There are therefore two questions: first, whether there is a building in existence which satisfies common law requirements or the statutory definition as the case may be, and, secondly, whether there are in existence in that building apertures sufficiently defined to give rise to a right to receive light through them. These questions may require to be considered in a number of contexts.

(1) Where a question arises as to whether enjoyment of light has occurred for the necessary period to establish a prescriptive right, the date of the construction of the dominant building may be in issue.
(2) The destruction or alteration of the dominant building may in some circumstances result in the right to light being lost. The effect of demolition and reconstruction is considered elsewhere in this book.[2] But in the case of a prescriptive right to light, it is clear that enjoyment for the necessary period is dependent on the continued existence of a building containing the apertures receiving light, or some other building which, by reason of the configuration of its apertures, can effectively be regarded as the successor thereto.
(3) Irrespective of issues of prescription, certain types of structure will not be regarded by the law as satisfying either the common law or statutory requirements for buildings or apertures capable of enjoying rights to light.

---

1 See Chapter 6 at **6.15–6.31**.
2 See Chapter 8 at **8.49–8.55**.

DECIDED CASES UNDER THE PRESCRIPTION ACT 1832, SECTION 3

4.3 In a number of cases, the courts have considered the italicised wording of the Act. The Act refers to 'other building'. These words have been held wide enough to include ecclesiastical buildings,[1] a picture gallery,[2] a greenhouse,[3] and a garage.[4]

4.4 In *Smith & Co (Orpington) v Morris*,[5] the county court judge gave consideration to the question as to whether a window was situated in a 'building' within s 3 of the Act. He stated that the principal elements for consideration were:

(1) did the structure give substantial shelter from the elements?;
(2) was it one which ordinarily required light by means of windows or fixed apertures?;
(3) did it have windows?;
(4) was it so attached to the soil as to pass under a conveyance of the land without specific mention?

In *Smith*, although the garage was open sided, it was held that this fact was not sufficient to deprive it of its character of a 'building'.

4.5 The position with regard to whether caravans and mobile homes are capable of constituting buildings for the purposes of the Prescription Act 1832, s 3 has never arisen. It is suggested that whether a caravan or mobile home is capable of constituting a building for the purposes of the statute is a question of degree, depending on the criteria identified in the case of *Smith & Co (Orpington) v Morris*, and in particular its degree of annexation to the land.

4.6 In *R v Rent Officer of Northamptonshire Registration Area, ex parte Allen*[6] the question arose as to whether a caravan was a 'house' for the purposes of the Rent Act 1977. The caravan was fully mobile, but was connected to services, although all services could be easily disconnected by hand. It was held that the caravan was not a house, in view of its mobility and the possibility of disconnecting services.

4.7 On the other hand, in *Elitestone Ltd v Morris*,[7] it was held that a chalet or bungalow which rested on concrete foundation blocks in the ground constituted a house protected by the Rent Act 1977. Lord Lloyd stated of the bungalow:[8]

---

1 *Ecclesiastical Commissioners v Kino* (1880) 14 ChD 213; *Attorney-General v Queen Anne Gardens and Mansions Co* (1889) 60 LT 759.
2 *Clifford v Holt* [1899] 1 Ch 698.
3 *Allen v Greenwood* [1980] Ch 119.
4 *Smith & Co (Orpington) v Morris* (1962) 112 LJ 702.
5 (1962) 112 LJ 702.
6 [1985] 2 EGLR 153.
7 [1997] 2 All ER 513, HL.
8 [1997] 2 All ER 516B.

> 'It is not like a portacabin, or mobile home. The nature of the structure is such that it could not be taken down and re-erected elsewhere. It could only be removed by a process of demolition ... if a structure can only be enjoyed in situ, and is such that it cannot be removed in whole or in sections to another site, there is at least a strong inference that the purpose of placing the structure on the original site was that it should form part of the realty at that site, and therefore cease to be a chattel.'

4.8 In the *Elitestone* case, the House of Lords reviewed earlier cases in which the distinction between chattels, and fixtures which form part of land was considered in the context of buildings. Relevant factors include the degree of annexation, and the purpose of annexation, in the context of which the ease with which the structure may be moved, is a relevant consideration. It is clear from the *Elitestone* case itself that the mere fact that the structure simply rests on the land without being actually attached to it will not prevent it becoming part of the land.

4.9 It is suggested that these cases provide helpful guidance as to the circumstances in which a mobile home or freestanding building not attached to land may constitute a building for the purposes of the Prescription Act 1832, s 3. It seems clear that, in general terms, a caravan if capable of being moved will not constitute a building, even if it is connected to services. In the case of large mobile homes which cannot readily be moved, and freestanding buildings which are, however, not permanently attached to the land, the question is one of degree, but it is submitted that there may well be circumstances in which they are capable of constituting 'buildings', provided that they have the appearance of buildings and contain apertures through which light is received.

4.10 In the somewhat unusual case of *Duke of Norfolk v Arbuthnot*,[1] an issue arose as to whether part of a church constituted a 'building'. The church in question was constructed in the form of a Latin cross with a central tower. The plaintiff claimed ownership of that portion of the church east of the tower, that would normally be occupied by the chancel, and erected a wall across the west end of it so as to separate it structurally from the rest of the church. The defendant pulled down part of this wall, alleging that the portion claimed by the plaintiff was the chancel of the parish church, and that even if it were not, the parishioners were entitled either by prescription at common law or by virtue of a lost grant, or under the Prescription Act 1832, s 3 to light from the part claimed by the plaintiff. The plaintiff established that he owned the eastern part of the building, and that it was not the chancel of the parish church. The defendant's claim to have the wall separating the east end of the church from the remainder removed, which was in the form of an iron grille, also failed. The defendant relied on common law prescription, the Prescription Act 1832, s 3, and a lost grant, but all three bases of claim were rejected. In relation to the Prescription Act 1832, Bramwell LJ doubted whether the church could be considered a building within s 3 of the 1832 Act, although he gave no reason for his (tentative) view on the point, which was not necessary for the decision nor referred to by the other members of the court. It is submitted that the dictum cannot be accorded

1 (1880) 5 CPD 390.

significant weight, given these points, the wording of the 1832 Act, and the other decided cases and what constitutes a 'building'. In *Ecclesiastical Commissioners v Kino*,[1] it was assumed that a church was a building capable of acquiring a right to light.

4.11 In *Harris v De Pinna*,[2] the issue arose as to whether a structure used for the storage of timber was a 'building' for the purposes of the 1832 Act. The structure consisted of several floors or stages, and was substantially constructed with upright timber standards fixed in stone bases built on solid piers. The standards were tied together with longitudinal baulks or cross-beams which supported floors or stages of solid planks, and were also connected by diagonal braces. The ends of the floors were open and unglazed, and served to admit light and air for drying timber. Light and air were received for the structure over the defendant's yard. The defendant commenced building over the yard, and the plaintiff, the owner of the structure, brought an action to restrain interference with light and air. It was held that the claim in relation to light failed. Two points were taken: the first was that the structure was not a 'building' within s 3 of the 1832 Act. At first instance, Chitty J accepted this argument, holding that although the structure was a structure, it was not a building within s 3.[3] The Court of Appeal did not find it necessary to decide the point, dismissing the claim on the ground that the structure contained no defined apertures through which light was received, Cotton LJ saying:[4]

> 'All that you protect is the access of light through the windows which have been substantially in the same place where they are at the time when the action is brought, for 20 years; and in my opinion it will not do in order to establish a right, to show that though at some time light did not come in through a particular access, at other times it did, and that sometimes it came in through one and sometimes through another opening, which was there in the structure of the building, which would admit light. Here we have evidence that the timber was stored and placed in these structures in different ways from time to time. What is the consequence? It may be, and the evidence of the plaintiffs has not negatived it, that at one time the timber would be so piled up that no light would come in from the aperture which there might be at, say, the eastern end of the building, and that when the timber was piled differently it came in through the eastern, and could not come in through the western aperture. Very true, during all that time the erection of the building may have enjoyed light, but it has not enjoyed, in my opinion, such access as will give a right to it to the occupier. In order to do that it must be shown that there has been a definite access, I do not say through a window, but through some part of the building and that there has been enjoyed in the building for the statutory period, the light which has come in through that definite mode or means of access.'

4.12 Decisions in the context of other legislation as to what constitutes a 'building' are of little assistance and, in *Harris v De Pinna*, Chitty J at first instance declined to treat as persuasive cases on the meaning of 'building' in the

1 (1880) 14 ChD 213.
2 (1886) 33 ChD 238.
3 Ibid at 249.
4 Ibid at 257.

Metropolitan Building Act 1855.[1] It is submitted that the word 'building' in s 3 is to be construed *ejusdem generis* with the earlier expressions, so that in general a building must have walls and a roof enclosing an interior space. Thus structures such as spectator stands[2] and walls[3] would not constitute a building, although they are undoubtedly structures.

THE TYPE OF APERTURE PROTECTED

Aperture must be defined

4.13 As is clear from the passage in *Harris v De Pinna* cited above, a right of light can be established only in relation to a defined aperture whose purpose is to admit light. An aperture used for an unglazed door will not qualify,[4] on the ground that admission of light through such an aperture is fluctuating and uncertain. Peterson J said:[5]

> 'If a door is at one time fully open and at another time only partially open, what is the aperture through which the light has been enjoyed, and what is the amount of light which has been enjoyed during the period of prescription.'

He also held that, in the particular context of s 3 of the Prescription Act 1832, it applied only to windows or apertures in the nature of windows and not to apertures with doors in them, which were primarily constructed for the purpose of being closed and thus excluding light. The position, therefore, seems to be that both at common law and under s 3, a prescriptive right to light cannot be acquired in respect of apertures with unglazed doors in them. This would not, however, apply to glazed doors which admit light even when closed.

4.14 Modern commercial buildings frequently employ glazed curtain walling supported by steel and concrete frames, as opposed to load-bearing masonry external walls. In such construction, it cannot be said that there are in reality 'apertures' at all. A court would, given the prevalence of the method of construction, be unlikely to find that such buildings are incapable of acquiring rights to light. It is submitted that the 'aperture' can properly be regarded as that part of the whole area between floor and ceiling slabs intended to admit light.

Partially obscured windows

4.15 Clearly, the fact that the window in question has curtains or blinds which are drawn at different times or seasons of the year does not prevent such a window being treated as enjoying a right to light. The same also applies where the

1 For use of the word 'building' in other statutory contexts, see eg Town and Country Planning Act 1990, s 336; Party Wall etc Act 1996, s 6.
2 Cf *City of Westminster v London County Council* [1902] 1 KB 326.
3 Cf *Mills and Rockleys Ltd v Leicester City Council* [1946] KB 315.
4 *Levet v Gas Light and Coke Co* [1919] 1 Ch 24.
5 [1919] 1 Ch 27.

window has external shutters capable of being opened and closed.[1] Permanent obstruction of the window by the dominant owner, for example by boarding up, may, depending on the circumstances, result in the aperture not acquiring a right to light, or in any acquired right to light being treated as abandoned.[2] In *Smith v Baxter*,[3] it was held that a permanent boarding up of two windows prevented them acquiring a prescriptive right to light, but the position was different with regard to another window which had been covered with shelving.

4.16 The right to light arises in relation to any part of the structure which contains a defined aperture for the admission of light, even though the aperture forms part of the structure of the building which also serves as a wall or roof, for example the glazed wall of a greenhouse or the glazed roof of a conservatory.[4] The dominant owner's right extends to the full size of the aperture, no account being taken of window frames or glazing bars.[5]

Apertures between different parts of the same building

4.17 In *Duke of Norfolk v Arbuthnot*,[6] the facts of which have already been outlined, Bramwell LJ expressed doubt as to whether a prescriptive right to light could arise in respect of light passing through part of a building owned by the plaintiff and thence via an arch to part owned by the defendant, on the ground that the arch existed for the common benefit of two buildings. Reasons for this doubt were not articulated, but it is a possible view that the right to light arises only in respect of apertures in the external envelope of a structure, so that no prescriptive right to light can arise in relation to the further diffusion of light once it has passed through the external envelope. Thus those whose premises derive light via a glazed atrium, for example, would not be protected.

4.18 It is suggested that this view is not correct. There is no logical reason why there should be no right to light which passes through part of a building before arriving at the plaintiff's premises. This view is supported by *Tisdall v McArthur & Co (Steel & Metal) Ltd*[7] in which it was held that the existence of a transparent glass roof over a yard which provided light to the plaintiff's windows did not prevent the acquisition of a prescriptive right to light.[8]

Incomplete/unoccupied premises

4.19 It appears that once a building is sufficiently structurally completed to be recognisably such, the fact that it remains unfinished will not prevent a right to

1 *Cooper v Straker* (1888) 40 ChD 21.
2 See, generally, Chapter 8 at **8.9–8.19**.
3 [1900] 2 Ch 138.
4 *Easton v Isted* [1903] 1 Ch 405.
5 *Turner v Spooner* (1861) 1 Drew and Sm 467 62 ER 457.
6 (1880) 5 CPD 390.
7 [1951] IR 228.
8 See also *Barnes v Loach* (1879) 4 QBD 494.

light arising by prescription. In *Courtauld v Legh*,[1] a house was structurally completed, the roof finished, the floors laid, and the windows put in, but not internally completed nor fit for habitation. It was held that a right to light in respect of the windows had been acquired. In *Collis v Laugher*,[2] it was held that for the purposes of the date of commencement of the 20-year period necessary to establish a prescriptive right to light under s 3 of the Prescription Act 1832, enjoyment commenced when the exterior walls of the building with the spaces for the windows were completed, and the building was roofed in, even though the windows themselves had not been installed. This case must of course be distinguished from the situation where the external walls are not constructed to a sufficient stage to have inserted in them the defined apertures for windows. Thus the construction of a steel and concrete frame for a building, without walling, would probably not give rise to an entitlement to a prescriptive right to light. Where a building enjoying rights to light is demolished, the rights it enjoys do not necessarily end for all time; if there is an intention on the part of an owner to rebuild they may be regarded as simply in abeyance.[3]

---

1 (1869) LR Exch 126.
2 [1894] 3 Ch 659.
3 See Chapter 8 at **8.49–8.50**.

Chapter 5
Acquisition of Rights to Light I – by acts of the parties

EXPRESS GRANT

5.1 It is comparatively rare for an easement of light to be created by express words of grant as between freeholders. More often are found deeds between owners of adjoining buildings, or provisions in conveyances of parts of land formerly in one ownership which contain covenants restricting buildings and other erections that can be constructed so as to protect existing rights to light.[1] There is no reason in principle, however, why an express grant cannot be effected. In order for a legal easement of light to be granted, a deed is required.[2] An equitable easement may be created otherwise than by deed.[3] An uncompleted agreement to grant a legal easement is a classic example of an equitable easement. If title to the servient land is registered, the easement, whether legal or equitable, must be protected by notice. A legal easement must be protected by registration on the title of the dominant land, up until which point it takes effect in equity only.[4]

5.2 In the case of unregistered land, an equitable easement created since 1925 is void against a purchaser for money or money's worth of a legal estate in the land subject to it, unless registered prior to completion of the purchase.[5] The fact that the purchaser has notice of it will not prevent the easement being void against him.[6] In the case of registered land, a person entitled to an equitable easement over registered land may apply to have notice of it registered and such easements may qualify as overriding interests under s 70(1)(a) of the Land Registration Act 1925.[7] For the effect of overriding interests on third parties, see *Ashburn Anstalt v Arnold (No 2)*.[8]

5.3 For an easement to be validly granted, the grantor must in general have sufficient interest in the servient land to create a valid easement over it. Easements granted over land belonging to third parties may, however, take effect by way of acquiescence or estoppel in some circumstances.[9] Likewise, if there is

---

1 See, eg, *Potts v Smith* (1868) LR 6 Eq 311.
2 Law of Property Act 1925, s 52.
3 Ibid, s 53.
4 This is so only if the title to the servient tenement is registered. Land Registration Act 1925, ss 19(2) and 22(2).
5 Land Charges Act 1972, s 4(6).
6 Law of Property Act 1925, s 199(1)(i).
7 See *Celsteel Ltd v Alton House Holdings Ltd* (1985) 2 All ER 562, and Chapter 1 at **1.14–1.16**. See Chapter 14.
8 [1988] 2 EGLR 64, CA.
9 See, eg, *ER Ives Investments Ltd v High* [1967] 1 All ER 504, CA.

an express grant of an easement over land to which the grantor has no title, but he then acquires title, he and his successors will be bound by estoppel.[1] Where the grantor has only a limited interest in the land over which he purports to grant the easement, the extent of the easement will be determined by his interest at the time of the grant, without taking into account subsequent events. So in *Booth v Alcock*,[2] the grantor of an easement of light had at the time of the grant only a lease over the servient tenement. He subsequently acquired the fee simple, but it was held that the grant was restricted in duration to the length of the lease which the grantor had at the date of the grant.

5.4 Where the rights of the grantor to dispose of his land are subject to statutory constraints, he cannot lawfully grant an easement in excess of his powers. This may arise on dispositions by trustees, or life tenants under the Settled Land Act 1925.[3] The importance of these restrictions, insofar as they apply to former trustees for sale, has been greatly reduced by the Trusts of Land and Appointment of Trustees Act 1996. Trustees of land have now all the powers of an absolute owner unless expressly restricted.[4] It remains the position that when authority is required the grant of an easement which is not authorised will be of no effect.[5]

5.5 In the same way as a competent grantor is required, no easement can be granted in excess of the interest of the grantee in the dominant tenement. This is consistent with the general principle that easements are appurtenant to land, so that they can only subsist for as long as the interest in land to which they relate subsists. Where the grant is to someone with a limited interest, who subsequently becomes the owner of the dominant tenement, the easement may enure for the benefit of the freehold if the terms of the grant contemplated that this should be the case.[6]

5.6 An easement of light may also be reserved by the vendor of land.[7] The reservation must normally be in clear terms.[8] Apart from this, an easement may be held to have been reserved by implication but such a reservation will be found to exist only where the facts are not reasonably consistent with any explanation other than such an easement was intended to be reserved.[9]

---

1 *Rowbotham v Wilson* (1857) 8 E&B 123; 8 HLC 348.
2 (1873) 8 Ch App 663.
3 See, eg, Settled Land Act 1925, s 49(1), which authorises the grant and reservation of easements, and s 41 of the same Act in regard to the grant of leases.
4 Trusts of Land and Appointment of Trustees Act 1996, s 6(1).
5 See eg *Oakley v Boston* [1976] QB 270 (consent required to grant of an easement under Ecclesiastical Leases Acts 1842 and 1858 but not obtained). See also *Re St Clement, Leigh-on-Sea* [1988] 1 WLR 720.
6 *Rymer v McIlroy* [1897] 1 Ch 528.
7 See Law of Property Act 1925, s 65.
8 *Wheeldon v Burrows* (1879) 12 ChD 31 at 49 per Thesiger LJ.
9 *Re Webb's Lease* [1951] Ch 808 at 829 per Jenkins LJ. *Peckham v Ellison* (1998) 77 P&CR D27, CA (right of way).

5.7 An express easement of light may be granted by a lease. The effect of such a grant was considered in *Frogmore Developments Ltd v Shirayama Shokusan Co*[1] in the context of its (alleged) inconsistency with intended development of nearby land. It was held that the grant of 'the right to free and unobstructed passage of light and air to the premises at all times' entitled the lessee to receive light at a level which did not fall below that required for the ordinary purposes for which the premises could be used.

GRANT BY IMPLICATION

5.8 An easement may be inferred where a conveyance or other document does not grant it expressly, but uses terms consistent with the existence of the easement. In *Roberts v Karr*,[2] the description of land in a release as abutting on a road was held to preclude the grantor from asserting that the grantee was not entitled to access over a verge which separated part of the land granted from that road.

5.9 An easement may be held to have been granted by implication, based on the intended use of the property the subject of a lease for sale.[3] In *Browne v Flower*,[4] Parker J considered the position of an implicit grant of an easement of light, saying:

> 'Once again, though possibly there may not be known to the law any easement of light for special purposes, still the lease of a building to be used for a special purpose requiring an extraordinary amount of light might well be held to preclude the grantor from diminishing the light passing to the grantee's windows, even in cases where the diminution would not be such as to create a nuisance within the meaning of recent decisions ...'

There seems no reason in principle why these words should be limited to the situation where the lessee or other grantee is claiming an extraordinary quantity of light. If the purpose for which premises are leased or granted contemplate the receipt of light in any quantity through existing or, indeed, proposed apertures a right to receive such light might arise by implication. This may well be of importance in the case of specialised premises, such as drawing offices, and will become more generally important if statutory requirements regarding health and safety at work lead to the imposition of a standard entitling employees to work in environments with direct sky illuminations. Current regulations require lighting at work places to be 'so far as is reasonably practicable, ... by natural light'.[5] This does not impose on the employer a duty to ensure that natural light is available, save except so far as it is 'reasonably practicable'. It would presumably not be the

---

1 (1997) ChD, unreported.
2 [1809] 1 Taunt 495.
3 *Lyttleton Times Co Limited v Warners Limited* [1907] AC 476; *Yankwood Limited v Havering London Borough Council* [1998] EGCS 75.
4 [1911] 1 Ch 219 at 226.
5 Construction (Health Safety and Welfare) Regulations 1996, reg 25.

case that it would be reasonably practicable to provide natural light where the terms on which the employer occupied the relevant premises did not confer on him a right to prevent the windows being obscured so as to limit or exclude natural light. It is, however, possible to envisage circumstances where it might be argued that since the contemplated purpose for which premises were being leased or purchased involved at least some obligation on the part of the purchaser to provide natural light to the work places of those whom he proposed to employ there, there was by implication a grant of an easement of light.[1]

GRANT UNDER THE RULE IN WHEELDON V BURROWS

5.10 This case[2] finds its foundations in the principle of implied grant. It is, in effect, an early formulation of s 62 of the Law of Property Act 1925 but the rights that pass are limited by comparison to that section, an exception being the agreement for a lease which does not count as a conveyance for the purposes of s 62.[3] The principle itself is neatly set out by Thesiger LJ:

> '... that, on the grant by the owner of a tenement of part of that tenement as it is then used and enjoyed, there will pass to the grantee all those continuous and apparent easements (by which, of course, I mean quasi-easements), or in other words all those easements which are necessary to the reasonable enjoyment of the property granted, and which have been and are at the time of the grant used by the owners of the entirety for the benefit of the part granted.'

5.11 The rule, therefore, usually operates on the sub-division of a parcel of land. For example, if a parcel of land under common ownership is divided into part A, which is retained and part B, which is disposed of, the rule confers by implication on the transferee of part B the benefits of any rights to light over part A that the former owner of both parts exercised over the land prior to its sub-division. The rule also applies where the common owner subdivides and sells the subdivided property simultaneously, retaining no land himself.

5.12 *Wheeldon v Burrows* was itself a case that concerned the right of access to light over the servient tenement. Access to light is regarded as both continuous and apparent and necessary for the reasonable enjoyment of the land and does not therefore suffer from the problems of easements (such as rights of way) for which proof of use or necessity is required.[4]

Thus, in *Swansborough v Coventry*,[5] Trindall CJ said:

---

1 For a case where the grant in a lease of a right to light was held not to be *instructed* by implication from surrounding circumstances, see *Frogmore Developments Ltd v Shirayama Shokusan Co Ltd* (1997) ChD, unreported. See **5.7**.

2 (1879) 12 ChD 31.

3 See *Borman v Griffith* [1930] 1 Ch 493.

4 For example, *Borman v Griffith* (above) – the case itself provides a useful review of the rule in *Wheeldon v Burrows* (above) at 499.

5 [1832] 9 Bing 305 at 309.

'It is well established by the decided cases, that where the same person possesses a house, having the actual use and enjoyment of certain rights, and also possesses the adjoining land, and sells the house to another person, although the lights be new, he cannot, nor can anyone who claims under him, build upon the adjoining land so as to obstruct or interrupt the enjoyment of those lights.'

Sale of part of land, where vendor retains the remainder

5.13 Where buildings on the land being disposed of have yet to be built but the vendor is aware, either at the time of the disposition or during any prior agreement for the disposition, that the land is being acquired for building purposes, the principle applies equally and the right attaches to the buildings when built.[1]

5.14 The transfer of rights by implication may itself be negatived or modified by circumstances, but the onus of establishing this is on the grantor. Therefore, where the grantor makes it clear in express terms that he intends to build on part A (the retained land), the grantee cannot complain if his access to light is restricted by such construction.[2] If, however, the grantee is aware of only a general intention to build, such as by describing the retained land as 'building land', then this is insufficient to negative the implication.[3]

5.15 Where a grantor who sells part of his land does not expressly reserve in that grant an easement of light in favour of the part he has retained, he will normally not be held to have reserved such a right by implication.[4] Such reservation should, therefore, be expressly stated in the grant. The general rule is that grants are construed against the grantor, and this principle applies to exclude, in general, the implication of reservations in favour of the grantor, as explained at **5.19**. The correct approach is for the court to interpret the terms of the grant by considering the instrument and the surrounding circumstances in conjunction.[5]

5.16 However, where a vendor disposes of two plots of land simultaneously, which are adjacent to each other, both conveyances are treated as grants under the rule in *Wheeldon v Burrows* and therefore each part acquires by implication the same easements over any other as it would if that other part had been retained by the vendor.[6] This rule applies equally to testamentary dispositions and voluntary conveyances inter vivos.[7]

---

1 *Frederick Betts Ltd v Pickfords Ltd* [1906] 2 Ch 87.
2 *Birmingham, Dudley & District Banking Company v Ross* (1888) 38 ChD 295.
3 *Broomfield v Williams* (1897) 1 ChD at 602. *Frogmore Development Ltd v Shirayama Shokusan Co Ltd* (1997) ChD, unreported.
4 *Wheeldon v Burrows* (1879) 12 ChD 31 at 49. See also **5.6**. For the effect of a reservation, see Law of Property Act 1925, s 65.
5 *St Edmundsbury and Ipswich Diocesan Board of Finance v Clark (No 2)* [1975] 1 All ER 772, CA; *Frogmore Developments Ltd v Shirayama Shokusan Co Ltd* (1997) ChD, unreported. For the extent of 'surrounding circumstances' see, generally, *Investors Compensation Scheme Ltd v West Bromwich Building Society* [1998] 1 All ER 98, HL.
6 *Russell v Watts* (1884) 25 ChD 559 – see especially Fry LJ at 584.
7 *Phillips v Low* [1892] 1 Ch 47.

Lease of part of land, where the landlord retains the remainder

5.17 As with an outright sale of land, the formal grant of a lease over part B of land of the lessor, will allow the lessee to acquire by implication, for the term of the lease, any right to the access of light over the retained land (part A), which it can be shown was actually enjoyed by the part let at the date of the lease.

5.18 During the term of that lease, any later lease or grant of the retained land must take effect subject to the right to the access of light to the let land.[1] If, however, there was never any formal grant of the original lease over the let land (eg there was an agreement only to create a lease), the rights of the original informal lessee may still be protected by registration or actual occupation of the part let.

5.19 Where a lessor, in demising part of his land over which light is received to his retained land, fails to reserve in favour of the part retained an easement of light over the part demised, the retained land will normally enjoy no right to light during the term of the lease.[2] For an easement of light to arise under the principle, it is not necessary for the common owner to be actually in possession of both parts of his land before he simultaneously disposes of both parts.[3]

5.20 The application of the principle was described by Mellish LJ in *Leech v Schweder*[4] as follows:

> 'It is perfectly established that if a man owns a house, and owns property of any other kind adjoining that house, and then either conveys the house in fee simple or demises it for a term of years to another person, a right to light unobstructed by anything to be erected on any land which at the time belonged to the grantor passes to the grantee.'

The implication may be negatived by surrounding circumstances, as where it is well known to the purchaser or lessee that the grantor or lessor intends to develop his retained land in a way which may interfere with the light to the buildings (actual or proposed) on the land conveyed or let.[5] The onus of negativing the implication of an easement lies on the grantor.[6]

LAW OF PROPERTY ACT 1925, SECTION 62

5.21 This is now the main way in which the right to easements which are not mentioned in the conveyance are impliedly granted and overlays the rule in

1 *Thomas v Owen* (1888) 20 QBD 225.

2 *Re Webbs Lease* [1951] Ch 808; *Frogmore Developments Ltd v Shirayama Shokusan Co Ltd* (1997) ChD, unreported. See also *Peckham v Ellison* (1998) 77 P&CR D27, CA.

3 *Barnes v Loach* (1879) 4 QBD 494.

4 (1874) 9 Ch App 463 at 472.

5 *Birmingham, Dudley and District Banking Co v Ross* (1888) 38 ChD 295; *Godwin v Schweppes Ltd* [1902] 1 Ch 926.

6 *Broomfield v Williams* [1897] 1 Ch 602; *Pollard v Gare* [1901] 1 Ch 834; *Swansborough v Coventry* (1832) 9 Bing 305; *Myers v Catterson* (1889) 43 ChD 470.

Wheeldon v Burrows. The section applies to conveyances made after 31 December 1881 which was when s 6 of the Conveyancing Act 1881, which preceded s 62 of the Law of Property Act 1925, came into effect.

5.22 Section 62 of the Law of Property Act provides that:

> '(1) A conveyance of land shall be deemed to include and shall by virtue of this Act operate to convey, with the land, all buildings, erections, fixtures, commons, hedges, ditches, fences, ways, waters, watercourses, liberties, privileges, easements, rights, and advantages whatsoever, appertaining or reputed to appertain to the land, or any part thereof, or, at the time of conveyance, demised, occupied, or enjoyed with, or reputed or known as part or parcel of or appurtenant to the land or any part thereof.
>
> (2) A conveyance of land, having houses or other buildings thereon, shall be deemed to include and shall by virtue of this Act operate to convey, with the land, houses, or other buildings, or outhouses, erections, fixtures, cellars, areas, courts, courtyards, cisterns, sewers, gutters, drains, ways, passages, lights, watercourses, liberties, privileges, easements, rights and advantages whatsoever, appertaining or reputed to appertain to the land, houses, or other buildings conveyed, or any of them, or any parts thereof, or, at the time of conveyance, demised, occupied, or enjoyed with, or reputed or known as part or parcel of or appurtenant to, the land, houses, or other buildings conveyed, or any of them, or any part thereof.'

5.23 By conveyance, is meant virtually any instrument which transfers or creates a *legal* estate in freehold or leasehold land.[1] The term does not include, therefore, agreements which create equitable interest only.[2] Where they apply, the general words of s 62 can only be excluded by express terms.[3]

5.24 Section 62 has the effect of passing to the transferee of land the benefit of existing easements, profits, privileges and rights which appertain to the land conveyed, or are indeed reputed to appertain to it, or which at the date of the conveyance are enjoyed with that land.

5.25 As an owner of land cannot have an easement over his own land, there is clear authority that s 62 operates only where there has been diversity of ownership, or occupation of the dominant or servient tenement prior to the conveyance. This is because where no such divergence exists there can be no easement to pass under s 62.[4]

5.26 However, strictly, the views of Lords Edmund-Davis and Wilberforce are *obiter dicta* albeit of high authority.[5] In the case of quasi-easements of light, it

---

1 Law of Property Act 1925, s 205(1)(iii).

2 *Borman v Griffith* [1930] 1 Ch 493. Which is of itself sufficient to create an express equitable easement – see **5.1**.

3 Law of Property Act 1925, s 62(4) – *William Hill (Southern) Ltd v Cabras Ltd* (1987) 54 P&CR 42 at 46.

4 *Sovmots Investments Ltd v Secretary of State for the Environment* [1979] AC 144 at 176C per Lord Edmund Davies. Lord Wilberforce expressed the same view.

5 For comment, see Harpum (1977) 41 *Conveyancer* 415; (1979) 43 *Conveyancer* 113; (1978) 42 *Conveyancer* 449.

appears in any event that where there is unity of occupation, s 62 is still capable of applying. This was decided in *Broomfield v Williams*.[1]

5.27 As with the rule in *Wheeldon v Burrows*, the presence of light over land is not difficult to show. Therefore, a right to the access of that light will be transferred under s 62 even where there has been a unity of ownership provided the right has been exercised by and for the benefit of the land conveyed and not just for the common benefit of the two properties. Where the land is not in common ownership no such problem arises. It should be noted that the court retains an equitable jurisdiction to rectify any conveyance which mistakenly transfers to a grantee more rights than were intended in a relevant contract for sale.

UNDER THE OBLIGATION NOT TO DEROGATE FROM GRANT

5.28 This principle is a general rule applying to all conveyances and is not restricted to cases involving easements. This is because it is based upon the presumed intention of the parties to the relevant grant. Therefore, in that a grantor should not do anything to render the disposal nugatory, the principle has been described as one 'of common honesty'.[2] The rights acquired pursuant to an application of the principle binds successors in title of the grantor and are available to successors in title of the grantee.

5.29 The principle finds clear judicial expression in the judgment of Parker J in *Browne v Flower*, where His Lordship said:

> 'But the implications usually explained by the maxim that no-one can derogate from his own grant do not stop short with easements under certain circumstances there will be implied on the part of the grantor or lessor obligations which a strict user of the land retained by him further than can be explained by the implication of any easement known to the law. Thus, if the grant or demise be made for a particular purpose, the grantor or lessor comes under an obligation not to use the land retained by him in such a way as to render the land granted or demised unfit or materially less fit for the particular purpose for which the grant or demise was made.'[3]

5.30 Therefore, the immunities acquired by virtue of the principle depend upon the common intention, to be gathered either from the express words of the grant or the circumstances in which it was made. No complaint can be made if an act by the grantor does not make the land granted unfit for a particular purpose or only achievable at a greater expense or with less convenience.[4]

---

1 [1897] 1 Ch 602.

2 *Harmer v Jumbil (Nigeria) Tin Areas Ltd* [1921] 1 Ch 200 at 235 and see *Johnston and Sons Ltd v Holland* [1988] 1 EGLR 264.

3 [1911] 1 Ch 219 at 225.

4 *O'Cedar Ltd v Slough Trading Company Ltd* [1927] 2 KB 123 at 127.

5.31 The principle has been applied so as to bind those deriving title from the grantor, irrespective of whether they have notice of the grantor's obligation.[1] In *Johnston and Sons Ltd v Holland*,[2] in which earlier cases were reviewed, the principle was held to apply to acts done by the grantor on land which he did not own at the date of the grant. This may be of considerable importance in rights of light situations, and may effectively preclude a vendor of land on which a building exists, or on which the erection of such a building is contemplated, from using land which he later acquires so as to interfere with the light received over it to the purchasers of the building, whether existing at the date of the sale or contemplated at that time. It is immaterial whether the purchaser's building would otherwise enjoy a prescriptive right to light.

UNDER STATUTORY PROVISIONS

5.32 Easements may be granted expressly by statute or may arise by the exercise or performance of powers or obligations contained in those statutes. One example of this is where a public body which compulsorily purchased land under a statutory power may need additional rights over adjoining land in order to carry out the purposes for which the land is being purchased. However, it should be noted that there is no implied right to create new easements which did not exist prior to the compulsory purchase[3] except insofar as they may exist as quasi-easements under either the rule in *Wheeldon v Burrows*, or s 62 of the Law of Property Act 1925.[4] This lack of creative power is confirmed by silence in the Acquisition of Land Act 1981, which is the primary Act by which the Government, local authorities and other bodies obtain land by compulsory purchase. Therefore, it is now the norm for specific Acts to contain express provision for the creation of new rights within their powers for compulsory purchase.

5.33 Where land is compulsorily purchased which has existing easements, these are transferred in the normal way under s 62 and the usual implications for successors in title apply. There are not many circumstances under which it would be envisaged that a right to light would specifically be required in an Act of Parliament, except, for example, insofar as the Ministry for Agriculture, Fisheries and Food requires land for experimental farms.

5.34 Another form of statutory provision which creates an easement of sorts, is that which permits the laying and repairing of pipes, wires and cables. These are not clear easements because the statutory undertaker does not acquire the land and as such there is no dominant tenement. This was considered in *Newcastle-under-Lyme Corporation v Wolstanton Ltd*[5] where Morton LJ agreeing with and quoting Evershed J at the first instance stated:

1 *Cable v Bryant* [1908] 1 Ch 259.
2 [1988] 1 EGLR 264, CA.
3 *Sovmots Investments v Secretary of State for the Environment* [1979] AC 144.
4 See **5.10–5.27**.
5 [1947] Ch 427 at 456.

> 'They have by force of the statute the exclusive right to occupy for the purposes of their statutory undertaking the space in the soil taken by the pipes ... but that exclusive right of occupation which continues so long as the Corporation carry on their undertaking, does not depend upon or involve the vesting in the plaintiff corporation of any legal or equitable estate in the land.'

5.35 The conclusion reached by JF Garner[1] is that these 'rights given by statute are *sui generis*, and fit in with no known other jurisprudence concept and amount to an exclusive right to occupy the space or can be occupied by the actual pipes themselves'. Acts which enable these activities include: the Electricity Act 1989,[2] the Telecommunications Act 1984[3] and the Water Industries Act 1991,[4] but once again in terms of rights to light these type of provisions are of little or no significance.

1 20 *Conveyancer* 208 at 213.
2 Schedule 4.
3 Schedule 2.
4 Section 159.

Chapter 6
Acquisition of Rights to Light II – by prescription

SUMMARY

6.1 An easement of light may be acquired by prescription in one of the following ways:

(1) by proving continuous enjoyment since time immemorial, which in practice means showing enjoyment back many hundreds of years and potentially since 1189. This is known as 'common law prescription'. Only freehold owners can claim the right by this means;
(2) by proving at least 20 years' continuous enjoyment back from the time when proceedings are issued. Such enjoyment must comply with the requirements of the Prescription Act 1832, and a claim is a prescriptive one based on that Act. Unique to rights to light, and only under this Act, a tenant may claim rights to light, both for and against a freehold owner and even against his own landlord;
(3) by claiming that light has been enjoyed for any period of at least 20 years and that enjoyment has been a fictitious grant of such a right by a person capable of making such a grant. Only freehold owners can claim the right by this means. This is known as a claim based on 'lost modern grant'. It saves having to prove enjoyment since 1189 and avoids having to prove enjoyment for at least 20 years back from the issue of proceedings as required by the Prescription Act 1832.

Any claim to rights to light can be based on any of these prescriptive heads of claim, and in some cases all three heads can be relied upon if the facts so warrant. It is rare, however, for a claim to be based (let alone succeed) upon common law prescription.

COMMON LAW PRESCRIPTION

6.2 The acquisition of an easement of light by prescription at common law requires proof of enjoyment from time immemorial, which in practical terms means from the beginning of legal memory being 1189, that being the first year of the reign of Richard I. The date was fixed by the Statute of Westminster in 1275 and remains fixed.[1]

6.3 As can be imagined, particularly with regard to the easement of light which depends on apertures in buildings for its enjoyment, proof of enjoyment back so

1 See, generally, Nash '1189 and the limit of legal memory' (1989) 139 NLJ 1763.

many centuries has increasingly become impossible. To overcome this, the courts have adopted a presumption that a right to light proved to have been long enjoyed, and without any evidence that enjoyment began at a date after 1189, was a right which had existed for a period commencing with the beginning of legal memory. Thus in *Aynsley v Glover*,[1] evidence of an 80-year-old witness was accepted as establishing the presumption of enjoyment since 1189, in circumstances where the date of building of the dwellings receiving light could not be proved.

6.4 It is equally possible to rebut the presumption by showing that the building can be proved to have been built at a date since 1189.[2] In the light of access to historical records such as Ordnance Survey maps and photographs, the National Monument Record maintained by English Heritage, local registers and Tithe and Enclosure maps it is often easier to rebut the presumption than establish it. In places such as the City of London, it is only in the case of certain churches which escaped the Great Fire, and a few other ancient buildings (such as exist in Cloth Fair near Smithfield) where the remotest possibility of establishing a common law prescriptive claim exists. The same may be true in places such as Bristol and York where 'ancient' buildings still exist.

6.5 It is also possible to rebut the presumption of long enjoyment by showing that at some time since 1189 the dominant and servient titles were in common ownership. The same result may occur where it can be shown that both tenements were in common possession (as opposed to common ownership – eg by a tenant) but that conclusion is not altogether clear.[3]

6.6 Enjoyment of light, if claimed by prescription at common law, must be by a freehold owner against a freehold owner. This is because the right, if acquired, depends on the presumption of a grant by the absolute owner of the freehold. Although there is an exception to this rule when claims under the Prescription Act 1832 are made (where a tenant may acquire an easement of light – see **6.17** and **6.30** for the detail of this), in claims made at common law, the grant must be for and against the fee simple.[4] The same point can arise where there is a limit on the capacity of the servient owner to grant an easement and where it would be ultra vires for the grant to have been made. Thus, in the case of the Church Commissioners where no consent can be shown to the grant, no grant can be presumed.[5] The same limitations may apply to fiduciaries, commoners[6] and the National Trust (where inalienable land is concerned). One other exception arises, rarely, where the claimant is a tenant with the right to enlarge his lease into

---

1 (1875) 10 Ch App 283.

2 See, eg, *Wheaton v Maple & Co* [1893] 3 Ch 48 – property built in 1852; *Bowring Services v Scottish Widows Fund and Life Assurance Society* [1995] 1 EGLR 158 – property shown to have been built after the Second World War where aerial photographs showed the bomb site after destruction of the predecessor building during the Blitz in 1940.

3 See Chapter 8 at **8.6–8.8**.

4 *Wheaton v Maple & Co* [1893] 3 Ch 63.

5 *Oakley v Boston* [1976] QB 270.

6 *Paine v St Neots Gas & Coke Co* [1938] 4 All ER 592; [1939] 3 All ER 812, CA.

a fee simple under s 153 of the Law of Property Act 1925.[1] In practice, it is important to check the capacity of the presumed grantor at any stage of the period for which enjoyment is claimed. Copyhold titles can still require consideration. In cases where a period prior to 1 January 1926 (on which date all copyholds were converted to freeholds) is material and the title of the dominant land was copyhold prior to that date for any period of the period of enjoyment relied upon, a number of different and difficult problems arise. Because it is rare to rely on such historic enjoyment, a summary of principles to be applied should suffice here.

(1) A copyholder may acquire a right to light against land owned by a third party, in the name of the Lord of the copyholders' manor.
(2) A copyholder may not acquire a right to light against his Lord unless the custom of the manor permits it. In many cases, the application of the principle that a use has a lawful basis (*omnia praesemuntur*) will allow the presumption that the custom was to allow the use.
(3) If enfranchisement of the copyhold was under the Copyhold Act 1894 or earlier Acts, the right to light will survive. It may not survive if enfranchisement was not statutory, and no rights to light were reserved to the copyholder.[2]

6.7 The enjoyment of the light claimed as an easement by prescription at common law must have been enjoyed 'as of right' and this means openly, without consent and without the use of force. (This rule is often described by textbooks in Latin '*nec vi* [ie not by force] *nec clam* [ie not secretly] *nec precario* [ie not by consent]'.) In the case of an easement of light it is hard to see how enjoyment can otherwise be than by the open use of a window, or other aperture, and in modern times force seems an inappropriate and unlikely vehicle for securing the enjoyment of light. However, in the context of modern neighbour disputes, it is not unknown for alleged obstructions to light to be torn down during the dead of night, if not during broad daylight. Recently, it has been held by the Court of Appeal (in a case concerning a right of way), that user enjoyed after its exercise becomes contentious (and which can be continued to be enjoyed only by the physical removal of obstructions), ceases to be as of right.[3] Thus, in the case of an easement of light, enjoyment after the matter becomes contentious (eg by forcible removal of an obstruction, or the cutting down of a tree, or hedge or even, possibly, the sending of a letter challenging the user) will not be as of right at common law. (Note, however, the different position which applies to the easement of light claimed under the Prescription Act 1832 at **6.21**, where enjoyment does not have to be as of right.) As to enjoyment by consent, evidence of permission other than in written form in light cases is rare, and mere acquiescence in the enjoyment (by not objecting to the aperture receiving light) will not prevent acquisition by prescription at common law, for such acquiescence is an essential ingredient in the establishment of the right by this

1 *Bosomworth v Faber* [1992] NPC 155, CA.
2 See *Derry v Sanders* [1919] 1 KB 223.
3 *Newnham v Wilsin* (1987) 51 P&CR 8.

means.[1] Enjoyment must not be inconsistent with a statute or custom. Thus enjoyment of light through an aperture in a building constructed in breach of planning control may not be capable of supporting a prescriptive claim at common law. As to custom, where the Custom of London applies, that too prevents a claim to the easement of light by prescription at common law.[2] It is thought that there is no longer a special custom in existence in York which affects light.[3]

6.8 It is possible to acquire the right to an easement of light by prescription at common law even though the enjoyment may have been by the dominant owner in mistake of his rights against the servient owner.[4] The explanation is that the claimant may believe that he has the right to the easement of light (eg from a grant) but this belief (in error) does not prevent the enjoyment from being acquiesced in by the servient owner who does not share the same belief.[5] It is only in the rare instance where both dominant and servient owners share the same (erroneous) belief as to the origin or existence of the right that it can be said that there is no assertion of any right which is being acquiesced in. Only then may such a shared belief prevent a claim in prescription at common law from succeeding.[6]

6.9 There is sometimes difficulty in establishing the knowledge of the servient owner of the enjoyment of the easement of light. For the purposes of claims under common law prescription, it must be shown that the freeholder has known of and acquiesced in the enjoyment.[7] The presence of a tenant on the servient land may in law affect the freeholder's knowledge. At common law (and note for the reasons set out at **6.15** the different situation which governs claims under the Prescription Act 1832), the actual or presumed knowledge of the freehold reversioner will determine how far he is bound by the presence of the apertures on the dominant land which are to acquire the right to the easement of light. It would seem that if the windows in the dominant land were there before the grant of the tenancy, the reversioner of the tenancy of the servient land will be bound.[8] The position where the windows were first opened during the currency of the tenancy of the servient land is less clear. The answer may depend on whether the windows had at the time the tenancy commenced the appearance of ancient lights.[9] In broad terms, it may be said that the longer the building is on the dominant land with its apertures in place, the more likely it is that the court will find in favour of a prescriptive claim succeeding and uphold the presumption

1 *Mills v Silver* [1991] Ch 271.
2 See **6.13**.
3 Ibid.
4 *Bridle v Ruby* [1989] 1 QB 169.
5 See *Mills v Silver* [1991] Ch 271.
6 See *Bridle v Ruby* above and also *Chamber Colliery v Hopwood* (1886) 32 ChD 549, where both servient and dominant owners believed that the enjoyment of the easement was for the term of the lease.
7 See **6.13**.
8 *Cross v Lewis* (1824) 2 B&C 686, 107 ER 538.
9 Ibid per Abbot CJ.

that the freehold reversioner of the servient land knew of it.[1] The extent of the servient owner's knowledge derived via an agent (eg a managing surveyor) must depend on the individual acts and circumstances.[2]

LOST MODERN GRANT

6.10 The doctrine of lost modern grant has in its origins the increasing difficulty which the courts encountered in establishing the presumption of enjoyment of an easement back to 1189. Thus, by analogy with the period of 20 years fixed by the Statute of Limitations 1623, it became possible to assert that enjoyment of an easement for 20 years, without any other lawful explanation, could be presumed to have had its origin in a grant. The grant was, of course, fictional. The word 'modern' no doubt refers to the fact that the presumed grant post-dates 1189.[3]

6.11 It is possible to establish acquisition of an easement of light by the application of the doctrine if it can be shown that there has been enjoyment both by and against the freehold owners of the dominant and servient tenements for a period of at least 20 years.[4] Although it has been argued that an easement of light cannot be acquired by the application of this doctrine (as considered by the Eire Supreme Court in *Tisdall v McArthur & Co*,[5] by reference to the obiter remarks of Farwell LJ in *Hyman v Van Den Bergh*),[6] there seems no logical reason why such an easement should not be capable of acquisition under this head.[7] The period of 20 years is not a fixed one (cf the Prescription Act 1832), and it can be claimed for any period of time during which the right was capable of being enjoyed. This is in contrast with claims under the Prescription Act 1832 where the relevant 20-year period must run continuously back from the date of the commencement of the action.[8]

6.12 If there is no evidence to show that the grant could not have been made (eg by incapacity of one of the parties, the absence of a requisite consent, or the fact of common ownership), the court will adopt the legal fiction that a grant was made.[9] It is only if there is evidence that it is impossible for a grant to have been made that the court will refuse to apply the fiction. Mere circumstantial evidence showing that a grant was unlikely will not displace the fiction.[10] However, the

---

1 *Pugh v Savage* [1970] 2 QB 373.
2 *Diment v Foot* [1974] 1 WLR 1427.
3 *Dalton v Angus* (1881) 6 App Cas 740, is the leading authority on the origin of the doctrine of lost modern grant.
4 *Simmons v Dobson* [1991] 1 WLR 720.
5 [1951] IR 228.
6 [1908] 1 Ch 167 at 176–178.
7 This view is supported by *Marlborough (West End) Ltd v Wilks Head and Eve* (1996) ChD, unreported, per Lightman J.
8 See **6.16**.
9 *Tehidy Minerals v Norman* [1971] 2 QB 528.
10 Ibid at 532, 552.

Law Commission and the Land Registry have recommended that legislation should be introduced to create a rebuttable presumption that an easement is abandoned if the party asserting the right cannot show it has been used during the last 20 years.[1]

6.13 Cases where it has been impossible to assert the fiction have arisen in the following circumstances.

(1) Where the presumed grantor cannot grant the right, for example a right of light over consecrated ground which cannot be granted by faculty.[2]
(2) Where there is evidence that the consent of a third party is required for a grant, which has never been obtained, such as the consent of the Church Commissioners.[3]
(3) Where the enjoyment of the right can be attributed to permission, or tolerance, such permission not being a grant in itself.[4] However, the enjoyment of the easement under a mistaken belief that the right has been conferred, or by the tacit acquiescence of the owner of the servient land will not preclude establishment of the right by application of the doctrine.[5]
(4) Where the Custom of London applies. This custom applies so as to give the right to freehold building owners within the area of the City of London to build on their 'ancient foundations' to any height without regard to the effect on neighbouring properties of the loss of light. Originally, the Custom extended only to houses, but in *Perry v Eames*,[6] the Custom was held to apply to non-residential premises, namely the Old Bankruptcy Court in Basinghall Street. Ancient foundations have not been satisfactorily defined in any modern authority, but it is suggested that the Custom applies to a freehold owner rebuilding within the 'footprint' of foundations formerly occupied by a building which has been demolished. Thus demolition of an existing building and replacement within that 'footprint', albeit with modern piled foundations, should be within the Custom. What is within the area of the City of London is capable of alteration by legislation, both primary and subordinate, and in any case on the fringe of the City it may be necessary to check the extent and location of the City of London Corporation's boundary with that of an adjoining London Borough. The City Solicitor can supply the information, both current and historic which may be required. It is not clear what is the effect of a building within the City boundary ceasing to be so as a result of boundary changes. It is thought that if redevelopment takes place at a date when all or part of the foundations of the building to be rebuilt are no longer in the City, the Custom may no longer apply as the building is not 'in the said City' according to the terms of the Custom. (The terms of the Custom as certified

1 See *Land Registration for the 21st Century* (Law Commission No 254) para 24.
2 *Re St Martin's Le Grand York* [1990] Fam 63.
3 *Oakley v Boston* [1976] QB 270.
4 *Bridle v Ruby* [1989] 1 QB 169.
5 Ibid; *Mills v Silver* [1991] Ch 271 and see **6.8**.
6 [1891] 1 Ch 658.

by the Recorder of the City of London in *Plummer v Bentham*,[1] are set out in Appendix 3.) The custom was applied in *Bowring Services v Scottish Widows Fund and Life Assurance Society*[2] demonstrating that in cases where no prescriptive right can arise under the Prescription Act 1832[3] the existence of the custom can be fatal to a claim based on lost modern grant, as well it might also be to a claim based on common law prescription. It is thought that the Custom of York has been abandoned and no longer survives, although no recent case has tested this proposition. By contrast, the custom in that city gave the right to build to any height on land which had not been built up, and that may account for its demise within what is now a fully developed city centre.

(5) Where the user lacks the qualities required for a prescriptive claim at common law (ie 'as of right' – or without force, secrecy or consent).[4]

6.14 Even though the doctrine relies on a fiction, a claimant or counter-claiming defendant seeking to assert a lost modern grant in his statement of case must set out the dates at, or before, or between which he alleges that grant was made.[5]

PRESCRIPTION ACT 1832, SECTION 3

6.15 The text of the material provisions of this Act (referred to in this part of the chapter as 'the 1832 Act') is set out in Appendix 1.

6.16 In summary form, and by way of introduction to the complex questions which arise under the 1832 Act, an easement of light can be acquired under s 3 of the 1832 Act provided:

(1) the light has been enjoyed for the benefit of *a building*;
(2) the light has been *enjoyed continuously for a period of at least 20 years* reckoned *back from the date on which the action challenging or asserting the right was commenced* (which is the date of the commencement of the action itself and not the date of a counter-claim asserting or challenging the right);
(3) the light has been enjoyed *without consent* of the servient owner or anyone on his behalf;
(4) the light has been enjoyed *without interruption*;
(5) the right is *not asserted against the Crown.*

6.17 The right may be claimed under the 1832 Act by a tenant of the dominant land, both against the freeholder of the servient land, and against any tenants of his. The principle will apply even where the freehold owner of the servient land is the same as the owner of the dominant land.[6] In practice, the precise extent of the

---

1 (1757) 1 Burr 248, 97 ER 297.
2 [1995] 1 EGLR 158.
3 See **6.13**.
4 See **6.7**.
5 *Tremayne v English Clays Lovering Pochin & Co* [1972] 1 WLR 657.
6 *Morgan v Fear* [1906] 2 Ch 406, affirmed by the House of Lords at [1907] AC 425.

rights to light (if any) acquired by a tenant under the 1832 Act will depend on the terms of any lease or underlease.[1] This is an important difference from other easements where enjoyment has to be both by and against the fee. It does not matter that the freehold owner of the servient land may be unable to make a grant, for example because of a statutory restriction on his rights. The Act operates without any presumption of a grant. It is quite permissible to claim a right to light not only under the Act, but also under the fiction of a lost modern grant – which in the latter case does require a presumption of a grant and thereby capacity to grant it.[2] The following important points of principle under s 3 should be noted.

The enjoyment of light must be for the benefit of a building

6.18 Whilst it is not strictly necessary to have 'apertures', in practical terms, the building cannot benefit from the enjoyment of light other than through openings through which light can pass.[3] It is not necessary to prove actual occupation of the building for actual enjoyment under s 3 to commence.

6.19 This is an important point when dealing with evidence as to the time during which there has been enjoyment under s 3. The date at which a building was completed to the extent of being able to enjoy light, which in most cases will be the time at which the structure can be said to have contained the apertures, will be the critical date for the start of the right rather than a later date when occupation commenced.[4] Thus evidence from the planning and building control departments of the relevant local authority and from those involved in the construction process such as architect, clerk of works or building contractor, may be important in dating the time from which the building was capable of enjoying the access of light.

6.20 'Building' has been defined by the court so as to include not just houses and offices but also:

- a greenhouse;[5]
- a church and a chapel;[6]
- a church in the City of London.[7]

But a structure for storing and seasoning timber and exhibiting it for sale was not a building within s 3 of the 1832 Act.[8] A modern example of a similar structure which would not be a building would be a car port.[9]

---

1 See Chapter 7.
2 See **6.4** and *Tapling v Jones* (1865) 11 HLC 290.
3 See, generally, Chapter 4.
4 *Courtauld v Legh* (1869) LR 4 Ex 126; *Collis v Laugher* [1894] 3 Ch 659. See also Chapter 4 at **4.19**.
5 *Allen v Greenwood* [1980] Ch 119.
6 *Ecclesiastical Commissioners v Kino* (1880) 14 Ch 213.
7 *A-G v Queen Anne Gardens & Mansion Co* (1889) 60 LT 759 – The Guards' Chapel in Westminster.
8 *Harris v De Pinna* (1886) 33 ChD 238.
9 See also Chapter 4 at **4.11** and **4.13**.

There must be continuous actual enjoyment of the right for at least 20 years back from the date on which the action asserting or challenging that right was commenced[1]

6.21 Unlike other easements claimed by prescription, s 3 of the 1832 Act does not require enjoyment of light to be 'as of right'. But there must be factual evidence of enjoyment.[2] Section 4 of the 1832 Act (see Appendix 1) has the effect that the claimant must show this continuous period of enjoyment calculated back from the commencement of the action, which in practical terms will be the date on which the claim form is issued by the court under either Part 7 or Part 8 of the CPR, or the date of issue of the High Court writ or county court summons in actions begun before 26 April 1999.[3]

6.22 In cases where the servient land is owned by infants, or tenants for life, or other persons with a disability (eg patients or persons under a disability) enjoyment of light against such persons for the period of their disability is still effective under s 3, as the right is said to be absolute and indefeasible if enjoyed for the 20-year period. Therefore, any periods of disability are not excluded by virtue of s 7 of the 1832 Act, which has no application to s 3. It is also important to note that the alternative 40-year period set out in s 2 of the 1832 Act does not apply to rights of light.[4]

6.23 For the right to have been 'actually enjoyed' there must be evidence that light was received by the building and so received as an easement. Thus blocking up of windows for long periods will prevent enjoyment[5] but not temporary obstructions, or nightly drawing of blinds, or closing of shutters for periods when a business is shut, for example during a weekend or Bank Holiday.[6] It must also be shown that enjoyment was between two different occupiers of the dominant and servient land. This is important where buildings are occupied by the same tenants of the same landlord, for in such a case the same tenants cannot acquire light against each other. (See below for the various situations which can arise under this head where landlord and tenant are concerned.) Whether modern style opaque advertising screens placed on the front of buildings while redevelopment of the interior is being carried out, amounts to the loss of actual enjoyment is a moot point. There must be a risk of the loss of actual enjoyment if the light received is substantially diminished for a fair period of time.

---

1 In practice, enjoyment for a period of more than 19 years may suffice – see below, and also Chapter 7 and Chapter 8 at **8.20**.

2 *Hyman v van den Bergh* [1908] 1 Ch 167 at 172; *Marlborough (West End) Ltd v Wilks Head and Eve* (1996) ChD, unreported.

3 *Colls v Home & Colonial Stores* [1904] AC 179.

4 *Perry v Eames* [1891] 1 Ch 658.

5 *Smith v Baxter* [1900] 2 Ch 138, and see Chapter 8 at **8.9–8.19**.

6 See Chapter 7 and Chapter 8 at **8.20–8.48** for prevention of acquisition by light obstruction notices and other means by which the enjoyment of the right may be interrupted.

The enjoyment must have been without consent or agreement in writing

6.24 Such consent or agreement must be in writing and may be signed either by the owner of the servient land, or by the dominant owner, or by a tenant of either, or someone else in occupation. It does not have to be signed by both parties. This means that a person with a lesser interest than the freehold can bind the freeholder – even without the knowledge or consent of the latter, and that is why well-drawn leases will contain provisions preventing tenants from agreeing to light being enjoyed by consent.[1]

6.25 What amounts to a written consent may sometimes be difficult to discern in certain deeds and documents. It is clear that a mere exception of the right to light will not amount to a consent under s 3. What is necessary is a provision which positively authorises the owner of the adjoining (servient) land to build as he pleases.[2] This is why in conveyances or transfers and in leases there is invariably an exception of light to the grantor coupled with a declaration that the grantor may build on his adjoining land to any height etc whether or not that interferes with the light enjoyed by the land conveyed, transferred or let.[3] A stone inscription reserving the right of the servient owner to build to a defined distance will not be an agreement in writing for the purposes of s 3.[4] The famous sign 'Ancient Lights' is not evidence of consent but rather an assertion that lights are being enjoyed.

There must not have been an interruption of the enjoyment

6.26 Section 3 of the 1832 Act states that the actual enjoyment of the light must have been for the full period of 20 years without interruption. Section 4 of the 1832 Act[5] states that, to be an interruption for the purposes of the Act, it must have been submitted to or acquiesced in for one year after the dominant owner has had notice of the interruption and of the person making the interruption or causing it to be made. What, therefore, is an 'interruption'? It is any obstruction of the enjoyment of the light caused by the servient owner (or by a third party) and the erection of buildings is an obvious example of this.[6] But a fluctuating obstruction such as packing cases or freight containers may not be an interruption.[7] A light obstruction notice registered under the Rights of Light Act 1959[8] will from the date of registration, whether as a contemporary, or as a final

1 *Hyman v Van Den Bergh* [1908] 1 Ch 167; *Marlborough (West End) Ltd v Wilks Head and Eve* (1996) ChD, unreported, per Lightman J, and see Chapter 7 at **7.4–7.6**.
2 *Haynes v King* [1893] 3 Ch 439.
3 See *Foster v Lyons* [1927] 1 Ch 219; *Willoughby v Eckstein* [1937] Ch 167.
4 *Ruscoe v Grounsell* (1903) 89 LT 426.
5 Set out at Appendix 2.
6 *Plasterers' Co v Parish Clerks' Co* (1851) 6 Ex 630.
7 *Presland v Bingham* (1889) 41 ChD 268.
8 See Appendix 2 for light obstruction notices. See also Chapter 7 at **7.11–7.14** and Chapter 8 at **8.31–8.34**. The term 'light obstruction notice' is not used in the Rights of Light Act 1959 but is a convenient shorthand for a notice registered under the provision of s 2.

notice, amount to an interruption if no action is taken by the dominant owner to challenge it by action within one year of such registration.[1]

6.27 It is necessary for the person creating the interruption to make it clear to the dominant owner who has created or authorised it. The mere fact that a building or structure is put up may not be enough.[2] Quite apart from placing the name of the servient owner on the offending structure, the service of a letter referring to the nature of the interruption and stating who has authorised it would be enough to satisfy s 4. A light obstruction notice under the Rights of Light Act 1959 when registered will contain a reference in the register to the person causing the Notice to be registered, and by s 3(6) of the 1959 Act, such registration is treated as an interruption under s 4 of the 1832 Act.[3] To disprove submission to or acquiescence in the interruption requires action to be taken which shows that the dominant owner has been unwilling to accept the interruption, and this opposition must be made clear to the servient owner by words, or actions. A solicitor's letter served on the servient owner, or the commencement and service of an action are the types of act which will displace any submission to or acquiescence in an interruption. In the case of the light obstruction notice under the Rights of Light Act 1959, opposition by an action claiming a right to light with a claim to set the notice aside would be enough. Uncommunicated objections or grumbles are not enough.[4] But it is very important to do any of these things within one year, and in most cases an immediate solicitor's letter (even as a protective measure prior to negotiations) is essential.

6.28 It is a by-product of s 4 that if there has been enjoyment for *over* 19 years followed by an obstruction which has not been acquiesced in for one year, and where an action is brought after 20 years have run (but within one year of the obstruction), the easement of light may be claimed under the 1832 Act – even though there has not been enjoyment for a full period of 20 years. This is sometimes known as the 'nineteen years and a day' rule. It is important to note that the enjoyment claimed must be for over 19 years (hence the 'day'), for if the action is commenced in a case where enjoyment prior to obstruction has been for only 19 years the action will fail as 20 years user cannot be established.

Examples

(1) A's building was constructed and the apertures were in place by 1 January 1979. B obstructs A's light (by a light obstruction notice 'LON') registered on 1 October 1998. If A brings an action on 1 June 1999 he can establish 20 years user and has not submitted to the interruption for one year.

---

1 Rights of Light Act 1959, s 3 set out at Appendix 1; *Bowring Services v Scottish Widows Fund and Life Assurance Society* [1995] 1 EGLR 158.

2 *Seddon v Bank of Bolton* (1882) 19 ChD 462.

3 See, generally, Chapter 7 at **7.14** and Chapter 8 at **8.37**.

4 *Dance v Triplow* [1992] 1 EGLR 190, CA; *Bowring Services v Scottish Widows Fund and Life Assurance Society* [1995] 1 EGLR 158.

(2) A's building was constructed and the apertures were in place by 1 January 1980. B obstructs A's light (as before by a LON) registered on 1 October 1998. If A brings his action before 2 January 1999 he is too soon for he cannot establish 20 years' enjoyment.

To preserve the nineteen years and a day rule where an interruption is caused by a light obstruction notice being registered, s 3(4) of the 1959 Act gives the dominant owner 'credit' for one year back from the date of the commencement of the enjoyment of light. Thus, in the second example, even if credit of one year is given back to 1 January 1979, any action brought before 2 January 1999 is too soon.

The right to acquire an easement of light under section 3 does not run against the Crown

6.29 This has the effect of rendering many servient owners subject to the fact that they cannot acquire rights to light against buildings which are in Crown ownership. This requires care to be taken in examining titles which are or which have been in Crown ownership. 'The Crown' will include not only Her Majesty in right of Her Crown (eg St James' Palace) and Her Royal Duchy of Lancaster (eg land to the south of the Strand), but also will include the Royal Duchy of Cornwall (eg the Kennington Estate in South London), the Crown Estate (eg Regent's Park in London), and Government Departments. The Crown may also feature as a freehold land owner following the dissolution of companies and the vesting in the Crown (or the appropriate Royal Duchy) as *bona vacantia*, or (following disclaimer by the Treasury Solicitor) in escheat. Before 1969 the Post Office was an office of the Crown and therefore an easement of light could not be acquired as against Post Office buildings. Other de-nationalised bodies may fall into the same category. In recent times, with sales of surplus NHS and MOD land in city centres, the exemption of the Crown is of some importance.[1] Custom (eg the Custom of London) cannot be used to prevent a right to light being acquired under s 3 of the 1832 Act.[2]

6.30 Because the easement of light can be acquired by and against persons with a lesser interest than a freehold, complex situations can arise where properties are the subject of claims to light which are tenanted.

Examples

(1) Block A is adjacent to Block B and the common owner of the freehold is landlord C. C grants a lease of Block A to D. C does not reserve any rights to light to himself, nor does he reserve the right to build on Block B to any height. D can acquire an easement of light for the benefit of Block A against his own landlord C and can prevent his landlord from rebuilding Block B in such a way that interferes with the light to Block A.

---

1 See *Perry v Eames* [1891] 1 Ch 658 and *Wheaton v Maple & Co* [1893] 3 Ch 48.

2 See **6.13**. See also *Salters Co v Jay* [1842] 3 QB 109, 114 FR 448; *Truscott v Merchant Taylors Co* (1856) 11 Exch 855, 156 ER 1074; *Perry v Eames* [1891] 1 Ch 658; all cases decided on the interrelation between s 3 of the 1832 Act and the Custom of London.

(2) The same facts arise as in (1) save that Block B is owned by E. Once again, C can prevent E from rebuilding in a way which interferes with the easement acquired under s 3.
(3) If the facts are the same as under (1) or (2) but there are a succession of tenants during the 20-year period of block A, each on the same terms, the result will be the same.[1] But if during that period a new lease is granted reserving rights to light to the landlord and the right to rebuild Block B, the tenant of Block A will not have acquired a right to light, as during the 20-year period he has enjoyed light by consent.[2]
(4) If a tenant of A surrenders the lease during the period, and the facts are as in (1) or (2) above, the successor tenant will have the right under s 3.[3]
(5) If the tenant of Block B acquires the reversion during the 20-year period and the tenant of Block A is holding on the terms set out in (1) above, the latter will have acquired the right under s 3.[4]
(6) If there is a surrender of the lease of Block A so that the freeholder of that Block obtains possession, he cannot acquire a right to light against Block B if he is still the owner of the freehold of it. He cannot acquire an easement against himself. But if by the time that the surrender and retaking of possession occurs he is no longer the owner of Block B, he can continue to assert his rights against it.[5]

6.31 It should be plain from the examples above that, in cases where the easement of light is in issue between buildings that are or have been let during the relevant 20-year period, great care must be taken to understand the history of the freehold title and the leasehold title and to see the leases that may have been granted by the dominant owner. Chapter 7 considers this further in the context of preventing rights to light from being acquired.

6.32 The effect of the Human Rights Act 1998 on the Crown's 'immunity' is considered in Chapter 15.

1 *Fear v Morgan* [1906] 2 Ch 415.
2 See *Haynes v King* [1893] 3 Ch 439.
3 *Fear v Morgan* [1906] 2 Ch 415.
4 *Richardson v Graham* [1908] 1 KB 39.
5 *Fear v Morgan* [1906] 2 Ch 415; *Richardson v Graham* [1908] 1 KB 39.

Chapter 7

Acquisition of Rights to Light III – prevention of acquisition

7.1 There are three ways in which an easement of light may be prevented from being acquired:

(1) by agreement between the dominant and servient owners (and in the case of tenanted properties by agreement between landlord and tenant);
(2) by physical interruption; and
(3) by use of the Rights of Light Act 1959.

BY AGREEMENT

7.2 It is open to the dominant and servient owners to agree that neither of them will acquire any light for, or against, the buildings on their respective titles. When there are sales off of parts of the property formerly in common ownership, it is commonplace to see the usual declaration that the purchaser will not be entitled to acquire any right to light against the land retained by the vendor or any successor as owner of that land. This will negate any implied grant under s 62 of the Law of Property Act 1925[1] or ss 19(3) and 22(3) of the Land Registration Act 1925, according to whether the title is unregistered or registered at the time of the disposition.

7.3 It is equally commonplace to see rights to light being reserved to a vendor, but as explained in Chapter 6 at **6.25**, that will not prevent a right to light being acquired under s 3 of the Prescription Act 1832[2] (or possibly by lost modern grant) by the purchaser or his successor unless it is also stated that any enjoyment is precarious; an example being the clause giving the adjoining owner (the former vendor) the right to build how he pleases.[3]

7.4 In the context of landlord and tenant, the only sure way of preventing acquisition by tenants, if no other difficulties such as those arising from the principle of non-derogation from grant, is to include provisions in a lease as set out at **7.5**. The same provisions should also be in any underlease or lesser interest, although it is thought that an absence of such terms would not allow the underlessee (or person claiming a derivative interest) to claim a right to light as the rights of such a person could not be greater than the headlessee. But the point is not entirely free from doubt in the light of the potentially wide scope of the

1 See Appendix 1.
2 See Appendix 1.
3 *Haynes v King* [1893] 3 Ch 439.

principle derived from *Fear v Morgan*[1] that a tenant can acquire a right to light under the 1832 Act in his own right and against the tenant of the common landlord.[2] It follows that there can be no acquisition of rights to light against the tenant of the common landlord if the claimant cannot establish that right against the landlord himself. An example of this arose in *Wheaton v Maple & Co*,[3] where the landlord was the Crown and, accordingly, no claim could be made against a tenant of the Crown. Likewise, where the common landlord has reserved rights to light to himself and has reserved the right to build to any extent on any of his adjoining land, one tenant of the landlord cannot assert a right to light against a neighbouring tenant of the same landlord.[4]

7.5 The provisions suggested are as follows:

(1) a term reserving all rights to light enjoyed by the demised property to the landlord. This stops any tenant claiming light independently of his landlord, and also enables the landlord to settle claims for interference without being obliged to account for any part thereof to the tenant in satisfaction of its interest. This ought to stop underlessees from claiming any right to light;
(2) a covenant preventing the tenant from asserting any claim to light against any neighbouring building of the landlord;
(3) a declaration that in respect of any neighbouring building of the landlord, he has the right to rebuild without limit;
(4) a covenant by the tenant not to stop up etc any windows on the demised property. This has more to do with preventing abandonment than acquisition, but is mentioned here for completeness;
(5) a covenant by the tenant to report any actual or threatened obstructions or light obstruction notices,[5] any planning applications and any adjoining owner notices. As under (4), this may have more to do with preventing the loss of rights. However, it is to be noted that, in the context of the light obstruction notice, as service of the proposed notice will invariably be on the tenants of the servient building and as the owner of that building will want to prevent acquisition of a right to light over it by the dominant building,[6] this reporting obligation is important.

7.6 Another form of agreement which will prevent a right to light from being acquired is to give permission to the dominant owner to build (up to a given

---

1 [1906] 2 Ch 415.

2 *Wheaton v Maple & Co* [1893] 3 Ch 48; *Willoughby v Eckstein* [1937] 1 Ch 167; *Blake and Lyons Ltd v Lewis Berger & Sons Ltd* [1951] 2 TLR 605.

3 [1893] 3 Ch 48.

4 See *Blake & Lyons Ltd v Lewis Berger & Sons Ltd* [1951] 2 TLR 605.

5 The term 'light obstruction notice' is not used in the Rights of Light Act 1959, but is a convenient shorthand for a notice registered under the provisions of s 2.

6 See **7.10**. See also s 7 of the Rights of Light Act 1959 which defines 'owner' as including a lessee for a term of years certain with not less than 7 years unexpired when the application to register the light obstruction notice is being made. A covenant against any such lessee applying to register a notice under the 1959 Act may be prudent and may be expressed independently or as part of the covenant referred to in (4) above.

height or according to defined plans) or to impose, by way of a restrictive covenant, a limit on building. In addition, it is agreed between the parties that any light enjoyed by the dominant owner pursuant to the permission granted is by consent. In London, it is common to find deeds regulating light in this way where both dominant and servient owners agree in such terms and, accordingly, neither have enforceable rights to light against each other, and can only enforce the terms of any restrictive covenant as to height etc.[1]

BY PHYSICAL INTERRUPTION

7.7 Prior to the implementation of a nationwide planning control regime from 1 July 1948, it was conventional to erect an obstruction (a 'spite screen') to prevent the acquisition of light under the 1832 Act. If that screen complied with s 4 of that Act and remained unchallenged for one year, a right to light could not be asserted under the 1832 Act in view of the 'interruption' caused by it. The Town and Country Planning Act 1947 which came into force on this date effectively put an end to the erection of spite screens, as planning consent was unlikely to be granted for a structure which was not only unsightly but which was also intrusive on the amenities of the neighbouring land.[2] Although the Town and Country Planning Act 1947 has been superseded, subsequent legislation has maintained and indeed extended the principle that 'development' (including building and engineering operations) requires planning permission.

7.8 Thus for over the past 50 years the primary manner of preventing light from being acquired has not been by means of the use of physical obstructions – whether classed as spite screens, or otherwise. Clearly, anything by way of a structure will usually need express planning consent under the Planning Acts.[3] The general development orders under successive town planning legislation permit certain works without the need to apply for planning permission. However, those orders have never allowed obstruction of the necessary size to be effective for this purpose.[4]

7.9 It is, however, important to note that the fact that a building has been erected and has been consented to may prevent the assertion of a right to light under the 1832 Act, if there has been submission to or acquiescence in it for one year.[5] In modern developments, it is not inconceivable that a building goes up apace while the parties' advisers discuss the pros and cons of its effect on the light to the dominant building. If one year has gone by, and the new building has been up for that time, an interruption has occurred and all rights under the 1832 Act

1 See Chapter 9 for further analysis of such deeds.
2 For planning law generally, see Chapter 13.
3 See Chapter 13 at **13.4** for the meaning of this expression.
4 See (currently) the Town and Country Planning (General Permitted Development) Order 1995, SI 1995/418. The main provisions relating to building operations are in Sch 2, Part 2.
5 See Chapter 6 at **6.26**.

are lost. It may be possible to fall back on lost modern grant, but not in the City of London.[1]

BY THE USE OF THE RIGHTS OF LIGHT ACT 1959

7.10 The Rights of Light Act 1959 (called in this part of this chapter 'the 1959 Act') came into force on 16 October 1959. Its provisions now set out the accepted manner in which rights to light can be prevented from being acquired.[2] The 1959 Act operates essentially by allowing the creation of a *notional* obstruction of light received by a building over the land of another. The terminology and procedures under the 1959 Act are set out in detail in Chapter 8 at **8.33**. In this chapter, we consider the practical aspects of operating the 1959 Act.

7.11 A light obstruction notice may be used in two situations in order to prevent a right to light from being obtained. First, where it is believed that the building on the dominant land is about to acquire the benefit of 20 years' user, the emergency procedure referred to below should be used. Even if the notice is challenged within one year of registration, if the evidence is such that the apertures in the building have not been in situ for 20 years (allowing if necessary for the 'nineteen years and a day' rule referred to in Chapter 6 at **6.28** and preserved by s 3(4) of the 1959 Act), the servient owner will have been successful in claiming that the building on the dominant land has not acquired a right to light. This may be of vital importance if the servient owner is planning his own development which would otherwise infringe the light to the building on the dominant land.

7.12 The second instance where the registration of the notice may be used to good effect in preventing the acquisition of a right to light is as follows. The owner of the servient land has plans to develop at some time in the future and is reasonably confident that of the dominant owners whose light may be affected by the development, some may not have acquired 20 years' user in respect of their buildings, and others may well not object to any notice within one year of registration. In the latter case, they will be deemed to have consented to an interruption[3] and unless they can rely on lost modern grant, they will be unable to assert any right to light. Clearly, there is a degree to which a gamble is being taken, but even if challenges are made to the notices within time, the servient owner can 'flush out' any problems in advance of the plans for development being finalised. This course may also avoid last-minute injunctions being threatened.

7.13 The effect of a light obstruction notice, once registered, is that it is intended to be equivalent to the obstruction of light to the dominant building across the servient land which would be caused:

---

1 See Chapter 6 at **6.13**.

2 See Appendix 1 for the text of the 1959 Act.

3 See Chapter 6 at **6.27–6.28**, Chapter 8 at **8.37**, and s 3(6) of the 1959 Act.

> 'by the erection, in such position on the servient land as may be specified in the application, of an opaque structure of such dimensions (including, if the application so states, unlimited height) as may be so specified.'[1]

As such, it amounts to an obstruction to the access of light to the dominant building and an interruption from the date of registration.[2] Such a notice will have that effect until it is cancelled. It will also have that effect until it has been registered for one year. In the case of a notice registered under a temporary certificate (see below), the notice will have effect only until the date fixed for its expiry (which cannot be longer than 6 months from registration), unless before that date application has been lodged with the local authority for registration of a notice based on a definitive certificate. The significance of the reference to one year is due to the need to tie in with s 4 of the Prescription Act 1832 and the concept of an 'interruption'.[3]

7.14 By s 3(6) of the 1959 Act, the notice, once registered, takes effect as if all persons interested in the dominant building have notice of it and on whose behalf it is registered. Unless and until any action is brought (within time), the persons interested in the dominant building are deemed to acquiesce in the obstruction caused by the notice, according to its terms. Once an action is brought, there is no longer any submission to or acquiescence in the notional obstruction. In order to maintain the 'nineteen years and a day' rule, s 3(4) gives the dominant owner the benefit of that rule by treating the commencement of enjoyment as having commenced one year earlier, if that would allow the dominant owner to challenge the notice under s 3(3). If the action fails, the court can direct that the dominant owner is deemed to have submitted to or acquiesced in the notice as if the action had not been brought (s 3(6) proviso).[4]

7.15 The first stage in any application to register a notice under the 1959 Act is, therefore, to decide the location and height of the notional obstruction. In practice, the height is left as an unlimited one. Of some difficulty is the need to take account of projections (this may require two notional obstructions placed against the faces of the servient buildings), and to take account of apertures on the dominant building where there is no doubt that a right to light exists, which calls for care in defining both the height and the width of the notional obstruction.

7.16 The second stage is to make an application in Form 1.[5] With this application should be lodged two copies of the proposed application in Form A to the Local Land Charges Rules 1977.[6] It is to this form that the plan of the suggested notional obstruction will be annexed. The Registrar will direct what notices should be given to those affected and who appear to have an interest in the

---

1 Section 2(2)(b) of the 1959 Act.

2 Section 3(1) of the 1959 Act.

3 See Chapter 6 at **6.27–6.28**.

4 See Chapter 6 at **6.28** for examples of the effect of s 3(4).

5 Prescribed by r 21 of the Lands Tribunal Rules 1996, SI 1996/1022 set out in Appendix 2. Form 1 is an application for the issue of a certificate that adequate publicity has been given to those affected by the proposed application to register the light obstruction notice.

6 SI 1977/985. See Appendix 2.

dominant building. In practice, the applicant will supply the Registrar with a list of all such persons. It is only in cases where there is doubt or difficulty that advertisements need to be directed, and if this is thought to be a possibility, a draft advertisement and suggested place for its publication should also be supplied to the Registrar on this application. In most cases, recorded delivery service with advice of receipt is recommended. It is sometimes necessary to serve a large number of occupational tenants in an office block, or a block of flats, but all have interests which may be affected and they must be served.[1]

7.17 The third stage is to give notice to all persons who appear likely to be affected by the registration of the notice, by serving a copy of the application on those directed to be served, and in such manner as the Registrar shall have directed at stage two.[2]

7.18 The fourth stage is to notify the Registrar that the directions as to service or notification have been complied with. This usually requires despatch of the recorded delivery and advice of receipt records with copies of all letters served and any newspaper or other advertisements placed. If satisfied, the Registrar will issue a definitive certificate that adequate notice has been given to those likely to be affected by the registration of the notice.[3]

7.19 The fifth stage is to apply for registration at the Local Land Charges Registry of the application (Form A) with the Registrar's definitive certificate of notice in Form 3 granted at stage four.[4] The registered notice will remain on the register for 21 years from the date of registration.[5]

7.20 In cases where there is exceptional urgency (eg the dominant owner is likely to be close to acquiring 20 years' enjoyment allowing for the credit of one year under s 3(4)) the emergency procedure may be invoked. This requires the making of an application to the Registrar of the Lands Tribunal for the issue of a certificate that, in the opinion of the Lands Tribunal, the case is one of exceptional urgency and that, accordingly, a light obstruction notice should be registered forthwith as a temporary notice, for such period as may be specified in the certificate. The period cannot exceed 6 months.[6] This is, in effect, an additional element to stage two under **7.16**. The applicant needs not only to have identified who is to be served and in what manner, but also why the matter is one of exceptional urgency. Form 1 is used for this purpose using the additional paragraph as regards exceptional urgency. It is prudent to have cogent evidence which can be placed before the Registrar in order to make out the case of exceptional urgency. The commonest reason is the fear (no doubt backed up by evidence of construction etc) that the dominant owner's building is about to

1 Lands Tribunal Rules 1996, r 22. See Appendix 2.
2 Ibid, r 22(3). See Appendix 2.
3 Ibid, r 24 and Form 3. See Appendix 2.
4 Local Land Charges Rules 1977, SI 1977/985, r 10, see Appendix 2.
5 Ibid, r 10(6)(b). See Appendix 2.
6 Section 2(3)(b) of the 1959 Act and Lands Tribunal Rules 1996, r 23. See Appendices 1 and 2.

acquire user of light for the 20-year period, and allowing for the 'credit' of one year under s 3(4). If the emergency certificate is granted in Form 2, that will allow registration of the notice in the Local Land Charges Register, for the period given in the certificate. It cannot last for more than 6 months.[1] The servient owner must then apply for a definitive certificate.

7.21 It is important to note the following practical features of this procedure.

(1) A temporary light obstruction notice will take effect as a notional obstruction and is something which will be an interruption from the date of registration.[2] It is, therefore, vital to challenge such a registration within one year from that date, for otherwise rights under the 1832 Act will be lost, and although reliance may be placed on the lost modern grant, that will be to no avail in the City of London where the Custom of London applies.[3] In practical terms, the challenge which should be made is to issue a claim form asserting the right to light for the benefit of the dominant building and asserting the fact that the light obstruction notice is an actionable interference to those rights. The same effect can be achieved by a counter-claim within one year in existing proceedings; see the definition of 'action' in s 7(1) of the 1959 Act. Note that no challenge can be made once the light obstruction notice has ceased to have effect.[4] This is important where temporary certificates are registered.

(2) Where a temporary light obstruction notice is registered, it is vital to complete the registration of the permanent light obstruction notice based on the definitive certificate before the expiry of the period specified for the temporary registration. If this is not done, there will be a break in the period of the year which is so vital if an interruption is to be claimed.

(3) A challenge to the issue of a certificate by the Registrar of the Lands Tribunal may be made by way of judicial review. A declaration to set aside sought by a claim form in an ordinary civil action and not in an application for judicial review is an abuse of the process and will be struck out.[5] In this context, it is important to note the need to ensure that the evidence placed before the Registrar should be as comprehensive as possible in order to avoid a later challenge that the evidence (eg of exceptional urgency) was so slender, or non-existent that the emergency certificate should be set aside.

(4) The issue of a certificate under the 1959 Act by the Registrar of the Lands Tribunal is not a decision which can be the subject of an appeal by way of case stated to the High Court.[6]

7.22 The 1959 Act applies to Crown land.[7] This includes land in which the Royal Duchies have an interest as well as land owned by government

1 Lands Tribunal Rules 1996, r 23(2).
2 *Bowring Services v Scottish Widows Fund and Life Assurance Society* [1995] 1 EGLR 158.
3 See Chapter 6 at **6.9**.
4 1959 Act, s 3(3) proviso.
5 *Bowring Services v Scottish Widows Fund and Life Assurance Society* [1995] 1 EGLR 158.
6 Ibid.
7 See s 4.

departments. Thus, it is possible for such bodies to use the 1959 Act to prevent the acquisition of light by adjoining owners, whereas the position remains that a right to light cannot be acquired against Crown land under s 3 of the Prescription Act 1832. Section 4 of the 1959 Act expressly preserves that position.

7.23 Finally, it is sometimes relevant to consider how far the 1959 Act affects right to light claims under the fiction of lost modern grant.[1] It is thought that although the words 'or otherwise' occur after the words 'by virtue of the Prescription Act 1832' in s 3(1) of the 1959 Act, in the context of determining the entitlement of the dominant owner to a right to light, the 1959 Act does not affect directly the fiction of lost modern grant. The concept of the light obstruction notice and its duration for one year is designed to challenge a right to light claimed under the 1832 Act. The framework of the 1959 Act does not fit into the fiction of a lost modern grant which can be alleged for any period, subject to the restrictions referred to in Chapter 6. The point has not, however, been decided. However, it might be open to a servient owner to assert the fact of registration in showing the impossibility of a grant during the time for which such registration had been effective. The same point might also be open to the servient owner to take when asserting abandonment.

1 See Chapter 6 at **6.10–6.14**.

Chapter 8
Extinguishment of Rights to Light

INTRODUCTION

8.1 A right to light may be extinguished in the following ways:

(1) by agreement between those interested in the dominant and servient tenements;
(2) by unity of ownership of the dominant and servient land;
(3) by permanent abandonment;
(4) by interruption;
(5) by demolition or alteration of the dominant building, in some situations;
(6) under certain statutory provisions relating to compulsory purchase and appropriation of land for planning purposes.

1. EXTINGUISHMENT BY AGREEMENT

8.2 An easement of light may be released by agreement between the owner of the dominant and servient tenements. Since an easement is an interest in land the release must be in writing,[1] and to effect a release of the legal estate ought to be by deed.[2] Care needs to be taken to ensure that all those entitled to and subject to the easement are parties to the deed, otherwise there is a risk that the objective may not be achieved. This could give rise to particular difficulties where not only the freeholder of the dominant building but also tenants are entitled to rights of light acquired under the Prescription Act 1832 by 20 years' user.[3] In these situations, there may be real uncertainty about the identity of the dominant owners, although clearly only those with legal interests in their land, and whose premises receive light through defined apertures over the servient land, will qualify. In the case of a building of multiple occupation, the task of tracing not only the occupying tenants, but also the owners of mesne interests in those parts of the building enjoying the rights to light may be laborious and fail to be exhaustive. This can cause problems where it is desired to redevelop the servient building in a way which may interfere with the dominant building's light.

8.3 In these cases, where it is desired to achieve agreement to extinguish rights to light, various expedients can be used. One is to obtain warranties and indemnities from those who appear to be the sole or main dominant owners, to the general effect that they:

(1) warrant that there are no other dominant interests;

---

1 Law of Property Act 1925, s 53.
2 Ibid, s 52.
3 See Chapter 6 at **6.17**, **6.24** and **6.30**.

(2) give indemnities against losses arising from any claims by either identified holders of interests in the dominant tenement or by potential claimants generally.

This approach has the merit of simplifying negotiations in a redevelopment situation, and also (subject to the solvency of the covenantors) has the effect of capping the developer's liability. It also discourages attempts by the covenantors to encourage claims by others, either in return for a share of any compensation achieved or as a lever to extract further concessions from the developer. On the other hand, it presupposes a willingness on the part of those giving the warranties and/or indemnities to expose themselves to possibly onerous liabilities, and is unlikely to be attractive except where substantial consideration passes in return.

8.4 Another approach is to rely on the Rights of Light Act 1959 (see below), combined with a deed of release executed by the known dominant owners. If a light obstruction notice[1] is registered under this Act and not challenged within a period of one year, the right to light is extinguished. Therefore, if the known dominant owners have bound themselves by agreement not to take steps to assert their rights, hence raise no challenge to the notice, once the notice has been in effect for one year (assuming no other claimants have commenced proceedings in the meantime) the possibility of such further claims is excluded. This procedure has the advantage of certainty, but involves a long timescale. Neither procedure, of course, itself guarantees that no adverse claims will be made. However, provided agreement has been reached with those having the major interests in the dominant tenement before the redevelopment starts, other claimants may, in practice, be reluctant to assert rights to the point of seeking interim injunctive relief to prevent building work proceeding, given the risk that they run on their undertakings in damages.[2] Equally, the failure to seek an interim injunction is likely to place substantial difficulties in the way of obtaining a mandatory order for removal of that part of the redevelopment which they allege infringes their rights at trial.[3] Hence there may be a need for a developer to factor in an element of calculated risk both as to whether all potential claims to rights to light have been identified and their agreement obtained, and whether any who did not fall within these categories in practice pose a threat to the development proceeding.

8.5 Deeds may make provision for determination of easements on notice. The precise terms of the provision for determination must be strictly complied with.[4] An easement may be extinguished by implied agreement, where the dominant owner authorises the servient owner to erect a building which must inevitably interfere with the easement of light. In these circumstances, the dominant owner is estopped from reasserting his right subsequently, on the ground that it would

1 The term light obstruction notice is not used in the Rights of Light Act 1959, but is a convenient shorthand for a notice registered under the provisions of s 2.

2 See Chapter 11 at **11.88**.

3 See Chapter 11 at **11.97–11.108**.

4 *Wallshire Limited v Advertising Sites Limited* [1988] 2 EGLR 167, CA.

be inequitable for him to do so.[1] In general, for the estoppel to be established, it must be shown that the dominant owner was aware of the existence of his right, or at least had a suspicion as to the true position.[2]

2. EXTINGUISHMENT BY UNITY OF OWNERSHIP

8.6 A man cannot have an easement over his own property.[3] Therefore, provided the freehold of both dominant and servient tenements is vested in the same person any easement of the one over the other is extinguished.

8.7 It appears to be the case that extinguishment operates only where the *freehold* of both tenements is vested in the same person. Accordingly, it does not operate where, for example, the same person owns the freehold of one tenement but simply a leasehold interest in the other. In such cases, it seems that whilst in practice a person in occupation of both properties in such circumstances cannot exercise the easement, it does not disappear but is simply suspended.[4] In *Simper v Foley*,[5] Page Wood V-C said:

> 'I apprehend it is clear that the effect of an union of the ownership of dominant and servient tenements for different estates is not to extinguish an easement of this description, but merely to suspend it so long as the union of ownership continues; and that upon a severance of the ownership the easement revives.'

8.8 In the case of easements of light, it is also to be remembered that under s 3 of the Prescription Act 1832 a right to light may be acquired in respect of and against land where the same person is the freeholder of both the dominant and servient tenements, but where the dominant (as well as possibly also the servient) tenements are in occupation of lessees.[6] It seems to follow that unity of ownership of dominant and servient tenements will not extinguish easements enjoyed by a lessee. Thus in *Richardson v Graham*,[7] the owner of a dominant tenement which had acquired a right to light by 20 years' user leased it to the plaintiffs, and then sold it (subject to the lease) to the defendant. It was held that the right to light continued during the term of the plaintiff's lease. The original owner of the dominant tenement could not have interfered with the easement without derogating from his grant to the plaintiffs, and the defendant could be in no better position. The right to light enured in favour of the plaintiffs against the defendant.

---

1 Cf *Taylor Fashions Limited v Liverpool Victoria Trustees Co Limited* [1981] 1 All ER 897; *Re Basham Deceased* [1987] 1 All ER 405. See also *Gillett v Holt* [1998] 3 All ER 917.

2 *Armstrong v Sheppard & Short Limited* [1959] 2 All ER 651; *Taylor Fashions Limited v Liverpool Victoria Trustees Co Limited* [1981] 1 All ER 897 at 912B.

3 *Kilgour v Gaddes* [1904] 1 KB 457.

4 *Thomas v Thomas* (1835) 2 CM&R 34.

5 (1862) 2 J&H 555 at 563.

6 *Frewen v Philipps* 11 CBNS 449; *Robson v Edwards* [1893] 2 Ch 146; *Morgan v Fear* [1907] AC 425. See Chapter 6 at **6.17**, **6.24** and **6.30**.

7 [1908] 1 KB 39.

3. PERMANENT ABANDONMENT

8.9 A right to light is a continuous easement, in the sense that enjoyment of it requires no human intervention.[1] A right to light is enjoyed by virtue of the configuration of the dominant tenement, not because any particular individual is using it at any particular moment.

8.10 However, the law recognises that a right to light may become abandoned. The general criteria required for abandonment of an easement were described by Lord Justice Buckley in *Tehidy Minerals Ltd v Norman*[2] as follows:

> 'Abandonment of an easement or of a profit à prendre can only we think be treated as having taken place where the person entitled to it has demonstrated a fixed intention never at any time thereafter to assert the right himself or to attempt to transmit it to anyone else.'

See also *Wilson's Brewery Ltd v West Yorkshire Metropolitan Borough Council.*[3]

8.11 It is clear, therefore, that an intention to abandon a right to light will only be established by clear evidence that the dominant owner has an intention no longer to rely on the right. Although (in theory) simple statements, documentary or, indeed, even oral evidence ought to suffice, provided repeated sufficiently often and emphatically. In practice, the issue is almost invariably one whose answer depends on the inferences to be drawn from external acts and circumstances surrounding the dominant and servient tenements. In some cases, the issue seems to have been approached simply as one involving an inquiry whether the acts of the dominant owner with respect to the apertures show an intention to no longer use them for the enjoyment of light. If the dominant owner blocks up his windows in a permanent way, and makes no use of them for a prolonged period, abandonment has been held possible.

8.12 On the other hand, in other cases, the courts have held that this is insufficient, and that the right to light will be held to have been abandoned only if, additionally, the owner of the servient land has acted in reliance on the actions of the dominant owner, so that he would be prejudiced if the right to light were held enforceable. The preponderance of authority is probably (just) in favour of the latter view.[4] On this view the doctrine of abandonment is similar to the doctrine of proprietary estoppel.[5] The alternative view, however, has some support, including at least one recent authority, and does have the merit of rendering unnecessary any inquiry as to whether the servient owner has suffered detriment. The authorities are reviewed below.

---

1 See Chapter 1.

2 [1971] 2 QB 528 at 553D.

3 (1977) 34 P&CR 224.

4 See Christine J Davis 'Abandonment of an Easement: Is it a question of intention only?' [1995] Conv 291.

5 For proprietary estoppel generally, see *Halsbury's Laws of England* (4th edn vol 16 (reissue) para 1072); *Snell's Equity* (30th edn 39–12).

8.13 It is submitted that, on the authorities, abandonment can occur in either way, although this has been expressly recognised in only one case.[1] Whichever approach the courts have adopted, it appears always to have been assumed that there could be no abandonment unless the dominant owner knew of his right.[2] This seems correct in principle. Just as acquisition of an easement of light by prescription is based on conduct and knowledge, abandonment should also be so based; unless the existence of what is being abandoned is known of by the possessor, he can hardly be said to have impliedly agreed to relinquish it.

8.14 In *Moore v Rawson*,[3] the plaintiff, who had in the wall of his building windows which were ancient lights, pulled down the wall and replaced it with a blank wall having no apertures 17 years before the action. The defendant subsequently, 3 years before the action, erected a building near to the plaintiff's new wall. About 3 years later, the plaintiff opened windows in the same position as the ancient lights in his new wall, and sued the defendant for obstruction. It was held that the action must fail, since the plaintiff had by his actions abandoned the right to light formerly enjoyed by the ancient lights. The decision was based on the ground that since the defendant had acted to his detriment by constructing his building without reference to the supposed right of the plaintiff, it would be unjust to grant an injunction. Abbott CJ also stated that by erecting a blank wall the plaintiff might have induced someone to buy the servient land.

8.15 *Moore v Rawson* was approved and followed in *Cook v Mayor of Bath*,[4] a case on obstruction of a right of way. In *Winter v Brockwell*,[5] a case pre-dating *Moore v Rawson*, the court applied the same principle. A parol (oral) licence was given by the dominant owner of a right to light and air received over a yard, to the servient owner to erect a skylight over the yard; the effect of this structure was to obstruct the light and air (the main problem apparently relating to smells). It was held that the dominant owner could not revoke the permission, once acted on, at all events without tendering to the servient owner a sum representing the expenses incurred in erecting the structure. This case might suggest that the dominant owner can re-assert his rights provided it is equitable for him to do so. Such a right is recognised in other contexts, probably in the doctrine of promissory estoppel.[6] However, the case should probably not be read as extending thus far. The structure could easily be removed without major damage to the fabric of the buildings surrounding the yard, and there were clearly issues of risk to health involved. The erection of substantial and permanent buildings by the servient owner was not, therefore, in question.

---

1 *Stokoe v Singers* (1857) 8 EL&BL 31, 120–121; see also **8.16**.

2 Cf *Obadia v Morris* (1974) 232 EG 333.

3 [1824] 3 B&C 332; 107 ER 756.

4 (1868) LR 6 Eq 177.

5 (1807) 8 East 308, 103 ER 359.

6 See, generally, *Halsbury's Laws of England* (4th edn vol 16 (reissue) para 1071). Sometimes called '*High Trees*' estoppel (see *Central London Property Trust Ltd v High Trees House Ltd* [1947] KB 130).

8.16 In *Stokoe v Singers*,[1] where the allegation of abandonment of the right to light failed, the dominant owner had blocked up his windows for 20 years; the apertures remained visible (the blocking up having been by means of rubble built up within them) as did the iron bars on the outside of the windows. A purchaser of the servient land then proposed to build so as to obstruct the windows, and the plaintiff, the successor to the dominant owner, then re-opened the windows. The judge's direction to the jury, approved on appeal, was to the following effect.

(1) The right to light to the plaintiff's windows continued until lost.
(2) There should be a verdict for the plaintiff unless:
    (a) his predecessor had by blocking up the windows manifested an intention of permanently abandoning them; or
    (b) they thought that the windows had been kept so closed as to lead the defendant to alter his position in the reasonable belief that the lights had been permanently abandoned.

This case recognises the two alternative methods of abandonment, one of which involves only the simple manifestation of an intention to abandon, without any alteration in the servient owner's position. This seems to have been the basis of the decision in *Lawrence v Obee*,[2] where a blank wall had replaced a window formerly in it for over 20 years. Although this was also a case in which the defendant had subsequently erected a building (an allegedly malodorous privy), it was not suggested (at least expressly) that this amounted to alteration of the servient owner's position. On the other hand, the decision may be explicable on this ground.

8.17 More recently, in *Marine and General Mutual Life Assurance Society v St James Real Estate Co Ltd*,[3] abandonment by simple evidence of intention has received backing in principle although the claim failed on the facts (since although the windows had been blocked up the apertures were retained, without the sills or reveals being broken). It was said that:

> 'It is clear that the windows were closed up in such a way that they could be reopened without keying into the brickwork of the walls. The procedure followed seems to have been, in summary, that a sleeve was put round the edges of the window, leaving the cill in place, and brickwork was laid within the sleeve. Thus, as appears from the photographs that were before me, the position of the apertures is clearly visible. Nevertheless I agree with the submission of the Defendant's Counsel that the closing up is solid, substantial and uses materials similar to the walls. I have no reason to doubt that, as Counsel submitted, the "infill" panels are perfectly capable of lasting the life of the building.'

8.18 Nevertheless, the court held applying *Tehidy Minerals Ltd v Norman*,[4] that the right to light had not been abandoned. The wall with windows had not been pulled down and replaced by a blank wall. Window apertures had been

---

1 (1857) 8 EL&BL 31, 120 ER 12.
2 (1814) 3 Camp 514, 170 ER 1465.
3 [1991] 2 EGLR 178.
4 [1971] 2 QB 528. See also **8.10**.

filled in with brick, but the sills remained and the position of the apertures was clearly visible.

8.19 By contrast, in *Smith v Baxter*,[1] the boarding up of windows for a prolonged period was held to amount to abandonment.[2] This suggests that the issue as to what degree of prominence in the obstruction of the window is required to evidence abandonment is ultimately one of fact.

4. INTERRUPTION

Actual interruption

8.20 Under the Prescription Act 1832, s 3,[3] 20 years' actual enjoyment of light gives rise to a right to light under that Act. However, by s 4 of the same Act:

> 'Each of the respective periods herein-before mentioned shall be deemed and taken to be the period next before some suit or action wherein the claim or matter to which such period may relate shall have been or shall be brought into question; and ... no act or other matter shall be deemed to be an interruption, within the meaning of this statute, unless the same shall have been or shall be submitted to or acquiesced in for one year after the party interrupted shall have had or shall have notice thereof, and of the person making or authorising the same to be made.'

8.21 The combined effect of ss 3 and 4 of the Prescription Act 1832 is that where light has been actually enjoyed for a period of more than 19 years prior to interruption, the right is capable of becoming 'absolute and indefeasible' under s 3, since no interruption for a period of at least one year, prior to the expiry of the 20-year period, is possible. However, until the period of 20 years has run, the dominant owner has no right capable of being relied on or giving rise to legal rights.[4] Thus, in *Lord Battersea v Commissioners of Sewers for the City of London*,[5] the plaintiffs sought an injunction to restrain the defendants from building so as to interfere with access of light to their premises. The buildings on the defendant's site had been demolished between May and October 1875. In 1895, the plaintiffs commenced proceedings against the defendants to restrain the construction of a new development on the defendants' land, asserting that their windows had since 1875 acquired a right to light under s 3 of the Prescription Act 1832. In July 1895, the plaintiffs sought an interlocutory injunction to restrain the defendants from building so as to interfere with the access of light. They claimed that since more than 19 years had passed since the old buildings on every part of the defendants' site had been pulled down, the defendants could do nothing to defeat the plaintiffs' right to light, even though the plaintiffs had not,

---

1 [1900] 2 Ch 138.
2 See also Chapter 4 at **4.15**.
3 See Chapter 6.
4 *Bridewell Hospital (Governors) v Ward, Lock, Bowden & Co* (1893) 62 LJ Ch 270; *Lord Battersea v Commissioners of Sewers for the City of London* [1895] 2 Ch 708.
5 [1895] 2 Ch 708.

at the time the motion for an interlocutory injunction came on for hearing, enjoyed the light for the full period of 20 years (because some of the buildings on the defendants' site had been demolished only in October 1875, hence the 20-year period would be completed only in October 1895).

8.22 The court held that the plaintiffs had not established their right to the light received by their premises over the defendants' land in its state following the demolition of the buildings in 1875. North J said:

> 'That section [ie s 4] to my mind, strongly bears out, on this point, what Section 3 says, because the period of years – the 20 years – is to be "next before the suit or action wherein the claim is made". What I am asked to do now is to say that it is quite sufficient that the 20 years shall be calculated, not 20 complete years before action, but 20 years, 19 years, and rather more of which is before action, the rest of the 20 years being made up during the continuance of the action. It seems to me that such a contention is directly contrary to the meaning of these two Sections. I think, therefore, that the action can only be brought after the period of 20 years has elapsed.'

8.23 However, the court's conclusion did not preclude the plaintiffs from relying on a right to receive light to their premises to the extent enjoyed over the defendants' land *prior* to the demolition of the defendants' buildings in 1875. Therefore, an interlocutory injunction was granted restraining the defendants from building higher than the buildings existing in July 1875 so as to obscure the plaintiffs' windows. Thus whilst the combined effect of ss 3 and 4 of the 1832 Act is that after enjoyment has existed for more than 19 years it is capable of ripening into an absolute and indefeasible right, the right arises only once the 20-year period has elapsed.

8.24 An interruption for the purposes of the 1832 Act requires either physical obstruction of the light or a notional obstruction under the Rights of Light Act 1959 (considered below). The physical obstruction may be due to the act of the servient owner or a stranger.[1] However, the mere commencement of legal proceedings by the servient owner does not amount to an interruption.[2] It is also established that the dominant owner's obstruction of his own light does not amount to an interruption within the meaning of the Act.[3] But such activity may be evidence of abandonment.

8.25 It is not established whether the interruption means *any* act which amounts to diminution of the light, even to a small (and possibly non-actionable) extent, or whether, in order to qualify as an interruption, the obstruction must be such as to be actionable. It is suggested that the latter must be the case, since the 1832 Act is concerned with rights to light, and if in a particular case an obstruction is not so substantial as to give rise to a claim, there seems no basis on which the provisions of the Act should be brought into play.

---

1 *Plasterer's Company v Parish Clerks Company* (1851) 6 Exch 630; *Davies v Williams* (1851) 16 QBD 546.

2 *Reilly v Orange* [1955] 2 QB 112.

3 *Smith v Baxter* [1900] 2 Ch 138.

8.26 In order to defeat the acquisition of a right to light under s 3, the interruption must be acquiesced in for one year. The notion of acquiescence implies knowledge that the obstruction exists. Submission or acquiescence is a 'state of mind', as Birkett LJ said in *Davies v Du Paver*.[1] The person in question, before he can be said to acquiesce, must have some notice of the existence of the obstruction. The mere presence of the obstruction is not enough for these purposes.[2] In *Seddon v Bank of Bolton*,[3] Fry J suggested in the course of argument that written notice was required,[4] but the actual point did not arise for decision since the court held that the plaintiff had failed to discharge the burden of proof in establishing her right to light. But at p 469 of the Report, Fry J did express the view, obiter, that the defendants had not shown the kind of notice which would have made the obstruction an interruption under s 4. Quite what notice is sufficient, other than expressly in writing, is open to debate. It is submitted that notice in writing is not necessary; it is, in practice, improbable that such notice would be given, and the terms of the 1832 Act do not expressly require it.

8.27 Assuming the dominant owner becomes aware of the obstruction, whether he acquiesced in its continuation for the one-year period is an issue of fact.[5] Evidence to negative acquiescence may take many forms. Clearly, the most decisive evidence of non-acquiescence is the commencement of legal proceedings to vindicate the right interrupted, although this is not an essential requirement.[6] Other types of evidence of non-acquiescence include:

(1) protests made in anticipation of the interruption;[7]
(2) refusal to act on a permission given by the servient owner (it being implicit in such permission that the existence of the right is denied);[8]
(3) other manifestations of dissent or dissatisfaction.

8.28 Section 4 of the 1832 Act refers to submission or acquiescence. The fact that something is submitted to reluctantly does not prevent it amounting to submission or acquiescence within s 4. In *Glover v Coleman*,[9] Brett J said:

> 'Acquiescence ... would mean not active agreement, but what might be called a tacit, a silent agreement, – a submission to a thing by one who is satisfied to submit. The question for the jury, therefore, upon a suggested acquiescence, would be, whether the plaintiff, although he has not specifically agreed that the thing should be done, has submitted to it, and has been satisfied to submit. Now, "opposition", on the other hand, I should say, would mean dissent or dissatisfaction manifested by some

---

1 [1953] 1 QB 184 at 203.
2 *Glover v Coleman* (1874) LR 10 CP 108; *Seddon v Bank of Bolton* (1882) 19 ChD 462. See Chapter 6 at **6.27**.
3 (1882) 19 ChD 462.
4 (1882) 19 ChD 462 at 464.
5 *Bennison v Cartwright* (1864) 5 B&S 1.
6 *Glover v Coleman* (1874) LR 10 CP 108.
7 *Davies v Du Paver* [1953] 1 QB 184.
8 *Ward v Kirkland* [1967] 1 Ch 194 at 231G–232F.
9 (1874) LR 10 CP 108 at 119.

> act of opposition. "Submitted to" in this part of the Section, seems to me to be something intermediate between a submission by one satisfied to submit and a dissatisfaction manifested by some act of opposition.'

In the same case, Grove J drew a distinction[1] between '*mere grumbling, or complaining to a member of his family, or expressing dissatisfaction to a third party*', which would not amount to an act of opposition, and '*protests . . . made to the party causing the interruption*', which would be capable of amounting to non-acquiescence.

8.29 In *Dance v Triplow*,[2] it was held that the following acts did not prevent the plaintiff from having acquiesced in an interruption of his right to light for more than one year:

(1) complaining to the local planning authority about a proposed revision of the planning consent obtained by the defendants;
(2) consulting solicitors concerning the defendant's use of a weed killer which had drifted across the boundary.

8.30 The same case also establishes that the burden of proving non-acquiescence lies on the dominant owner once the interruption has lasted for more than one year. This is consistent with the general rule that it is for the person asserting the right to light to establish their case.[3]

Notional interruption

8.31 The Rights of Light Act 1959 (in this section and in Chapter 7 referred to as the 1959 Act) introduces a statutory method of interruption without the need for the erection of a physical obstruction. The mechanism provided by the Act is a light obstruction notice, a notional physical obstruction notionally erected on the land of the giver of the notice. Registration of the light obstruction notice as a local land charge is deemed to constitute notice to those affected. The light obstruction notice remains effective for one year, this period mirroring the length of time during which an obstruction must continue under s 4 of the Prescription Act 1832. If those affected by the notice fail to take and protect their rights within the one-year period, their rights to light will be extinguished to the same extent as if an actual physical obstruction had been erected for that period in the position specified in the light obstruction notice.

8.32 The 1959 Act was passed to remedy two problems which had arisen as a result of the Second World War. The first was that during the War many buildings had been destroyed, and by the time the Act was passed had not been rebuilt. This led to the possibility of rights to light being acquired by neighbouring buildings over the sites on which these buildings had formerly stood. Secondly, the enactment of the Town and Country Planning Act 1947 required planning permission for the erection of physical obstructions which

1 (1874) LR 10 CP 108 at 121.
2 (1992) 1 EGLR 190; (1991) 64 P&CR 1.
3 Cf *Seddon v Bank of Bolton* (1882) 19 ChD 462.

were formerly used to prevent the acquisition of rights to light under the Prescription Act 1832. In practice, the need for planning permission resulted in the practice of erecting such obstructions falling off. The combined effect of these matters was perceived to give rise to a risk that many areas of land might be sterilised for development in future. A committee under Mr Justice (later Lord Justice) Harman (this is commonly known as 'the Harman Committee') was appointed to consider the problem, and reported in May 1958.[1] The Harman Committee Report sets out the problem, and provides a useful guide to the interpretation of the 1832 Act, which resulted from it.[2]

8.33 Sections 2 and 3 of the 1832 Act lay down the basic framework. The basic concept is the creation by s 2 of a notional obstruction brought into being by a notice under the section. Although the Act does not define such a notice except in terms of its being a notice under s 2, such notices are generally referred to as 'light obstruction notices', and this terminology will be used here. Section 2(1) provides that for the purposes of preventing the access and use of light from being taken to be enjoyed without interruption, any person who is an owner of land ('the servient land') over which light passes to a dwellinghouse, workshop or other building ('the dominant building') may apply to the local authority in whose area the dominant building is situated for the registration of a light obstruction notice. By s 7(1), the term 'owner' bears a special meaning. It applies to:

(1) the freeholder;
(2) a tenant under a fixed-term lease having not less than 7 years unexpired;
(3) a mortgagee in possession where the interest mortgaged is either the freehold or a lease with not less than 7 years unexpired.

8.34 The key provision of the Act is s 3(1), which provides that once a light obstruction notice is registered under the Act the access of light to the dominant building across the servient land shall be treated as obstructed to the same extent, and with the like consequences, as if an opaque structure, of the dimensions specified in the application:

(1) had on the date of registration of the notice been erected in the position on the servient land specified in the application, and had been so erected by the person who made the application; and
(2) had remained in that position during the period for which the notice has effect and had been removed at the end of that period.

8.35 A light obstruction notice is therefore notionally a physical obstruction of light to the dominant building received over the servient land. The obstruction ceases to have effect after one year;[3] this ties in with s 4 of the Prescription Act 1832, set out at **8.20**. There is no need for the notional obstruction to remain in position for more than one year to be effective as an interruption under the 1832

---

1 Report of the Committee on the Law Relating to Rights of Light (Cmnd 473).
2 See Appendix 3 for relevant extracts.
3 See s 3(2)(b).

Act, and equally a period of less than one year would not be sufficient. As has been pointed out above, since no interruption of less than one year can be effective under the 1832 Act to prevent the 20-year period being established, enjoyment for more than 19 years is capable of ripening into a prescriptive right.[1] The 1959 Act applies the same regime to notional obstructions created by light obstruction notices, by s 3(4). The actual wording of the subsection is to the effect that where at any time during the period for which a light obstruction notice is in force:

> 'the circumstances are such that if the access of light to the dominant building had been enjoyed continuously from a date one year earlier than the date on which the enjoyment thereof in fact began, a person would have had a right of action in any court ... in respect of the registration of the notice, that person shall have the like right of action ...'.

8.36 By s 7(1), 'action' includes a counter-claim.[2] Where the notional obstruction creates an actionable interference to the dominant building, the owner has the same right of action in respect of the registration of the notice as he would have had in respect of a physical obstruction of the same dimensions as those described in the notice. The remedies available are declaratory relief, and an order directing cancellation or variation of the notice, as the court may determine.[3] Cancellation of the light obstruction notice would generally be predicated on the basis of the court deciding that the entire obstruction was unlawful, a variation on a decision that only part of the obstruction created an actionable interference.[4] For obvious reasons, injunctive relief is not available. The 1959 Act makes no provision for an award of damages suffered by reason of the notional obstruction. This is no doubt consistent with the absence of any *actual* obstruction, since there has been no interference with the light in fact received by the dominant building.

8.37 As has been seen in relation to s 4 of the 1832 Act, the issue of acquiescence is relevant in deciding whether there has been an interruption of the light for a sufficiently long period to defeat the acquisition of a prescriptive right.[5] The 1959 Act introduces for the purposes of s 4 of the 1832 Act a special regime in relation to light obstruction notices. The two key features of the regime are:

(1) registration of the light obstruction notice is deemed to be notice of the obstruction to all those interested in the dominant building;
(2) until the light obstruction notice is challenged in legal proceedings, all persons interested in the dominant building are deemed to acquiesce in the obstruction, but from the date of legal proceedings no person is deemed to acquiesce in the obstruction.[6]

---

1 See **8.21**.
2 Now a Part 20 claim under the CPR.
3 See s 3(5).
4 See *Hawker v Tomalin* [1969] 20 P&CR 550.
5 See **8.27–8.30**.
6 See s 4(6).

Thus where the 1959 Act applies, it is unnecessary to enquire into either the state of mind of the person alleged to have acquiesced or as to whether the acts in relation to the obstruction amounted to acquiescence: it is simply necessary to see whether legal proceedings to challenge the notice were commenced within one year of its registration, even if not by the particular claimant. There is a proviso that if the court dismisses a particular claimant's claim, it may direct that the regime shall continue to apply as if the action had not been brought. The purpose of this is to prevent the light obstruction notice from being deprived of effect by virtue of an unsuccessful claim. The court's power is discretionary.

8.38 The 1959 Act lays down a number of detailed requirements as to:

(1) the giving of notice to those likely to be affected by a light obstruction notice before such a notice is registered;
(2) the form of the notice;
(3) registration of the notice.

The aim of these provisions are twofold: first, they are designed to ensure that those interested in the servient land become aware of the proposed registration of the light obstruction notice, and do not lose their rights by failing to challenge within the one-year period from registration the notice, in circumstances where they had no notice of the proposal to register it. Secondly, there is the need to protect purchasers of the dominant building; since there will be no physical evidence of a light obstruction notice visible on inspection of the dominant building, a purchaser might be led to conclude that windows looking over the servient land had acquired prescriptive rights to light. It is therefore necessary to ensure that light obstruction notices are registered in some publicly available register for inspection by prospective purchasers. The 1959 Act achieves this by providing that light obstruction notices are to be registered as local land charges under the Local Land Charges Act 1975.

8.39 Before an application can be made to a local authority for registration of a light obstruction notice, appropriate publicity must be given to the proposed application. The 1959 Act deals with this in s 2(3), by providing that an application is to be accompanied by a certificate issued by the Lands Tribunal.[1] The certificate may be in one of two alternative forms:

(1) a certificate under s 2(3)(a) certifying that adequate notice of the proposed application has been given to all persons who in the circumstances existing at the time when the certificate is issued appear to the Lands Tribunal to be persons likely to be affected by the registration of a notice in pursuance of the application;
(2) a certificate under s 2(3)(b) certifying that in the opinion of the Lands Tribunal the case is one of exceptional urgency, and that accordingly a notice should be registered forthwith as a temporary notice for such period as may be specified in the certificate.

1 Established under the Lands Tribunal Act 1949.

Certificates issued under s 2(3)(a) are known as definitive certificates, and those issued under s 2(3)(b) as temporary certificates. The purpose of a temporary certificate is to enable a light obstruction notice to be erected where otherwise the period of 19 years uninterrupted enjoyment of light would be completed before the procedure for obtaining a definitive certificate, and registration, could be effected. In order to prevent the emergency certificate procedure being used to bypass the definitive certificate procedure, provision is made for emergency certificates to have only a limited life, following which a definitive certificate must be obtained.

8.40 The procedure for obtaining certificates is laid down in Part VI of the Lands Tribunal Rules 1996.[1] Rule 21 provides that an application for a certificate of the Lands Tribunal under s 2 of the 1959 Act is to be in Form 1 in Sch 1 to the Rules.[2] It must be accompanied by two copies of the application which the applicant proposes to make to the local authority in whose area the dominant building is situated. By r 22, on receipt of an application the Registrar of the Lands Tribunal is to determine what notices are to be given whether by advertisement or otherwise to persons who appear to have an interest in the dominant building, the subject of the proposed application. The Registrar must require the applicant to provide any documents or information which it is in his power to provide. By r 22(3), the notices that the Registrar determines shall be given under r 22 must be given by the applicant, who is to notify the Registrar in writing once this has been done setting out full particulars of the steps he has taken.

8.41 In the case of an application for a definitive certificate, the Registrar will require the following information:

(1) the identities of all those interested in the dominant building who could qualify as 'owners' within the 1959 Act, s 7;
(2) the business addresses and registered offices of the person so identified;
(3) the full address and location of the dominant building.

The proposed applicant will be required to write letters to all those so identified, giving them notice of the proposed application to the local authority, and enclosing a copy of that proposed application and any plan which is to accompany it.

8.42 The identity of the potential 'owners' may be capable of ascertainment from a property search at the Land Registry: however, such a search may not reveal the names of all potential owners: leases for terms of less than 21 years are not registrable under the provisions of the Land Registration Act 1925 as amended,[3] and there is therefore a risk that potential owners may not be traced by a Land Registry search. There is therefore usually a requirement imposed that a copy of the proposed application to the local authority be sent to the dominant

1 SI 1906/1022.
2 See Appendix 2.
3 See Land Registration Acts 1986 and 1997.

building addressed simply to the 'occupier'. Following notification to the Lands Tribunal that the relevant notices have been served, the Registrar will issue the definitive certificate in Form 3 in Sch 1 to the Lands Tribunal Rules.[1]

8.43 Where the application includes an application for a temporary certificate authorising the registration forthwith of the proposed notice, the applicant will need to include in his application details of the reasons which make the case one of exceptional urgency. It is desirable to accompany the application in these circumstances by an affidavit verifying the facts.[2] Strictly, such evidence is not necessary in the first instance (though the Registrar may require it). Whether there is an accompanying affidavit or not, the application should contain a full explanation of the reasons for the application being made as one of urgency. An example of the type of situations where this would be the case would be if the dominant building had been completed 18 years or thereabouts prior to the application, so that there was a real risk of the 19-year period elapsing shortly.

8.44 A temporary certificate cannot last longer than 6 months.[3] Form 1 in Sch 1 to the Rules envisages a composite application both for a temporary and definitive certificate. The Registrar may, therefore, grant a temporary certificate in respect of a proposed application, and give directions at the same time as to the notices to be given to those affected, preparatory to the grant of a definitive certificate. The applicant can then, having given the appropriate notification to those likely to be affected by the light obstruction notice, apply to the Registrar for the definitive certificate, and obtain it within the 6-month period.

8.45 It is not possible to challenge the Registrar's decision to issue a temporary certificate except by way of judicial review proceedings under RSC Ord 53, as set out in Sch 1 to the CPR.[4] Once the relevant certificate has been obtained, the applicant applies to the relevant local authority (in whose area the dominant building is situated) for registration of the notice in respect of which the certificate has been given as a local land charge under the Local Land Charges Act 1975. The procedure is governed by the Local Land Charges Rules 1977.[5] By r 10(1), an application is to be in Form A and be accompanied by the certificate of the Lands Tribunal. On receipt of the application and certificate, the registering authority (ie in the local authority for the purposes of the Local Land Charges Act 1975 in whose area the dominant building is situated) must register the notice in accordance with r 6. Rule 6(1) provides for registration by reference to the land in the area of the registering authority, and r 6(2) provides for the registration by entering in the part of the register appropriate for that charge the particulars specified in Sch 2 to the Local Land Charges Rules 1977 in relation to that Part.

---

1 See Appendix 2.

2 Affidavit evidence may be adduced before the Lands Tribunal under Lands Tribunal Rules 1996, rr 33 and 38.

3 Lands Tribunal Rules 1996, r 23(2).

4 *Bowring Services Ltd v Scottish Widows Fund and Life Assurance Society* [1995] 1 EGLR 158.

5 SI 1977/985. See Appendix 2.

The relevant part of the register for light obstruction notices is Part 11.[1] Part 11 requires information with regard to the notice to be entered under the following heads.

(1) Description of charge.
(2) Description of dominant building.
(3) Name and address of applicant and short description of his interest in the servient land.
(4) Position and dimension of structure to which registration equivalent.
(5) Date of temporary Lands Tribunal certificate (if any) and of its expiration.
(6) Date of definitive Lands Tribunal certificate.
(7) List of documents filed.
(8) Date of registration.

8.46 Form A in Sch 1 to the Local Land Charges Rules 1977 envisages that the application will be accompanied by a plan showing the location of the servient land and the position of the notional obstruction on it. The form of application envisages that the notional obstruction will be of unlimited height. Normally, the notional obstruction will be shown on the plan attached to the application, but the form of application also allows for the possibility of notional obstructions on all the boundaries of the servient land. One advantage of the notional obstruction introduced by the 1959 Act is that it is possible to 'position' it so as to obstruct windows in any position irrespective of the practical problems of erecting an actual obstruction of the requisite dimensions and in the desired position. This can be important where the dominant building has acquired an extra storey. The notice can be positioned to obstruct the new windows without interfering with the windows lower down, which may already enjoy indefeasible rights.[2]

8.47 It must be remembered that the Lands Tribunal will not issue a definitive or temporary certificate without having before it the draft application to the local authority. It is not therefore possible to register a light obstruction notice in a form different from that in respect of which the Lands Tribunal has issued its certificate.

8.48 Where a temporary certificate accompanies the application to the registering authority, the registering authority is to cancel the registration of the notice if no definitive certificate has been filed, on the expiration of the period of operation of the temporary certificate.[3] Where a notice is registered following the issue of a temporary certificate, and the applicant subsequently obtains a definitive certificate before the temporary certificate expires, the period of 12 months within which the light obstruction notice must be challenged under s 3(2) of the 1959 Act runs from the date of registration of the notice pursuant to

---

1 See Local Land Charges Rules 1977, r 3. See Appendix 2.

2 Contrast the practical problem faced by a servient owner erecting an actual obstruction to upper windows and lower windows enjoying established light – see *Tapling v Jones* (1865) 11 HLC 290.

3 Local Land Charges Rules 1977, r 10(6).

the temporary certificate. So in *Bowring Services Limited v Scottish Widows Fund and Life Assurance Society*,[1] the plaintiff failed in its effort to challenge a light obstruction notice in circumstances where on 12 August 1991 the light obstruction notice was registered pursuant to a temporary certificate, which was expressed to expire within 4 months unless a definitive certificate was lodged. The definitive certificate was issued on 8 October 1991. The plaintiff commenced proceedings to challenge the light obstruction notice in October 1992, more than 12 months after the initial registration of the light obstruction notice, but within 12 months of the issue of the definitive certificate. It was held that the plaintiff's challenge had been made too late to prevent the notice being effective as an interruption of the plaintiff's enjoyment of light. The court also dismissed the plaintiff's argument to the effect that the Registrar's decision to issue the temporary certificate was invalid, holding that the only way of challenging this would be by way of judicial review proceedings.

5. DEMOLITION OR ALTERATION OF THE DOMINANT BUILDING

8.49 Since a right to light inherently depends on the existence of defined apertures in a building, the disappearance of the building, or the relevant part containing the apertures may affect whether the right to light continues to exist. This question raises similar issues as to whether there has been abandonment by blocking up windows,[2] but goes further, considering complete demolition of the dominant building, or demolition and/or remodelling of the wall in which the windows enjoying rights to light are situated.

8.50 Dealing first with demolition, it is clear in principle that the demolition of the dominant building may result in the disappearance of rights to light enjoyed with it but, equally, that this is not necessarily the case. In *Ecclesiastical Commissioners v Kino*,[3] a church containing windows enjoying rights to light was demolished. The owner of neighbouring land asserted that the effect of this demolition was to bring to an end the rights to light enjoyed by the windows. This argument was rejected. It was held that the fact that there was no existing window did not prevent the plaintiffs obtaining an injunction, on the basis that they intended to rebuild making use of the pre-existing right to light for the new building. The effect of the demolition was simply to suspend enjoyment of their rights.[4]

8.51 Where the dominant building undergoes alterations, so that the windows enjoying rights to light are replaced by new windows, whether the right to light is lost depends on a number of matters. The general principle is that alterations to

1 [1995] 1 EGLR 158.
2 See **8.17–8.18**.
3 (1880) 14 ChD 213.
4 See also *Staight v Burn* (1869) 5 Ch App 163.

windows will not destroy the right to light enjoyed by them, provided there is coincidence between at least part of the old and the new apertures.[1] The right to light, however, will not extend to those portions of new apertures opened in the dominant building which do not coincide with the apertures which previously enjoyed a right to light, nor, obviously, to wholly new apertures (unless and until they acquire prescriptive rights to light of their own). Where the new operations coincide partially with the old ones, the claimant is entitled to have his prescriptive rights protected. It is thought that in such cases damages may be awarded for the whole loss to the building,[2] on the basis that the obstruction of the new lights inevitably involves obstruction of the old.

8.52 Thus where a window enjoying rights to light is increased in size, the right to light applies to only that portion of the larger aperture which is coincident with the pre-existing window, but equally the right to that portion is not lost by the enlargement. Where the effect of the alteration is to *reduce* the size of the existing window, the position is that the right to light remains, but the dominant owner cannot complain about any subsequent building work of the servient owner which obstructs the light received from the newly reduced window, if the light would have remained adequate notwithstanding the obstruction if the window had remained at its original size.[3] In *Ankerson v Connelly*,[4] the defendant redeveloped his land, and reduced the size of windows enjoying rights to light, resulting in the light received being reduced by at least three-quarters. The plaintiffs, owners of the servient tenement, then erected hoardings sufficient to obstruct the defendant's windows in their altered condition. There was evidence that but for the reduction in size the obstruction would not have caused actionable interference to the windows. It was held that the defendant had no right to complain.

8.53 In *WH Bailey & Son Limited v Holborn & Frascati Limited*,[5] the same principle was applied where the obstruction to the window arose not directly from the dominant owner's acts, but by acts of another servient owner, to which the plaintiff had assented. Sargant J said:[6]

> 'I think myself that the true view of the law is suggested by a passage in the 8th edition of Gale on Easements where at p. 547 the learned author says: "It would seem clear that after an alteration in an ancient window whereby its size was decreased, the dominant proprietor would not be entitled to prevent the erection of buildings which, though obstructing the altered window, would not, before the alteration, have caused an illegal obstruction within the rule laid down in *Colls'* case. This principle was applied in *Ankerson v. Connelly*". Converting that passage from a negative proposition into a positive proposition and applying it not to an alteration

1 *Tapling v Jones* (1861) 11 CBNS 283; (1862) 12 CBNS 826; (1865) 12 CBNS 166; 11 HLC 290.
2 On the principles discussed in Chapter 11 at **11.50**.
3 *Ankerson v Connelly* [1906] 2 Ch 554; [1907] 1 Ch 678.
4 [1906] 2 Ch 544; affirmed [1907] 1 Ch 678.
5 [1914] 1 Ch 598.
6 [1914] 1 Ch 602–603.

of a window but to an alteration of the light coming over adjoining property brought about with the assent or permission of the owner of the dominant tenement, it seems to me that it is true to say that an obstruction of light coming over adjoining property acquiesced in or consented to by the owner of the dominant tenement does not entirely negative his right to an easement of light over other adjoining property, though it does not give him any further right over that second adjoining property, so as to prevent the erection of a building which he could not have prevented had he not assented to the prior obstruction of light over the first adjoining property.'

8.54 Where the effect of the alterations to the dominant building is to destroy the identity between the old and the new apertures, the right to light may be lost. *De minimis* coincidence will not be enough to preserve the right.[1] It is therefore of practical importance for a dominant owner who proposes to carry out work to a building enjoying rights to light both to keep an accurate survey record of the position of any such windows which are to be demolished, and to ensure that the new apertures are in the same position as the old. In *News of the World Limited v Allen Fairhead & Sons Limited*,[2] a claim to rights to light in respect of a redeveloped building replacing an original building enjoying such rights failed for lack of proof of the position of the original windows. This was so even though the court accepted that there was some coincidence between certain of the old and new apertures, albeit the extent was unclear.

8.55 Where the plane of the window, or the position of the wall in which it is situated are altered, whether the right to light is preserved cannot be answered simply by reference to coincidence between the old and the new aperture. The court's approach has been to uphold the continuation of rights to light provided the light continues to be received by the dominant building in the same general position as when the pre-existing window was in existence. In *National Provincial Plate Glass Insurance Co v Prudential Assurance Co*[3] Fry J said:

> '... I find nothing whatever in the statute [ie the Rights of Light Act 1832] which refers expressly to a window or aperture. I find in the statute a reference to the access of light, and in my view the access of light might be described as being the freedom with which light may pass through a certain space over the servient tenement ...'

The principle has been applied to:

(1) replacement of a dormer window with a skylight;[4]
(2) setting back a wall, replacing in it windows in the same position and of the same sizes as in the original wall;[5]
(3) setting back of a wall, and insertion in it of a window at a different angle to the original.[6]

---

1 *Ankerson v Connelly* [1906] 2 Ch 554; [1907] 1 Ch 678.
2 [1931] 2 Ch 402.
3 (1877) 6 ChD 757 at 764.
4 *National Provincial Plate Glass Insurance Co v Prudential Assurance Co* (1877) 6 ChD 757.
5 *Barnes v Loach* (1879) 4 QBD 494.
6 *Bullers v Dickinson* (1885) 29 ChD 155.

6. EXTINGUISHMENT UNDER STATUTORY PROVISIONS

8.56 Part IX of the Town and Country Planning Act 1990 (in this section referred to as 'the 1990 Act') provides for certain local authorities to acquire land compulsorily for development and planning purposes.[1] By s 237 of the 1990 Act:

> '(1) Subject to subsection (3), the erection, construction or carrying out, or maintenance of any building or work on land which has been acquired or appropriated by a local authority for planning purposes (whether done by a local authority or by a person deriving title under them) is authorised by virtue of this section if it is done in accordance with planning permission, notwithstanding that it involves—
> (a) interference with an interest or right to which this section applies, or
> (b) a breach of a restriction as to the user of land arising by virtue of a contract.
> (2) Subject to subsection (3), the interests and rights to which this section applies are any easement, liberty, privilege, right or advantage annexed to land and adversely affecting other land, including any natural right to support.
> . . .
> (4) In respect of any inference or breach in pursuance of subsection (1), compensation—
> (a) shall be payable under section 63 or 68 of the Lands Clauses Consolidation Act 1845 or under section 7 or 10 of the Compulsory Purchase Act 1965, and
> (b) shall be assessed in the same manner and subject to the same rules as in the case of other compensation under those sections in respect of injurious affection where—
> (i) the compensation is to be estimated in connection with a purchase under those Acts, or
> (ii) the injury arises from the execution of works on land acquired under those Acts.
> (5) Where a person deriving title under the local authority by whom the land in question was acquired or appropriated—
> (a) is liable to pay compensation by virtue of subsection (4), and
> (b) fails to discharge that liability,
> the liability shall be enforceable against the local authority.
> (6) Nothing in subsection (5) shall be construed as affecting any agreement between the local authority and any other person for indemnifying the local authority against any liability under that subsection.
> (7) Nothing in this section shall be construed as authorising any act or omission on the part of any person which is actionable at the suit of any person on any grounds other than such an interference or breach as is mentioned in subsection (1).'

The effect of this provision is that private rights (including easements of light) are overridden, where they affect the use of land held for planning purposes where development is carried out in accordance with planning permission. This applies

---

1 See 1990 Act, s 226. For the meaning of 'required' see *Chesterfield Properties v Secretary of State for the Environment* [1997] NPC 122.

not only to development by the Local Planning Authority itself but also to any person deriving title from it.[1]

8.57 In *R v City of London Council, ex parte Master Governors and Commonalty of the Mystery of the Barbers of London*,[2] it was held first that where a local authority has acquired and held land for planning purposes, s 237(1) of the 1990 Act enabled land initially acquired or appropriated for planning purposes, and developed, to be redeveloped notwithstanding that the effect of the development was to interfere with rights to light, and, secondly, that the section applied notwithstanding that the local authority had itself covenanted with the dominant owner not to obstruct its light and air.[3]

8.58 Where land acquired compulsorily is subject to a right of light, the acquiring authority is neither obliged nor empowered to acquire those rights compulsorily. The dominant owner in respect of such an easement is not entitled to a notice to treat, but only to compensation for the injury. Where land acquired has the benefit of an easement, that easement will pass to the acquiring authority.[4]

8.59 Various statutes empower public and private bodies to acquire land compulsorily. Such acquisition is generally subject to the Land Compensation Act 1961, the Compulsory Purchase Act 1965, and the Acquisition of Land Act 1981. Where land compulsorily acquired has the right of an easement, that easement will pass to the acquiring authority.[5] Generally, when powers are given by statute to acquire land compulsorily, the whole of the landowner's interest must be purchased, unless the relevant provision authorises acquisition of a lesser right, such as an easement.[6] So in *Sovmots Investments Ltd v Secretary of State for the Environment*,[7] it was held that a local authority's power to purchase compulsorily land for housing did not extend to the compulsory creation of easements for services, and of access and support, incidental to the compulsory purchase of a number of maisonettes in an open complex which was not itself intended to be acquired. Lord Wilberforce said:

> 'A power to acquire a right over land cannot authorise compulsion of an owner of land not being acquired to grant new rights over that land.'

Where land is acquired compulsorily, its value will be assessed taking into account the benefit of any easement of light it enjoys, as part of its open market value.

---

1 See 1990 Act, s 236(8).
2 [1996] 2 EGLR 128.
3 But see *Thames Water Utilities Ltd v Oxford City Council* (1999) 77 P&CR D16, holding that s 237 did not authorise breaches of covenant by subsequent use of buildings erected under the section.
4 See *Halsbury's Laws of England* 4th edn vol 8(1) (reissue) paras 30–31.
5 [1977] 2 All ER 385, HL.
6 Ibid at 393g.
7 Land Compensation Act 1961, s 5(2).

8.60 Where the effect of compulsory acquisition is to interfere with a right to light enjoyed over the land compulsorily acquired, the general principle is that if the interference would have been actionable, but for being authorised by statute, the dominant owner has no right to action.[1] Instead, he may make a claim for compensation for injurious infliction of his land, depending on the statutory provisions under which the compulsory acquisition has been authorised. Such a claim may be made under s 68 of the Lands Clauses Consolidation Act 1845, or s 10(1) of the Compulsory Purchase Act 1965. The measure of compensation is, in principle, the same as for damages in tort. The damage must not be too remote.[2] When the obstruction of light interferes not only with windows in the claimant's building enjoying rights to light, but also with windows not enjoying such rights, compensation may be claimed for the effect on the building as a whole, not limited to damage arising from obstruction of the windows enjoying rights to light. This was decided in *Re London Tilbury and Southend Railway Company and Gowers Walk School Trustees*.[3] The basis for the decision was that the obstruction to the windows in the building which did not enjoy rights to light inevitably obstructed the light received by the windows that did.

Lord Esher MR said:

> 'If … a person puts up buildings, the inevitable consequence of their erection being to obstruct ancient and modern lights, should not be taken to have foreseen that in obstructing the one he would obstruct the others. If that were proved in a common law action the plaintiff would be entitled to damages for the whole of the consequences of the wrongful act of obstructing ancient lights, which would include damage to the new as much as to the old lights. If so, it seems to me obvious that compensation must be given under the statute to the same extent.'[4]

Lindley LJ stated:

> '… they [the railway company] have infringed the rights of the trustees by darkening certain ancient windows, and as a consequence of that they have diminished the value by an amount found by the arbitrator to be 1450*l*. That is the necessary consequence of their wrongful act. On what principle are the railway company not to pay for that diminution in value? The railway company say they might have blocked up all the modern windows; but to this the trustees may reply, that more than this has been done, that their rights have been infringed, and that, though no action will lie because the infringement is authorized by an Act of Parliament, their case falls within the 16th section of the Railways Clauses Act, and that the consequence is that full compensation must be made, which full compensation is the difference between the value of the land as it was and as it is at present.'[5]

---

1 See *Brown v Heathlands Mental Health NHS Trust* [1996] 1 All ER 133.

2 *Rickett v Metropolitan Railway* (1867) LR 2 HL at 175.

3 (1889) 24 QBD 326, decided under s 16 of the Railways Clauses Consolidation Act 1845. Cf the same principle applied in the award of damages at common law. See Chapter 11 at **11.50–11.51**.

4 Ibid at 329–330.

5 Ibid at 332.

Lopes LJ put the matter succinctly:

> '... having regard to the position of the windows of the school buildings, it is physically impossible to obstruct the light to the new, without at the same time obstructing the light to the ancient windows.'[1]

8.61 However, it is clear that no claim will be for injury which could not have been caused at common law,[2] although it seems that establishing a diminution in the value of the claimant's land may not be an essential pre-requisite to a claim.[3] No claim lies for temporary interference caused by the execution of works, as opposed to the permanent obstruction resulting from the construction (once complete) on the land acquired.[4] The measure of compensation relates to injury to the land of the claimant, not to a loss personal to the landowner or relating to some particular use of his land.[5] There is no claim for a 'ransom' which the landowner might have sought to extract to grant a release of his rights.[6] This is in contrast to his private law position, where damages may be assessed on this basis, if an injunction is refused. Compensation is normally assessed by the Lands Tribunal,[7] acting either under the relevant statutory provision or s 1 of the Land Compensation Act 1961.

1 (1889) 24 QBD 326 at 332–333. See also Chapter 11 at **11.50**.
2 *Wildtree Hotels Ltd v Harrow London Borough Council* [1998] 3 All ER 638, CA.
3 *Eagle v Charing Cross Railway* (1867) 2 CP 638.
4 *Wildtree Hotels Ltd v Harrow London Borough Council* (above).
5 *Argyle Motors (Birkenhead) Ltd v Birkenhead Corporation* [1974] 1 All ER 201, HL.
6 *Wrotham Park Settled Estates v Hertsmore Borough Council* [1993] 2 EGLR 15, CA.
7 See Chapter 11 at **11.119–11.127**.

Chapter 9
Deeds Regulating Rights to Light

GENERALLY

9.1 It is not particularly uncommon for there to exist deeds regulating rights to light enjoyed by buildings over other buildings, particularly in major established city centres. The most common situation in which they are employed is where one building owner wishes to erect a building which may interfere with a dominant owner's existing rights to light. They may also be used when two (or more) building owners wish to facilitate development of their sites by mutual release and/or registration of their rights enjoyed over each other's properties. There are no other prescribed forms of deed and, in practice, their phraseology and content differ quite widely[1] depending on the degree of the parties' interests, the objectives of each party, and the content in which the deed is made. In this chapter are considered, first, typical provisions which may occur in such deeds, secondly, the distinction between 'restrictive' and 'permissive' deeds, thirdly, the legal effectiveness of rights to light deeds and, finally, drafting issues.

TYPICAL PROVISIONS

9.2 The terms which are normally incorporated in rights to light deeds, and problems which arise on their interpretation, vary considerably. The following are normally to be expected.

Payment of compensation

9.3 Where the parties have agreed that a sum is to be paid for permission to erect a new building, the deed will provide for this. It is desirable that a time for payment should be specified, and that if the sum to be paid is compensation for the effect of a new building, the coming into force of the permission for the new building is expressed to be conditional upon such payment.

9.4 In some cases, the deed will simply contain a recital that the sum has been paid. The function of recitals is to narrate the history leading up to the making of the agreement in question or to express in general terms the intention with which the agreement was made.[2] Recitals are an aid to construction, but they cannot control, cut down or qualify operative parts of the contract which are clear.[3] The effect of a recital that a certain sum has been paid is not, in equity, conclusive

1 For forms of grants of easements of light generally, see *Encyclopaedia of Forms and Precedents* Vol 13(1) (Butterworths, 1996 reissue), paras [5550]–[5557].

2 See Lewison *The Interpretation of Contracts* 2nd edn (Sweet & Maxwell, 1997) para 9.09.

3 Ibid, paras 9.10, 9.11.

against an original party, but may be relied on by a subsequent purchaser provided he has no notice of non-payment.[1]

Defining the rights infringed

9.5 It is usual, where the deed is intended to give permission for a development which would infringe the dominant owner's right to light, for the deed to state the fact that the dominant owner has certain rights which will be affected by the new development of the servient owner. Although desirable, draftsmen seldom think to incorporate a plan and elevation showing the affected windows. The purpose of such a provision is to make it clear that the subject matter of the deed is relaxation of existing rights to light enjoyed by the covenantor. It is also normal for the deed to contain a provision either in the recitals or the operative parts that the relevant windows of the covenantor are 'ancient lights', or more explicitly that they enjoy prescriptive rights to light. The effect of such a provision is to prevent arguments arising as to whether in fact such rights to light are enjoyed. A distinction may be drawn between provisions which define the existing status of windows and ones which govern the future, for example by precluding the subsequent acquisition by the windows of prescriptive rights.[2]

Defining the extent of the development permitted

9.6 This subject gives rise to problems of interpretation in many cases, although these can be avoided with good drafting.

9.7 The first matter to be addressed is what exactly the deed permits. Many deeds are framed by reference to a particular proposed building to be erected by the servient owner, and provide that the servient owner is at liberty to erect a building as shown on certain drawings, which are defined as 'the works'. This provision is often reinforced by a provision to the effect that the consent is limited to the execution of the works as defined 'but not further or otherwise' or by a provision that the works cannot be varied without the consent of the dominant owner.

9.8 The two questions most likely to arise from such provisions are:

(1) what is the position if 'the works' are demolished or destroyed. Can the servient owner rebuild them without the consent of the dominant owner?;
(2) is the servient owner entitled to replace the works with a new building which does not have any greater effect on the light enjoyed by the dominant owner than the works, albeit that the new building is in a different configuration?

---

1 Lewison *op cit*, para 9.18, and see Law of Property Act 1925, s 68.
2 *Marlborough (West End) Ltd v Wilks Head and Eve* (1996) ChD, unreported.

Freedom of dominant owner to alter his building

9.9 Deeds of this kind normally contain a provision which entitles the covenantee (dominant owner) to alter his building, notwithstanding that the light to the permitted building is affected. Frequently, this is backed up by a provision that the light to the relevant windows of the permitted building is to be regarded as enjoyed by the consent of the owner of the dominant building. In some cases, these rights are qualified – in effect the covenantee (dominant owner) gives cross-covenants that he will not alter his building in future, or replace it with any building which affects the lights received by the permitted building to more than a certain extent. This is often defined again by reference to light angles.

Reference to the Prescription Act 1832

9.10 It is frequently provided that the agreement is to enure for the benefit and burden of both parties, and to apply to successors in title, and to be an agreement within s 3 of the Prescription Act 1832, so that there is to be no prescriptive acquisition of a right to light in respect of the permitted building. It is possible for such terms to bind the freeholder of the dominant land even though he is not a party and the tenant of that land has entered into such an agreement.[1]

Glazed bricks provision

9.11 At common law, reflected light is ignored in ascertaining the extent of loss of light. This also applies to light reflected from glazed bricks of the servient owner's wall, on the ground that there is no power to compel the servient owner to maintain the reflective surface in position or to clean it.[2] Rights to light deeds, however, often make provisions to the effect that the new building shall contain glazed surfaces and that these shall be maintained.

Determination

9.12 The deed may or may not make provision for determination on notice or on certain events. In practice, determination provisions are not greatly favoured, as they raise difficult questions for funding sources, apart from the obvious risk of them being invoked at inconvenient times and giving rise to greater expense.

RESTRICTIVE AND PERMISSIVE DEEDS

9.13 A restrictive deed is one which, on its true construction, limits the permission either to a defined profile, or (in some cases) to one particular building. A permissive deed is one which grants permission in wider terms and has the effect of authorising restriction of light to the dominant tenant provided

---

1 See Chapter 6 at **6.24**.

2 *Dent v Auction Mart Co* (1866) LR 2 Eq 238 at 251–252. See Chapter 2 at **2.7** and **9.32–9.33**.

that the terms of the provision are not exceeded. Which category a deed falls into is often a matter of considerable difficulty and one of practical importance when replacement or alteration of the authorised building comes to be considered.

9.14 Where the words of the deed are not clear, it is necessary to approach these questions by considering all the terms of the deed, and the matrix of fact including anything which would have affected the way in which the language of the document would have been understood by a reasonable man.[1] However, evidence of the subjective intention of the parties is not admissible. Thus in *Rabin v Gerson Berger Association Limited*,[2] it was held that evidence of the advice of counsel was not admissible to interpret a deed prepared on the basis of that advice. Likewise, oral evidence is generally inadmissible to add, vary or contradict the deed.[3]

9.15 The importance of the distinction is that whereas under a restrictive deed no deviation from the approved plan(s) can be allowed, a permissive deed may be interpreted to allow an alternative scheme provided it has no greater effect than the permitted scheme on the light concerned.

9.16 A related point is whether the deed prohibits rebuilding of the permitted development, in the event of its accidental destruction. Whilst each deed is different, it is suggested that, in general, on this question it is inherently unlikely (assuming the deed is not clear on the point) that the parties could have intended that the benefit of the deed should be lost in the event of accidental destruction of the building authorised by it, for example in the case of fire, given that the deed is intended to have permanent effect. It can hardly have been intended that the covenantee should enjoy a windfall of this magnitude even if the deed was restrictive in terms of the development allowed. It would, of course, in this case be necessary to rebuild the development in the prescribed form.

9.17 Whether in a particular case a deed is restrictive or permissive, depends on its wording and other admissible evidence. Use of the words 'but not further or otherwise' is not conclusive. The real question in every case is 'what are the essential parameters to which the permitted building must conform?'

9.18 It is thought, first, that even where the deed incorporates floor plans, it will not normally be interpreted as restricting changes to the internal layout of the permitted building which can have no effect on the light situation.

9.19 Where the deed incorporates a detailed set of drawings with plans and elevations, but prohibits development apart from that specifically authorised, it may be difficult to determine whether the deed prohibits any alteration in the

---

1 *Investors Compensation Scheme Ltd v West Bromwich Building Society* [1998] 1 All ER 98, HL; see also *Prenn v Simmonds* [1971] 3 All ER 237; *Reardon Smith Line Limited v Hansen-Tangen* [1976] 3 All ER 570, HL.

2 [1986] 1 All ER 374. See *Investors Compensation Scheme Ltd v West Bromwich Building Society* [1998] 1 All ER 98 at 114J, per Lord Hoffmann.

3 *Jacobs v Batavia and General Plantations Limited* [1924] 1 Ch 287; *Rabin v Gerson Berger Association Limited* [1986] 1 All ER 374; Lewison *op cit*, para 2.07.

building permitted, for example by altering fenestration or architectural details, or remodelling the external appearance in other ways. It is thought that, in general terms, the intention of the parties must be taken to be to authorise buildings falling within a particular envelope, so that provided the external dimensions are not altered such works are permitted. It cannot have been the presumed intention of the parties that all repairs and improvements to the permitted building should be prohibited.

9.20 This leaves open the difficult question of whether it is open to the servient owner to completely replace the permitted building provided he does so within the same envelope as the original building. This is a question of construction of the deed, but it is thought that, in general, where permission is granted for a single building it is not open to the servient owner to do this, since once the permitted building has been demolished it ceases to exist, and no new building is covered by the deed. The question then arises as to whether the servient owner is entitled to build at all on this land without the permission of the dominant owner. It is respectfully submitted that unless the deed contains express provisions to the contrary, he remains entitled to do this, but cannot build in a way which would infringe the lights of the dominant owner to a greater extent than would have been permissible at common law had the permitted building not been constructed. In other words, the effect of the demolition is simply to render the relevant provisions of the deed 'spent', and to lead to reversion to the common law position.

9.21 The more closely the permitted building is defined by scale-plans, elevations and sections incorporated in the deed, and particularly where it contains a provision that no variation in the permitted building may be made, the less easy it will be to argue that the permitted plan can be deviated from, subject to the right of the servient owner to repair the building once erected.

9.22 Where the permitted building is not described very fully in the deed, or where the deed incorporates 'light angles', difficult points may arise. Where the deed incorporates elevations or sections which show the relationship of the proposed building and the dominant owner's building, possibly with lines running from the dominant owner's windows upwards towards the sky congruent with the extremities of the outline of the permitted building, it may more readily be inferred that it is the intention of the parties that any building whose height does not intersect a line drawn from the same point at the same angle is permitted.

9.23 Some support for this general approach is provided by *Cemp Properties (UK) Limited v Dentsply Research and Development Corporation (No 2)*.[1] In that case, a deed executed in 1934 allowed the servient owner to erect a new building. The deed provided that he should:

> 'have full liberty and power to erect the new building in accordance with the plan annexed hereto but not otherwise.'

1 [1989] 2 EGLR 196.

The plan showed a three-storey building which permitted light to the bottom sill of a window (described as window B in the deed) at an angle of 54.5° from the horizontal. The permission given by the deed was determinable on notice. Morritt J said:[1]

> 'The other point at issue is whether the 1934 deed would permit the erection of a new building so as to infringe the rights to light of the five apertures to the same, but to no greater extent than the 1934 deed allowed. The third recital states that the building owner:
>
> > ... is desirous of erecting ... new buildings of greater height which threaten to interfere with the ancient lights ... and to diminish the access of light and air ... and the plan annexed hereto indicates the manner in which such ancient lights will be effected.
>
> The plan referred to merely shows the flank wall of the proposed new building consisting of a ground and three upper floors topped by a parapet. Various light angles are shown, the material one being a line which shows that the top of the parapet permits the access of light to window B at an angle of 55.5°. There is no other indication of the nature or design of the new building.
>
> Clause 1 provided that:
>
> > ... the building owner and the persons rightfully claiming under it shall have full liberty and power to erect the said new buildings in accordance with the said plan annexed hereto but not otherwise.
>
> Clause 2 enabled the owners of 1–5 Poland Street at any time thereafter to raise the height or alter the elevation of 1–5 Poland Street or to pull down and erect any new buildings according to such plans and elevations and in such manner as they should consider proper.
>
> ...
>
> In my judgment the 1934 deed authorised any building provided that it did not infringe the rights to light to the five apertures to any greater extent than the plan indicated. The permission granted was not expressed to be temporary. The purpose of the deed and the plan showed that the parties were concerned only with position and height of the flank wall of the proposed new building. The parties were not concerned at all with which particular bricks formed the wall and the parapet. In my judgment, therefore, on a proper construction of the 1934 deed, the owners of the site were entitled to put up a new building with a flank wall facing 1–5 Poland Street in the same position and to the same height as shown on the plan.'

9.24 In the *Cemp* case, the two important features of the deed were that the outline of the new building was shown purely schematically, and there was a light angle shown running from a particular window sill. The use of a light angle or angles tends to show that there is less concern with the particular permitted building, and that the true intent is simply to prevent construction beyond the line formed by the angle.

---

1 [1989] 2 EGLR 196 at 202C–E.

9.25 The further question arises as to the impact of the permission granted on pre-existing common law rights. It is thought that even if the deed is restrictive (in the sense that it permits only a particular building), it will not prohibit work which does not infringe the common law rights of the dominant owner as they pre-dated the deed and the erection of the building. In other words, it is open to a servient owner to build on his land, and for those purposes to demolish and rebuild the permitted building provided those common law rights are not infringed. This will be of importance if some parts of the permitted building do not infringe the dominant owner's common law rights. This would clearly be the case in relation to parts of the permitted building which are either too low or too distant from the dominant owner's building to have any effect on the light it enjoyed before the permitted building was erected. In other words, it is not open to the dominant owner to argue that because the deed permits only a particular building to be erected, he retained complete control over demolition or alterations to that building even if the relevant parts of the building have no effect on his common law rights. His rights of control extend only to those parts of the building which require permission under the deed if not to constitute an infringement of his common law rights.

LEGAL EFFECTIVENESS

9.26 Although the fact that rights to light deeds are frequently employed suggests that legal effectiveness is unquestioned, their legal enforceability can raise difficult questions.

Between original parties

9.27 No difficulty arises in principle where questions of enforcement arise between original parties to the deed. Ordinary contractual principles apply, so that both benefit and burden of the deed are fully enforceable.

Position of successors in title

9.28 Rights to light deeds may have a somewhat hybrid quality, imposing various types of obligations, such as obligations not to build (or only to build to a certain extent), obligations to pay money, obligations to build and retain reflective wall coverings, and acknowledgements that light is enjoyed by licence only. As far as the position of successors in title is concerned, each of these categories can raise different questions.

9.29 Insofar as the deed in question restricts building, it could be regarded as imposing a restrictive covenant. On the other hand, deeds are usually couched in terms of permissions, and it is not clear whether the fact that permission is limited of itself means that the permission is to be regarded as a species of restriction on the use of land. On balance, it is thought that provisions in rights to light deeds which grant permission 'but not further or otherwise' can be regarded as restrictive covenants, restricting the use of the land burdened. Assuming this is the case, the benefit of the restrictive covenant is taken by the owners of the land intended to be benefited, provided the benefit of the covenant is annexed to the land. In the case of covenants entered into after 1925, s 78(1) of the Law of Property Act 1925 effects automatic annexation.[1] It is essential that the covenantee retains land capable of being benefited, and that it must be capable of being ascertained with reasonable certainty.[2]

9.30 As regards the burden of restrictive covenants, in the case of covenants entered into after 1925, they are not enforceable against purchasers for valuable consideration unless registered under the Land Registration Act 1925 or the Land Charges Act 1972.[3] It would therefore be prudent in the case of rights to light deeds to ensure that they are duly noted on the register of the covenantor's title.

9.31 In the case of other covenants, it is necessary to distinguish between transmissibility of benefit and burden. Dealing first with benefit, a successor in title may enforce a covenant provided:

(1) it touches and concerns land;
(2) it relates to clearly identifiable land;
(3) it has been entered into with someone having an interest in the land intended to be benefited;[4]
(4) the person seeking to enforce the covenant must have an interest in the land;[5]
(5) the agreement must show an intention that the benefit of the covenant be transmissible.

9.32 In practice, it is likely that these requirements will be satisfied in many cases. The question of the transmission of the burden of covenants is, however, more problematic, since in the case of both positive covenants and negative covenants which are not restrictive covenants, the general rule is that successors in title are not bound. This rule was reaffirmed in *Rhone v Stephens*.[6] It is subject to various statutory exceptions,[7] but these are unlikely to have much practical impact. It follows that terms requiring a building owner to construct or maintain a light-reflecting finish on the walls of his building are not in principle enforceable against successors in title.[8] However, such provisions are capable of coming within the principle relating to benefit and burden laid down in such cases as *Halsall v Brizell*,[9] under which where a right over property is enjoyed on the condition of performance of a positive obligation, enjoyment of the right

1 *Federated Homes v Mill Lodge Properties* [1980] 1 All ER 371.
2 *Formby v Barker* [1903] 2 Ch 539; *Renals v Cowlishaw* (1879) 11 ChD 866.
3 Land Registration Act 1925, ss 20, 50; Land Charges Act 1972, s 2(5).
4 See Law of Property Act 1925, s 78(1).
5 Ibid; *Smith v River Douglas Catchment Board* [1949] 2 All ER 179, CA.
6 [1994] 2 AC 310.
7 For example s 33 of the Local Government (Miscellaneous Provisions) Act 1982; s 106 of the Town and Country Planning Act 1990.
8 Cf *Dent v Auction Mart Co* (1866) LR 2 Eq 238.
9 [1957] Ch 169.

may be restrained if the positive obligation is not performed. Thus, in *Halsall v Brizell*, a deed relating to the development of land contained provisions granting rights of way to owners of individual plots, and further provisions imposing on them an obligation to contribute to common upkeep costs. It was held that a successor to an original covenantor who owned the plot was liable to contribute to the upkeep costs, Upjohn J saying:

> 'If the defendants did not desire to take the benefit of this deed, for the reasons that I have given they could not be under any liability to pay the obligations thereunder. They do desire, however, to take the benefit of this deed. They have no right to use the sewers which are vested in the plaintiffs, and I cannot see that they have any right, apart from the deed, to use the roads of the park which lead to their particular house ... the defendants cannot rely on any way of necessity nor on any right by prescription, for the simple reason that, when the house was originally sold in 1851 to their predecessor in title, he took the house on the terms of the deed of 1851 which contractually bound him to contribute a proper proportion of the expenses of maintaining the roads and sewers, and so forth, as a condition of being entitled to make use of those roads and sewers. Therefore it seems to me that the defendants cannot, if they desire to use their house as they do, take advantage of the trusts concerning the user of the roads contained in the deed and the other benefits created by it without undertaking the obligations thereunder. On that principle it seems to me that they are bound by this deed, if they desire to take its benefits.'

9.33 It is clear that the principle does not extend so as to oblige the successor to a covenantor to perform positive obligations if he wishes to take any benefit under a deed, but is restricted to those obligations intimately connected with his enjoyment of property rights.[1]

9.34 In relation to provisions in rights to light deeds, the light to windows of a building is deemed to be enjoyed by permission of the covenantee, s 3 of the Prescription Act 1832 makes specific provision for this in its wording:

> 'unless it shall appear that the same was enjoyed by some consent or agreement expressly made or given for that purpose by deed or writing ...'

No reference is made to registration, hence it is thought that such provisions are effective whether or not the deed is registered.

DRAFTING ISSUES

9.35 Deeds should always contain plans and sections of the existing and proposed buildings sufficient to establish the precise parameters of the permissions or limitations confirmed or imposed in the text. These should be cross-referred to the relevant paragraphs of the operative part of the deed. In

---

1 *Rhone v Stephens* [1994] 2 AC 310 per Lord Templeman; distinguishing *Tito v Waddell (No 2)* [1977] 3 All ER 129. See also *Thamesmead Town Ltd v Allotey* [1998] 3 EGLR 97, CA.

some cases, it may be useful to supplement these with isometric preparations of the affected area, to show the relationship of the relevant buildings.

9.36 The draftsman should address specifically the following issues.

(1) Whether the deed is permissive or restrictive in terms.[1]
(2) Whether provision is to be made as to alterations to the permitted building, and whether there are to be terms alluring to changes in its configurations, finishes, colour, glazing treatment, and size.
(3) Where the size or height of new building is restricted, whether the restrictions apply to the whole building, or only to those parts which affect the relevant light. There is normally no point in preventing alterations to, or expansion of, part of a new building remote from that which gives rise to rights to light issues.
(4) It should be made clear that instructions apply only to the exterior or bulk of any new building, not to its external layout.
(5) The position in the event of accidental destruction of the permitted building should be covered. Normally, rebuilding to the same design should be allowed, but it may also be prudent to address the situation which may arise in the event of a change in construction giving uneconomic or refused planning permission.
(6) Whether the instructions should remain in force once the dominant building ceases to exist may require consideration. Normally, the dominant owner would expect to be able to protect his position in this eventuality.

9.37 Certain general points, common to all deeds, require to be taken into account.

(1) In order to be legally effective, it is desirable that all those interested in each property be parties to the deed, including mortgagees. Otherwise, there is a risk that the deed may prove impossible to enforce against a recalcitrant owner of some interest in one of the areas of land concerned. There may also, of course, be difficulties for a party who seeks to rely on the deed if he or his predecessor was not a party.
(2) Where the deed on its true construction is intended to be made with a party, and that party is named in the deed, that party is entitled to enforce covenants of the covenantor even though he has not himself executed the deed. The rationale of this rule is that since there is no obligation placed on the covenantee, it is not essential that he should have executed the deed before he can enforce it.
(3) Even where obligations are imposed on the covenantee, he may be able to enforce the deed notwithstanding that he has not executed it.[2] Where the covenantor has not executed the deed, he will not be bound at law but he may be bound in equity if he takes the benefit of property under the same

1 See **9.13–9.25**.
2 *Morgan v Pike* (1854) 14 CB 473; *Northampton Gas Light Co v Parnel* (1855) 15 CB 630.

deed.[1] Section 1 of the Law of Property (Miscellaneous Provisions) Act 1989 has relaxed the requirements for the execution of a deed, by removing certain formal requirements. However, by s 1(2), an instrument is not to be a deed unless it makes clear on its face that it is intended to be a deed by the person making it or the parties to it whether by describing itself as a deed or expressing itself to be executed or signed as a deed or otherwise. The deed must also be validly executed. Section 1(3) of the same Act prescribes the method of execution of a deed by an individual.

(4) Section 56(1) of the Law of Property Act 1925 extends those persons who may take the benefit of a covenant, by enabling any party who can show that, as a matter of construction, the benefit of a covenant is intended to be vested in him to take the benefit of it even though he is not named as a party to the deed.[2]

(5) It is normal for rights to light deeds to recite the interest of each of the parties to the deed in the property concerned, as freeholder, mortgagee, lessee or otherwise. In practice, depending on the subject matter of the deed, it may not be necessary for those holding only short-term leases to be parties, and this may not be practical in the case of a building of multiple occupation. It is, of course, always necessary to bear in mind that if such parties enjoy rights to light which are to be infringed by a development of a neighbouring building, their rights will not be affected by agreement between the freeholders of their building and the owner of the site on which the new building is to be erected. It is necessary, therefore, to make separate provision for compensation for their loss, assuming the right to claim such compensation is not excluded by the terms of their leases (in practice, relatively unlikely except where the new building is owned by their lessor).

(6) Where the deed provides for an easement to arise in the future, the rule against perpetuities applies. Therefore, the deed must be framed to ensure that the easement cannot arise further in the future within 21 years after the expiration of lives in being or a specified number of years not exceeding 80.[3] When land is not described at the date of the grant as part of the dominant tenement, a provision for it to be designated as such in the future will be used for perpetuity.[4]

---

1 *Formby v Barker* [1903] 2 Ch 539.

2 *Re Ecclesiastical Commissioners for England's Conveyance* [1936] Ch 430; *Beswick v Beswick* [1968] AC 58. See also **9.38** in respect of rights under the Contracts (Rights of Third Parties) Act 1999.

3 Perpetuities and Accumulations Act 1964, s 1(1).

4 *London and Blenheim Estates Ltd v Ladbroke Retail Parks Ltd* [1993] 4 All ER 157, CA.

THE EFFECT OF THE CONTRACTS (RIGHTS OF THIRD PARTIES) ACT 1999 ON EXPRESS GRANTS OF EASEMENTS OF LIGHT AND OTHER AGREEMENTS IN CONNECTION WITH RIGHTS TO LIGHT

9.38 The Contracts (Rights of Third Parties) Act 1999 reforms the rule of privity, which, in general terms, prevents a person who is not a party to a contract enforcing that contract, or taking a benefit under it.[1] The Act allows a person who is not a party to a contract to enforce a term of it if either the contract expressly provides that he may, or if the term sought to be enforced purports to confer a benefit on him. The latter alternative right to enforce is excluded if it appears that the parties did not intend the term to be enforceable by the third party.[2]

9.39 The third party who claims the right to enforce the term must be expressly identified in the contract, either by name, or as a member of a class, or as assuming a particular description. But he need not be in existence when the contract is entered into.[3]

9.40 The remedies available to a third party are those remedies which would have been available to him had he been a party to the contract, but any enforcement is subject to and must be in accordance with any terms of the contract.[4]

9.41 Section 2 of the 1999 Act contains restrictions upon the manner and extent to which the principal parties can rescind, vary or extinguish rights under the contract so as to affect the third party's rights. The remaining sections of the Act[5] concern procedural matters in enforcement proceedings by the third party, and specific exception of contracts from the Act.

9.42 The impact of the Act upon the agreements relating to rights to light would appear to be as follows.

(a) The Act affects only the rights of a third party to enforce a term of the contract where it expressly says he may, or where the term is for his benefit. The third party cannot be liable for the burden of agreements unless he is an actual party to the agreement.

(b) Agreement to grant rights to light may, conceivably, confer a benefit on others, such as adjoining landowners. Unless the contracting parties define who is the third party with the (potential) right to enforce the term, the Act

---

1 The Act came into force on 11 November 1999, but does not apply to contracts entered into between that date and 11 May 2000, unless the contract specifically provides that the Act is to apply to it. In respect of contracts made after 11 May 2000, the application of the Act is as described above.

2 Section 1(1) and (2). See Appendix 1.

3 Section 1(3).

4 Section 1(4) and (5).

5 Sections 3–8.

will have no bearing on the matter whether there is an express provision as to third party enforcement, or whether there is a purported conferment of benefit.[1] Thus, it is only where the contract to grant the right has, as its aim, the inclusion of others as beneficiaries of the grant, that the Act will have any relevance.

For instance, if there is a contract for the sale of land between *A* and *B*, and *A* is retaining adjoining land, and *A*, as a term of the contract, agrees to execute a grant of light over his retained land in *B*'s favour, only *C*, another adjoining landowner, could not enforce that term.[2] But if such a contract incorporated a further term that *C* could ask for a grant of light in his favour from *A*, or if *C* was defined in the contract as a person in existence and having the potential right to enforce the term, the Act would give *C* the right to do so.

(c) The same principles set out at (b) above will apply to other contracts concerning rights to light, such as agreements to vary such rights, or to extinguish or release them. In the case of such variation and release, one foreseeable difficulty created by the Act is the right of third parties, such as tenants in one of the buildings affected, to claim the benefit of a contract to vary or release rights. For example, it may be that a variation or release has been agreed between the parties in terms by which it is intended that such tenants are *not* to have rights to light which they may enjoy varied or released. Conversely, the parties may want to bind everyone to a variation or release, in which case the agreement should be carefully drawn so as to achieve this. In the former case, the parties to the agreement should exclude the right of third parties to enforce any terms under the Act by expressly stating that: (i) the parties do not intend that any terms of the agreement are to be enforceable by any person not a party; and (ii) (for the avoidance of doubt) rights conferred by the Act are excluded from persons who might otherwise be within its scope. In the latter case, where the aim of a variation or release is to encompass all those with potential rights to light, there should be no need to consider any exclusion or modification of rights under the Act in view of the fact that all persons who are intended to be caught by the variation or release are either parties, or will be made expressly subject to the burden of the agreement by those having a higher title.[3]

9.43 In general terms, the Act requires the parties, and those drafting agreements for them, to consider whether any terms are going to have an effect on the rights of third parties, and whether such third parties ought to have the right to enforce any terms of the agreement between the principal parties. It is suggested that, in the context of rights to light, the answer to the last question will be no, and, therefore, the sensible course is to exclude the Act expressly.

---

1 Section 1(1) and (3).

2 Even s 56 of the Law of Property Act 1925 could not come to his aid: *Beswick v Beswick* [1968] AC 58 and see **9.37**(4) above.

3 See Chapter 8 at **8.3**.

Chapter 10

Proceedings for Infringement of Rights to Light I – Causes of Action, Parties, Limitation and Venue

CAUSES OF ACTION

10.1 Actionable interference with a right to light constitutes the tort of private nuisance. The term 'nuisance' is properly applied only to such unreasonable user of land as interferes with the enjoyment by the plaintiff of rights in land.[1] There is a peculiarity in claims for nuisance for infringement of easements (including rights of light) that the action can succeed only if an easement is established to exist. Generally, ordinary claims for nuisance depend simply on whether the matters complained of are an actionable wrong under the general law.[2]

10.2 It is established that no claim lies for invasion of privacy by overlooking or obstruction of a view or prospect.[3] Where the right to light is protected by a contract, an action lies against the contract breaker under the terms of the agreement. The same applies where breach of a right to light deed is in question.

10.3 Restrictive covenants may have the effect of preventing the erection of buildings which interfere with light, and they may also be employed to protect privacy and views by prohibiting the erection of buildings on the land burdened by the covenant. Restrictive covenants may, in appropriate cases, be in force against the owner for the time being of the servient land by the owner for the time being of the dominant land, even where there is no privity of contract or estate between them.[4]

PARTIES

Claimants

10.4 It is established that in order to maintain an action in private nuisance, a plaintiff must have interest in land.[5] Therefore, a person on premises as a mere

---

1 Newark *The Boundaries of Nuisance* (1949) 65 LQR 480, cited by Lord Goff of Chieveley in *Hunter and Others v Canary Wharf Ltd* [1997] AC 655, HL at 687G, and referred to in *Hussain v Lancaster City Council* (1998) 77 P&CR 89, CA per Hirst LJ at 108–109.

2 For the requirements of the tort of nuisance generally, see *Halsbury's Laws of England* 4th edn vol 34, reissue (1997) paras 9–14 and 16–30.

3 See, generally, Chapter 2 at **2.3**.

4 For the law of restrictive covenants, see Francis *Restrictive Covenants over Freehold Land: A Practitioners' Guide* (Sweet & Maxwell, 1999).

5 *Hunter and Others v Canary Wharf Ltd* [1997] AC 655, HL.

licensee has no right of action.[1] Thus, in principle, a right of action is available to freeholders, tenants in occupation, and others with a legal right to occupy the premises affected but not to licensees.[2] In the case of tenants, the protection extends only to those in whom the tenancy is vested at the date of the wrong, hence a tenant who has assigned his interest cannot make a claim, even if he subsequently resumes possession following the absconding of the assignee. Presumably, the same rule would apply where, following the insolvency of the assignee and the disclaimer by its liquidator of the term of the lease under the Insolvency Act 1986, a vesting order is made in favour of the original tenant or an intermediate assignee under ss 181 and 182 of that Act.

10.5 Those who have legal interests in the premises, whether as freehold or leasehold, may maintain an action in nuisance provided the injury to light affects the permanent value of their interest. Thus in *Shelfer v City of London Electric Lighting Co*,[3] it was held that a reversioner had a right of action where his property was injured by vibration from the operation of a generating station. In *Jesser v Gifford*,[4] it was held that a reversioner could sue in respect of damage caused by obstruction to ancient lights.[5]

Defendants

10.6 The liability of the actual tortfeasor is undoubted: it is not necessary to establish that he owns the servient tenement. Thus in the case of a building infringing a right to light, the contractor erecting the building may be liable for creating the nuisance.[6] Liability of the tortfeasor continues in respect of consequential damage, even after he has parted with possession of the building and is unable to remedy the situation.[7] It is not necessary for the tortfeasor to have any interest in the land in question. Liability may also arise not only in respect of acts actually done, but also in respect of acts authorised, where the person in question has power to prevent the acts being done. So in *Chartered Trust Plc v Davies*,[8] a landlord of a shopping mall was held liable to one of his tenants for authorising the erection of a pawnbrokers' sign outside an adjacent unit, and failing to prevent queuing by prospective customers of the pawnbroker

1 *Hunter and Others v Canary Wharf Ltd* [1997] AC 655, HL at 692 per Lord Goff of Chieveley overruling *Khorasandjian v Bush* [1993] 3 All ER 669, CA. For the position of premises occupied collectively by companies in the same group as licensees, see *Butcher Robinson & Staples Ltd v London Regional Transport* [1999] 36 EG 165. See also Murdoch 'Who can sue in Nuisance?' *Estates Gazette* 1999 No 28 (17 July 1999), p 120 and Chapter 11 at **11.33**.

2 For the distinction between a lease and a licence, see *Street v Mountford* [1985] AC 809, and generally *Hill & Redman's Law of Landlord and Tenant* paras [549]–[900]. In general, a person in exclusive possession of premises paying rent will be considered a tenant.

3 (1895) 1 Ch 287, CA.

4 (1767) 4 Burr 2141.

5 See also *Wilson v Townend* (1860) 1 Drew & Sm 324; *Shadwell v Hutchinson* (1829) 3 C&P 615.

6 *Thompson v Gibson* (1841) 7 M&W 456.

7 *Rosewell v Prior* (1701) 12 Mod 635, 639.

8 [1997] 2 EGLR 83, CA.

in the common parts of the mall.[1] In *Lippiatt v South Gloucestershire County Council*,[2] a landowner was held liable for repeated acts of nuisance committed on neighbouring land by travellers whom it knew to be based on its land.

10.7 An occupier of land is liable for a nuisance even though he has not created it, if he continues it while in occupation.[3] An occupier is also liable for nuisance created after he becomes the occupier if he has actual or constructive notice of its existence, or if he continues a nuisance with actual or constructive notice of its existence, and does not take reasonable steps to bring it to an end.[4] Making use of a building which constitutes a nuisance amounts to adoption.[5]

10.8 Where a person purchases a building which is let to tenants, he is liable for nuisance created by the original reversioner, even though he has no right to abate the nuisance under the terms of the lease.[6]

10.9 Therefore, in general, the persons who are likely to be responsible in law for nuisances caused by the erection of obstructions to light will include the following:

(1) the building contractor erecting the building;
(2) the landowner on whose land the building is being erected, if the building is being erected with his authority;
(3) the tenant or other occupier directly authorising the erection of the building in question.

10.10 Where the servient tenement changes hands, the new owner will be liable for continuing the nuisance. Where the servient property is the subject of a lease, the general rule is that the landlord is not liable for nuisances committed by his tenant unless he has authorised the tenant to commit the nuisance. But where the landlord has powers of management of his property sufficient to pursue the cessation of the nuisance, he may remain liable if he fails to exercise them.[7] The court will not grant an injunction against a landlord who is not able under the terms of the lease to take any steps to restrain future continuation of the nuisance.[8]

10.11 In many cases, leases contain tenant's covenants prohibiting any acts by the tenant on the demised premises which constitute a nuisance. It is thought that the existence of such a covenant, coupled with failure by the landlord to take

---

1 Cf the earlier case of *Hilton v James Smith & Sons (Norwood) Ltd* [1979] 2 EGLR 44.
2 (1999) *The Times*, 9 April, CA.
3 *Rosewell v Prior* (1701) 12 Mod 635; *Thompson v Gibson* (1841) 7 M&W 456.
4 *Goldman v Hargrave* [1966] 2 All ER 989, PC; *Leakey v National Trust for Places of Historic Interest or Natural Beauty* [1980] 1 All ER 17, CA; *Sedleigh-Denfield v O'Callaghan* [1940] 3 All ER 349, HL.
5 *Sedleigh-Denfield v O'Callaghan* [1940] 3 All ER 349 at 358 per Viscount Maugham.
6 *Sampson v Hodson-Pressenger* [1981] 3 All ER 710.
7 *Smith v Scott* [1973] 1 Ch 314; *Elizabeth v Rochester on Midway City Council* 26 April 1983, CA; *Hussain v Lancaster City Council* (1998) 77 P&CR 89, CA; *Chartered Trust Plc v Davies* [1997] 2 EGLR 83.
8 *Celsteel Ltd v Alton House Holdings Ltd* [1986] 1 All ER 608, CA.

steps to enforce such a covenant in the event of the tenant obstructing a neighbour's light, might be sufficient, on the principles discussed above, to make the landlord liable to the dominant owner whose light has been interfered with. It is clear that the grant by the landlord of a lease to a developer requiring or authorising the erection of a building which will interfere with a right to light would also be sufficient to result in him incurring liability.[1] In *Tetley and Others v Chitty and Others*,[2] it was held that the landlord of a go-cart track was liable for nuisance caused to those living in the vicinity, since the noise was an ordinary necessary consequence of the operation of the go-carts, and there had been implied consent to the creation of the nuisance. On the other hand, it is clear that a landlord is not liable for nuisances committed by his tenant elsewhere than at the demised premises.[3]

10.12 Where the landlord re-lets premises after a nuisance upon them has been created, if he knew or ought to have known of the nuisance before re-letting, he is liable for the nuisance which occurs.

10.13 One point to be considered, in selecting the appropriate defendant, is the extent of the remedy being sought. In *Barnes v Allen*,[4] the court refused to grant a mandatory injunction to require a building to be demolished for infringement of light, where the action was brought against the lessee alone, without joining the freeholder. This decision is clearly correct. It cannot be right to order the destruction of property in which a person has an interest without them having an opportunity to go before the court, save in exceptional circumstances.

10.14 It may be necessary to join the freeholder in cases where there is doubt whether a claim against a lessee alone will succeed. For example, a claim based on the Prescription Act 1832 might not succeed against the lessee alone (because of an interruption) and a claim based on lost modern grant would require joinder of the freeholder.

LIMITATION

10.15 An interference with a right to light constitutes the tort of nuisance. Under the Limitation Act 1980, s 2, claims must be brought within 6 years of the date the cause of action accrues. The interference with a right to light constitutes a continuing nuisance, with a right of action accruing afresh every day.[5] However, damages can be recovered for only that part of the loss which arose during the relevant period before the commencement of proceedings or, arguably, the assessment of damages.[6]

---

1 Cf *Burt v Victoria Graving Dock Co* (1882) 47 LT 378; *Winter v Baker* (1887) 3 TLR 569; *Jenkins v Jackson* (1888) 40 ChD 71; *Tetley v Chitty* [1986] 1 All ER 663.

2 [1986] 1 All ER 663.

3 *Hussain v Lancaster City Council* (1998) 77 P&CR 89, CA.

4 (1927) 164 LT Jo 83.

5 See Chapter 11 at **11.41** note 2.

6 *Hardy v Ryle* (1829) 9 B&C 603.

10.16 In some cases, the dominant owner has a concurrent claim for breach of contract, if the right to light arises pursuant to an agreement – either an express grant, or a covenant (eg in a lease) not to obstruct light to certain windows. The limitation period for claims based on simple contracts is 6 years from the date of the breach. Whether the defendant will be deemed to be in continuing breach of contract during every day that this state of affairs continues will depend on the wording of the contract. In some cases, the breach may be a single breach committed on a certain date. This could arise, for example, if there were an agreement to construct a particular new building in a certain way so as not to obstruct the dominant owner's right to light. Once the new building has been constructed otherwise than as agreed, the cause of action is complete. In most cases, however, where there is a simple covenant not to obstruct windows, it is thought that the breach continues as long as the state of affairs exists.[1] Where the obligation is contained in a deed, under s 8 of the Limitation Act 1980, the period of limitation is 12 years.

10.17 By the proviso to s 36(1) of the Limitation Act 1980, it is provided that the time-limits, inter alia, relating to ss 2, 5 and 8 of that Act shall not apply to any claim for, inter alia, an injunction or other equitable relief, except insofar as such time-limit may be applied by the court by analogy in like manner as the corresponding time-limit under any enactment repealed by the Limitation Act 1939 was applied before 1 July 1940. By s 36(2) of the Limitation Act 1980, it is provided that nothing in that Act affects any equitable jurisdiction to refuse relief on the ground of acquiescence or otherwise.

10.18 Historically, limitation periods depend entirely on statutory provisions. Those provisions did not in general apply to suits in equity, which, prior to the Judicature Act 1873, were the only way that claims for injunctions could be made. It is, therefore, theoretically possible for a dominant owner to commence proceedings for equitable relief without being bound by the limitation periods in the Limitation Act 1980. However, such a claim is likely to be barred by the equitable doctrine of laches.[2] It is unclear whether the doctrine of laches can apply so as to debar the claimant from equitable relief even if he starts his action within the relevant limitation periods laid down by the 1980 Act. It is thought that, in general, it ought not to apply, given that Parliament has laid down a period during which the right of action should be available.[3] In practice, given that interference with rights to light is a continuing cause of action, the issue is unlikely to arise directly, although it may be of relevance in considering whether to grant a mandatory injunction at trial to obtain the removal of the offending structure.[4]

---

1 Cf *Midland Bank Trust Company v Hett Stubbs & Kemp* [1979] Ch 384.

2 See *Lindsay Petroleum Company v Hurd* (1874) LR 5 PC 221; *Nelson v Rye* [1996] 2 All ER 186.

3 Cf *Re Pauling's Settlement Trusts* [1962] 1 WLR 86.

4 See Chapter 11.

VENUE

10.19 Actions for infringement of rights to light may be brought in the High Court and the county court, and are governed by the Civil Procedure Rules 1998 ('CPR') as supplemented by Practice Directions ('PD') issued under the authority of the Civil Procedure Act 1997, s 5. Guidance and the appropriate venue is provided by the High Court and County Courts Jurisdiction Order 1991.[1] Transfer between High Court and county court is regulated by Part 30 of the CPR.

10.20 Claims of nuisance involving rights to light will normally be initiated under Part 7 of the CPR, and are wholly to be assigned to the multi-track unless they are very straightforward. The Particulars of Claim must comply with CPR Part 16, and should contain the following.

(a) A statement of the claimaint's interest in the land injured (whether as owner, tenant or exclusive licensee).
(b) A statement that there is a building on the claimant's land through the windows in which an easement of light is enjoyed. The relevant windows should be shown on plans and elevation drawings attached to the Particulars of Claim.[2]
(c) A statement that the defendant is the owner or occupier of certain land, or that (in the case of a non-occupying defendant) he is carrying out activities (eg building works) on certain land.
(d) The injury (actual or threatened) to the claimaint's rights should be set out.
(e) Claims for damages, prohibitory or mandatory injunctive relief, and declarations as appropriate. Any special damage should be set out in detail.
(f) The claim must contain a statement of value where there is a mandatory claim.[3]
(g) Where an injunction or declaration is sought, the claim must comply with CPR PD16 para 9.1

10.21 The claimant may attach to or serve with his statement of case a copy of any document which he considers necessary to his claim, including an expert's report.[4] This may be useful where such a report has been finalised before proceedings are commenced.

10.22 Frequently, where building work is about to start, or is in progress, which threatens to interfere with the claimaint's light, an application for an interim injunction will be required. CPR, r 25.2 allows an interim injunction to be granted before proceedings are started in urgent cases.[5]

---

1 SI 1991/24, as amended.
2 CPR, r 16.3.
3 CPR, r 16.3.
4 CPR PD16 para 16.3(3).
5 See also Chapter 11 at **11.7–11.11**. The considerations relating to interim injunctions are also discussed in Chapter 11. For civil procedure generally, see *Civil Court Service* (Jordans).

Chapter 11

Proceedings for Infringement of Rights to Light II – Remedies

GENERAL OVERVIEW OF REMEDIES AVAILABLE

11.1 The law provides various remedies in respect of infringements of rights to light. These may be considered under the following heads.

(1) Abatement.
(2) Damages at common law.
(3) *Quia timet* and interim injunctions.
(4) Final injunctions.
(5) Damages in addition to or lieu of an injunction ('equitable damages').
(6) Declaratory relief.

11.2 The decision which remedy to claim, and in what terms, is a matter of considerable practical importance for those aggrieved by a threatened or actual infringement of a right to light. This is particularly the case where the claimant seeks an injunction. One particularly frequent dilemma which a claimant may face is whether to apply to the court for an interim injunction in advance of trial to restrain the defendant from commencing and/or further continuing with building works which the claimant alleges will (when the resulting building is complete) obstruct his light. It is a virtually invariable requirement of the grant of such an injunction that the claimant must give an undertaking to compensate the defendant for any loss the defendant suffers if it transpires that the injunction ought not to have been granted ('undertaking in damages'). This can expose a claimant to the possibility of incurring onerous liabilities, where the allegedly infringing building is a sizeable commercial development, where the delay between the grant of an interim injunction and the trial of the case may be months, if not longer. On the other hand, the courts have moved to, or at least very close to, a position where failure to apply for an interim injunction is itself treated as a reason for both refusing a mandatory final injunction to remove the obstructing development and denying the claimant the right to damages calculated on the basis (more favourable to the claimant than the normal measure) that he is entitled to be compensated for the loss of the bargaining position which his right to injunctive relief gives him.[1] Thus failure to act promptly may result in effective loss of the right to prevent the obstruction taking place.

11.3 The assessment of damages also gives rise to areas of difficulty. The principles governing common law damages are entirely separate from those governing equitable damages. Equitable damages, granted most frequently in

1 See **11.108**.

lieu of a final injunction, are intended to reflect the loss due to the permanent infringement of the claimant's right, as well as past loss.[1]

11.4 In addition to legal remedies, the law in theory recognises certain limited forms of self-help by way of abatement of a nuisance.[2] In early medieval times, from which the common law originates, self-help was not regarded with disfavour, and indeed even private war was recognised. The modern climate, however, is decidedly against self-help, and it is suggested that an aggrieved party should resort to it only in unusual circumstances. It remains, nevertheless, of more than academic relevance.

PROCEDURAL MATTERS

11.5 Of the remedies enumerated above, the first, abatement, does not require recourse to court proceedings. The remainder can be sought only in such proceedings. It is therefore necessary to refer briefly to the procedure for claims in relation to rights to light in the civil courts.

11.6 The civil courts at first instance in England and Wales are the High Court of Justice, and the county courts. The High Court is part of the Supreme Court.[3] The county courts are also established by statute, and are located throughout the country on a regional basis.[4] From both High Court and county courts, appeals lie (with permission of the court of first instance or the Court of Appeal) to the Court of Appeal, and thence (with permission) to the House of Lords, the ultimate Court of Appeal for the whole of the UK. Certain matters may be referred to the European Court of Justice and the European Court of Human Rights, although these are very unlikely to involve rights to light.

11.7 Following the coming into force of the Civil Procedure Rules 1998 ('CPR') on 26 April 1999, a complete recasting of civil procedure has occurred in relation both to the High Court and the county courts, and the Court of Appeal. Prior to that time, civil procedure was governed by the Rules of the Supreme Court 1965 in the High Court, and the County Court Rules 1981 in the county courts. It is therefore necessary to bear this in mind when considering the terminology used in cases. Two particular points of nomenclature should be noted: under the CPR the person initiating a claim is known as the 'claimant', and the person defending the claim as the 'defendant'. In previous terminology, the person initiating a claim was known as the 'plaintiff', and this term occurs universally in the cases decided before the CPR came into force. In the text of this book, the term 'claimant' is generally used, in accordance with modern usage, save in the cases (in practice numerous) where discussion occurs of cases where

---

1 See **11.119** et seq.

2 See **11.12–11.26**.

3 Established originally in 1873; see now Supreme Court Act 1981.

4 See County Courts Act 1984. Their location is wholly unrelated to counties, a local government unit which itself no longer exists in many areas of the country.

the term 'plaintiff' is used. Secondly, the CPR refer to injunctions obtained prior to trial as *interim* relief, the former description being *interlocutory* relief.

11.8 The CPR are divided into Parts, supplemented by Practice Directions which relate to the individual Parts and give detailed guidance on the procedure to be followed. Certain former Rules of the Supreme Court 1965 ('RSC') and County Court Rules 1981 ('CCR') are preserved, for the time being, in Schs 1 and 2 to the CPR respectively. Under the CPR, there are common rules relating both to the High Court and the county court. A claimant generally initiates proceedings by one of two procedures, known from the relevant Parts of the CPR as a Part 7 claim and a Part 8 claim respectively. Part 7 claims are appropriate where there are contested issues of fact. A Part 8 claim is appropriate where the claimant either seeks the court's decision on the question which is unlikely to involve a substantial dispute of fact or where it is required by the rule or a Practice Direction.[1] In relation to a Part 8 claim, the evidence on which the claimant relies must normally be served with the claim,[2] and the provisions relating to defence and reply in the CPR do not apply. In practice, rights to light disputes are likely to be dealt with under the Part 7 procedure, save where the only issue concerns the interpretation of a document.

11.9 The choice of venue for commencement of proceedings is governed by the CPR, including Practice Directions supplementing them. Currently, where proceedings are for damages, a claim cannot be started in the High Court if the value is less than £15,000.[3] Subject to this, the choice between High Court and county court depends on the complexity of the facts, legal issues, remedies or procedures involved, and the importance of the claim. Part 30 of the CPR provides for transfer of cases from High Court to county court, and vice versa.

11.10 It frequently arises in rights to light claims that the claimant, before trial, wishes to restrain the defendant from continuing with the erection of a building which, as he alleges, will obstruct his right to light. Under the CPR, '*interim* injunctions' are sought pursuant to CPR, Part 35. In the case of exceptional urgency, it is possible to obtain an interim injunction before proceedings are started.[4]

11.11 Appeals lie to the Court of Appeal, with leave of the court of first instance or the Court of Appeal. In general, leave to appeal is more likely to be granted on points of law.[5]

1 CPR, r 8.1.
2 CPR, r 8.5.
3 CPR, PD7, para 2.1.
4 CPR, r 25.2.
5 See Court of Appeal Practice Direction, paras 2.9, 2.10. For guidance on practice generally, see *Civil Court Service* (Jordans). This is regularly updated and contains the full text of the CPR and Practice Directions, together with procedural tables, commentary and forms.

ABATEMENT

General

11.12 Abatement is a remedy achieved by the act of the aggrieved party, by physical removal of the structure which interferes with the light to which that party is entitled. The remedy is hedged around with a number of restrictions discussed below and is best avoided if at all possible, given the increasing disfavour shown by the courts to self-help remedies. Nevertheless, it remains available, and is described below. In *Burton v Winters*,[1] Lloyd LJ said:[2]

> 'Ever since the assize of nuisance became available, the courts have confined the remedy by way of self-redress to simple cases such as an overhanging branch, or an encroaching root, which would not justify the expense of legal proceedings, and urgent cases which require an immediate remedy.'

In the light of these criteria, it is thought that the practical ambit of abatement in rights to light disputes is limited; few cases involving rights to light are as simple or urgent as those given by Lloyd LJ.

Abatement and the criminal law

11.13 Not the least of the risks of attempting abatement is that it could potentially involve commission of a crime, if it transpired that the actions carried out were beyond what the law allows. In general, damage to the property of another is a criminal offence. Under s 1(1) of the Criminal Damage Act 1971:

> 'A person who without lawful excuse destroys or damages any property belonging to another intending to destroy or damage any such property or being reckless as to whether any such property would be destroyed or damaged shall be guilty of an offence.'

It has been held that 'damage' includes permanent or temporary impairment of value or usefulness, as well as physical harm.[3] Thus the simple removal from the ground and laying down on the ground of a fence alleged to have stopped light, for example, would fall within the statute.

11.14 Section 5(2) to (4) of the Criminal Damage Act 1971 provides as follows:

> '(2) A person charged with an offence to which this section applies shall, whether or not he would be treated for the purposes of this Act as having a lawful excuse apart from this subsection, be treated for those purposes as having a lawful excuse –
>
> ...
>
> (b) if he destroyed or damaged or threatened to destroy or damage the property in question ... in order to protect property belonging to himself or another or a right or interest in property which was or which he

1 [1993] 3 All ER 847, CA.

2 Ibid at 851; see also *Cooperative Wholesale Society Limited v British Railways Board* (1995) NPC 200, (1995) *The Times*, 20 December. See **11.19**.

3 *Morphitis v Salmon* [1990] Crim LR 48, DC.

believed to be vested in himself or another, and at the time of the act or acts alleged to constitute the offence he believed –

(i) that the property, right or interest was in immediate need of protection; and

(ii) that the means of protection adopted or proposed to be adopted were or would be reasonable having regard to all the circumstances.

(3) For the purposes of this section it is immaterial whether a belief is justified or not if it is honestly held.

(4) For the purposes of subsection (2) above a right or interest in property includes any right or privilege in or over land, whether created by grant, licence or otherwise.'

It is submitted that a person who destroyed a building or fence which he believes obstructs his light could, depending on the facts, avail himself of a defence under s 5(2) of the Act. For the purposes of s 5(2), 'property' bears the extended definition in s 5(4), clearly wide enough to include an easement of light. This is to be contrasted with the interpretation of 'property' in s 10(1) of the Act, in which property is defined as:

> 'Property of a tangible nature, whether real or personal ...'

The defendant would, however, have to show that he had an honest belief, first, that his easement of light 'was in immediate need of protection', and secondly, that the means of protection adopted 'were ... reasonable having regard to all the circumstances'. However, he does not have to show that the belief he actually entertained was justified, provided it was honestly held (see s 5(3)).

11.15 It ought, therefore, in principle, to be possible for a defendant to secure his acquittal provided he can establish the necessary honest belief. However, he may well face certain difficulties. First, his alleged honest belief that his easement 'was in immediate need of protection' might well be challenged. It could be said with some force that, given the availability of civil legal remedies for interference with light, and given that the interference with light does not cause any direct or permanent damage to the dominant owner's property, there would be no honest basis for such a person to believe that his easement was in immediate need of protection. Further, the word 'immediate' involves the application of an objective test. There must be evidence on which it could be said that the defendant believed that immediate action had to be taken to do something that would otherwise be a crime in order to prevent the immediate risk of something worse happening.[1]

11.16 It is further a question of whether acts of this kind could be said to be 'in order to protect property'. Once again, the test is objective. It could be said against a defendant in these circumstances that the removal of the building or screen in question was not carried out for this purpose, given the availability of remedies by Act of law.

11.17 Finally, reference should be made to s 9 of the Theft Act 1968, under which the offence of burglary is committed by someone who enters a building as

1 *Johnson v DPP* [1994] Crim LR 673, DC.

a trespasser with the intention, inter alia, 'of doing unlawful damage to the building or anything therein'.[1] The criteria of unlawful damage are the same as in the Criminal Damage Act 1971. The offence applies only where there is entry to a 'building', which it seems may also include an unfinished building.[2] Therefore, although abatement is not directly prohibited by criminal law, there is a far from negligible risk that a person purporting to exercise a power of abatement might face a criminal charge.

Limit of the remedy

11.18 Returning to the limitations on the right of abatement in civil law, the right to carry out works of abatement may be exercised both on the dominant owner's land and on the land of the servient owner (in practice, of course, the latter situation is more likely).[3] The right to abate, however, arises only when an interference with the easement has occurred, and not on account of a threatened interference alone. Thus in *Morrice v Baker*,[4] Haughton J said:

> '... you have come too soon, to cast this down before it was made, for if he have an intent to build a wall, and lays the foundations, you ought not to disturb him for this his inception, you cannot pull this down.'

11.19 The acts of abatement must go no further than strictly necessary to abate the nuisance. Thus in *Greenslade v Haliday*,[5] the plaintiff, who had a right to irrigate a meadow by placing a dam of loose stones across a small stream and occasionally a board or fender, fastened the board by means of two stakes which had never been done by his predecessors. The defendant who had rights on the same stream, removed the stakes and the board also. It was held that the defendant was entitled to remove the stakes, which gave the board a character of permanency, but was not entitled to remove the board. Tindal CJ said:

> ... the defendant has done more than she ought to have done. The board in dispute was fastened by stakes, which was not usual; but the defendant, instead of removing the stakes alone, removed the board also. If a party who had a right to a stone weir were to erect buttresses, one who should oppose the erection of the buttresses could not justify demolishing the weir as well as the buttresses.'

Similarly, in *Lagan Navigation Co v Lambeg Bleaching, Dyeing and Finishing Co*,[6] the cutting away of banks to allow the escape of flood water was held unjustifiable because the defendant failed to prove it had not caused unnecessary damage. In *Cooperative Wholesale Society v British Railways Board*,[7] where abatement of a nuisance caused by a decrepit wall was in issue, it was held that the

1 Theft Act 1968, s 9(1) and (2).
2 Cf *R v Manning* (1871) LR I CCR 338.
3 *R v Rosewell* (1699) 2 Salk 459; *Thompson v Eastwood* (1852) 8 Exch 69.
4 3 Bulst 196 81 ER 165.
5 (1830) 6 Bing 379, 130 ER 1326.
6 [1927] AC 226.
7 (1995) NPC 200, (1995) *The Times*, 20 December.

right extended only to demolishing the wall, not rebuilding it. And in the case of light, where only part of a building erected by the servient owner obstructs the dominant owner's light, the dominant owner is entitled only to pull down so much of the new building as actually obstructs the light.[1] If there is a choice between possible methods of abatement, that which causes the least damage must be selected.[2] However, if either alternative would interfere with third party rights, or those of the public, it cannot be adopted, and it then becomes necessary to adopt that which is more onerous to the wrongdoer.[3] Unnecessary damage during the course of abatement will be an actionable trespass.[4] However, where reasonable abatement inevitably involves further adverse consequences to the offending obstruction, it is submitted that the person carrying out the abatement works is not on that account liable: for example, if demolition of the offending part of the building inevitably involves the removal or collapse of other parts.[5]

11.20 In general, a person wishing to carry out abatement works on the land of another must give that other notice, except in the case of emergency or where there is a danger to persons or property and no reasonable opportunity to give notice.[6] It follows that in the not uncommon case of obstruction to light caused by trees, the dominant owner is within his rights to abate the interference with light by cutting down so much of the servient owner's trees as overhang his land.[7] However, two members of the Court of Appeal stressed that it would be desirable to give notice in all cases.[8] Kay LJ said:

> 'No-one but an ill-disposed person would do such an act without previous notice. There was no emergency in this case. The defendant has acted in an unneighbourly manner, and I cannot help thinking he intended to cause annoyance.'

The Court of Appeal deprived the defendant of the costs of the action. It would seem, therefore, it would be prudent in all cases for notice to be given. Further, in the House of Lords, Lord McNaughten suggested[9] that the rule would not necessarily apply:

> 'to the case of trees so young that the owner might remove them intact if he chose to lift them, or to the case of shrubs capable of being transplanted ...'

11.21 It is not entirely clear whether the right to carry out abatement works to trees exclusively on one's own side of the boundary without notice to the neighbour whose trees they are is limited to removing those lengths of the tree's

---

1 *Penruddock's case* (1597) 5 Co Rep 100(b); *James v Haywood* (1630) 1 William Jones 221; *Cooper v Marshall* (1757) 1 Burr 259.
2 *Roberts v Rose* (1865) LR 1 Ex 82.
3 Ibid, per Blackburn J at p 89.
4 *Lagan Navigation Co v Lambeg Bleaching, Dyeing and Finishing Co* [1927] AC 226.
5 Cf *Kawkwell v Russell* (1856) 2 LJ Ex 34.
6 *Jones v Williams* (1843) 11 M&W 176; *Lemmon v Webb* [1894] 3 Ch 1 at 13, per Lindley LJ.
7 *Lemmon v Webb* [1894] 3 Ch 1; [1895] AC 1.
8 See Lopes LJ at [1894] 3 Ch 18, and Kay LJ at [1894] 3 Ch 24.
9 [1895] AC 1 at 7.

boughs which project over the boundary, or whether in addition the dominant owner may reach across the boundary, by means of a lopper or hedge cutter for example, to cut further portions of the tree lying on the servient owner's side of the boundary. In *Lemon v Webb*, it is clear that the Court of Appeal proceeded on the basis that only those portions on the dominant owner's side of the boundary could be cut, but in the earlier case of *Pickering v Rudd*[1] the defendant had removed a Virginia Creeper growing in the plaintiff's garden, but which had spread over the side of the defendant's house, by means of ropes and scaffolding suspended over the plaintiff's garden without touching the surface of the plaintiff's premises. Lord Ellenborough directed the jury that the question was whether in removing the mischief the defendant had done any damage to the tree which might have been avoided, upon which there was a verdict for the defendant. This case might support the proposition that, provided there is no actual touching of the ground on the other side of the boundary, leaning over the boundary at higher level to cut trees which constitute a nuisance is permissible.

11.22 It is, however, submitted that *Pickering v Rudd* should be approached with caution, and that the better view is that expressed in *Lemmon v Webb*. Further, in *Anchor Brewhouse Developments Ltd v Berkeley House (Docklands Developments) Ltd*,[2] it was held that trespass to land caused by the oversailing of a crane jib entitled the landowner to injunctive relief, a decision incompatible with the reasoning of Lord Ellenborough in *Pickering v Rudd* that no trespass was committed if a bullet was fired across a field but did not fall to the ground in the field. It appears established from the *Anchor Brewhouse* decision, and earlier authorities referred to therein,[3] that trespass to airspace is always actionable.

11.23 In the result, it is submitted that it is not permissible to overhang the boundary in order to remove those portions of a tree which give rise to a nuisance. Therefore, in the not uncommon case of nuisance caused by fast growing conifers, where the majority of the foliage obstructing the light forms a comparatively high but narrow column on the servient owner's land, topping of such trees would be permissible only with due notice to the servient owner, save where an emergency arises.

11.24 Finally, the abatement must not give rise to a breach of the peace. This is in line with the general reluctance of the court to sanction self-help. Thus in *Hale De Portibus Maris*,[4] it is said:

> 'Any man may justify the removal of a common nuisance either at land or by water, because every man is concerned in it ... but because this many times occasions tumults and disorders, the best way to reform public nuisances is by the ordinary courts of justice.'[5]

---

1 (1815) 4 Camp 219.
2 [1987] 2 EGLR 173.
3 In particular, *Kelsen v Imperial Tobacco Company Great Britain and Ireland Ltd* [1957] 2 QB 334; *Woollerton and Wilson Ltd v Richard Costain Ltd* [1970] 1 WLR 411.
4 1 Harg Tracts 87.
5 Cited with approval by Kay LJ in *Lemmon v Webb* [1894] 3 Ch 1 at 19.

Relationship of abatement with legal proceedings for the same wrong

11.25 Abatement by act of a party will prevent a subsequent claim in legal proceedings for the same remedy.[1] But there seems no reason why a claim should not be maintained for damage sustained prior to the abatement,[2] because since interference with light is a continuing nuisance, damage is suffered every day whilst the nuisance continues prior to the abatement. The contrary dictum of Lord Atkinson in *Lagan Navigation Co v Lambeg Bleaching, Dyeing and Finishing Co*[3] to the effect that exercise of the right of abatement destroys any right of action in respect of a nuisance is probably to be regarded as confined to claims for abatement or future loss alone.[4]

11.26 It was formerly an open question as to whether the right to pursue the remedy of abatement survived legal proceedings in which a mandatory injunction to remove the nuisance was refused. Clearly, it would not be exercisable if the court dismissed the claim on the basis that no easement was found to exist, but in other cases, if the court either at the interim stage or the final stage of the action refused a mandatory injunction, the position was less clear: in *Lane v Capsey*,[5] Chitty J in the context of the failure of a claim for a mandatory injunction at trial, left the point open. In *Burton v Winters*,[6] it was held by the Court of Appeal that a right of abatement did not survive the conclusion of legal proceedings in which a mandatory injunction was refused. Conversely, there is no obligation to exercise a right of abatement as a precondition of exercising a right to claim damages or an injunction.[7] In *Leakey v National Trust of Places of Historic Interest or Natural Beauty*,[8] Megaw LJ said:[9]

> 'But in any event, if there were such a right of abatement, it would . . . be because my neighbour owed me a duty. There is, I think, ample authority that, if I have a right of abatement, I also have a remedy in damages if the nuisance remains unabated and causes me damage or personal injury.'

---

1 *Baten's case* (1610) 9 Co Rep 53b and 55a. *Burton v Winters* [1993] 3 All ER 847 at 851d.
2 *Kendrick v Bartland* (1679) 2 Mod Rep 253.
3 [1927] AC 226 at 244.
4 Cf *Clerk & Lindsell on Torts* 17th edn, para 29–24.
5 [1891] 3 Ch 411.
6 [1993] 3 All ER 847, CA.
7 *Lemmon v Webb* [1894] 3 Ch 1 at 24, per Kay LJ; *Smith v Giddy* [1904] 2 KB 448; *Job Edwards v Birmingham Navigations* [1924] 1 KB 341 at 356, per Scrutton LJ; *Bradburn v Lindsay* [1983] 2 All ER 408.
8 [1980] 1 All ER 17.
9 Ibid at 34.

DAMAGES AT COMMON LAW

General principles

11.27 In this section are considered damages awarded at common law for nuisance. The subject of damages awarded in addition to or in lieu of an injunction (equitable damages) is dealt with separately at **11.115** and following.

11.28 Damages at common law are normally awarded to compensate the plaintiff for wrong done. In certain limited circumstances, the court may award aggravated or exemplary damages.[1] The principle governing an award of compensatory damages is that the measure of such damages is:

> 'That sum of money which will put the party who has been injured, or who has suffered, in the same position as he would have been in if he had not sustained the wrong for which he is now getting his compensation or reparation.'[2]

11.29 A general principle is that damages for nuisance are not recoverable if they are too remote. For damages to be recovered from the wrongdoer, it is necessary to establish:

(1) that the wrongdoer has caused the damage concerned;
(2) that damage of the type which has occurred was a reasonably foreseeable consequence of the wrongdoer's acts or omissions.[3]

So in *The Wagon Mound (No 1)*,[4] it was held that there was no liability for an oil spill in a harbour which resulted in a fire due to ignition of some oil which in turn had been lit by a fire which had started in cotton waste floating on the surface of the water. The ignition of the cotton waste had occurred due to sparks from the plaintiff's welding operations. It was held that damage of this kind was not reasonably foreseeable.

11.30 Where, however, the type of damage is foreseeable, but its extent is not, all damages are recoverable even if the extent of the injuries suffered by the plaintiff is greater than could have been foreseen.[5] But the limit to this principle is illustrated by *Balfour Beatty Construction (Scotland) Ltd v Scottish Power Plc.*[6] In that case, the pursuer received a supply of electricity from the defender under contract, at a construction site where it was constructing an aqueduct. The power supply failed whilst the pursuer was in process of conducting a continuous pour of concrete, for which electricity was essential. As a result of the failure of the supply the entire day's work was rendered abortive. It was held that the pursuer

---

1 See **11.8**.
2 Per Lord Blackburn in *Livingstone v Rawyards Coal Co* (1885) 5 App Cas 25 at 39.
3 *Overseas Tankship (UK) Ltd v Morts Dock and Engineering Co Ltd The Wagon Mound (No 1)* [1961] 1 AC 388.
4 Ibid.
5 *Hughes v Lord Advocate* [1963] AC 837; *Parsons v Uttley Ingham & Co Ltd* [1978] QB 791.
6 (1994) 71 BLR 20, HL.

was not entitled to recover, since damage arising from failing to achieve a continuous pour was not of a foreseeable kind.

11.31 Where, however, damage of a particular kind is foreseeable, the defendant is liable for all loss of that kind, and recovery is not reduced by the fact that the plaintiff is, for example, abnormally sensitive. This is sometimes referred to as 'the egg shell skull' rule.[1] The wrongdoer 'must take the victim as he finds him'.[2] Thus if the plaintiff is unusually susceptible either physically or mentally,[3] the risk of this increasing the plaintiff's loss is on the defendant. However, the defendant is not obliged to take the plaintiff as 'a quarrelsome litigious perfectionist'.[4]

Loss due to plaintiff's impecuniosity

11.32 As a general rule, a defendant is not responsible for increased loss which flows solely from the plaintiff's impecuniosity.[5] However, this principle does not apply in relation to failure to mitigate loss, or where the impecuniosity is not the sole cause of the loss in question.[6]

Recovery on behalf of third parties

11.33 The general principles governing title to sue are dealt with in Chapter 10. This section covers the scope of an individual claimant's claim. It is a well-established general rule that a claimant can recover in tort only in respect of his own loss, and not in respect of loss suffered by others.[7] This may have important ramifications in the case of claims for damage caused by loss of light. A distinction must be drawn between claims relating to injury to the value of the property affected, and loss of amenity claims. In the former case, the nature of the claim or claims is for injury to a property interest. A party with an interest in the building (whether in possession or reversion), which he can show has been damaged by the injury to the light to the building, is entitled to maintain a claim in respect of damage to his interest. Thus there may be claims by occupying tenants, mesne landlords and the freeholder. On the other hand, it is not possible, generally, for any of such parties to claim for loss which in truth falls on others. Thus if, for example, company A owns the building, but its subsidiary, company B, occupies the building as tenant of company A, both company A and company B have separate claims, but it is not possible for company B to claim for the whole

---

1 See *Dulieu v White* [1901] 2 KB 669.
2 Per Lord Wright in *Bourhill v Young* [1943] AC 92 at 109.
3 See *Kremin v Duke Street Investments Ltd* (1992) CILL 806.
4 Ibid at 809.
5 *Liesbosch Dredger v SS Eddison* [1933] AC 499.
6 *Dodd Properties (Kent) Ltd v Canterbury City Council* (1980) 1 WLR 433; *Mattocks v Mann* (1992) *The Times*, 19 June.
7 There are some circumstances where, in contrast, a party may recover substantial damages even though he has suffered little or no loss, if this was envisaged when the contract was made (*Linden Gardens Trust Ltd v Kenesta Sludge Disposals Ltd* [1993] 3 WLR 408, HL).

loss.[1] Where the occupying entity (or entities) are simply licensees, they cannot maintain a claim even for their own loss.[2]

11.34 It is, therefore, important that *all* those who have suffered loss as a result of an infringement of light who have an interest in the building are found in the action as claimants, if full recovery is to be achieved. Equally, from a defendant's point of view, care needs to be taken when considering issues of payment of compensation for loss of light, and compromises of actions in which some (but not all) of those interested in the affected building pursue claims. A practical view may need to be taken as to whether, on the one hand, to take the risk of further claims, or on the other hand, to insist on some type of indemnity from those who are claimants against the possibility of future claims.[3]

11.35 On the other hand, where the claim is for inconvenience and loss of amenity, only those who actually suffer such loss may claim it.[4]

11.36 In the case of 'one man' companies, the court may, in appropriate circumstances, be prepared to allow the proprietor of the company to recover loss which, nominally, has been sustained by the company, on the ground that in reality that loss has been sustained by the proprietor. Thus in *Esso Petroleum v Mardon*,[5] plaintiffs who were individuals were held entitled to recover damages from the defendant for breach of contract and misrepresentation which led them to enter a lease of a filling station, although the lease had actually been taken in the name of a company which they owned. In *DHN Food Distributors Ltd v Tower Hamlets Borough Council*,[6] a claim by a holding company for disturbance following compulsory purchase was allowed even though the premises in question were occupied by a subsidiary. The court held that it was possible to look at the realities of the situation and pierce the corporate veil. Conversely, in *Kremin v Duke Street Investments Ltd*,[7] an individual plaintiff was held entitled to recover loss sustained by private companies he controlled, arising from claims for, inter alia, nuisance caused to the plaintiff.

---

1 *Richard Roberts v Douglas Smith Stimson* (1988) 46 BLR 50; possibly the principle does not apply where the holding company has no claim of its own – *George Fisscher (Great Britain) Ltd v Multi Construction Ltd* (1992) CILL 795.

2 *Butcher Robinson & Staples Limited v London Regional Transport* (1999) 36 EG 165, [1999] 36 EG 165. See also Chapter 10 at **10.4**.

3 See Chapters 8 and 9 at **8.3** and **9.37**, point (5).

4 Although in *Credit Suisse v Beegas Nominees Ltd* [1994] 1 EGLR 76 the (corporate) plaintiff tenant of a building recovered general damages for breach of a repairing covenant in a lease for inconvenience experienced by staff and customers, no consideration seems to have been given to the question of whether the tenant was entitled to claim on behalf of such third parties and it is suggested the decision is suspect. In *Yankwood v London Borough of Havering* [1998] EGCS 575, it was suggested that the award was on the basis of being intended to compensate the plaintiff for loss of business.

5 [1975] QB 819.

6 [1976] 3 All ER 462, CA.

7 (1992) CILL 806.

Claims by reversioners

11.37 There may be many interests in the dominant land. In the case of a freehold owner in possession, no difficulty arises. He is not only directly affected by the infringement of light but is the owner of the whole interest in the dominant land, and, therefore, competent to claim in respect of all damage. Where the interest in the dominant land is split between a tenant or tenants and reversioners, the general rule is that each party holding an interest in the land is entitled to maintain an action in respect of his own loss. In the case of those whose interests are not in possession (mesne tenants, and freeholders), it is now well established that they are entitled to bring claims for the injury to their interest, provided the interference with the land is of a sufficiently permanent nature to affect the value of that interest.[1] The requirement that the injury must be of permanent character would, presumably, exclude transient obstructions which have no effect on the value of the interest of the plaintiff. In the case of the erection of a permanent obstruction, no difficulty is likely to arise but the position may be less clear cut where the obstruction is, though temporary, potentially more than transient, for example due to scaffolding which will be struck when the relevant building work is complete. But it is thought that an obstruction can still be regarded as permanent even if it is not constructed of orthodox building materials, and may be readily removed, if the evidence shows that it is intended that it shall remain permanently in position.[2]

11.38 It is clear that the calculation of the damage suffered by a reversioner for injury to light is potentially complex. Relevant factors will include the length of the occupational lease, the length of the interest held by the reversioner (if he is not the freeholder) and the effect on the income received by the reversioner as a result of the interference. If the injury to the claimant is small, applying normal valuation principles, it is generally less likely that the claimant would be granted an injunction, as opposed to being left to his remedy in damages.[3] In practice, the court is generally likely to be more receptive to claims for injunctions brought by occupiers rather than to claims from reversioners, at least where the amount of damage to the reversion is small.

Retention of rights to light by reversioner by agreement

11.39 Under s 3 of the Prescription Act 1832, a leaseholder can acquire a prescriptive right to light against both his landlord and other tenants of his landlord.[4] To counter this, leases may contain a clause along the lines that the lessee:

---

1 *Jesser v Gifford* (1767) 4 Burr 2141; *Shadwell v Hutchinson* (1829) 3 C&P 615 (claim by trustee); *Battishill v Reed* (1856) 18 CB 696; *Metropolitan Association v Petch* (1858) 5 CBNS 504.

2 *Metropolitan Association v Petch* (1858) 5 CBNS 504; *Baxter v Taylor* (1832) B&Ad 72; cf *Mumford v Oxford Worcester and Wolverhampton Railway Company* (1856) 1 H&N 34.

3 *Shelfer v City of London Electric Lighting Co* [1895] 1 Ch 287 and see **11.89–11.108**.

4 *Morgan v Fear* [1907] AC 425.

'shall not be or become entitled to any right of access to light or air to the demised premises which would in any way restrict or interfere with the user of the remainder of the building or any adjoining or neighbouring or nearby property for building or any other purpose.'

11.40 The effect of such provisions in relation to prescriptive claims is considered in Chapter 7.[1] But they may also, if suitably worded, operate both to preclude light claims by the lessee against both the landlord and third parties, and reserve to the landlord the right to claim the damages for full value of the infringement as if he were in possession, on the argument that the lessee will have reduced his bid for the premises owing to the absence of protection against interference with light. The validity of the argument of course depends on the facts of each case. It may be very difficult, in practice, to show any loss where the premises have been disposed of on a long lease prior to the infringement occurring.

Continuing after an initial award of damages

11.41 Interference with light is a continuing nuisance, in other words one whose effect is regarded by the law as carrying on from day to day as long as the interference remains in place. Three corollaries follow from this.

(1) The plaintiff is entitled to recover damages in respect of the whole period of his ownership during which the interference with light continues.
(2) Successive owners can sue in respect of the damage occurring during their ownership since the cause of action is a continuing one.[2]
(3) If the damages are to be assessed as at the date of trial, but the plaintiff is entitled to bring successive actions in the future, as long as the injury continues.

11.42 The principles governing successive awards of damages now have limited practical importance given that all courts now have power to grant injunctive relief, or damages in lieu. But prior to the middle of the nineteenth century, the common law courts could award only damages (but not injunctions) and, conversely, courts of equity could not award damages. Successive claims for damages for infringement of light were, therefore, common.[3]

11.43 Thus in *Shadwell v Hutchinson*,[4] the plaintiff brought an action for obstruction of lights to a building. The principal argument of the defendant was that he was entitled to rely on the Custom of London, under which buildings on ancient foundations could be raised to any height.[5] The court having ruled

1 See Chapter 7 at **7.6** in particular.
2 *Whitehouse v Fellows* (1861) 10 CBNS 765; *Delaware Mansions Ltd v Westminster City Council* [2000] BLR 1, CA.
3 The common law courts were first empowered to grant injunctions in relation to nuisance by the Common Law Procedure Act 1854, ss 79–81. The Chancery Court was empowered to award damages in lieu of an injunction by the Chancery Amendment Act 1858 ('Lord Cairns' Act').
4 (1829) 3 C&P 615.
5 For the Custom of London, see Chapter 7.

against the defendant both on this point and on the argument that the plaintiff as a trustee could not maintain the action, the jury awarded one shilling damages. In subsequent proceedings between the same parties,[1] the plaintiff made a claim for damages for the obstruction caused by the infringing building from 28 November 1828 to the time of the second action. It was admitted that the obstruction of light was in just the same state as at the time of the former action. The plaintiff was awarded damages of £100.

11.44 From the plaintiff's point of view, the need to bring successive actions was obviously unsatisfactory. Historically, its consequences were mitigated by the practice which grew up in the common law courts of awarding what were in effect penal damages in the second action if the obstruction to light was not removed. Thus in *Shadwell v Hutchinson*, the damages in the second case of £100 were clearly assessed by the jury at a figure designed to deter the defendant from maintaining the obstruction. In *Battishill v Reed*,[2] a case of wrongful encroachment rather than interference with rights to light, the defendant paid 30 shillings into court, which he claimed was sufficient to compensate the plaintiff for the actual damage. The jury were directed to consider whether the amount paid into court was sufficient to cover the actual damage, and decided that it was. On appeal, it was held that the Jury were right, Jarvis CJ saying:

> 'I think the Jury did right to give, as they generally do, nominal damages only in the first action; and if the defendant persists in continuing the nuisance, then they may give such damages as may compel him to abate it, but not, as was insisted here, the difference between the original value of the premises and their present diminished value.'

11.45 All the judges in *Battishill v Reed* recognised that it would not be permissible for the plaintiff to call evidence of the diminution in the value of his building caused by the obstruction, on the ground that this would be inconsistent with the principle on which damages were awarded. It would not be open to a claimant to make a claim based on permanent injury to the capital value of his building, and at the same time be able to pursue successive claims for injury accruing from day to day.

11.46 A partial alleviation of the inconvenience of having to take successive proceedings is provided by the principle that damages are to be assessed down to the date of the assessment.[3] Thus in the case of a continuing cause of action, damages can be assessed not simply from the date of commencement of the cause of action to the date proceedings were issued, but to the date of trial or assessment of damages, if later.

---

1 (1830) 4 C&P 335.

2 (1856) 18 CB 696.

3 This was formerly embodied in RSC Ord 37, r 6, but is not reproduced in the CPR. However, it is thought that the principle continues to apply. See *Hole v Chard Union* [1894] 1 Ch 294, CA for an example of the former principle.

11.47 Although the rule that interference with light is a continuing cause of action remains of importance for the purposes of the Limitation Act 1980,[1] the importance of these rules has for other purposes been at least greatly reduced by changes in the structure and powers of the superior courts effected originally in the nineteenth century. First, by virtue of s 2 of the Chancery Amendment Act 1858 the Court of Chancery, where it had jurisdiction to entertain an application for an injunction or specific performance, might award damages in addition to or in substitution for an injunction or specific performance. Formerly, the Court of Chancery had no power to award damages.[2] This provision, therefore, both enabled the Court of Chancery to award damages and empowered it to award damages in addition to or in lieu of an injunction. Since the fusion of common law and equity (see below), all civil courts have power to award damages, so the first extension of the power of the Court of Chancery effected by the 1858 Act is of no practical importance. However, the power to award damages in lieu of an injunction remains important.[3] It gives rise to a power to withhold an injunction in favour of compensating the plaintiff by way of damages not only for loss suffered up to trial but for the permanent prospective loss of his right to light. Damages in lieu of an injunction (equitable damages) are considered below.[4]

11.48 Secondly, by virtue of the Judicature Acts 1873 to 1875, the formerly separate common law and Chancery Courts were amalgamated into the unified structure. All of the Supreme Court, including the High Court of Justice, divisions of the High Court and the Court of Appeal administer both common law and equity.[5] The same court may award common law damages, of injunctive relief, and equitable damages. The county court has the same jurisdiction.[6]

11.49 It is not clear whether it still remains open to a claimant to follow the former practice and pursue successive actions for damages only. It is suggested that this is technically possible, but unwise, for the following reasons:

(1) Given the availability of injunctive relief in every court, and the power to award damages in lieu of an injunction, the claimant would be obliged in his first action to specify whether he is claiming damages at common law or in lieu of an injunction.[7] If no damages in lieu of an injunction are sought in the first action, the claimant would probably be held to have disentitled himself from injunctive relief or damages in lieu in future.

(2) The court would probably not be prepared to award in effect penal damages in the second action, since the purpose of such damages was to dissuade the defendant from continuing with the wrong, whereas the court would have

1 See Chapter 10 at **10.15**.

2 See **11.110**.

3 The actual provisions of the Act were repealed but have been held to have been preserved by subsequent legislation, see *Leeds Industrial Co-operative Society v Slack* [1924] AC 851. See now Supreme Court Act 1981, s 50; County Courts Act 1984, s 38(1).

4 See **11.109–11.127**.

5 See now Supreme Court Act 1981, s 49.

6 County Courts Act 1984, s 38.

7 *Jaggard v Sawyer* [1995] 2 All ER 189, CA per Millett LJ.

had power in all cases to grant the claimant an injunction, which was not the position prior to the nineteenth-century reforms discussed above. Therefore, the court would not now award such damages, confining the claimant to actual loss established.

(3) Having regard to point (1), arguably the second claim could be struck out under CPR, r 3.4 on the basis that the second claim infringes the principle laid down in *Henderson v Henderson*[1] that:

> '... the court requires the parties ... to bring forward their whole case, and will not (except under special circumstances) permit the same parties to open the same subject of litigation in respect of a matter which might have been brought forward as part of the subject matter in contest ... The plea of res judicata applies except in special cases, not only to points upon which the court was actually required by the parties to form an opinion and pronounce a judgment, but to every point which properly belonged to the subject of litigation, and which the parties, exercising reasonable diligence, might have brought forward at the time.'

Measure of damages at common law

11.50 The basic measure of damages for injury to land caused by nuisance is diminution in the value of the land.[2] This will, therefore, be the appropriate measure where the injury is permanent, and is not subsequently abated by the removal of the offending obstruction, either voluntarily or by reason of a court injunction. The claim is not restricted to that suffered by the particular part of his building which enjoys ancient lights, but extends to diminution in the value of the whole of his building, including those parts whose windows do not enjoy ancient light.[3] Such damages are sometimes termed 'parasitic', in that the plaintiff is entitled to recover not only the loss caused by the obstruction of apertures enjoying the easement but also loss caused by the darkening of those which do not. The principle seems clearly established where the same obstruction affects not only ancient lights but also windows which enjoy no rights to light in the same building. In such cases, the claimant is entitled to sue for loss to the building as a whole.[4] It seems that the principle also extends to entitle the claimant to claim

1 *Henderson v Henderson* (1843) 3 Hare 100 per Wigram V-C at 114–115. See also *Talbot v Berkshire County Council* [1994] QB 290. The principle applies only where the subject matter of the second action could have been determined in the first: *Barrow v Bankside Agency Ltd* [1996] 1 WLR 257, *Neasham v John Thompson* (1999) 24 March, CA (transcript reference LTA 1998/7547/1). The courts have recently moved away from the strict application of the principle (*Barrow v Bankside Agency Ltd* [1996] 1 WLR 257; *Neasham v John Thompson* 24 March 1999, CA (transcript reference LTA 1998/7547/1)). In *Bradford and Bingley Building Society v Seddon* [1999] 4 All ER 216, it was held that mere re-litigation in circumstances falling short of cause of action or issue estoppel did not necessarily give rise to abuse of process, and that the maintenance of a second claim which could have been part of an earlier one, or which conflicted with an earlier one, should not in itself be regarded as an abuse of process. In such cases, the claimant was not required to establish special circumstances to justify his litigation.

2 *Hunter and Others v Canary Wharf Ltd* [1997] AC 655, HL.

3 *Re London Tilbury and Southend Railway Company and Gowers Walk School Trustees* (1889) 24 QBD 326; *Scott v Goulding Properties Limited* [1973] IR 200.

4 Ibid.

not only for injury to the building with ancient lights, but also the depreciation to other buildings or land which will be affected by the obstruction. So in *Griffith v Richard Clay & Sons Limited*,[1] the plaintiff owned two houses fronting a street, the front windows of which were ancient lights. He also owned a piece of land to the rear of the houses, and adjacent thereto. The defendants wrongly obstructed the plaintiff's ancient lights. The plaintiff's houses were dilapidated, and he intended to demolish them and redevelop the whole site (including the land at the rear) as a warehouse or factory. It was held that he was entitled to recover not only for diminution in the value of the houses but also for the effect of the wrongful obstruction on the value of the land at the rear. Cozens Hardy MR stressed that the plaintiff's site taken as a whole was small (48 × 43 feet) and obviously must be used as one building site. He stated:

> '... the plaintiff is entitled to recover for all the damage caused which was the direct consequence of the wrongful act and so probable a consequence that, if the defendant had considered the matter, he must have foreseen that the whole damage would result from that act ...'[2]

11.51 In *Wills v May*,[3] the plaintiff was held entitled to recover for loss due to diminution in value not only of the house whose ancient lights were obstructed but also the neighbouring house which he proposed to redevelop along with it, notwithstanding that the neighbouring house's site might not be immediately ripe for development. Thus 'parasitic' damages may be recovered in two situations.

(1) Where the obstruction of ancient lights also obstructs windows which have no right to light, damage for all the loss to the building is recoverable.
(2) Where the obstruction of ancient light affects the value of neighbouring property owned by the claimant which it is foreseeable will be developed by the claimant together with the property whose ancient lights are obstructed.[4]

11.52 Where a nuisance causes physical damage to property, the remedial cost may in appropriate circumstances be recoverable, but it is difficult to conceive of such a claim being made for loss of light, except (conceivably) if the effect of obstructing the ancient light to a greenhouse were to cause damage to an exotic plant.[5]

11.53 Where the effect of the loss of light results in the premises losing amenity value, damages may be recovered. Such damages may include damages for injury to health, and inconvenience. There is a lack of authority on how such damages should be calculated in practice, although in *Bone v Seale*,[6] it was said that the

---

1 [1912] 2 Ch 291.
2 Ibid at 298.
3 [1923] 1 Ch 317.
4 See also *Horton v Colwyn Bay and Colwyn Urban District Council* [1908] 1 KB 327, and Hudson 'Parasitic Damages for Loss of Light' 39 Conv, p 116.
5 For the possibility of a greenhouse acquiring a right to an exceptional quantity of light, see Chapter 3 at **3.14**.
6 [1975] 1 All ER 787, CA.

court should follow the principles applicable to damages for loss of amenity in personal injury cases.[1] It is also appropriate to have regard to claims by tenants against landlords for breach of covenant, insofar as they shed light on the approach of the court to claims based on loss of amenity suffered by occupiers of premises due to unlawful activities. Such cases, however, should be approached with caution given the wide difference between the effect of loss of light and such matters as dust, noise from building works, and other physical disturbances.[2]

11.54 Probably, a claimant who suffers loss of light may maintain a claim for damages for injury to health caused by the loss of light, if it is the foreseeable consequence of the defendant's wrongful act. Certainly, damages for inconvenience are recoverable.[3]

11.55 Damages for economic loss are undoubtedly recoverable in claims for nuisance, subject to issues of remoteness and foreseeability. Thus in *Dodd Properties (Kent) Limited v Canterbury City Council*,[4] damages for nuisance were awarded representing dislocation of the plaintiff's business during the period when building works were carried out. In *Andreae v Selfridge & Co*,[5] damages for loss of business due to noise and vibration caused by building works were awarded. In *Collingwood v H & C Stores*,[6] damages were awarded for obstruction to the plaintiff's premises by the erection of a hoarding, assessed by reference to loss of trade. In *Yankwood Limited v Havering London Borough Council*,[7] again damages were awarded by reference to interference with business. Another possible claim could be extra expense of installing and running additional lighting systems, or having the existing lighting on for longer each day (though in practice claims of the latter kind are hard to prove). Provided it is reasonably foreseeable, loss sustained by inability to let the premises is recoverable: this is certainly the position in claims for breach of covenant for quiet enjoyment,[8] on the basis that such damages fall within the first limb of the rule in *Hadley v Baxendale*,[9] as arising in the usual course of things. Given that the test of reasonable foreseeability in contract is more restrictive than in tort,[10] there seems no reason why such damages should not be recoverable in tort.

11.56 In cases involving trespass, the courts have made awards of damages assessed by reference to a reasonable sum for the use made by the defendant of

---

1 See also *Halsey v Esso Petroleum Co* [1961] 1 WLR 683; *Bunclark v Hertfordshire CC* [1977] 2 EGLR 114.

2 For some examples of damages awards covering these factors, see Franklin 'More Heartache: A Review of the Award of General Damages in Building Cases' 8 Const LJ 318.

3 *Moore v Buchanan* (1966) 197 EG 565 (a right of way case).

4 [1980] 1 All ER 928, CA.

5 [1938] Ch 1.

6 [1936] 3 All ER 200.

7 [1998] EGCS 75.

8 *Mira v Aylmer Square Investments Limited* [1990] 1 EGLR 45.

9 (1854) 9 Exch 341.

10 *Czarnikow v Koufos* [1969] 1 AC 350, and see McGregor *Damages* 16th edn (Sweet & Maxwell, 1997), para 259.

the claimant's land. Thus in *Whitwham v Westminster Brymbo Coal Company*,[1] the defendants tipped spoil on the plaintiffs' land. Damages were assessed not by reference to the diminution in the value of the land, but by reference to a reasonable licence fee which the plaintiffs could have sought in return for granting the defendants the facility. Lindley LJ said:[2]

> 'The Plaintiffs have been injured in two respects. Firstly, they have had the value of their land diminished; secondly, they have lost the use of their land, and the Defendants have had the use of it for their own benefit. It is unjust to leave out of sight the use which the Defendants have made of this land for their own purposes, and that lies at the bottom of what are called the wayleave cases.'

The same principle has been applied in subsequent cases:[3]

11.57 In *Stoke on Trent City Council v W & J Wass Limited*,[4] Nicholls LJ said:[5]

> 'It is an established principle concerning the assessment of damages that a person who has wrongfully used another's property without causing the latter any pecuniary loss may still be liable to that other for more than nominal damages. In general, he is liable to pay, as damages, a reasonable sum for the wrongful use he has made of the other's property. The law has reached this conclusion by giving to the concept of loss or damage in such a case a wider meaning than merely financial loss calculated by comparing the property owner's financial position after the wrongdoing with what it would have been had the wrongdoing never occurred. Furthermore, in such a case it is no answer for the wrongdoer to show that the property owner would probably not have used the property himself had the wrongdoer not done so.'

11.58 In *Lawson v Hartley-Brown*,[6] this principle was applied to a case of trespass by building works, by a landlord constructing additional floors on top of a building demised (together with its air space) to the tenant. Damages were assessed by reference to a reasonable figure that would have been agreed, taking into account the advantage to the defendant, and the disturbance and potential loss of profit to the plaintiffs, at 1½ times the annual rent payable by the plaintiffs to the defendant.

11.59 This measure of damages is likely to have relatively limited application in the field of rights to light. If the obstruction is permanent in nature, the claimant is likely to seek injunctive relief: if it is refused, damages in lieu of an injunction will be assessed on the basis of the principles discussed below.[7] If the claimant, at the time he commences proceedings, is not entitled to injunctive relief his damages for permanent obstruction will normally be assessed by reference to the diminution in value of his land. However, the 'wayleave measure' may, it is

---

1 [1896] 2 Ch 538, CA.
2 [1896] 2 Ch 538 at 542.
3 See, eg, *Penarth Engineering Company v Pounds* [1963] 1 Lloyd's Rep 359; *Inverugie Investments v Hackett* [1995] 1 WLR 713, PC.
4 [1988] 3 All ER 394.
5 Ibid at 402.
6 (1995) 71 P&CR 242.
7 See **11.09–11.127**.

thought, be an appropriate basis of claim for a temporary obstruction to light: the claimant and the defendant would notionally have bargained to allow the defendant to infringe the claimant's right, and reached a figure taking into account the benefit and cost to both sides. The same general approach would probably be adopted by the court in assessing the measure of damages for trespass by oversailing by a crane on a construction site, which is subsequently removed, and other similar transient acts of trespass.

Interest

11.60 By s 35A of the Supreme Court Act 1981 and s 69 of the County Courts Act 1984, courts have power to award interest on damages. In general, where the damages represent compensation for financial loss, the claimant will be granted interest at a reasonable commercial rate over the period from the date the loss was sustained, until judgment. The appropriate rate is one which properly compensates the claimant, not one taking into account the profit the defendant wrongfully made out of withholding the money. In commercial cases, interest is intended to reflect the rate at which the claimant would have had to borrow money to supply the place of that which was held. The special position of the individual claimant should be disregarded.[1] Where the claimant is at all material times in credit at the bank, the interest should be assessed by reference to the amount of interest lost by the claimant, rather than a borrowing rate.[2]

11.61 Where the claimant is awarded a sum assessed by reference to wrongful use of land, interest is not awarded, on the ground that it would produce a double recovery situation.[3]

Taxation

11.62 In *British Transport Commission v Gourley*,[4] it was held that in awarding damages, account must be taken of the tax which would have been payable on the sums which have been lost as a result of the tort. For the rule to apply, it is necessary that:

(1) the sums for the loss of which the damages awarded constitute compensation would have been subject to tax;
(2) the damages awarded to the claimant would not themselves be subject to tax.

11.63 Where the claim is for diminution in value to land, the first factor will not arise. If the claimant deals in land, so that the land is trading stock, the rule in *BTC v Gourley* will not apply, because the claimant will be liable to tax on the asset. Interest is normally taxable at the hands of the recipient, hence again the rule in *BTC v Gourley* will not apply. Where appropriate, the court can

1 *Tate & Lyle Distribution v GLC* [1982] 1 WLR 149; *Shearson Lehman Hutton Inc v Maclaine Watson & Co Ltd (No 2)* [1990] 2 All ER 723.
2 *Amstrad Plc v Seagate Technology Inc & Another* (1997) 86 BLR 34.
3 *Whitwam v Westminster Brymbo Company* [1896] 1 Ch 894.
4 [1956] AC 185.

investigate the claimant's tax position in detail. The court should not necessarily ignore the effect of taxation where the damages are taxable, if this would be to produce over-compensation to the claimant.[1]

11.64 Care should be taken when releasing existing rights to light to ensure that, so far as possible, the party releasing those rights does not unwillingly incur either a capital gains tax,[2] or income tax charge. The release of the right may be a disposal of an asset within ss 21 and 22 of the Taxation of Chargeable Gains Act 1992, noting in particular s 22(1)(c). In addition, it may be open to the Inland Revenue in certain cases to treat sums paid for releases as gains within the technical and complex provisions of s 776 of the Income and Corporation Taxes Act 1988, thus causing an income tax charge under Case VI of Schedule D to arise. Under s 776(11), it is possible to seek advance clearance if it is thought that this section may apply. In any event, tax advice taken before any deal is done is a wise precaution. Finally, if a release is expressed to be for consideration in money or money's worth, Stamp Duty will be payable on the document recording the release, *ad valorem*, at the rate in force when the agreement is made, unless certified to be for value under the current threshold for *ad valorem* duty.

GENERAL PRINCIPLES AND CLASSIFICATION OF INJUNCTIONS

General

11.65 An injunction is a command by the court directed to a particular person to do or abstain from doing a certain act or acts. In a sense, all court orders granting a remedy require certain things to be done, but many types of court order are not injunctions, for example a judgment for a sum of money, or an order that one party pay the other's costs. Relief by way of injunction was originally granted by the Court of Chancery alone. The Court of Chancery administered a system of rules known as 'Equity', hence injunctions are a species of *equitable relief*. The distinction between injunctions and other court orders is that injunctions fall within the category of relief by way of ordering a particular person to do or to abstain from something which the Court of Chancery could have ordered.

11.66 Historically, injunctions were granted by the Court of Chancery either to support an equitable right or to support a legal right, where the remedies provided by the common law courts were not strong enough. At common law, it was not possible for a plaintiff directly to ensure that a continuing nuisance by way of infringement of light was ended by an order of the court. All he could do was to bring successive claims for damages, and rely on the jury to in effect put a stop to the defendant's wrongful conduct by a penal award of damages. Equity, however, would award an injunction to restrain legal wrongs, including the

1 *Amstrad Plc v Seagate Technology Inc & Another* (1997) 86 BLR 34.
2 See Taxation of Capital Gains Act 1992.

commission of a nuisance such as interference with light. However, in the case of a nuisance, equity could not grant an injunction until the plaintiff had established the claim in an action in one of the common law courts (Kings Bench, Common Pleas and Exchequer) which could award only damages. Following the report of a Royal Commission in 1851, the common law courts were given a limited right to grant injunctions, by the Common Law Procedures Act 1854, and the Court of Chancery a right to award damages under the Chancery Amendment Act 1858. Ultimately, by the Supreme Court of Judicature Act 1873, the separate systems of court were amalgamated, and every division of the High Court has power to award remedies including injunctions and damages. The county court has parallel jurisdiction under the County Courts Act 1984.[1]

Classification of injunctions

11.67 Injunctions may be classified in various ways.

(1) *Prohibitory/mandatory*. A prohibitory injunction prevents certain acts being done, whereas a mandatory injunction requires the defendant to take positive steps. In the context of rights to light, a typical prohibitory injunction would be one preventing the defendant from building so as to obstruct the claimant's light. A mandatory injunction would be one requiring the defendant to remove so much of a building as obstructs the plaintiff's light.
(2) *Final/interim*. A final injunction is one which the court grants at the trial of the action, and which will (almost invariably) be phrased so as to have permanent effect. An interim injunction is one granted prior to the trial of the action, to protect the plaintiff's rights prior to trial. It is not uncommon, for example, for a claimant in a rights to light case to seek an interim injunction to prevent the defendant from starting or continuing building which may infringe the claimant's rights to light until the case can be tried.

Quia timet/other injunctions

11.68 A *quia timet* injunction is granted to prevent a wrong before it occurs, where there is a very strong probability that substantial harm would be caused to the claimant which would not be adequately remedied by a damages claim. This is sometimes expressed in the phrase that the claimant would suffer 'grave damage'.[2]

Without notice/with notice injunctions

11.69 An injunction without notice is one granted on an application by one party without the other party being given notice, whereas a with notice injunction is one which is granted after hearing both parties. Without notice applications for injunctions are exceptional, and normally arise in two situations. First, where the case is one of exceptional urgency, so that the claimant needs

1 See, further, *Civil Court Service* (Jordans). See **11.11**, note 5.
2 *Redland Bricks Ltd v Morris* [1970] AC 652.

instant intervention from the court without time being allowed for the normal notice to be given to the defendant enabling the defendant to participate. Secondly, certain types of application for interim injunctions would have their purpose defeated were the defendant initially to be notified of them, for example applications for injunctions to restrain the defendant from disposing of or dealing with his assets prior to trial (so-called 'Freezing' orders).[1]

11.70 All injunctions are subject to certain overriding requirements. Under s 37(1) of the Supreme Court Act 1981:

> 'The High Court may by order (whether interlocutory or final) grant an injunction ... in all cases where it appears to the court to be just and convenient to do so.'[2]

11.71 Although the power to grant an injunction is by the terms of the statute unlimited, where, as in the case of rights to light, the injunction is sought in order to protect a legal right, it is of course necessary for the claimant to establish that he has such a right. It is not sufficient for the claimant to argue that he has an expectation or hope of acquiring such a right in the future. In the case of a claim based on a right to light, it would not be possible for a claimant to seek an injunction on the ground that he has a prescriptive right to light, if the necessary period has not elapsed, nor would he be entitled to object to the registration of a notice under the Rights of Light Act 1959 on the ground that its effect will be to prevent him acquiring such a right.[3] The grant of an injunction, like all other equitable relief, is discretionary. Relief may be refused if the court concludes that the claimant had acted unconscionably, even if his legal right is established.

QUIA TIMET AND INTERIM INJUNCTIONS

11.72 The grant of an interim injunction[4] can be regarded, in its simplest form, as a 'holding operation' until the action is heard at trial. As with other types of injunctions, interim injunctions may be sought to prevent a wrong before it occurs (*quia timet*); or to prevent a wrong continuing (prohibitory); or to require the defendant to take some positive steps to remedy a wrong (mandatory). As a result, the grant or refusal of an interim injunction is a very important matter that can have a profound effect on both parties in practical and financial terms.

11.73 The application for an interim injunction is not, however, a mini-trial. The only evidence given to the court is by witness statement or affidavit and this will not be subjected to the rigours of cross-examination. Whilst this approach may seem deficient, it is consistent with the court's desire not to express an opinion on the merits of the case until the full action is heard, even though a

---

1 See CPR Part 25 for interim relief (including freezing orders) generally.

2 The position in the county court is the same, subject to certain statutory restrictions that are not material for claims in relation to rights to light – see County Courts Act 1984, s 38(1).

3 See Chapters 7 and 8 at **7.10–7.23** and **8.31–8.48**.

4 Formerly known as 'interlocutory' – see **11.7**.

defendant can ultimately be sent to prison for breaching the terms of an interim injunction.

11.74 The principles guiding the court's equitable discretion to grant an interim injunction are set out in *American Cyanamid Co v Ethicon Ltd*[1] by Lord Diplock. Lord Diplock set out a three-stage test.

(1) Is there a serious issue to be tried?
(2) Would damages be an adequate remedy for a party injured by the court's grant of, or failure to grant, an injunction?
(3) Where does the 'balance of convenience' lie?

These principles, while of general application, should not be read as if they were set in stone[2] and it will be seen that they are subject to variations and may in some cases be entirely inappropriate. In any event, the '*American Cyanamid* Principles' rest upon the foundation of s 37(1) of the Supreme Court Act 1981, which allows the court to grant an injunction only where it is 'just and convenient to do so'.

Is there a serious issue to be tried?

11.75 Lord Diplock adopted a threshold test to separate the wheat from the chaff. In this instance, the application of a strict test is tempered by the level of inquiry that the court can undertake upon the evidence placed before it. Lord Diplock therefore rejected the view previously held of the need to show either 'a probability that the plaintiffs are entitled to relief' or a 'strong prima facie case that the right which he seeks to protect in fact exists'.[3] Instead, he continued:

> 'The court no doubt must be satisfied that the claim is not frivolous or vexatious; in other words, that there is a serious issue to be tried.'[4]

11.76 As to what these words mean, Lord Diplock specifically rejected the idea of a percentage based threshold test:

> 'The purpose sought to be achieved by giving to the court discretion to grant such injunctions would be stultified if the discretion were clogged by a technical rule forbidding its exercise if upon that incomplete untested evidence the court evaluated the chances of the plaintiff's ultimate success in the action at 50 per cent or less, but permitting its exercise if the court evaluated his chances at more than 50 per cent.'[5]

In general, therefore, this hurdle is fairly easily satisfied and all that has to be seen for a 'serious issue to be tried' is whether the claimant has prospects of success which exist both in substance and reality. Thus, a claimant will be unsuccessful where he relies on a cause of action unknown to English law, or a cause of action that is clearly unarguable on the facts presented.[6]

---

1 [1975] AC 396, HL.
2 *Cayne v Global Natural Resources Plc* [1984] 1 All ER 225, CA, per May LJ at 237.
3 [1975] AC 396 at 407G.
4 Ibid.
5 Ibid.
6 See *Mothercare Ltd v Robson Books Ltd* [1975] FSR 466 at 474; *Morning Star Co-operative Society Ltd v Express Newspapers Ltd* [1979] FSR 113.

An investigation as to the adequacy of damages

11.77 Damages can be an alternative method of giving relief to the wronged party. Therefore, once the court has established that there is a serious issue to be tried, the following inquiry is to be made, in four stages.

> '[i] [T]he court should first consider whether, if the plaintiff were to succeed at trial in establishing his right to a permanent injunction, he would be adequately compensated by an award of damages for the loss he would have sustained as a result of the defendant's continuing to do what was sought to be enjoined between the time of the application and the time of trial.
>
> [ii] If damages in the measure recoverable at common law would be adequate remedy and the defendant would be in a financial position to pay them, no interlocutory injunction should normally be granted, however strong the plaintiff's claim appeared to be at that stage.
>
> [iii] The court should then consider whether, on the contrary hypothesis that the defendant were to succeed at the trial in establishing his right to do that which was sought to be enjoined, he would be adequately compensated under the plaintiff's undertaking as to damages for the loss he would have sustained by being prevented from doing so between the time of the application and the time of the trial.
>
> [iv] If damages in the measure recoverable under such an undertaking would be an adequate remedy and the plaintiff would be in a financial position to pay them, there would be no reason upon this ground to refuse an interlocutory injunction.'[1]

This approach of looking at the relevance of the availability of an adequate remedy in damages was confirmed by Lord Goff in *R v Secretary of State for Transport, ex parte Factortame Ltd (No 2)*.[2]

The 'balance of convenience'

11.78 This stage of the test applies only where a doubt exists, as to the adequacy of the respective remedies in damages available to either party or both. Thus, by this stage, the court has examined the basic legal foundation of the cause of action and assessed the availability and adequacy of financial recompense. Assessing the 'balance of convenience', however, allows the court to step back and take the practical realities of the situation into account.

11.79 Unfortunately, the search for this balance of convenience is not aided by any hard and fast rules. The courts do not have a closed list of factors that should be taken into account. As such, any decisions as to the balance of convenience must be taken on a case-by-case basis. Yet despite this obvious reluctance to fetter their equitable discretion, the courts have set out a number of guiding principles.

---

1 *American Cyanamid Co v Ethicon Ltd* [1975] AC 396 at 408C–E. Subdivisions [i] to [iv] have been inserted for clarity of exposition.

2 [1991] 1 AC 603.

(1) *The risk of injustice.* The balance to be ascertained is more fundamental and weighty than mere 'convenience' would suggest and should be considered against the background of s 37(1) of the Supreme Court Act 1981. This emphasis on injustice is confirmed by Lord Diplock in another case: *NWL Ltd v Woods*,[1] where he stated:

> 'In assessing whether what is compendiously called the balance of convenience lies in granting or refusing interlocutory injunctions in actions between parties of undoubted solvency the judge is engaged in weighing the respective risks that injustice may result from his deciding one way rather than the other at a state when the evidence is incomplete.'

(2) *The status quo.*

> 'Where other factors appear to be evenly balanced it is a counsel of prudence to take such measures as are calculated *to preserve the status quo*.'[2]

As to when in time the 'status quo' applies, it was held in *Garden Cottage Foods Ltd v Milk Marketing Board*[3] that this meant the state of affairs immediately before the issue of the writ, ignoring minimal periods of time, unless the plaintiff is guilty of unreasonable delay.

(3) *Special factors.*

> '[T]here may be many other special factors to be taken into consideration in the particular circumstances of individual cases.'[4]

There is some argument as to whether the exceptions, which will be discussed below,[5] to the *American Cyanamid* Principles can be incorporated within the 'special factors' hereto referred rather than forming specific principles for clearly distinguishable circumstances. It is submitted that if they were to be incorporated within the 'special factors' then the exceptions may well encompass the rule and this can not have been what Lord Diplock intended.

(4) *The merits of the case.*

> '[I]t may not be improper to take into account in tipping the balance the relative strength of each party's case as revealed by the affidavit evidence adduced on the hearing of the application. This however should be done only where it is apparent upon the facts disclosed by evidence as to which there is no credible dispute that the strength of one party's case is disproportionate to that of the other party.'[6]

The courts have generally been reluctant to give any greater prominence than that of 'tipping the balance' to the relative strengths of each party's case. However, in *Series 5 Softwear Ltd v Clarke*,[7] Laddie J did not approach

---

1 [1979] 1 WLR 1294, HL at 1306G.
2 *American Cyanamid v Ethicon Ltd* [1975] AC 396 at 408G per Lord Diplock.
3 [1984] AC 130, HL.
4 [1975] AC 396 at 409D per Lord Diplock.
5 See **11.78**.
6 [1975] AC 396 at 409B–C per Lord Diplock.
7 [1995] 1 All ER 853.

this aspect as one of last resort. Like Lord Diplock, he held that the court must be able to come to a clear view as to the strength of each party's case on credible evidence, but once that was so, the view taken would immediately be a factor that the court could take into account when assessing the 'balance of convenience'.

While it may be expecting too much of the court not to look at, or form a view of, the relative strengths of each party's case, it is likely that courts will continue to be reluctant to express their decisions on this basis alone when dealing with cases which fall within the *American Cyanamid* Guidelines.

Exceptional cases

Quia timet injunctions

11.80 The principles which govern the grant of an interim injunction to prevent a wrong before it occurs differ both in substance and terminology. Instead of the court assessing whether there is a serious issue to be tried, the fundamental question becomes whether there is a probability that damage will accrue to the claimant in the future. The level of probability required will, however, depend upon whether the plaintiff is seeking a prohibitory or mandatory order. It is clear that in relation to the latter there must be a 'very strong probability upon the facts that grave damage will accrue to him in the future'.[1]

11.81 Once this has been assessed, the normal inquiry into the adequacy of damages, if the court does not grant the *quia timet* injunction and the damage actually accrues, should be considered.

Where the grant or refusal of an interim injunction would finally dispose of the action

11.82 This may occur either because, as a matter of law, there would be nothing left for the unsuccessful party's interest to proceed upon at trial, or looking at the commercial realities of the situation the court's decision to grant or refuse the injunction renders it uneconomic for the unsuccessful party to continue to prosecute or defend. In either event, the grant of the interim injunction could not properly be regarded as a 'holding operation' and thus this is a type of case which falls outside of the *American Cyanamid* guidelines.

11.83 This was expressly confirmed by Lord Diplock in *NWL Ltd v Woods*,[2] who went on to state that where this was the case:

> 'the degree of likelihood that the plaintiff would have succeeded in establishing his right to an injunction if the action had gone to trial, is a factor to be brought into the balance by the judge in weighing the risks that injustice may result from his deciding the application one way rather than the other.'[3]

---

1 *Morris v Redland Bricks Ltd* [1970] AC 652, HL at 665G per Lord Upjohn.
2 [1979] 1 WLR 1294 at 1306D.
3 Ibid, 1307B–C.

However, the required strength of the case on the merits has not been defined with any consistency by the courts. While some cases have required 'an overwhelming case on the merits',[1] others have demanded only some assessment of the merits which show them to be 'more than merely a serious issue to be tried'.[2] Once again, the best touchstone is the level of potential injustice that would result from grant or refusal. One can expect that where the grant or refusal of the interim injunction would finally dispose of the action, the higher the potential for injustice and the more concerned the courts will be about the merits of either party's case.

Mandatory interim injunctions

11.84 While the court has jurisdiction to grant a mandatory interim injunction, it is a very exceptional form of relief. This is because the requirement that a positive act should be done to repair some omission or to restore the prior position by undoing some wrongful act, whilst still a 'holding operation' is a draconian requirement that may well have severe practical and financial consequences, resulting in injustice.

11.85 Consequently, the courts have adopted a different approach to these forms of interim injunctions as can be seen from *Shepherd Homes Ltd v Sandham*.[3] This approach now finds its clearest expression in the judgment of Chadwick J in *Nottingham Building Society v Eurodynamics Systems*:[4]

> 'First, this being an interlocutory matter, the overriding consideration is which course is likely to involve the least risk of injustice if it turns out to be "wrong" in the sense described by Hoffmann J [ie granting an injunction to a party who fails to establish his right at the trial (or would fail if there was a trial) or alternatively, in failing to grant an injunction to a party who succeeds (or would succeed) at trial].
>
> Secondly, in considering whether to grant a mandatory injunction, the court must keep in mind that an order which requires a party to take some positive step at an interlocutory stage, may well carry a greater risk of injustice if it turns out to have been wrongly made than an order which merely prohibits action, thereby preserving the status quo.
>
> Thirdly, it is legitimate, where a mandatory injunction is sought, to consider whether the court does feel a high degree of assurance that the claimant will be able to establish his right at a trial. That is because the greater the degree of assurance the claimant will ultimately establish his right, the less will be the risk of injustice if the injunction is granted.
>
> But, finally, even where the court is unable to feel any high degree of assurance that the claimant will establish his right, there may still be circumstances in which it is appropriate to grant a mandatory injunction at an interlocutory stage. Those circumstances will exist where the risk of injustice if [the] injunction is refused sufficiently outweigh the risk of injustice if it is granted.'

---

1 As in *Cayne v Global Natural Resources Plc* [1984] 1 All ER 225 per Everleigh LJ.
2 *Lansing Linde Ltd v Kerr* [1991] 1 All ER 418, CA.
3 [1971] 1 Ch 340.
4 [1993] FSR 468 at 474.

For a case where the necessary 'high degree of assurance' was established, see *London and Manchester Assurance Co Ltd v O & H Construction Ltd and Another.*[1]

11.86 Although rare, mandatory interim injunctions have been granted to preserve, amongst other things, the claimant's rights to ancient lights. In both *Daniel v Ferguson*[2] and *Von Joel v Hornsey*,[3] the defendants were required to remove the section of building works, erected after service of a writ, which obstructed the ancient lights pending trial of the action. It should be noted that the inequitable conduct, displayed by both defendants in trying to rush through their building works and thus make service of the writ ineffective, was clearly a factor which influenced the court's decision. 'It is right that buildings thus run up should be pulled down at once, without regard to what the result of the trial may be.'[4]

11.87 The importance of equitable conduct on the part of both the claimant and defendant was expressly highlighted in relation to *quia timet* injunctions in the case of *Morris v Redland Bricks Ltd.*[5] However, the points made later apply equally to mandatory *quia timet* interim injunctions. It would seem, therefore, that given the court's reluctance to grant a mandatory interim injunction, there is little point in applying for one in all but the most extreme circumstances. However, the courts have on the occasion of determining whether to grant a final injunction referred to the plaintiff's failure to apply for an interim injunction as grounds for refusing the grant of the final injunction.[6]

Undertaking in damages

11.88 It is an almost invariable requirement of the grant of an interim injunction that the claimant gives an undertaking in damages, to safeguard the defendant if it subsequently transpires that the injunction should not have been granted.[7] The principles governing such undertakings were set out by Neill LJ in *Cheltenham and Gloucester Building Society v Ricketts*[8] as follows:

> 'From the authorities the following guidance can be extracted as to the enforcement of a cross-undertaking in damages.
>
> (1) Save in special cases an undertaking as to damages is the price which the person asking for an interlocutory injunction has to pay for its grant. The court cannot compel an applicant to give an undertaking but it can refuse to grant an injunction unless he does.

---

1 [1989] 2 EGLR 185.
2 [1891] 2 Ch 27.
3 [1895] 2 Ch 774.
4 *Daniel v Ferguson* [1891] 2 Ch 27 at 30 per Lindley LJ.
5 [1970] AC 652 – see especially 666.
6 *Blue Town Investments Ltd v Higgs and Hill PLC* [1990] 1 WLR 696. But see *Oxy Electric v Zainuddin* [1990] 2 All ER 902; *Snell & Prideaux Ltd v Dutton Mirrors Ltd* [1995] 1 EGLR 259, CA (Hoffmann LJ) and see **11.97–11.102**.
7 *Smith v Day* (1882) 21 ChD 421.
8 [1993] 4 All ER 276, CA at 281d–282f.

(2) The undertaking, though described as an undertaking as to damages, does not found any cause of action. It does, however, enable the party enjoined to apply to the court for compensation if it is subsequently established that the interlocutory injunction should not have been granted.

(3) The undertaking is not given to the party enjoined but to the court.

(4) In a case where it is determined that the injunction should not have been granted the undertaking is likely to be enforced, though the court retains a discretion not to do so.

(5) The time at which the court should determine whether or not the interlocutory injunction should have been granted will vary from case to case. It is important to underline the fact that the question whether the undertaking should be enforced is a separate question from the question whether the injunction should be discharged or continued.

(6) In many cases injunctions will remain in being until the trial and in such cases the property of its original grant and the question of the enforcement of the undertaking will not be considered before the conclusion of the trial. Even then, as Lloyd LJ pointed out in *Financiera Avenida v Shiblaq* [1990] CA Transcript 973 the court may occasionally wish to postpone the question of enforcement to a later date.

(7) Where an interlocutory injunction is discharged before the trial the court at the time of discharge is faced with a number of possibilities. (a) The court can determine forthwith that the undertaking as to damages should be enforced and can proceed at once to make an assessment of the damages. It seems probable that it will only be in rare cases that the court can take this course because the relevant evidence of damages is unlikely to be available. It is to be noted, however, that in *Columbia Pictures Industries Inc v Robinson* [1987] 3 All ER 338, [1987] Ch 38 Scott J was able, following the trial of an action, to make an immediate assessment of damages arising from the wrongful grant of an Anton Piller order. He pointed out that the evidence at the trial could not be relied on to justify ex post facto the making of an ex parte order if, at the time the order was made, it ought not to have been made (see [1987] 3 All ER 338 at 378, [1987] Ch 38 at 85). (b) The court may determine that the undertaking should be enforced but then direct an inquiry as to damages in which issues of causation and quantum will have to be considered. It is likely that the order will include directions as to pleadings and discovery in the inquiry. In the light of the decision of the Court of Appeal in *Norwest Holst Civil Engineering Ltd v Polysius Ltd* [1987] CA Transcript 644 the court should not order an inquiry as to damages and at the same time leave open for the tribunal at the inquiry to determine whether or not the undertaking should be enforced. A decision that the undertaking should be enforced is a precondition for the making of an order of an inquiry as to damages. (c) The court can adjourn the application for the enforcement of the undertaking to the trial or further order. (d) The court can determine forthwith that the undertaking is not to be enforced.

(8) It seems that damages are awarded on a similar basis to that on which damages are awarded for breach of contract. This matter has not been fully explored in the English cases though it is to be noted that in *Air Express Ltd v Ansett Transport Industries (Operations) Ltd* (1979) 146 CLR 249 Aicken J in the High Court of Australia expressed the view that it would be seldom that it would be just and equitable that the unsuccessful plaintiff "should bear the burden of damages which

> were not foreseeable from circumstances known to him at the time". This passage suggests that the court in exercising its equitable jurisdiction would adopt similar principles to those relevant in a claim for breach of contract.'

In practice, the consequences of an undertaking can be immense. Claimants need to consider carefully whether by obtaining interim relief they may expose themselves to onerous liabilities, particularly when the effort of such relief is to hold up construction of a large commercial building, resulting in loss of rent, contractor's standing time and financing costs, all of which would certainly support a claim on the undertaking. The dilemma is compounded by the court's adoption of a general practice that failure to apply for an interim injunction may well debar the claimant from obtaining a final injunction.[1] Clearly, an early assessment of the severity of the injury with expert advice is required. Recourse may also be had to the court's powers to order advance disclosure of documents.[2]

FINAL INJUNCTIONS

11.89 At trial, in deciding whether the appropriate remedy is damages or an injunction, the courts apply the following principles, laid down in *Shelfer v City of London Electric Light Company*,[3] a case in which the claim related to nuisance by noise and vibration, arising out of the operation of a steam-powered power station. AL Smith LJ said:[4]

> 'In my opinion, it may be stated as a good working rule that –
>
> (1) if the injury to the plaintiff's legal rights is small,
> (2) and is one which is capable of being estimated in money,
> (3) and is one which can be adequately compensated by a small money payment,
> (4) and the case is one in which it would be oppressive to the defendant to grant an injunction
>
> then damages in substitution for an injunction may be given.
>
> There may also be cases in which, though the four above-mentioned requirements exist, the defendant by his conduct, as, for instance, hurrying up his building so as if possible to avoid an injunction, or otherwise acting with a reckless disregard of the plaintiff's rights, has disentitled himself from asking that damages may be assessed in substitution for an injunction.
>
> It is impossible to lay down any rule as to what, under the differing circumstances of each case, constitutes either a small injury, or one that can be estimated in money, or what is a small money payment, or an adequate compensation, or what would be oppressive to the defendant. This must be left to the good sense of the Tribunal which deals with each case as it comes up for adjudication. For instance, an injury to the plaintiff's legal right to a window and a cottage represented by £15 might well be held not to be small but considerable; whereas a similar injury to a warehouse or

---

1 See **11.97–11.102**.
2 See CPR, r 31.16 and *Burrells Wharf Freeholds v Galliard Homes Ltd* [1999] CILL 1526.
3 [1895] 1 Ch 287.
4 [1895] 1 Ch 322–323.

other large building represented by ten times that amount might be held to be inconsiderable. Each case must be decided upon its own facts; but to escape the rule it must be brought within the exception. In the present case, it appears to me that the injury to the plaintiff is certainly not small, nor is it in my judgment capable of being estimated in money, or of being adequately compensated by a small money payment.'

11.90 This statement of the law has generally, been adopted in subsequent cases. In *Colls v Home and Colonial Stores*,[1] Lord Lindley referred to it with approval, citing it as a case in which it was explained that the general rule that where a legal right is continuously infringed an injunction to protect it ought to be granted was subject to qualification. The words of AL Smith LJ have frequently been quoted subsequently with approval, and applied.[2] However, other authoritative views have been expressed. These differ from those of AL Smith LJ in two respects, more of emphasis than substance. First, AL Smith LJ expressed himself in terms which suggests that unless the tests he laid down were satisfied, an injunction ought to be granted. However, in *Colls v Home and Colonial Stores*,[3] Lord MacNaghten took the view that the court should incline towards the grant of damages in lieu of an injunction unless there were specific factors pointing towards the grant of an injunction:

'In some cases, of course, an injunction is necessary – if, for instance, the injury cannot fairly be compensated by money – if the defendant has acted in a high-handed manner – if he has endeavoured to steal a march on the plaintiff or to evade the jurisdiction of the court. In all these cases an injunction is necessary, in order to do justice to the plaintiff and as a warning to others. But if there is really a question as to whether the obstruction is legal or not, and if the defendant has acted fairly and not in an unneighbourly spirit, I am disposed to think that the court ought to incline to damages rather than an injunction.'

11.91 In *Kine v Jolly*,[4] in which a mandatory injunction to remove part of a house was granted at first instance, but overturned on appeal, Vaughan-Williams LJ somewhat enigmatically stated:

'I propose to apply either the test laid down by Lord MacNaghten in *Colls v Home and Colonial Stores Ltd* or that laid down by A.L. Smith L.J. in his judgment in *Shelfer v. City of London Electric Lighting Company*.'[5]

He went on to hold that it was impossible to say that there ought to be any injunction upon the ground that the defendant has acted in a high-handed manner, or has shown a desire to steal a march on the plaintiff, or to evade the jurisdiction of the court. He stated that both parties had acted honestly in accordance with what they believed and not unreasonably. On the other hand,

1 [1904] AC 179.
2 *Slack v Leeds Industrial Co-operative Society* [1924] 2 Ch 475; *Price v Hilditch* [1930] 1 Ch 500; *Pugh v Howells* (1984) 48 P&CR 298; *Deakins v Hookings* [1994] 1 EGLR 190; *Jaggard v Sawyer* [1995] 2 All ER 189, CA; *Gooden v Ketley* [1996] EGCS 47, CA.
3 [1904] AC 179.
4 [1905] 1 Ch 480.
5 Ibid at 495.

Cozens-Hardy LJ thought that 'the tendency of the speeches in the House of Lords in *Colls v Home and Colonial Stores Ltd* is to go a little further than was done in *Shelfer v City of London Electric Lighting Co*' and that, as a general rule, the court ought to be less free in granting mandatory injunctions than it was previously.[1] The third member of the court, Romer LJ, delivered a dissenting judgment.

11.92 It is suggested that there is no difference between AL Smith LJ and Lord MacNaghten save one of emphasis. Both recognise that certain conduct of the defendant may lead to the court being more ready to grant a mandatory injunction, but Lord MacNaghten is in effect saying that unless such conduct is shown to have occurred the court would tend towards refusing an injunction, whereas AL Smith LJ would cast the burden on showing that an injunction should not be granted by reason of the defendant's conduct, on the defendant.

11.93 In *Fishenden v Higgs and Hill Ltd*,[2] the Court of Appeal expressed the view that the *Shelfer* case did not lay down rigid rules. Lord Hanworth MR said that the rules in the *Shelfer* case should be read together with the later cases of *Colls* and *Kine v Jolly*, and that the court should incline against an injunction if possible. Romer LJ took the view that AL Smith LJ did not intend to say and did not in fact say that in all cases where the conditions he laid down were not satisfied an injunction should be granted. Maugham LJ indicated disapproval of AL Smith LJ's 'good working rule'.

11.94 The *Shelfer* principles do not apply universally. In the case of restrictive covenants, the normal rule is that a plaintiff is entitled to an injunction. So in *Doherty v Allman*,[3] Lord Cairns LC observed of the remedy of injunction for a breach of a negative covenant that:[4]

> '... if there had been a negative covenant, I apprehend, according to well-settled practice, a Court of Equity would have had no discretion to exercise. If parties, for valuable consideration, with their eyes open, contract that a particular thing shall not be done, all that a Court of Equity has to do is to say, by way of injunction, that which the parties have already said by way of covenant, that the thing shall not be done; and in such case the injunction does nothing more than give the sanction of the process of the Court to that which already is the contract between the parties. It is not then a question of the balance of convenience or inconvenience, or of the amount of damage or of injury – it is the specific performance, by the Court, of that negative bargain which the parties have made, with their eyes open, between themselves.'

11.95 However, the court retains a discretion even in such cases to award damages in lieu of an injunction whether the breach is of a positive or negative stipulation.[5] Likewise, the *prima facie* remedy for a continuing trespass (or one which may take place at some future date) is an injunction. The availability of an

1 [1905] 1 Ch 480 at 504.
2 (1935) 153 LT 128.
3 (1878) 3 App Cas 709.
4 Ibid at 719–720.
5 *Chiska Ltd v Hammersmith and Fulham London Borough Council (No 2)* (1999) *The Independent*, 19 July.

injunction as a remedy in this situation was considered in *Patel v WH Smith (Eziot) Ltd*, by Balcombe LJ:[1]

> 'What, then, are the principles which a court should apply in a case of this type? It seems to me that, first, prima facie a landowner, whose title is not in issue, is entitled to an injunction to restrain trespass on his land whether or not the trespass harms him. In support of that proposition there are two comparatively recent cases at first instance. The first is *Woollerton and Wilson Ltd v Richard Costain Ltd*, which was a reserved judgment of Stamp J ...[2] Stamp J. said:
>
> > "It is in my judgment well established that it is no answer to a claim for an injunction to restrain a trespass that the trespass does no harm to the plaintiff. Indeed, the very fact that no harm is done is a reason for rather than against the granting of an injunction: for if there is no damage done the damage recovered in the action will be nominal and if the injunction is refused the result will be no more nor less than a licence to continue the tort of trespass in return for a nominal payment."
>
> To the like effect is the decision, also at first instance, of Walton J. in *John Trenberth Ltd v National Westminster Bank Ltd*[3] and I cite a short passage from the judgment, where the judge accepted a submission by counsel for the plaintiff:
>
> > "when one is dealing with the direct physical invasion of a right of property by a trespass one is very close to the line of cases stemming from *Doherty v Allman* which decide that an injunction to enforce a negative stipulation in a contract goes almost as of course.[4] The parties, having agreed that something shall not be done, the court simply says that what the parties have agreed shall not be done." '

However, the courts have more recently relaxed this approach.[5] The court is more disposed to grant a prohibitory than a mandatory injunction, although the reluctance to grant an injunction of the latter kind is less marked than at the interim stage since all the facts will be known, hence the risk of injustice inherent in the grant of a mandatory injunction will not be present.

11.96 Thus in *Redland Bricks Ltd v Morris*,[6] the plaintiff complained of the defendant's excavation on neighbouring land which had rendered the plaintiff's land unstable. The cost of restoring the support to the plaintiff's land was £30,000, and the value of that land £12,000. The House of Lords held that an injunction ought not to be granted against the defendant requiring it to carry out works of this extent, although the judge would have been justified in imposing on the defendants an obligation to do some reasonable and not too expensive works which might have a reasonable chance of preventing further damage. Lord Upjohn said:[7]

---

1 [1987] 1 WLR 853, 858–859, CA. See also *Harrow London Borough Council v Donohue* [1993] NPC 49, CA.
2 [1970] 1 WLR 411, 413.
3 (1979) 39 P&CR 104, 108.
4 (1878) 3 App Cas 709, CA.
5 See **11.100** and case cited there.
6 [1970] AC 652.
7 Ibid.

'1. A mandatory injunction can only be granted where the plaintiff shows a very strong probability on the facts that grave damage will accrue to him in the future ... It is a jurisdiction to be exercised sparingly and with caution, but in the proper case, unhesitatingly.

2. Damages will not be a sufficient or adequate remedy if such damage does happen ...

3. Unlike the case where a negative injunction is granted to prevent the continuance or recurrence of a wrongful act the question of the cost to the defendant to do works to prevent or lessen the likelihood of a future apprehended wrong must be an element to be taken into account: (a) where the defendant has acted without regard to his neighbour's rights, or has tried to steal a march on him or has tried to evade the jurisdiction of the court or to sum it up, has acted wantonly and quite unreasonably in relation to his neighbour he may be ordered to repair his wanton and unreasonable acts by doing positive work to restore the status quo even if the expense to him is out of all proportion to the advantage thereby accruing to the plaintiff ... (b) but where the defendant has acted reasonably, although in the event wrongly, the cost of remedying by positive action his earlier activities is most important for two reasons. First, because no legal wrong has yet occurred (for which he has not been recompensed at law and in equity) and, in spite of gloomy expert opinion, may never occur or possibly only on a much smaller scale than anticipated. Secondly, because if ultimately heavy damage does occur the plaintiff is in no way prejudiced by his action at law and all his consequential remedies in equity.'

11.97 In the context of rights to light, the issues as to the grant or refusal of an injunction at trial will be as follows.

(1) If the claimant has applied for and obtained an interim injunction restraining the infringing development, should a final injunction to this same effect be granted?
(2) If the claimant has either not applied for, or been refused such an interim injunction, should a mandatory injunction to order the removal of the infringing development be granted?

11.98 The answers to these questions vary from case to case. The court's discretion is wide. If the *Shelfer* guidelines are satisfied, an injunction will be refused. But there are a wide variety of circumstances to be considered. The most important factors are:

(1) the extent of the injury to the claimant;
(2) whether there has been an interim injunction applied for or granted;
(3) the defendant's conduct.

The decisions exhibit a general reluctance to order completed buildings to be pulled down. So, in *Wrotham Park Estate Co Ltd v Parkside Homes Ltd*,[1] a mandatory injunction was sought to secure the demolition of houses constructed

1 [1974] 1 WLR 798.

in breach of a restrictive covenant. The court refused to grant a mandatory injunction, Brightman J saying:[1]

> 'It would in my opinion be an unpardonable waste of much needed houses to direct that they now be pulled down ... no damage of a financial nature has been done to the plaintiffs by the breach of the layout stipulation. The plaintiff's use of the Wrotham Park Estate has not been and will not be impeded. It is totally unnecessary to demolish the houses in order to preserve the integrity of the restrictive covenants imposed on the rest of area 14.'

11.99 In *Bracewell v Appleby*,[2] when both the first and second factors came into play the issue arose as to whether a mandatory injunction should be granted preventing future use of a right of way which the defendant had wrongfully used for access to a new house, which had not been fully constructed at the date the plaintiff's rights were asserted, but which was completed and inhabited at the date of trial. The court refused an injunction on the ground that it would have the effect of rendering the house uninhabitable. The plaintiff had not sought an injunction until the house was actually constructed. In *Jaggard v Sawyer*,[3] another case involving the construction of a house in breach of a restrictive covenant, the court refused a mandatory injunction to remove the house, and awarded damages in lieu. The court held that the injury to the plaintiff's rights was small, that it could be adequately compensated by a small money payment, and that it would be oppressive to the defendant to grant an injunction. It was relevant also that the plaintiff had not sought an interim injunction, and that the defendants had not acted in blatant and calculated disregard of the plaintiff's rights.

11.100 The general reluctance of the court to grant a mandatory injunction which would prevent the continued use of newly constructed buildings is strikingly illustrated in *Gooden v Ketley*,[4] a case of trespass by building works. The plaintiff sought the removal of a manhole, drains and wall, constructed when the defendant built three blocks of flats on his land and, it was alleged and found, constituted trespass on the plaintiff's land. It was held that a mandatory injunction should be refused, on the ground that the case was one where the injury to the plaintiff's legal right was small, it was capable of being estimated in money, and could adequately be compensated by a small money payment. Further, the case was one in which it would be oppressive to the defendant to grant an injunction. The court further held that in considering oppression, there was a range of cases to be considered, at one end of which the defendant might have acted openly and in good faith and in ignorance of the plaintiff's rights, and at the other end in full knowledge that he was invading the plaintiff's rights and hoping to present the plaintiff with a fait accompli. In the instant case, whilst the defendant had acted deliberately, it was not an appropriate one for the grant of an injunction, although an award of aggravated damages was upheld. This case

1 [1974] 1 WLR 811B.
2 [1975] 1 Ch 408.
3 [1995] 2 All ER 189, CA.
4 [1996] EGCS 47.

seems to extend the ambit of the court's discretion to refuse a mandatory injunction in the case of trespass considerably from that which underlies the authorities considered at **11.95**. This seems to be in line with the more relaxed approach recently apparent in relation to injunctions to restrain breaches of covenant, discussed at **11.94**.

11.101 In *Snell & Prideaux Ltd v Dutton Mirrors Ltd*,[1] again the basis for refusal of a mandatory injunction to remove an obstruction to a right of way was related to the failure by the plaintiff to seek an interim injunction despite being given an opportunity to do so, before the offending building works were carried out. The court took into account that the defendants were acting in good faith, and the fact that the plaintiffs had an alternative access to their building from the front, and had made virtually no use of the right of way obstructed for many years.

11.102 In *Gafford v Graham*,[2] a case of building in breach of a restrictive covenant, an injunction to have the offending structure removed was refused both on the ground of hardship and on the ground that the owner of the dominant tenement had with full knowledge of his rights, omitted to seek an interim injunction, even though the defendant's conduct had shown blatant and calculated disregard for the plaintiff's rights. The plaintiff's willingness to accept compensation was also relevant. Indeed, in the earlier case of *Blue Town Investments v Higgs & Hill*,[3] it was held that these factors were decisive. Although in *Oxy Electric v Zainuddin*[4] Hoffmann J criticised the *Blue Town* decision, he explained his criticism when giving judgment in *Snell & Prideaux Ltd v Dutton Mirrors Ltd*[5] in the following terms:

> 'Finally on the remedy, I should mention that Mr West, in submitting that his client should be granted a mandatory injunction, relied upon a decision of my own in *Oxy Electric Ltd v Zainuddin* [1991] 1 WLR 115 as support for the proposition that the fact that the plaintiffs did not apply for an interlocutory injunction was immaterial to whether they should be granted a final one at the trial. That case goes no further than deciding that failure to apply for an interlocutory injunction is not a reason for striking out the action as frivolous and vexatious. It by no means follows that it is not a matter to which regard may be had in deciding whether a final injunction should be granted. In this case, it was quite clear that delaying the commencement of the works on the defendants' land until this action had been determined was going to involve a risk of financial loss to the defendant. The question was, who should bear the risk of that financial loss if their claim turned out to be wrong? The defendants offered the plaintiffs the opportunity of preserving the status quo on condition that they were willing to give a cross-undertaking which would impose that risk upon them. That the plaintiffs declined to do. In those circumstances, the defendants, being advised that they had an arguable case, went ahead and averted the loss by going forward with the building. In my judgment, that was not an unreasonable thing for them to

1 [1995] 1 EGLR 259.
2 (1998) 77 P&CR 73.
3 [1990] 2 All ER 897.
4 [1990] 2 All ER 902.
5 [1995] 1 EGLR 259.

> do. In those circumstances, I think it would be quite wrong to penalise them by ordering their building to be torn down.'

11.103 In two earlier cases, mandatory injunctions were refused. In *Kine v Jolly*,[1] an injunction to have a building infringing a right to light pulled down was refused. The court treated the case as one where there had been no sharp practice or unfair conduct on the part of the defendant, and where the damage had not been irremediable, and where damages would be adequate compensation.

11.104 In *National Provincial Plate Glass Insurance Co v Prudential Assurance Company*,[2] a mandatory injunction was refused on the grounds that the infringing building would not seriously affect the occupation of the plaintiff's house, and that the injury done to the plaintiffs was done by an integral part of a very important building scheme, and that a portion of that scheme actually benefited the plaintiff.

11.105 On the other hand, in other cases the court has been prepared to grant a mandatory injunction at trial to compel the removal of the infringing building. In *Smith v Smith*,[3] the plaintiff raised a wall from 9 foot 6 inches to 26 foot 8 inches about 8 feet from the plaintiff's windows, despite protests by the plaintiff. The plaintiff claimed that the erection of the wall had darkened his rooms, especially the kitchen and scullery, and his workshop which was rendered useless for the work of a cabinet maker and upholsterer. He adduced evidence that the rooms facing the party wall were so darkened that they could scarcely be used except by artificial light; that the workshop was rendered almost useless for its purpose; that the house had become almost uninhabitable; that the health of some of the inmates had been affected and the plaintiff's wife and children had been obliged to leave. The main defence was delay and acquiescence. The court dismissed the defence. Sir George Jessell MR said:

> 'Without laying down any absolute rule, in the first place it is of great importance to see if the defendant knew he was doing wrong, and was taking his chance about being disturbed in doing it.
>
> The next point for consideration is the materiality of the injury to the plaintiff ... but that alone was not sufficient; all the circumstances of the case must be taken into consideration, not only the injury to the plaintiff but also the amount which has been laid out by the defendant.
>
> In the present case the injury was most serious to the plaintiff, and he could not be compensated without the defendant buying the house, also as regards the defendant I am not satisfied that any considerable sum has been laid out upon his building. Again the plaintiff was occupier of the house, so that it was a personal injury to him ...'

Interestingly, the order of the court provided that if there was a dispute as to whether the defendant had pulled down a sufficient extent of the wall, it was to be referred to a named surveyor.

---

1 [1905] 1 Ch 480.
2 (1877) 6 ChD 757.
3 (1875) LR 20 Eq 500.

11.106 In *Pugh v Howells*,[1] the defendants built a two-storey extension to their house, next door to the plaintiff's house, thereby affecting the light to the plaintiffs' kitchen. When the plaintiffs observed that the defendants were carrying out work their solicitors wrote to the defendants' solicitors asking them to disclose any plans. The reply was unhelpful and the defendants completed the extension to roof level over a bank holiday weekend. The court of first instance refused an injunction, and awarded the plaintiffs £500 damages in lieu. The Court of Appeal granted a mandatory injunction for removal of that part of the extension above ground floor level, on the ground, first, that the defendants' conduct, in proceeding in the teeth of complaints by the plaintiffs and advice from their own expert was such as to merit serious criticism. Further, that it was not possible to say that the injury to the plaintiffs' rights was insignificant. Similarly, in *Cudmore-Ray v Pajouheshnia*,[2] a mandatory injunction was granted when the defendant had hurried up the building works and acted with reckless disregard for the plaintiff's rights.

11.107 In *Deakins v Hookings*,[3] another case concerning an extension to a property which affected the plaintiff's house in which she lived, a mandatory injunction was granted on the ground that the injury to the plaintiff was significant, since the rooms affected formed part of her house.

11.108 The position may be summarised as follows.

(1) The court will almost never grant a mandatory injunction at the interim stage, before the rights of the parties have been finally determined.
(2) The court will grant a mandatory injunction at the stage of trial only with reluctance. Material factors in deciding whether to grant a mandatory injunction (as opposed to damages) are:
   (i) the extent of the injury to the claimant's premises;
   (ii) the extent of the personal effect on the claimant and other occupiers of the loss of light;
   (iii) the social utility of the defendant's development which infringes the light;[4]
   (iv) the cost to the defendant of removing the offending building;
   (v) whether the claimant applied for an interim injunction before the offending building was in place, to restrain further work;
   (vi) the degree of blameworthiness on the part of the defendant, including:
      (a) whether the defendant was acting innocently, in ignorance of the claimant's rights, or was indifferent as to whether such rights were being breached or not;
      (b) whether the defendant disregarded protests by the claimant before work started, or during work;

1 (1984) 48 P&CR 298, CA.
2 [1993] CLY 4040.
3 [1994] 1 EGLR 190.
4 See also in this context *Greenwich NHS Trust v London & Quadrant Housing Trust* [1998] 3 All ER 437 and **11.133**.

(c) whether the defendant showed a deliberate intention to flout the claimant's rights by hurrying on work so as to create a fait accompli;
(d) whether the defendant received and, if so, ignored expert advice that what he was doing would infringe the claimant's rights.

Choice between equitable damages and prohibitory or mandatory injunctive relief

11.109 It might seem at first as though the grant of a prohibitory injunction was, in principle, far less objectionable than a mandatory injunction since the defendant is not required to take any positive steps, and hence it can be argued that a prohibitory injunction in perpetuity, to protect the claimant's rights, is of little disadvantage. But consideration will show that this is not always so. If, for example, the defendant has suspended building works in response to demands by the claimant, or indeed in compliance with an interim injunction, his situation may, in practice, be unenviable. Apart from the costs of suspending work (already discussed in relation to undertakings in damages in connection with interim injunctions),[1] the future inability to complete the building except by omitting some infringing portion thereof may, in practice, pose great difficulties. In modern office buildings, plant rooms, and tenure farms, air-conditioning units are frequently located at high level, ie those parts of the building most likely to be the subject of complaint by a plaintiff. Omitting them may pose grave difficulties in enabling the building to function. The committed part may be structurally important, and there is the question of compliance with building regulations to be considered. Finally, it may be necessary for a revised planning permission to be obtained in order to authorise the building in the form it will finally take, if a prohibitory injunction is granted. Of course, in the case of minor residential extension many of these considerations will not apply, but it is necessary to bear them in mind when consideration is given to the grant of even a prohibitory injunction at trial, as opposed to a mandatory injunction.

11.110 An important factor is the court's power to award damages in lieu of an injunction. This is now enshrined in s 50 of the Supreme Court Act 1981:

> 'Where the Court of Appeal or the High Court has jurisdiction to entertain an application for an injunction or specific performance, it may award damages in addition to, or in substitution for, an injunction or specific performance.'

This provision was originally contained in the Chancery Amendment Act 1858, s 2 ('Lord Cairns' Act'). The original wording of s 2 of the 1858 Act was as follows:

> 'In all cases in which the Court of Chancery has jurisdiction to entertain an application for an injunction against any breach of any covenant, contract or agreement, or against the commission or continuance of any wrongful act, or for the

1 See **11.88**.

specific performance of any covenant, contract, or agreement, it shall be lawful for the same court, if it shall think fit, to award damages to the party injured either in addition to or in substitution for such injunction or specific performance, and such damages may be assessed in such a manner as the court shall direct.'[1]

11.111 Under Lord Cairns' Act, the Court of Chancery was given a discretion whether to award damages in lieu of an injunction. But the effect of refusing an injunction would of course, in practice, enable the defendant to carry on with the wrongful act. Therefore, equitable damages are assessed on the basis that they compensate the claimant not only for the wrong he has suffered up to the date of trial, but also for the fact that he will, in practice, be losing his rights in perpetuity.[2]

11.112 The distinction between prohibitory and mandatory injunctions, so important at the interim stage, is as already noted of less significance at trial, although the courts have historically shown considerable reluctance to order the removal of permanent building works on a substantial scale. This underlines the importance to a claimant of seeking interim prohibitory relief at the earliest possible moment. In some cases, the effect of a prohibitory injunction may be just as drastic as a mandatory one. This is particularly the case if the building is part completed, since refusal of permission for completion may make it impossible, for various technical reasons, for the building to be occupied and used. This is apart from problems with obtaining revised planning permission and Building Regulation consent for the truncated version which will result from the grant of a prohibitory injunction.

11.113 The terms of an injunction are a matter of the court's discretion. In the drafting of an injunction, it must be remembered that the remedies for breach of the terms of an injunction are by way of sequestration and committal for contempt of court. It is therefore important that the order clearly sets out what the defendant is required to abstain from doing, or to do. In the case of a prohibitory injunction, the injunction ought to make it clear what the defendant is prohibited from doing. In the case of a prohibitory injunction, it was said by Lord MacNaghten in the *Colls* case,[3] that the order should be in general terms restraining the defendant from erecting any building so as to cause a nuisance or illegal obstruction to the plaintiff's ancient windows. He also suggested that if the Act came to trial before the defendant's building was completed, there should be liberty to the plaintiff to apply for a further mandatory injunction or damages within a fixed time after the building was completed. This was intended to meet the case, presumably, where it is not clear whether the building as completed will constitute an actionable interference. Examination of orders made in decided

---

1 For the subsequent history of the provision, see *Leeds Industrial Co-operative Society Ltd v Slack* [1924] AC 851 at 861–862. The county courts have concurrent jurisdiction to award injunctions, specific performance, and damages in lieu thereof (County Courts Act 1984, s 38).

2 See **11.115–11.127**. And see Jolowicz 'Damages in Equity – A Study of Lord Cairns' Act' [1975] CLJ 224.

3 [1904] AC 179 at 194.

cases show that these suggestions have been followed.[1] Modification of the standard form may be required to take account of those parts of a proposed new building which are uncontroversial. Alternatively, it may be in some cases appropriate to define the outline of the building which is permitted.

11.114 In the case of mandatory injunctions, the court will generally refuse to grant an injunction in terms which require constant supervision by the court.[2] It is therefore important to define precisely the extent of the defendant's obligations. One possible solution in the case of uncertainty is for the order to provide for reference to a surveyor or other expert.[3] Alternatively, the order may be framed by reference to a plan showing the area to be demolished. It may be appropriate to suspend the operation of an injunction for a reasonable period to avoid hardship to the defendant or occupiers of the building, and the time for compliance should be specified in the order, and should be reasonable having regard to all the circumstances, including the need to arrange contractors, obtain statutory permissions etc. It would be highly unusual for the operation of an injunction not to be suspended pending appeal. Normally, this is done by inserting in the order a provision that provided a notice of appeal is entered within a certain time the operation of the injunction is to be suspended until final determination of the appeal.

THE AWARD OF DAMAGES UNDER THE COURT'S EQUITABLE JURISDICTION

11.115 Such damages are awarded in addition to or in lieu of injunctions, under powers originally conferred by the Chancery Amendment Act 1858, s 2, known as Lord Cairns' Act.[4] They can be awarded only where the claimant is entitled to claim an injunction. It is clear that the date at which the claimant must establish his entitlement to an injunction is the date of commencement of the proceedings. In *Holland v Worley*,[5] Pearson J, having read s 2 of the Chancery Amendment Act 1858, said:

> 'It only arises when the Court of Chancery has jurisdiction to grant an injunction. It can only apply to those cases in which the court could have granted an injunction, at all events at the time of the filing of the Bill.'

That this is the position has been confirmed in *Jaggard v Sawyer*:[6]

> '(4) The power to award damages under Lord Cairns' Act arises whenever the court "has jurisdiction to entertain an application" for an injunction or specific performance. This question must be determined as at the date of the writ. If the

1 See, eg, *Higgins v Betts* [1905] 2 Ch 210 at 218; *Andrews v Waite* [1907] 2 Ch 500 at 510–511.
2 *Co-op Insurance Society Ltd v Argyll Stores (Holdings) Ltd* [1997] 3 All ER 297, HL.
3 As in *Smith v Smith* (1875) LR 20 Eq 500 at 505.
4 See **11.110**.
5 (1884) 26 ChD 578.
6 [1995] 2 All ER 189, where Millett LJ said (at p 205d).

court would then have had jurisdiction to grant an injunction, it has jurisdiction to award damages instead. When the court comes to consider whether to grant an injunction or award damages instead, of course, it must do so by reference to the circumstances as they exist at the date of the hearing.

(5) The former question is effectively one of jurisdiction. The question is whether, at the date of the writ, the court *could* have granted an injunction, not whether it *would* have done (see *City of London Brewery Co v Tennant* (1873) LR 9 Ch App 212). Russell LJ put it neatly in *Hopper v Rogers* [1974] 3 All ER 417 at 419, [1975] Ch 43 at 48, when he said that the question was "whether ... the judge could have (however unwisely ...) made a mandatory order". There have been numerous cases where damages under Lord Cairns' Act were refused because at the date of the writ it was impossible to grant an injunction or specific performance: for one well-known example, see *Lavery v Pursell* (1888) 39 Ch D 508. The recent case of *Surrey CC v Bredero Homes Ltd* [1993] 3 All ER 705, [1993] 1 WLR 1361 appears to have been a case of this character.'

11.116 An example of the application of this rule is provided by *Fritz v Hobson*.[1] Equitable damages were granted notwithstanding that subsequent to the commencement of proceedings the nuisance in question had been abated. The plaintiff's failure to apply for or obtain an interim injunction, which might otherwise be held to be a factor which would prevent him being awarded an injunction at trial, is not a bar to his claiming equitable damages as such.

11.117 In *Surrey County Council v Bredero Homes Ltd*,[2] the defendant developed a housing estate more intensively than permitted by restrictive covenants in the transfers to it. The plaintiff covenantees took no steps to restrain this development by way of claim for an injunction or specific performance. After the defendant had disposed of all the houses, the covenantees commenced claims for damages, based on a sum equal to the payment that might have been extracted from the defendant in return for agreed modifications to the covenants so as to authorise the more profitable development which had in fact been carried out. It was held that the plaintiffs were entitled only to nominal damages, since by the time the action had commenced there was no prospect of the plaintiffs being awarded equitable relief. Clearly, if the claimant at the time he started proceedings is no longer the dominant owner at the time those proceedings are commenced, he could not have any prospect of claiming any relief apart from damages for the loss of business and discomfort he suffered from the infringement of light whilst he was in occupation. Equally, if the right to light arose under a deed, and the defendant is not at the date of the proceedings the owner of the servient land, there would be no prospect of an injunction, and hence no claim except to common law damages. Where the claimant claims a *quia timet* injunction, there is jurisdiction to award equitable damages, but such damages will be awarded solely in respect of the damage to be sustained in the future by injuries which the injunction, if granted, would have prevented.[3]

---

1 (1880) 14 ChD 542.

2 [1993] 3 All ER 705, CA.

3 *Leeds Industrial Co-operative Society v Slack* [1924] AC 851.

11.118 Equitable damages are to compensate the plaintiff for all loss, past and prospective.[1] Past loss would cover matters which would form the subject of a claim at common law, for example discomfort and injury to business. In the case of trespasses, a defendant can be ordered to pay daily damages representing the value to the defendant of the wrongful use.[2] But where as in the case of infringement of light, the infringement is permanent, the better view seems to be that the court, if it refuses an injunction, will award global damages for both past loss and prospective loss, without differentiation.

11.119 The method of calculation of damages, where an injunction has not been granted, was summarised by Millett LJ in *Jaggard v Sawyer*:[3]

> 'Prima facie the measure of damages in either case for breach of a covenant not to build a house on neighbouring land is the diminution in the value of the plaintiff's land occasioned by the breach. One element in the value of the plaintiff's land immediately before the breach is attributable to his ability to obtain an injunction to prevent the building. Clearly a defendant who wished to build would pay for the release of the covenant, but only so long as the court could still protect it by the grant of an injunction. The proviso is important. It is the ability to claim an injunction which gives the benefit of the covenant much of its value. If the plaintiff delays proceedings until it is no longer possible for him to obtain an injunction, he destroys his own bargaining position and devalues his right. The unavailability of the remedy of injunction at one and the same time deprives the court of jurisdiction to award damages under the Act and removes the basis for awarding substantial damages at common law. For this reason, I take the view that damages can be awarded at common law in accordance with the approach adopted in *Wrotham Park*, but in practice only in the circumstances in which they could also be awarded under the Act.'

11.120 The actual method of calculation was described thus by Sir Thomas Bingham MR:

> '[The trial judge] valued the right at what a reasonable seller would sell it for. In situations of this kind a plaintiff should not be treated as eager to sell, which he very probably is not. But the court will not value the right at the ransom price which a very reluctant plaintiff might put on it. I see no error in the judge's approach to this aspect.'

The approach in *Jaggard v Sawyer* has subsequently received support from the Court of Appeal decision in *Gafford v Graham*.[4]

11.121 Damages, therefore, fall to be assessed by reference to the amount which the dominant owner could reasonably have expected to receive for their release, discounting any ransom element. The same approach had been adopted in *Bracewell v Appleby*,[5] a case relating to a right of way where Graham J. said:

---

1 *Fritz v Hobson* (1880) 14 ChD 542.
2 *Whitwham v Westminster Brymbo Coal Company* [1896] 2 Ch 538.
3 [1995] 2 All ER 189 at 196–197, CA.
4 (1998) 77 P&CR 73.
5 [1975] 1 All ER 993.

> '... I think that for the purpose of estimating damages they [i.e. the Plaintiffs] and the other servient owners in Hill Road, albeit reluctant, must be treated as being willing to accept a fair price for the right of way in question and must not be treated as if they were in the extremely powerful bargaining position which an interlocutory injunction would have given them if it had been obtained before the Defendant started operations and incurred expense.'

11.122 The decided cases give relatively limited guidance as to the amount of awards. The most usual starting point is to consider the profit which the defendant has made as a result of the wrongful act, and make an award which reflects a part of this profit, on the ground that the defendant would notionally have been prepared to give up some profit element in order to secure his objective. In *Bracewell v Appleby*, the defendant had built a house on a plot of land. Access to the house could be gained only down a private road, but the defendant had no right to use the private road for such purposes. The court assessed the likely net value of the house at £5,000. The defendant was not a professional developer, and had built the house for his own occupation. The court concluded that he would have been prepared to pay a substantial sum for the privilege of doing so, and awarded damages of £2,000. In *Wrotham Park Estate Co Limited v Parkside Homes Limited*,[1] a case concerning a breach of a restrictive covenant by the construction of a house, the sum awarded amounted to approximately 5 per cent of the benefit obtained by the defendant. In *Jaggard v Sawyer*, the basis of the calculations is not apparent from the report.

11.123 The starting point is sometimes the one-third figure which, in the compulsory purchase case of *Stokes v Cambridge Corporation*,[2] was applied to assess the percentage of the developer's profit which the holder of a ransom strip would seek as a condition of releasing the strip. The analogy is not perfect, because in the *Stokes* case it was assumed that an inducement to the holder of the ransom strip would be that its own land would benefit from the development, which can seldom be the case in a rights to light situation. It is in any event difficult to apply the principle where the infringing development is of no direct financial benefit to the defendant, for example if it is part of his residence, or where indeed the infringing development actually involves the defendant incurring a loss.

11.124 A further point is that, in rights to light cases, it is seldom that the true comparison is between the defendant's site undeveloped and developed, as opposed to a comparison between the defendant's site with the existing building, and with a reduced or reconfigured building so as to avoid infringing the claimant's right. Defendants not infrequently argue that had the claimant proved unreasonable in negotiations, it would have been open to them to redesign their building so as to avoid infringing the light, without any loss of floorspace or architectural charm, and hence the amount that the claimant should be looking for is minimal.

---

1 [1974] 2 All ER 321.
2 (1961) 13 P&CR 77.

11.125 The court, in assessing the damages, will generally be assisted by expert valuation evidence, directed to the question of the benefit achieved by the defendant as a result of the infringement.[1] An alternative approach to calculation of such damages but using the same principle was adopted in *Carr-Saunders v Dick McNeil Associates Limited*.[2] Millett J awarded damages for obstruction to light on the same general principles but calculated them differently. He said:[3]

> 'I am entitled to take into account not only the loss of light and the loss of amenity generally, due to such factors as loss of sky visibility, the impression that the building at the rear is now closer than it was (though that is an optical illusion), the loss of sunlight and other such matters, in short, the general deteriorating quality of the environment. Also I have to bear in mind the fact that in any negotiations between the Plaintiff and the Defendants the Plaintiff would certainly not be satisfied with the £3,000 which Mr Anstey considers appropriate. He would have a bargaining position because, unless he were bought out, the Defendants would be inhibited in their development. In *Wrotham Park Estate Co. Limited v. Parkside Homes Limited* this approach was applied to the award of damages for breach of restrictive covenant; and in *Bracewell v. Appleby* it was applied to damages for obstruction to a right of way. In my judgment the same approach ought to be adopted where damages are awarded, in lieu of a mandatory injunction, for the interruption of the right to light to ancient windows ...
>
> Accordingly I am entitled to take account of the servient owner's bargaining position and the amount of profit which the Defendants would look to in the development of their site. I have no evidence of the amount of profit which the Defendants are expected to make from their development ... but I have evidence of the general loss of amenity. To that extent, it seems to me that the Court is entitled to approach the question on the basis that damages are awarded in lieu of an injunction, and not merely in compensation for the loss of the actual legal right. If the mandatory injunction had been granted, the building would have been pulled down and the Plaintiff would have been restored not only to its direct light, but also to sky visibility, a pleasant view of brickwork and a sloping roof, sunlight and so on.
>
> I have little material to guide me, except the £3,000 or thereabouts must be the absolute minimum figure. Doing the best I can and taking into account, I hope, all of the considerations which have been pressed on me by both sides, of the evidence that I have heard and, indeed, of my own view, I award general damages of £8,000.'

11.126 The importance of this case is that:

(1) damages were assessed by reference to what was in effect a multiplier of the actual loss, rather than by reference to a percentage of the profit that the defendant made;
(2) damages were assessed by reference to loss of amenity, as well as to financial loss.

It is not entirely clear whether Millett J was treating the plaintiff as entitled to have his damages assessed as including a ransom element. If so, the decision

1 See, eg, *Gafford v Graham* (1998) 77 P&CR 73.
2 [1986] 2 All ER 888
3 Ibid at 896b.

would be inconsistent with *Bracewell v Appleby*, and Millett J's own later judgment in *Jaggard v Sawyer* (where, however, *Carr-Saunders v Dick McNeil Associates* was not cited). Given the judge's citation of *Bracewell v Appleby*, it seems unlikely that he intended to adopt a different approach, however. On this basis, *Carr-Saunders* can be regarded as simply another approach to the assessment of damages in the way pointed by earlier cases, and approved in *Jaggard v Sawyer*.

11.127 These are not the only possible methods of calculating equitable damages. In *Gafford v Graham*,[1] an award was made based on the diminution in value of the plaintiff's property, on the basis that this would have been reflected in the sum which might reasonably have been demanded as a quid pro quo for relaxing the covenant. In *Marine and General Mutual Life Society v St James Real Estate Co Ltd*,[2] the court had regard to a settlement of a claim between the defendant and a neighbouring dominant owner.

THE CROWN

11.128 No injunction (final or interim) can be granted in general against the Crown,[3] save in prerogative proceedings (including judicial review).[4] This applies to emanations of the Crown, importantly (for present purposes) the Crown Estates Commissioners.[5]

11.129 Crown immunity does not extend to bodies created by statute (eg local authorities). However, it is established that where the legislative has entrusted a statutory body with functions to be discharged in the public interest, and has given that body power to acquire and hold land for the purpose of discharging that function, private easements affecting the land will not be enforced by injunction or damages. The aggrieved party's remedy lies exclusively in a claim under compulsory purchase legislation.[6] For compulsory purchase and extinguishment under statutory powers, see **8.7**.

DECLARATORY RELIEF

11.130 The court has power at trial to declare the respective rights of the parties. Declaratory relief may be appropriate where it is important to establish the parties' rights for the future. Examples would include:

---

1 (1998) 77 P&CR 73.
2 [1991] 2 EGLR 178.
3 See *Halsbury's Laws* 4th edn, vol 24 (reissue), para 824.
4 See Supreme Court Act 1981, s 31 and *M v Home Office* [1993] 3 All ER 537, HL.
5 For the position of the Crown Estate see *Halsbury's Laws* 4th edn, vol 12(1) (reissue), paras 278ff.
6 *Brown and Others v Heathlands Mental Health NHS Trust* [1996] 1 All ER 133.

(1) where disputed questions relating to a rights to light deed have been resolved;
(2) where disputed questions as to the rights enjoyed by one party under an agreement, or by virtue of an easement, have been resolved;
(3) where disputed questions as to whether such rights have been lost by abandonment or delay have been resolved.[1]

More generally, it is often prudent to include a claim for declaratory relief where the primary issues relate to damages and an injunction, so as to establish the entitlement to light in the future.

11.131 Historically, the general power to grant declarations was reserved to the Courts of Equity, having first been conferred by the Court of Chancery Act 1850, s 14. Until 1883, courts would only grant declarations ancillary to claims for other relief, but it has since then been possible to claim a declaration as a free-standing remedy.[2] However, the jurisdiction of the court will be exercised in general only in relation to legal rights, subsisting in future, of the parties represented in the litigation. Further, those whose rights are not affected have no locus standi to seek a declaration.[3]

11.132 A further limitation is that the court will not grant a declaration in relation to rights which may arise in the future, but which depend on a contingency which may or may not happen and are to that extent hypothetical. However, where the right depends on a contingency which is practically certain to occur, the right is for the purposes of declaratory relief regarded as a future right and not hypothetical.[4] Further, the court will not grant a declaration if its effect would be to open the floodgate to numerous similar claims, for example as to whether a party is entitled to terminate a contract.[5]

11.133 There was formerly believed to be a rule that the court would not grant a declaration when giving judgment by consent or without trial, for example where there was judgment in default of defence or notice of intention to defend. It has, however, been stated that this is simply a rule of practice, and the court will grant a declaration where the undefended claim is for a breach of contract and it would not otherwise be clear that the contract is at an end by reason of the defendant's repudiation.[6] There seems no reason in principle why the same position should not apply in relation to rights to light. In *Greenwich Healthcare NHS Trust v London & Quadrant Housing Trust and Others*,[7] where the issue concerned whether a proposed realignment of a road would interfere with a right of way, Lightman J expressed the law as follows:

---

1 See, eg, *Ankerson v Connolly* [1906] 2 Ch 544, *affirmed* [1907] 1 Ch 678, CA.
2 See RSC Ord 15, r 16, in Sch 1 to the CPR.
3 See, eg, *Meadows Indemnity Co Ltd v Insurance Corporation of Ireland Plc* [1989] 2 Lloyd's Rep 298, CA. But see *Re S* [1995] 3 All ER 290, CA.
4 *Powell and Thomas v Evans Jones & Co* [1905] 1 KB 11; *Re S* [1995] 3 All ER 290, CA.
5 *Midland Land Reclamation Ltd and Leicestershire County Council v Warren Energy Ltd* [1997] CILL 1222.
6 *Patten v Burke Publishing Co Ltd* [1991] 2 All ER 821.
7 [1998] 3 All ER 437.

'The question now arises whether I can grant a declaration that if the plaintiff proceeds with the development the defendants have no entitlement to an injunction or damages in respect of any breach of the restrictive covenant but that their rights (if any) are limited to a claim for compensation in proceedings before the Lands Tribunal; and that the defendants have no entitlement to an injunction in respect of any interference with the right of way, but their remedy (if any) is limited to an award of damages.

In *F v. West Berkshire Health Authority (Mental Health Act Commission intervening)* [1989] 2 All ER 545 at 570, [1990] 2 AC 1 at 81 Lord Goff pointed to the width of the jurisdiction conferred on the court by RSC Ord 15, r 16 to grant binding declarations of rights, and the three conditions to be satisfied if that jurisdiction is to be exercised. These conditions are that the question under consideration is a real question; that the person seeking the declaration has a real interest; and that there has been proper argument. In *Camilla Cotton Oil Co v. Granadex SA, Shawnee Processors Inc v Granadex SA* [1976] 2 Lloyd's Rep 10 at 14 Lord Wilberforce said that special circumstances may justify the grant of a declaration that a person is not liable in an existing or possible action, and that careful scrutiny is required before such a declaration is granted, most particularly as to the utility of such a negative declaration. In *Patten v. Burke Publishing Co Ltd* [1991] 2 All ER 821, [1991] 1 WLR 541 Millett J emphasised the importance of the consideration whether the paramount duty of the court to do the fullest justice to the plaintiff to which he is entitled can be fulfilled without such a grant of a declaration.

In this case there is a real question whether the defendants have a right to an injunction or damages in respect of the restrictive covenant and to an injunction in respect of the easement; the plaintiff has a very real interest in obtaining the declarations sought; and I have heard full argument. Further the grant of a negative declaration that the plaintiff is not exposed to possible action seeking such relief is a matter of the highest utility since it is the precondition to the ability of the plaintiff to secure the building of a new modern national health service hospital and the provision of national health care services. Justice to the plaintiff cannot be done without the grant of this relief.

I am quite satisfied that I have jurisdiction to grant the declarations sought and that I should do so. One special feature of this case is that the declarations sought extend to the entitlement of the defendants, not to proprietary rights eg to easement or the benefit of restrictive covenants, but to their entitlement to the equitable remedy of injunction. The jurisdiction of the court to grant declarations must extend to entitlement both to proprietary rights and to particular remedies. The circumstances in which the discretion may be properly exercisable in case of declarations as to entitlement to particular remedies may be rare, but circumstances may exist when a declaration eg that a defendant is not entitled to specific performance, rectification or an injunction, is necessary if a period of damaging (or indeed paralysing) uncertainty is to be avoided and indeed the occasion for an unwarranted ransom demand is to be removed.'

11.134 Despite the width of the jurisdiction, the limitations on the court's grant of declaratory relief can be important in two situations in particular. First, where a potential developer is contemplating the purchase of a site, overlooked by buildings with windows which may enjoy prescriptive rights to light, there is no readily available way of trying the issue whether, if the purchase proceeds, the development will be possible without running into rights to light difficulties. The developer will have no interest in land capable of giving him locus standi unless and until his purchase proceeds and the court is unlikely to be prepared to assist a *prospective* purchaser with a declaration. Secondly, the court is unlikely to be prepared to entertain a claim for a declaration as to light unless there is some substantive issue between the parties. Therefore, a dominant owner who wishes to ensure that his title to ancient lights is secure has no readily available method of confirming this.[1]

11.135 The court may grant final, but not interim, declaratory relief against the Crown.[2]

1 Although the servient owner can of course call the dominant owner's rights into question by a light obstruction notice under the Rights of Light Act 1959; see Chapter 8.

2 Crown Proceedings Act 1947, s 21.

Chapter 12
Measurement and Valuation of Light

METHODS OF MEASUREMENT

Percy Waldram

12.1 In September 1928, Percy Waldram, the well-known light expert, gave a paper entitled *Daylight and Public Health* to the Commission Internationale de L'Eclairage. In that paper, he reminded his audience that:

> '... the "ancient light" law of England, which gives the owner of windows over 20 years old an indefeasible right to an adequate access of light and air, is often quoted as a piece of comparatively modern legislative interference with commercial development. It is however as old as English law, and that was copied direct from Roman law.'

12.2 In his summing up, he drew attention to the most important aspects as to why loss of light should be measured when he stated:

> '(a) that positions from which no sky at all is visible at table height are inadequately lit for ordinary purposes, such as continued clerical work, and
> (b) that it is undesirable that rooms should be constructed, or used for habitancy, or for clerical or other ordinary work over long periods, unless they have at least some sky visible from table height over some reasonable portion of their area.'

12.3 He also urged the members to be wary of the claims that 'whitened obstructions, light walls and ceilings and other expedients for mitigating gloom' worked when the surfaces became dirty and no longer operated with any benefit, especially on dull days. Indeed, in earlier papers, Percy Waldram categorically stressed that the human eye cannot be trusted when dealing with light levels. He gave as an example the fact that light in any ordinary room lit by windows from one side only falls away very quickly indeed as the distance from the window increases, for the amount of visible sky decreases very rapidly. Yet the human eye is not necessarily aware of this.

12.4 In summary, Percy Waldram highlighted three main points:

(1) for healthy living, man must have, and is legally entitled to have, an adequately lit room;
(2) light must be direct from the sky, and not from artificial light or from reflected surfaces; and
(3) the human eye cannot be trusted for measuring light.

What is meant by light in rights to light terms?

12.5 In a room, light is normally found consisting of three parts, namely:

(1) sunlight;
(2) artificial light; and
(3) skylight or what is often referred to as daylight.

Sunlight is not relevant in most rights to light cases, and, clearly, artificial light must also have no place. (An argument is often voiced that artificial lighting should be taken into account because when there are deep plan offices, it is clearly impossible to rely upon daylight, but legally this has not yet proved to be an adequate challenge.)

12.6 It is daylight which is relevant, but daylight consists of three components:

(1) the externally reflected component;
(2) the internally reflected component; and
(3) the sky component.

The absolute level of daylight at a point in a room is the result of many stages of attenuation and reflection. Indeed, to predict it accurately requires an intricate calculation, normally based upon the standard method of calculating the ratio of internal illuminants to external illuminants under a simple sky brightness pattern. This ratio is called the daylight factor.

12.7 The externally reflected component consists of light reflected from adjoining buildings, obstructions or other objects, and obviously can vary considerably. The second component, being the internally reflected component, comprises light received within a room from the walls, ceilings, floors and objects in the room in question and, similarly, can vary tremendously depending on decorative preferences. However, the third component, known as the sky component, comprises light direct from the sky and this can be measured accurately based upon an agreed standard. The uncertainty of external and internal reflection becomes irrelevant in rights to light calculations because it is ignored and, instead, the calculations are based on a sky of uniform brightness. All glazing is ignored, and generally the framework to windows. It is the sky through the apertures or unglazed openings which counts.

12.8 Clearly, there can be a wide variation in the amount of light from the sky at any one time, whether it is sunny or cloudy, whether external buildings are glazed or in dark bricks, or ceilings are black or white, and for all these reasons light meters cannot be used in assessing rights to light claims. Indeed, light meters are of value only for moments in time, for example when photographs are being taken or when deciding whether a cricket match should continue or not. They are never used in determining whether a room has lost light.

12.9 It was the work of Percy Waldram, and his father before him, which led to a standard being adopted for a uniform sky. Imagine a man lying on his back in the middle of a field with nothing on the horizon. In a theoretical sense, he has a dome of sky over his head, touching the horizon on all sides. See Figure 12.1. In order to make any calculations with regard to skylight penetration, there has to be an assumption of uniform sky brightness or luminance coming from this dome of sky.

12.10 Sky brightness varies unpredictably in temperate climates. It depends on the height of the sun above the horizon and on the various cloud formations. The amount of light in a room lit by daylight is proportional to sky brightness. The intensity of light coming from a window varies with time unpredictably and over a wide range of conditions. A standard had to be set and the figure of 500 foot candles illumination was adopted by the National Physical Laboratory in 1928 as being the average condition of sky brightness found in towns in Great Britain over the greater part of winter days, over long periods in late autumn and early spring, over substantial but less lengthy periods in early autumn and late spring, and on wet days in summer. It was felt that over these periods and, therefore,

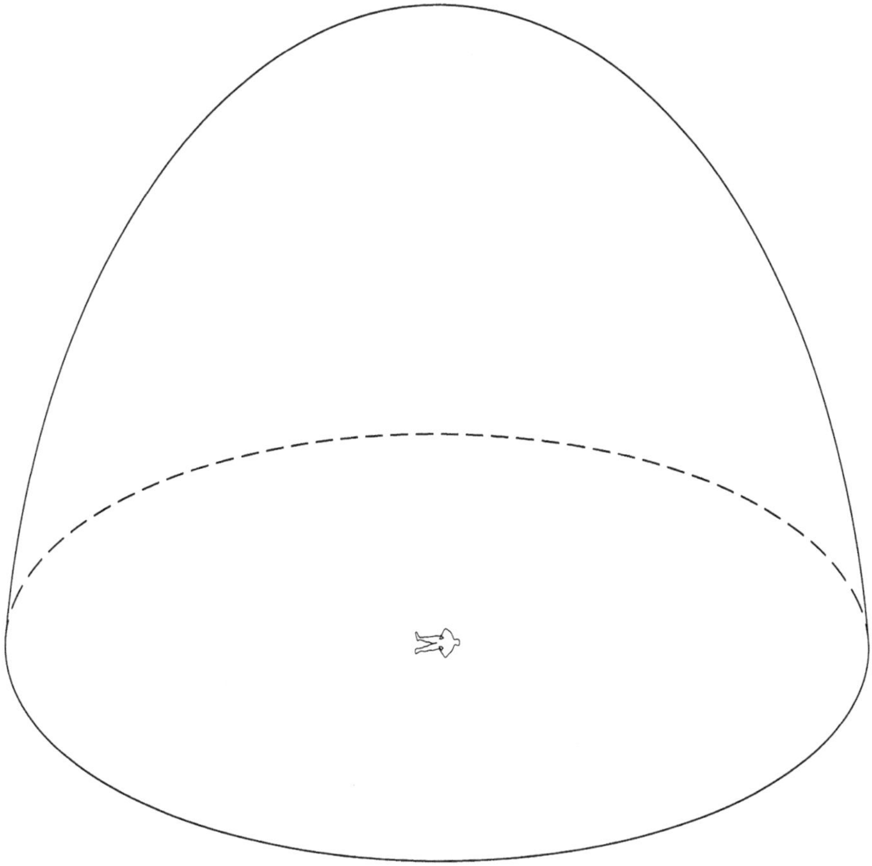

Figure 12.1: The dome of sky

over a great part of the year, reasonable people would normally expect to have adequate light for ordinary purposes.

12.11 On 5 March 1928, Percy Waldram's paper *The Estimation of Damage in Ancient Lights Disputes* was read at the Surveyors Institution and he confirmed:

> '... the brightness of the sky on such a moderately dull day has been standardised, at least for this country, by the National Physical Laboratory at 500 foot candles, ie such a sky brightness as would cause a white card open to a complete hemisphere of sky (as when laid on a flat roof higher than all surrounding buildings) to be as bright as it would be were it exposed to a measured illumination of 500 foot candles; or when exposed to half a hemisphere of sky (as when laid upon the cill of an unobstructed window) to be as bright as it would be were it exposed to a measured illumination of 250 foot candles.'

The maximum light coming from the sky as you lie in a field is therefore 500 foot candles; 500 foot candles is 500 lumens per square foot (or approximately 500 lux).

What is being measured?

12.12 Percy Waldram and his father spent considerable time in 1912 measuring and valuing daylight illumination in public and private buildings and came to the conclusion that:

> '... for ordinary purposes, comparable with clerical work, the natural illumination at which average reasonable persons would consistently grumble was that which represented 1/250 (0.4%) of the outside illumination which would fall on a window cill from an unobstructed quartersphere of sky, of the same brightness as that of the patch of sky which illuminated the position under consideration. This grumble point is, of course, the same as 1/500 or 0.2% of the light which would fall from an unobstructed hemisphere of uniform sky onto a flat roof.'

Indeed, this quotation from 'The Illuminating Engineer' of April/May 1923 went on to confirm that this basic conclusion had '... survived the drastic test of many closely contested ancient light cases'. In other words, the grumble point was agreed as 0.2 per cent which equals 1 foot candle or 1 lumen per square foot. A lumen per square foot is a measure of illumination equal to that provided by a candle one foot away from you, providing enough light to read a newspaper. Thus one lumen per square foot or one foot candle has become the standard by which rights to light is measured within a room.

12.13 In 1932, the Commission Internationale de L'Eclairage met at Cambridge and resolved three further issues:

(1) that the use of contour lines be adopted ... in all questions;
(2) that table height should be regarded as 85cm (ie 850mm or at that time, taken in imperial, as 2 ft 9 in); and
(3) that less than 0.2 per cent daylight should be regarded as inadequate for work involving visual discrimination.

There was an appreciation that 0.2% was the barest minimum, but recognising that there should normally be more lumens per square foot available even directly from the sky, without taking into account the additional benefit of reflected light both external and internal.

12.14 With the basic criteria above, the measurement being ascertained is the loss of light which will occur between the existing 0.2 per cent contour in any given room and the position of the 0.2 per cent contour when the development outside the room is constructed.

How is it measured?

12.15 As a result of 'an enormous amount of uncongenial work', Percy Waldram devised a method in the 1920s in which the three dimensions needed in order to measure light were translated into two dimensions. He produced what is called the Waldram diagram based upon the principles of Mercator's projection. Waldram concluded that:

> 'the adjusted flat projection of the quartersphere of sky which affords the light received by an unobstructed window cill ... in which all the angular scales are so adjusted that the area of sky represented by one square inch anywhere onto a diagram so adjusted has precisely the same lighting value.'

If such a diagram is drawn 20 in × 10 in or 200 sq in in area, every square inch of sky projected onto it will represent 0.5 per cent of the daylight to sill ratio.

12.16 Figure 12.2 shows a Waldram diagram based on an unglazed aperture, ie disregarding the glazing bars and frame of the actual window.[1] Waldram sums up the benefit of his diagram saying:

> '... from the worst lit positions in the given interiors, or from any number of doubtful positions, the sky visible through the window, windows or skylight over any obstructions which may be present is plotted by its angular co-ordinates on a suitable measuring diagram, representing the quartersphere of visible sky. The divisions (of the diagram) are so adjusted as to represent by the area any piece of the visible sky its power of illuminating a surface at the point under consideration. This plotting can usually be done from the plans and sections ...'

12.17 Before translating information onto a Waldram diagram, it is necessary to have as full and as precise details as possible of all relevant buildings on the site and adjoining sites. When acting for a developer this involves accurate dimensions of the bulk of the existing building on the site which is soon to be demolished. Similar details are required for the new building proposed for the site and its exact positioning relative to the existing building. It is the bulk that is significant and details of windows, doors etc are not relevant. Each adjoining owner's building must be positioned in exact relationship with the existing building and the building proposed. Details are needed of the size of every window, or aperture which obtains light, and the thickness of the structural walls. The size of the rooms behind the apertures is also of importance. Indeed,

---

1 Cf Chapter 4 at **4.16**.

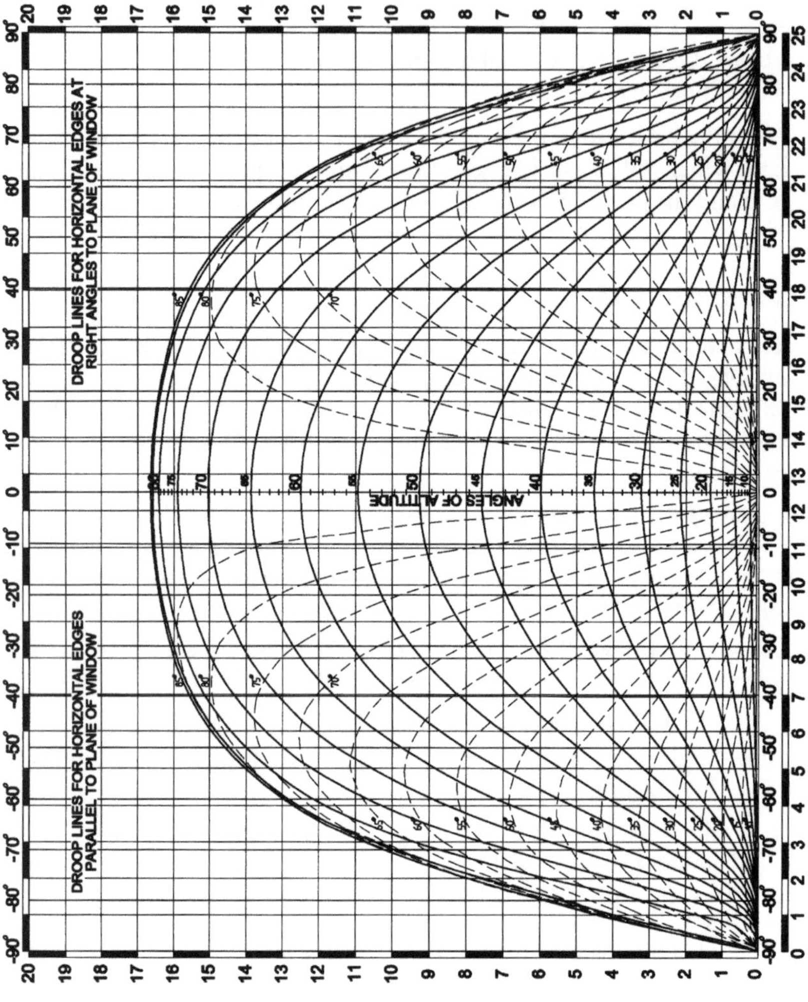

Figure 12.2: A Waldram diagram

when acting for a developer it may well be impossible to obtain access to adjoining owners' buildings. The developer may not wish to communicate with adjoining owners, and therefore presumptions must be made on the actual room sizes behind the windows. With regard to a valuation, room sizes are vitally important, and indeed possible alternative room layouts need consideration. This is dealt with later in this chapter at **12.33**.

12.18 When analysing each adjoining building in turn, it must be remembered that the developer's building and other adjoining owners' buildings may not be the only buildings which affect the light penetration. There could be other buildings adjoining which cut out light such as, in London, Tower 42 (formerly the NatWest tower), the Canary Wharf tower, or Centre Point. Any building which is visible from an adjoining owner's property from rooms likely to be affected, must be plotted on the analysis.

12.19 Land surveyors are often used to produce the data required for an accurate study and they are equipped with modern technology to assess heights of buildings and their positions. Ordnance Survey maps can be invaluable.

12.20 When the data is collected, a plan, sections and elevations of the respective buildings need to be drawn to scale before being plotted on the Waldram diagram. First a grid system is set up in every room likely to be affected by the new development. The grid is positioned at 850mm above floor level, or at the working plane, all as agreed in 1932. Then it is necessary to find the position of the 0.2 per cent contour based upon the existing building which stands on the site. Having discovered this, the same exercise is carried out to ascertain where the 0.2 per cent contour will move to in each room once the new building is constructed.

12.21 Figure 12.3 shows in plan a room with one window and the site next door. The existing building on the site is shown shaded and the proposed new building in solid dashed outline. A point is chosen on the grid where it is anticipated that the existing 0.2 per cent contour will be. Using a protractor, the angles to the window reveals are measured in each direction with the 0 position of the protractor based on the reference point. The window reveals are then transferred to the Waldram diagram. The angles of every corner of every relevant obstruction outside the window are also measured and transferred to the Waldram diagram. This would include Centre Point or the Canary Wharf tower if they were visible and affected the calculation. The Waldram diagram will have a number of vertical lines on it defining these angles.

12.22 The same exercise is carried out in section as shown at Figure 12.4. Here the existing building is shown shaded for easy reference. Care must be taken to draw in the correct angle relating to each specific corner or projection of the building prior to transferring it onto the Waldram diagram. Again, all buildings which could possibly affect the light entering the window must be recorded.

12.23 Figure 12.5 shows a completed Waldram diagram with the outline of the window and the existing adjoining building. It is then possible to ascertain how

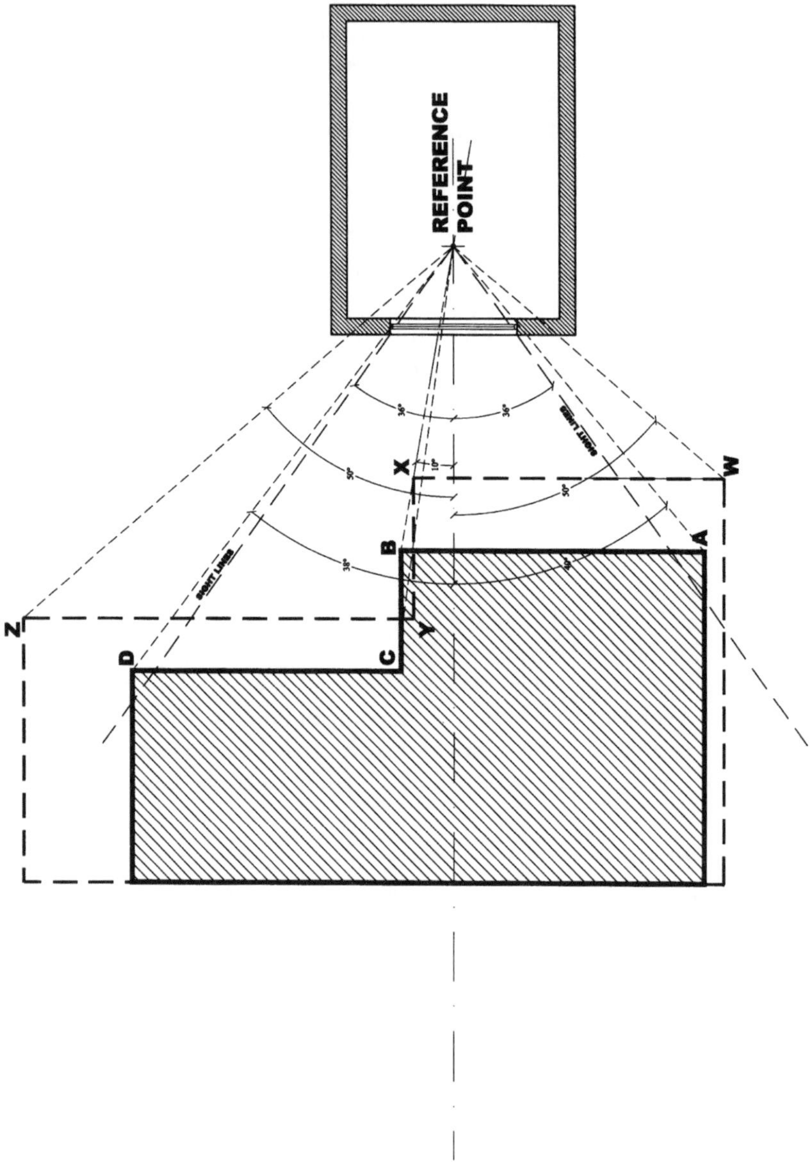

Figure 12.3: Plan of room with one window

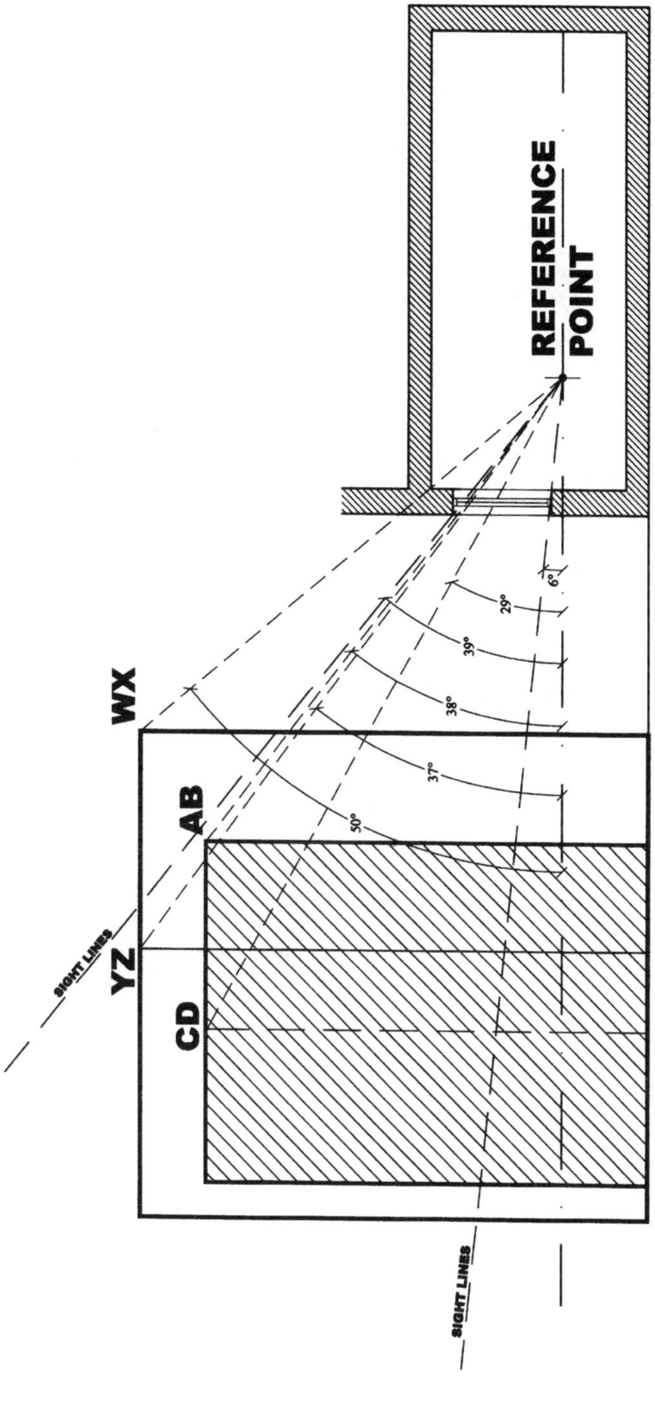

Figure 12.4: Section through room

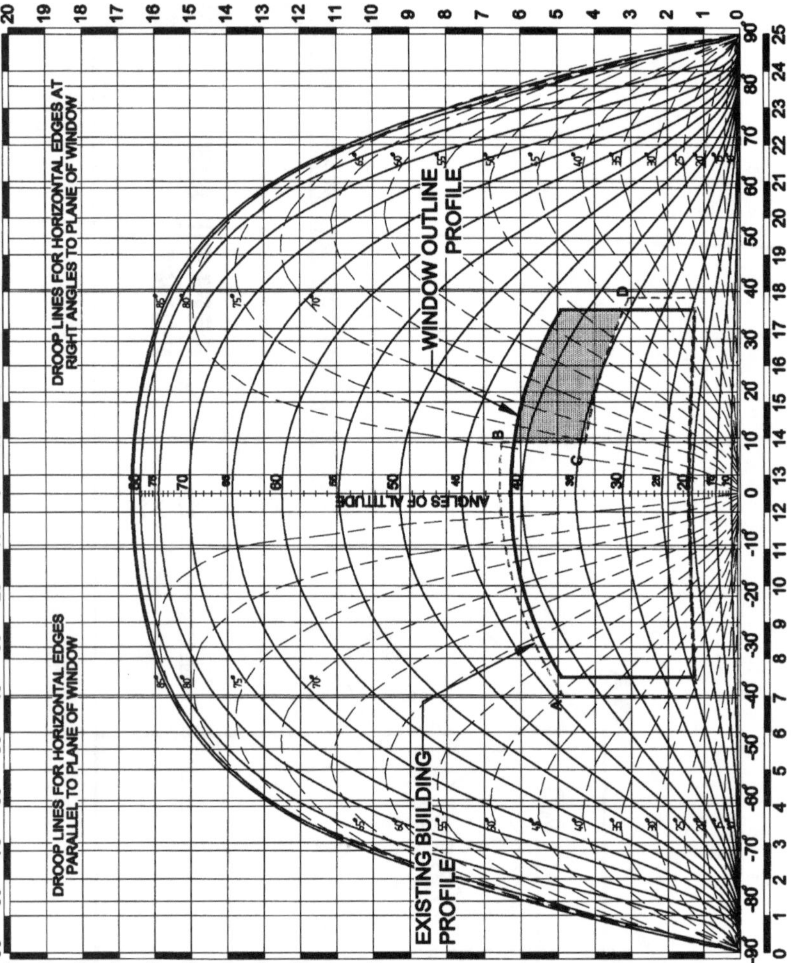

Figure 12.5: Waldram diagram with existing building

much of the sky remains visible. Is it 0.2 per cent? Figure 12.5 shows more than 0.2 per cent remaining and therefore another reference point further back in the room must be chosen and the process repeated until only 0.2 per cent remains visible through the window. The process has to be repeated often enough to allow for the entire 'as existing' contour to be drawn in as all the points of reference of 0.2 per cent are joined together. The process is then repeated in exactly the same way to draw in the 'as proposed' contour but anticipating that it is likely to have moved closer to the window (see Figure 12.6). On plan, the result is shown in Figure 12.7. The shaded area was 'in darkness' when the existing building stood on the site. The hatched area shows the additional area which will now be in darkness with the new building in position.

12.24 Sometimes, rights to light deeds have to be considered when measuring loss of light to a property. A deed between two parties may allow the developer to build a new building to a certain height and profile and the adjoining owner is not able to complain. It is only if the developer wishes to build a building which transgresses these controls that an assessment needs to be made. Instead of assessing the contour with the existing building standing on the site, the 'existing building' has to be assumed to be a building of the height and profile set out on the deed. This is what is plotted first on the Waldram diagram prior to the new building being plotted. The first contour plotted, therefore, is for the allowed building under the deed prior to plotting the 0.2 per cent contour for the proposed building. The interpretation of rights to light deeds is considered in Chapter 9.

12.25 The development of more advanced computers has allowed for software to be written to take away the tedium of preparing Waldram diagrams. The software is based upon the principles of trigonometry and allows for immense flexibility when a developer is designing a new building. Once all base data has been put into a computer, the software can analyse a variety of possible schemes for the site and the developer can decide what kind of risk he might want to take. Rights to light advisers work closely with architects to produce an acceptable scheme. (This has the additional benefit of providing information such that daylighting and sunlighting analyses for planning can also be prepared.)

12.26 A very rough and ready method of starting off gauging where the light contour might fall can be undertaken using what is called the 'no sky line'. Where there are two close parallel buildings, this is a good initial ready reckoner. See Fig 12.8 where the no sky line passes under the head of the adjoining owner's window from the working plane and over the top of the building standing immediately alongside. On the working plane, you can see how there is light on the side of the line closest to the window and no light behind it. Indeed, Percy Waldram advised that the no sky line lies at about 0.1 per cent or 0.15 per cent. When setting off to find the 0.2 per cent contour, therefore, it is important to start in front of this line closer to the window.

12.27 Although in early rights to light cases, the 45° angle has been cited as relevant, it has no basis or validity in rights to light work. Figure 12.9 shows in

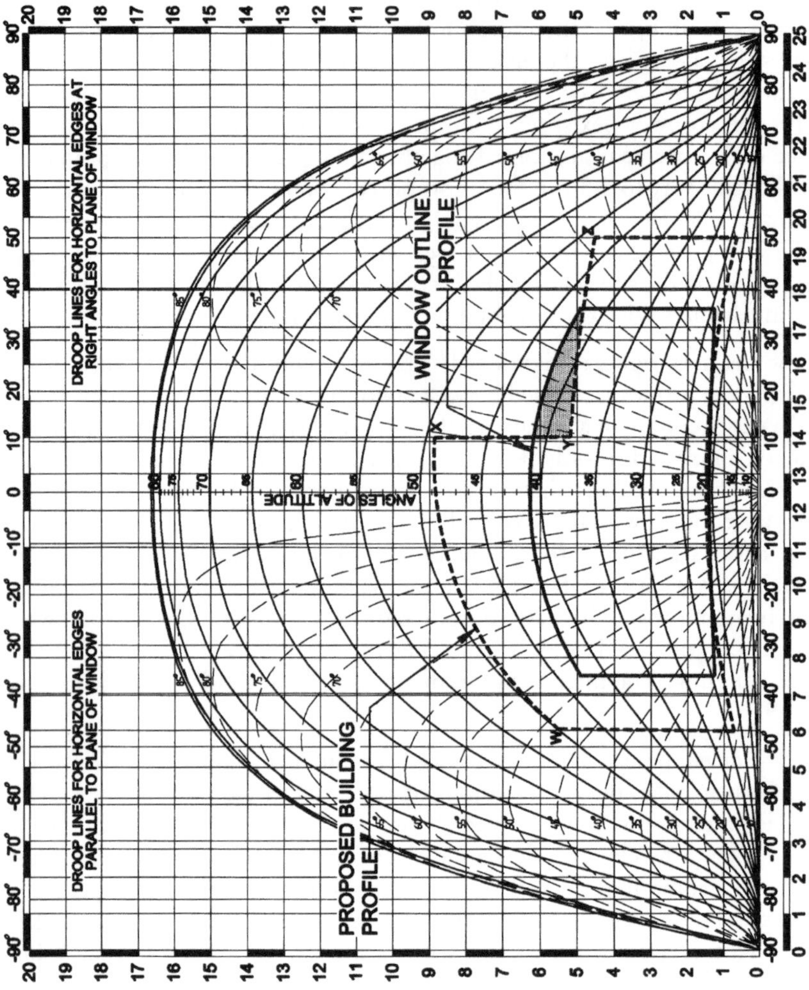

Figure 12.6: Waldram diagram with approximately 0.2 per cent remaining

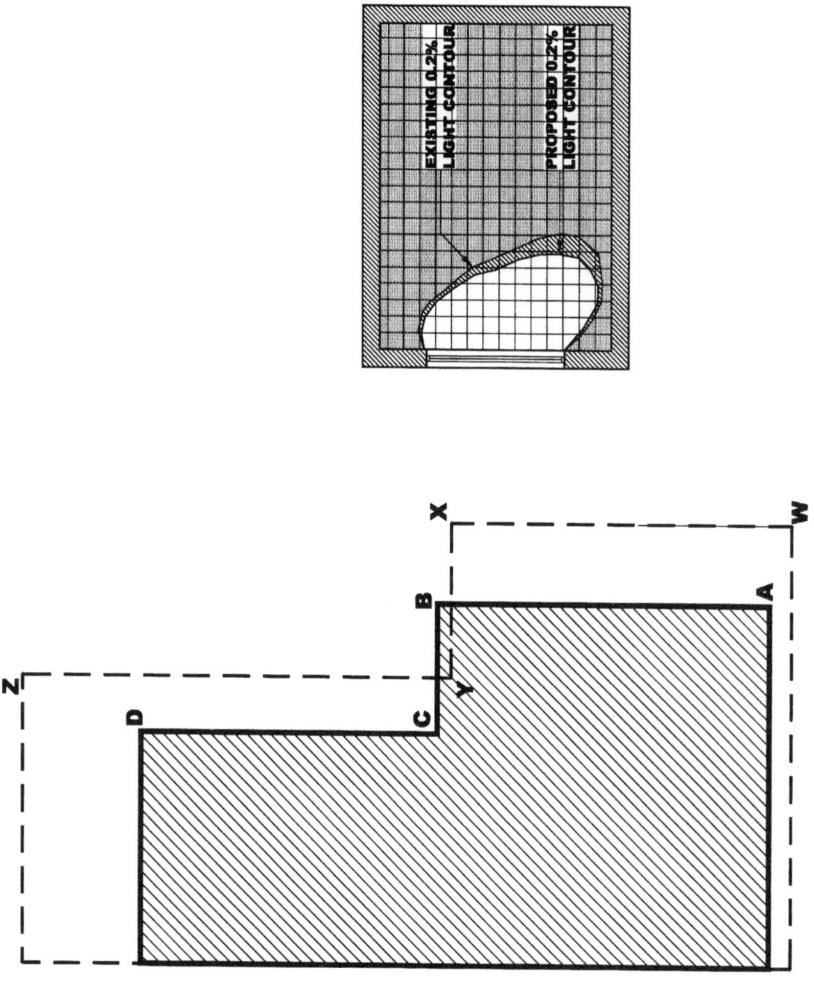

Figure 12.7: Plan showing loss hatched

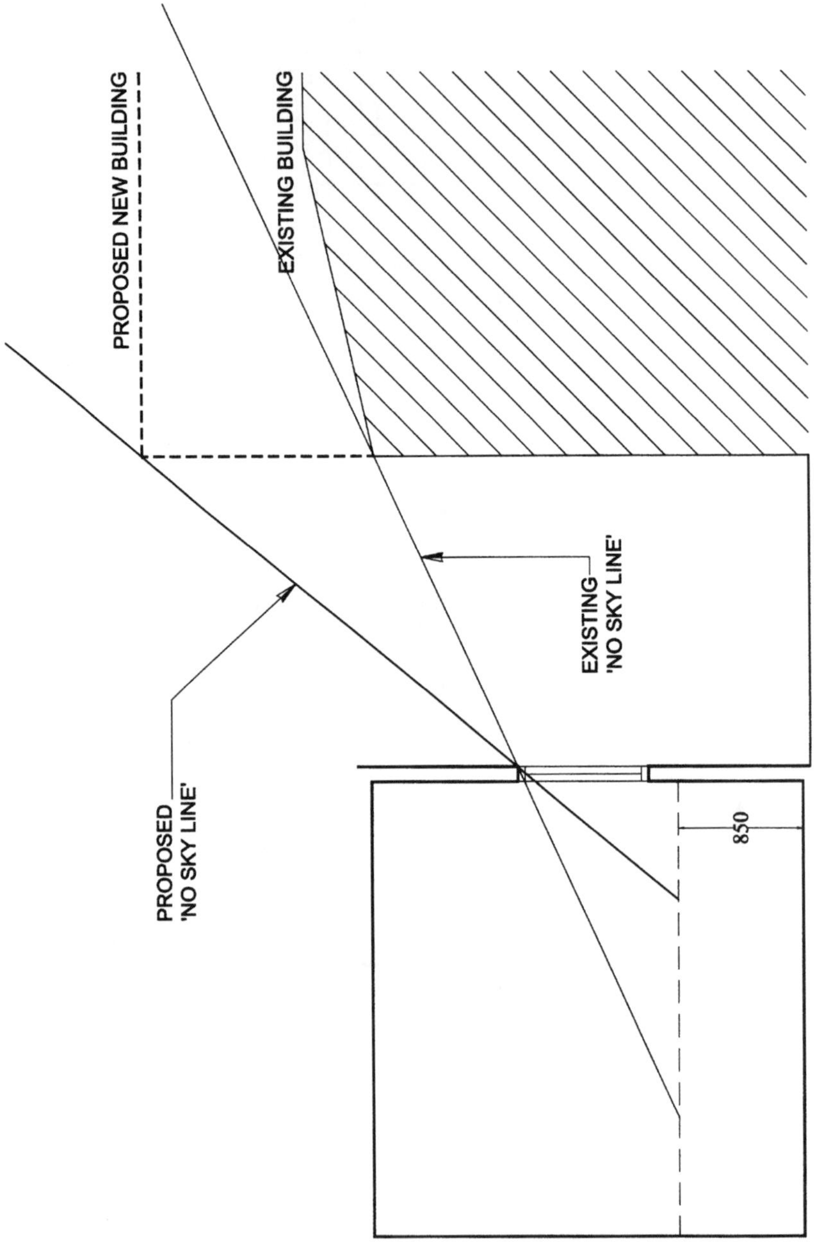

Figure 12.8: The 'no sky line'

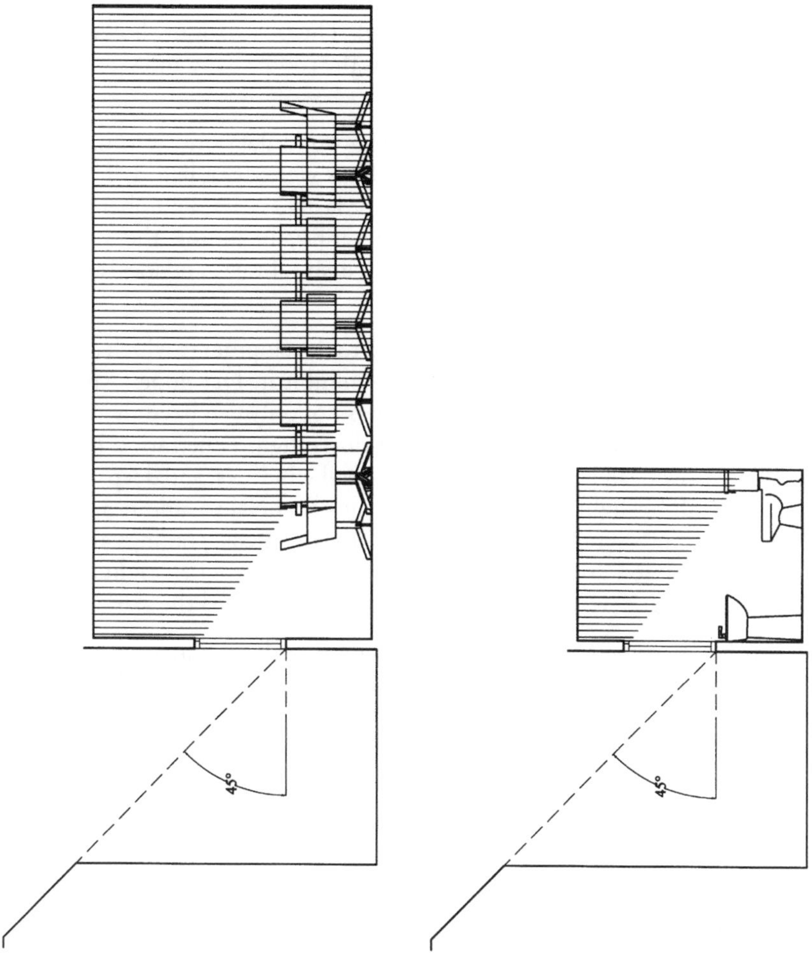

Figure 12.9: The 45° angle

two simple pictures how irrelevant it is. This is whether the line is taken from the sill of the lowest window or through the head. The boardroom shown will be badly lit but the bathroom will be well lit – it is the room shape and size which is significant.

12.28 Research is necessary to provide background data on the siting of old buildings, window positions, and when buildings were demolished. The use of aerial photographs can be invaluable. During the last 30 years, a number of major companies have specialised in aerial photography, including the Ordnance Survey. In addition, planning authorities, the British Library, and local authority libraries can all be of assistance.

12.29 There are some key factors with regard to developments which can assist in maintaining light penetration or positively inhibit it. Developers should be aware that providing balconies to new buildings not only can have an impact on adjoining buildings but will dramatically cut down light penetration into their own building. Low head heights, narrow and small windows, and deep cheeks to mansards also inhibit light penetration. It is not beneficial to adjoining owners for a developer to raise enclosing parapet walls to roof areas – railings are better. The use of brise soleil are considered solid obstructions when rights to light analyses are being undertaken, and glass canopies are treated the same way.

12.30 It is helpful when adjoining owners' buildings have windows with high head heights and roof lights. The Georgians knew what they were doing when they built their houses with tall narrow windows.

VALUATION OF LOSS OF LIGHT

The area measurement

12.31 The measurements undertaken above produce an area of loss between the old and the new contour positions. However, before any assessment is made, any gain must be off set against losses. This is accepted practice within rooms, but it is not accepted practice to off set gains at one end of a building against losses at the other end where completely different areas of the building are affected.

12.32 The size and shape of a room are highly significant. The area of the whole room is directly relevant to the outcome and must be assessed first. Reference has been made to what was called 'the 50/50 rule'. Basically, if one-half of a room remained lit such that adequacy was achieved, then the adjoining owner affected by the development could not complain. The contour at the half-way point was called the 'grumble line'. Although this rule no longer applies, it is a good starting point when assessing a room. Indeed, if one room is actionably injured, then other rooms which have losses only at the rear would also come into the loss calculations – these are called parasitical injuries. If there are rooms with losses only at the rear, they are not actionably injured and no compensation should be paid.

12.33 Each room, whatever its shape or size can be divided into four. John Anstey in his book *Rights of Light*[1] refers to each 25 per cent in turn as '... very serious loss, serious loss, fairly important loss and not very important loss'. The first area of the very serious loss is known as the front zone or the front 25 per cent of a room; the next 25 per cent with the serious loss is known as the first zone; the next 25 per cent of the room, the zone of fairly important loss, is known as the second zone; and the final 25 per cent of the room is known as the makeweight area. Although it seems easy to divide a room into four, it must be appreciated that a room is not lit in a simple fashion. First, a room is unlikely to be 100 per cent lit. It is normally about 98.5 per cent lit as you will inevitably obtain unlit areas in the corners immediately to the left and right of a window. This clearly affects the calculation. Indeed, it is possible to obtain a shaft of light passing through a window and lighting one side portion only of a room to the back wall. Figure 12.10 shows the 25 per cent front zone actually to the side and back of the room! Consideration must also be given to possible different layouts in a building. Cellular offices are a perfectly valid alternative to open plan areas.

12.34 In any analysis, good light should be present for at least 25 per cent of a room. If light is lost from this area the matter is serious as there is 'very serious loss'. Any loss within this area is multiplied by 1.5 so the area is always increased to account for the significant damage. The area of the room between 50 per cent and 25 per cent well lit is considered a standard area and is called the first zone loss. There is no multiplication to enhance the area of recorded loss but all other measurements are equated to this first zone. The area between 50 per cent and 75 per cent would be argued as being an area not actionable in itself, but actionable if it forms part of a loss in the front 50 per cent of the room. The area calculated is therefore taken as one-half and the loss multiplied by 0.5. The rear or makeweight part of the room is taken at one-quarter the area, so the multiplication factor is 0.25.

12.35 Figure 12.11 shows a typical analysis of a number of floors in a building and the analysis of loss equating all the areas to the equivalent of the first zone loss. This table is utilised in all rights to light assessments and is known therefore as the equivalent first zone ('EFZ') table.

12.36 The weighting does, however, change depending on the circumstances of the particular case. When the loss is actionable, ie in the front or first zone, then any makeweight loss is promoted to the second zone and receives a 0.5 weighting rather than a 0.25 weighting. However, when losses are not actionable in some parts of a building, then any second zone loss is demoted and receives a 0.25 weighting rather than a 0.5 weighting, and the totals are then added in to other losses in other parts of the building which are actionable.

1 Published on behalf of The Royal Institution of Chartered Surveyors by RICS Books (3rd edn, January 1998).

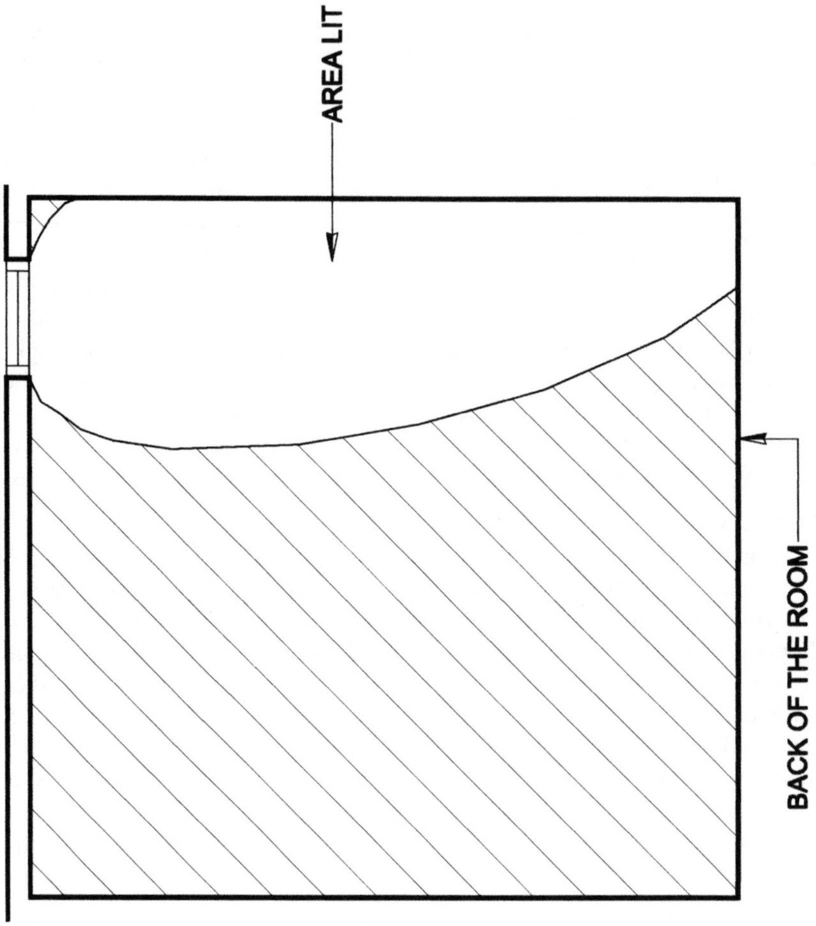

Figure 12.10: The zoning peculiarity

Rights of Light Calculations
EFZ Table - Existing and Proposed

Room Ref	Floor	Room Area (Sq.M.)	1/4 Room Area	0.2% Before	0.2% After	Loss	Front	Zone 1	Zone 2	MWT	EFZ Sq.M.	EFZ Sq.Ft.
ROOM-00-01	0	8.81	2.20	0.73	0.02	0.71	0.71	0.00	0.00	0.00	1.06	11.41
ROOM-00-02	0	12.72	3.18	0.83	0.44	0.39	0.39	0.00	0.00	0.00	0.59	6.35
ROOM-00-03	0	17.73	4.43	0.57	0.37	0.20	0.20	0.00	0.00	0.00	0.30	3.23
ROOM-00-04	0	16.14	4.03	0.71	0.69	0.03	0.03	0.00	0.00	0.00	0.04	0.43
ROOM-01-01	1	11.26	2.82	0.91	0.79	0.12	0.12	0.00	0.00	0.00	0.18	1.94
ROOM-01-02	1	19.05	4.76	1.40	0.37	1.03	1.03	0.00	0.00	0.00	1.54	16.58
ROOM-01-03	1	16.74	4.18	1.69	0.68	1.00	1.00	0.00	0.00	0.00	1.51	16.25
ROOM-02-01	2	27.67	6.92	3.87	2.30	1.58	1.58	0.00	0.00	0.00	2.37	25.51
ROOM-02-02	2	20.46	5.12	1.14	1.06	0.09	0.09	0.00	0.00	0.00	0.13	1.40
ROOM-02-03	2	16.89	4.22	2.10	0.48	1.62	1.62	0.00	0.00	0.00	2.43	26.16
ROOM-02-04	2	40.29	10.07	9.82	3.84	5.98	5.98	0.00	0.00	0.00	8.98	96.66
ROOM-03-01	3	22.57	5.64	17.25	15.77	1.49	0.00	0.00	1.16	0.33	0.37	3.98
ROOM-03-02	3	72.14	18.04	26.88	15.03	11.85	3.00	8.85	0.00	0.00	13.35	143.70
ROOM-03-03	3	6.92	1.73	4.48	2.88	1.60	0.00	0.58	1.02	0.00	1.09	11.73
Totals:		**309.39**	**77.34**	**72.38**	**44.72**	**27.69**	**15.75**	**9.43**	**2.18**	**0.33**	**33.94**	**365.33**

Figure 12.11: A typical EFZ table

Valuation

12.37 First, a decision must be taken as to what proportion of the rent of the affected property could be said to be being paid for the amount of light penetrating the property. This has been a matter of debate over many years but in major city centres, particularly where higher rents are involved, it is felt currently that no more than £5 per square foot of the annual rent represents the value of light. There is still considerable argument about how much of the rent should be taken in every case. It is worth viewing John Anstey's book on rights to light where he gives a number of alternative graphs which conclude that it is a matter for the two experts to agree at the beginning. Local letting agents should be able to provide evidence of local rental levels as a starting point.

12.38 Valuation advice is important, particularly when deciding upon an appropriate Years' Purchase ('YP') yield since this is the final part of the process to produce the capital figure relating to the damage. The rental figure for the light is multiplied by the EFZ and then the YP. The valuer advising must be told that rights to light injuries are valued on the basis of a freeholder in possession, even if the property is an investment property, and even though there may be several subsidiary interests in the dominant tenement which have to be taken into account. The value of the rights to light injury depends upon the unexpired term of the leases and also whether landlords have reserved all rights of light to themselves.

12.39 As a simple example, consider a freeholder with a headlessee who has 7 years remaining on his lease and a sub-tenant with 4 years. Let us assume the loss is 500 sq ft and the element of rent relating to light is £5 per square foot per annum. The annual rent is therefore £2,500. Assuming the appropriate yield is 6 per cent (and so the YP multiplier is approximately 16.5), the capitalised figure is £41,250. The sub-tenant has 4 years to go before the end of the term of this sub-lease and the head lessee 7 years to run. The total sum of £41,250 must be divided equitably between the three parties. Let us now consider that from a valuer's point of view, using Parry's 'Valuation Tables'. Within Parry's tables is the 'Present Value of £1 per annum' table. This sets out the capitalisation factors to be applied to the annual income stream at various rates of return. (They assume rental income receivable annually in arrears but are still used in some areas of valuation including rights to light.)

12.40 The perpetuity figure at 6 per cent is actually 16.6667 and therefore the true payment is £41,666.75 to be divided between the parties. For the sub-tenant with 4 years to run, the 6 per cent column for 4 years has a YP of 3.4651. The headleaseholder with 7 years has a YP of 5.5824 and from this must be deducted the tenant's 3.4651 to give 2.1173. The freeholder has the remainder of 16.6667 – 5.5824 to give 11.0843. The sub-tenant therefore gets £8,662.52 (20.79%), the headleaseholder £5,291.68 (12.70%) and the freeholder £27,712.55 (66.51%). (If there had been any rent review in either the headleaseholder's term or the sub-tenant's term, then the YP calculation would reflect only the period to the next rent review because the loss of light would be taken into account at that review.)

12.41 In rights to light discussions, the sum of £41,666.75 is referred to as 'the book value'. All parties should be satisfied with their proportion but remember that the YP can change depending on when the valuation is carried out and, although most sums are agreed prior to the damage occurring, the loss should really be valued at the exact point in time when damage accrues.

APPLYING THE LAW

12.42 It has been stated earlier that the size and shape of a room is of great importance when assessing loss of light and how serious it is. To reiterate, it is generally agreed that provided more than 50 per cent of a room remains lit in commercial properties, then there is no injury and no action. However, when the amount of space lit falls below 50 per cent, then there is potentially actionable damage.

12.43 This cannot be taken as a guide when dealing with residential properties. It is clear that judges are inclined to side with the adjoining owner whose light is damaged, particularly when a developer can be seen to be making profit from a scheme. It seems from the cases before the courts that even rooms lit to 55 per cent may not be adequately lit.

12.44 In commercial properties, an affected adjoining owner, who has rooms damaged such that less than 50 per cent remains well lit, can then claim for other rooms which might be damaged only in the rear portion. This comes under the heading of parasitical injuries. Parasitical injuries are also relevant when a developer has to pay well over book value when paying damages. This arises because the adjoining owner or dominant owner has the basic right to obtain an injunction.

12.45 It is impossible to be sure when an adjoining owner would obtain an injunction relating to commercial adjoining premises. However, it must be remembered that if a room is already poorly lit, ie only 25 per cent or less, then any reduction in the light to this area would almost inevitably be regarded as a serious loss, and a plain case for an injunction. Even if the damage is relatively minor, the available light is held to be invaluable because there is so little of it, and any developer could be in jeopardy by reducing penetration further.[1]

12.46 The book value can be enhanced not just by one-and-a-half times its value but enhanced to whatever sum the adjoining owner might ask for, although this is normally by up to three or four times the book value. The adjoining owner has the ability to seek an injunction and is in a powerful position. The courts have on many occasions affirmed that they will not countenance a wrongdoer

1 For the principles giving the grant of injunctions, see Chapter 11 at **11.72–11.108**.

effectively compulsorily purchasing the right of the dominant owner.[1] This is when what could be called the 'wayleave' principle comes into operation. Basically, it is no longer satisfactory to look at the area of loss in the adjoining owner's building and try to ascertain an enhancement factor. The only sensible way of reaching any kind of negotiated settlement is for some sharing of the developer's profit to be agreed.[2]

12.47 The developer, who is raising his building to a greater extent than a previous building, is benefiting from the value of the extra floor space. It is the value of this additional extra floor space, which the developer could not realise if the adjoining owner obtained an injunction, which may have to be shared in profit terms with the adjoining owner (or owners if there are more than one). An analysis is made of this additional floor space which is then valued to ascertain the profit level for the developer. Building costs must be taken into consideration but the final profit element could be shared, if there is extremely serious damage, on a 50/50 basis between the badly affected adjoining owner and the developer.

12.48 In the case of deeds with restrictive covenants, similarly the adjoining owner could end up with one-half of the profit of the extra floor space which can be built only if the restrictive covenant is released. Indeed, the adjoining owner may even ask for other benefits and is clearly in an extremely strong position.

---

1 See eg *Anchor Brewhouse Developments Ltd v Berkeley Homes (Docklands Developments) Ltd* [1987] 2 EGLR 173; *London & Manchester Assurance Co Ltd v O & H Construction Co Ltd* [1989] 2 EGLR 185; *Deakins v Hookings* [1994] 1 EGLR 190.

2 For the principles on when the court awards damages in lieu of an injunction, see Chapter 11 at **11.109–11.127**.

Chapter 13
Rights to Light and Planning Law

SUMMARY

13.1 This chapter examines the relationship between rights to light and planning law, as established under the Planning Acts. These regulate development, including building works. Generally, planning provision is required for such works.

13.2 In deciding whether to grant planning permission, local planning authorities are guided by policies including ones which are designed to protect sunlight, daylight and views. Such criteria are both wider and narrower than those governing rights to light. Wider, in that view and direct sunlight are considered, narrower in that planning law does not directly protect private rights, and cannot be invoked by an aggrieved landowner to restrain his neighbour from infringing his rights to light. He may try to persuade the local planning authority to refuse planning permission, or challenge the grant of such permission by judicial review.[1] Planning law is concerned with public rights and duties, and the decision whether to grant or refuse permission is taken by public bodies in the public interest.

13.3 It is also important to appreciate that:

(1) the grant of planning permission does *not* grant protection from private law claims for infringement of rights to light;
(2) the criteria generally applied in deciding whether to grant or refuse planning provision are *not* the same as those used by the courts in deciding whether a right to light has been infringed.

THE EXTENT TO WHICH LIGHT IS PROTECTED BY PLANNING LAW AND POLICIES

13.4 Development of land is regulated by the provisions of the Planning Acts.[2] Under this legislation, development as defined in s 55 of the Town and Country Planning Act 1990 may be carried out only if planning permission has been granted[3] by the local planning authority ('LPA') or the Secretary of State for the

---

1 See Rules of the Supreme Court 1965, Ord 53, as contained in Sch 1 to the CPR.
2 Comprising the Town and Country Planning Act 1990, Planning (Listed Buildings and Conservation Areas) Act 1990, Planning (Consequential Provisions) Act 1990, Planning (Hazardous Substances) Act 1990, Town and Country (General Permitted Development) Order 1995, SI 1995/418.
3 Under s 57 of the Town and Country Planning Act 1990.

Environment, Transport and the Regions ('the Secretary of State').[1] LPAs are certain designated local authorities. 'Development' is defined as including building and engineering operations.[2] Such development is termed 'operational development', in contra-distinction to development involving change of use. Although under the Act it is in principle necessary to apply for and obtain planning permission for any development of land, this requirement is in practice relaxed. Under the Town and Country Planning (General Development) Order 1988,[3] blanket planning permission is granted for certain types of development falling within the parameters of the Order. And under the Town and Country Planning (Use Classes) Order 1988,[4] certain changes in the use of land are deemed not to involve material changes of use and hence do not require planning permission.

13.5 The decision whether to grant or refuse planning permission is one for the LPA, or in certain cases the Secretary of State.[5] Where planning permission is refused, an appeal lies in accordance with regulations either to the Secretary of State, or to a person appointed by him. From thence, an appeal may lie to the High Court on a point of law.[6] A general account of planning law is beyond the scope of the present work.[7]

13.6 In deciding whether to grant or refuse planning permission, the LPA must normally apply the provisions of the development plan[8] unless material considerations indicate otherwise. The development plan is the plan prepared by the LPA under its statutory duties under the Planning Acts. The responsibility for preparing development plans has historically been laid on various local authorities. There is, for example, no development plan covering the whole of England and Wales. Various changes in local authority organisation, and the differing paces with which each local authority has proceeded with the preparation of a development plan mean that there is now something of a patchwork of approved plans in different areas. In principle, approved plans are likely to comprise either:

(1) a unitary development plan ('UDP') for the area in question; or
(2) a local plan or plans; or
(3) the structure plan.

---

1 In the case of local planning authorities, see Town and Country Planning Act 1990, ss 70 to 72; in the case of the Secretary of State, see Town and Country Planning Act 1990, ss 77 to 79. The Secretary of State also has the power to provide for the grant of planning permission by development order by virtue of s 59.

2 See Town and Country Planning Act 1990, s 55(1).

3 SI 1988/1813, revoked by the Town and Country Planning (General Permitted Development) Order 1995, SI 1995/418.

4 SI 1988/764.

5 See Town and Country Planning Act 1990, ss 77 to 79.

6 Ibid, s 288.

7 The most comprehensive work is the *Encyclopedia of Planning Law* published in six volumes (Sweet & Maxwell).

8 Town and Country Planning Act 1990, s 54A.

LPAs, and the Secretary of State on appeal, must also take account of central government policy, as embodied in official statements and Planning Policy Guidance notes ('PPGs').[1]

THE RELEVANCE OF RIGHTS TO LIGHT IN THE DECISION-MAKING PROCESS

13.7 The general rule is that since planning powers are to be exercised in the public interest, private rights (or the absence thereof) are not directly relevant to decisions as to their exercise.

> 'The planning system does not exist to protect the private interests of one person against the activities of another.'[2]

13.8 It should follow that the concerns of private individuals are not relevant to the planning process. In practice, things are not so clear, for two reasons.

(1) First, in formulating the UDP, the LPA is required by law to include policies to conserve the natural beauty and amenity of land in its area, and to improve the physical environment. LPAs must also have regard to central government guidance. Policies designed to protect light and views of existing residents are almost universally incorporated in UDPs. The criteria used were formerly those in a Department of the Environment publication of 1971: *Sunlight and Daylight: Planning criteria and design of buildings.* This has now been superseded by a BRE report: *Site Layout Planning for Daylight and Sunlight: A guide to good practice*. (There is also a British Standard covering daylight.)[3] UDPs tend to adopt the standards of one of these documents, and by reference to these to lay down detailed criteria to protect daylight to existing buildings, restricting the height and distance of any new building which may affect the windows of existing buildings in terms of light and lost sky visibility.[4] These standards can be considerably more stringent than common law rights to light in restricting new development.

(2) Planning case-law shows that it is legitimate to take into account visual amenities of existing residents when granting or refusing planning permission for a new building. In *Wood-Robinson v Secretary of State for the Environment*,[5] the LPA refused permission for the erection of a house in the grounds of a block of flats, on the ground that it would spoil the residents' views. The developer appealed unsuccessfully to a planning inspector and to the High Court. Its argument was that private interests (ie the residents' view) were irrelevant to planning. The court held that whether protection of

1 See, generally, [1999] JPL 568.
2 See PPGI (February 1997), para 64.
3 See **13.23** for a further description of those documents.
4 See, further, **13.23**.
5 [1998] JPL 976.

the view in the public interest was a legitimate planning consideration was for the decision-maker (ie the inspector) to decide. Note that the residents could not have sued the developer for blocking their view of the house once it had been erected, since there is no common law right to a view.

13.9 This discussion is consistent with previous cases which established that an LPA can refuse planning permission for development that would harm private interests, provided the decision can be justified on planning grounds, ie that it relates to the character of the use of land. Courts have upheld:

(1) restrictions on development round a radio telescope to prevent interference (*Stringer v Minister of Housing and Local Government*);[1]
(2) a refusal of permission for a concrete plant that would harm a nearby precision engineering factory through dust (*RMC Management Services v Secretary of State for the Environment*);[2]
(3) a refusal of permission for conversion of a house into two flats, resulting in each occupier suffering noise disturbance from the other (*London Borough of Newham v Secretary of State for the Environment*).[3]

13.10 In *Brewer v Secretary of State for the Environment*,[4] the would-be developer sought to rely on the *absence* of a common law right to light as a ground for granting planning permission. A planning inspector granted permission on appeal. He found that the proposed development (a house extension) would substantially harm the light received by the windows of an adjacent property.

13.11 However, he accepted that because the developer proposed to register a light obstruction notice against the adjacent property,[5] the effect of which (if unchallenged for the necessary period) would be to prevent the adjacent owner asserting a right to light, this harm was not relevant. The court overturned the decision and held that the inspector had been wrong to take the presence or absence of a common law right to light into account. The case suggests that the absence of a right to light will *not* justify the grant of permission (unless normal planning criteria are satisfied).

13.12 Thus planning law can take into account private interests provided there is a sufficient planning justification, but the existence or otherwise of a right to light does not justify departing from normal planning policies.

---

1 [1971] 1 All ER 65.
2 (1972) 222 EG 1593.
3 [1986] JPL 607.
4 [1988] 2 PLR 13. For light and obstructing notices and their effect, see Chapter 7 at **7.10–7.14** and Chapter 8 at **8.31–8.37**. For further discussion of the *Brewer* decision, see **13.22**.
5 See Chapter 8.

THE EFFECT OF PLANNING PERMISSION ON PRE-EXISTING RIGHTS TO LIGHT

13.13 The effect of the grant of planning permission for the erection or alteration of a building which when erected or altered will infringe established rights to light, is not to deprive the dominant owners of their existing private law rights or confer immunity from claims for nuisance. So in *Hunter v Canary Wharf Ltd*,[1] Lord Hoffmann said:[2]

> '... I am not suggesting that a grant of planning permission should be a defence to anything which is an actionable nuisance under the existing law. It would, I think, be wrong to allow the private rights of third parties to be taken away by a permission granted by the planning authority to the developer.'

13.14 *Wheeler v JJ Saunders Ltd*[3] illustrates this principle. Planning permission was granted for a pig farm, the operation of which caused nuisance to an adjoining owner through smells. The adjoining owner brought legal proceedings to restrain it. The owner of the pig farm argued that the effect of the grant of planning permission was to authorise that which would otherwise have been a nuisance, and hence that the plaintiff had been deprived of a right of action in respect of it. He relied on the decision in *Gillingham Borough Council v Medway (Chatham) Dock Co Ltd*.[4]

13.15 In an earlier case, *Allen v Gulf Oil Refining Ltd*,[5] the Court of Appeal was concerned with a nuisance that arose from an oil refinery built with statutory permission. The Court held that a planning authority had no jurisdiction to authorise nuisance save insofar as it had the statutory power to permit the change of the character of the neighbourhood. However, in the *Gillingham Borough Council* case, the Court of Appeal distinguished *Allen* in which planning permission for the development of a commercial port had resulted in the use of roads in the neighbourhood by heavy goods vehicles 24 hours a day. The Court held that the planning permission was not a licence to cause nuisance, but where the permission relates to development or change of use then the question of nuisance falls to be decided with reference to the neighbourhood with that use or development and not by reference to the neighbourhood as it previously existed.

13.16 In *Wheeler*, reliance was placed by the defendant on the *Gillingham Borough Council* case. The Court of Appeal, however, held that in the *Wheeler* case the grant of planning permission had not changed the character of the neighbourhood, since the defendant's farm had prior to the planning permission been used for pig breeding, although on a different part of the farm property.

---

1 [1997] AC 655, HL.
2 Ibid at 710D.
3 [1995] 2 All ER 697, CA.
4 [1993] QB 343.
5 [1981] AC 1001.

13.17 In *Greenwich Health Care NHS Trust v London and Quadrant Housing Trust*,[1] the court granted declaratory relief to the effect that an injunction would not be available to restrain an interference with an easement because the proposed development was 'necessary to achieve an object of substantial public and local importance and value'. The case probably does not support the proposition that the grant of planning permission for such a project will prevent the owner of easements affected from seeking an inspection. There was in that case no opposition to the development, and the decision can be justified on other grounds.

13.18 It appears, therefore, that the law as it stands at present may be summarised as follows.

(1) The grant of planning permission does not directly affect private rights, whether to light or other rights.
(2) The grant of planning permission does not authorise a nuisance.
(3) Insofar as the *character of the neighbourhood* is relevant in deciding whether a nuisance has occurred, the effect of the grant of permission may be relevant, insofar as it leads to a change in the character of the area.[2]

The present state of the law is not entirely satisfactory; equating the grant of planning permission for a development which *potentially* changes the character of an area with actual changes to that character is illogical and runs counter to the clearcut principle in *Allen*. The implied transfer of the functions of protection of neighbours from nuisance to the planning process in such cases also seems somewhat naïve given the conflicting pressures on planning decision-makers. However, it is submitted that this question is unlikely to arise in the context of rights to light, where the character of the neighbourhood is not in issue.

13.19 Nevertheless, the grant of planning permission may indirectly affect the exercise of rights to light. Regulations[3] require that publicity be given to certain applications for planning permission. The purpose of the Regulations is to ensure that those who may be affected (in the broad sense) by the grant of planning permission receive due notice of it. Sometimes, particularly in the case of large or controversial developments, the local planning authority may hold a consultation exercise, notified in the local press, at which plans and/or a model of the proposed development may be displayed at the town hall, or the developer may hold meetings to explain the proposed development's main features. A dominant owner who is notified of a proposed development in this way will need to consider promptly whether he should apply for a *quia timet* or interim injunction in private law proceedings. If a dominant owner fails to act promptly to seek the court's protection once he becomes aware of the threat to his rights, he may be denied not only a restrictive injunction at trial but also substantial damages he could have obtained had he obtained (or at least applied for) a *quia*

1 [1998] 3 All ER 437.
2 See the comment on the *Wheeler* case at [1995] JPL 619 at 632.
3 See the Town and Country (General Development Procedure) Order 1995, SI 1995/419, art 8; see also the Listed Buildings Act 1990, s 73.

timet or interim prohibitory injunction (see Chapter 11, especially **11.97–11.127**.)

CURRENT PLANNING POLICIES RELATING TO LIGHT

13.20 There are no national planning policies specifically related to the protection of light to existing buildings. However, in practice, there are often local objections to development based on loss of light, either generally, or specifically with regard to sunlight or views.

13.21 In general disputes, following the decision in *Wood Robinson v Secretary of State for the Environment* (see **13.8**), planning permission is unlikely to be refused simply on the ground that a view enjoyed by an existing property will be lost. In exceptional cases, local planning policies may provide for protection of views which are of acknowledged importance. Development which would interfere with such views will be refused, although, in practice, this is relatively rare.[1]

13.22 In *Brewer v Secretary of State for the Environment*,[2] it was held that an inspector appointed by the Secretary of State had erred in law in granting planning permission for a residential extension seriously interfering with light to the neighbouring property, in reliance on the fact that the neighbour had registered a light obstruction notice under s 2 of the Rights of Light Act 1959. It was held that planning was concerned with land use in the public interest, and in general the presence or absence of private rights was irrelevant. This must of course now be read subject to the *Gillingham Borough Council* decision.[3]

13.23 Rather more common are questions relating to sunlight and daylight. In deciding whether the interference with light to existing buildings is unacceptable in planning terms, local planning authorities are likely to have regard to the following non-statutory material.[4]

(1) British Standards Institution *Code of Practice for daylighting* (British Standard BS8206: Part 2 1992).
(2) Building Research Establishment Report BR209:1991 – *Site Layout Planning for Daylight and Sunlight. A Guide to Good Practice.*
(3) *Sunlight and Daylight Planning Criteria and the Design of Buildings* (Department of the Environment, 1971).

13.24 BS8206: Part 2 1992 (as amended) contains a code of practice for daylighting. The purpose of the standard is stated in the Foreword as being 'intended to enhance the well being and satisfaction of people in buildings'. The

---

1 For example, views of St Paul's Cathedral in London are protected – see Regional Planning Guidance 3, Strategic Guidance for London Planning Authorities, Annex A (set out in volume 6 of the *Encyclopedia of Planning Law* (Sweet & Maxwell).

2 [1988] 2 PLR 13; see also **13.10**.

3 See **13.14**.

4 See also **13.8**.

Foreword cautions that 'careful judgment should be exercised when using the criteria for other purposes, particularly town planning control'.

13.25 Paragraph 4 of the BS Code of Practice states that unless an activity requires the exclusion of daylight, a view out-of-doors should be provided irrespective of its quality. Paragraph 5 states that sunlight should be admitted unless it is likely to cause thermal or visual discomfort to the users, or deterioration of materials. It is stated that in 'interiors in which the occupants have a reasonable expectation of direct sunlight should receive at least 25 per cent of probable sunlight hours'. Probable sunlight hours are the number of hours annually during which the sun shines on unobstructed ground taking cloudiness into account. The standard further states that 5 per cent of probable sunlight hours should be received during the winter months. Paragraph 5 continues by suggesting that the general illumination from skylight should be such that there is not excessive contrasts between the interior and the view outside, and that if electric lighting is not normally to be used during daytime the average daylight factor should be not less than 5 per cent. If electric lighting is to be used through daytime, the average daylight factor should not be less than 2 per cent. These criteria apply where a predominantly day-lit appearance is required. The standard further suggests that even if a predominantly day-lit appearance is not required in dwellings, it is recommended that the average daylight factor be at least 1 per cent in bedrooms, 1.5 per cent in living rooms and 2 per cent in kitchens.

13.26 Paragraph 6 of the Code of Practice states that in relation to task lighting the principles of lighting design using daylight are the same as those for electric lighting. It is necessary both to achieve a given level of illumination and to take account of the circumstances that determine its quality.

13.27 The Code of Practice lists recommended minimum proportions of glazing the view in deep side-lit rooms. It also lists recommended illuminances in an appendix, and contains sections on the design of supplementary electric lighting, sunlight shading, energy efficiency, and conservation of materials.

13.28 Although the Code of Practice is aimed at the design of new buildings, its principles can be adapted to an assessment of the qualitative impact on existing properties of new development. In particular, paragraph 5 of the Code of Practice could be used to assess what would be acceptable in terms of loss of sunlight and illumination.

13.29 The Building Research Establishment ('BRE') report is designed to prescribe good practice on the layout plans of new development to achieve daylight and sunlight. Paragraph 2 deals with daylight to existing buildings, and the impact of new development. It states that:

> 'if any part of a new building or extension ... suspends an angle of more than 25° to the horizontal, then the diffused daylighting of the existing building may be adversely affected. This will be the case if either the vertical sky component ... is less than 27% and less than 0.8 times its former value; or the area of the working plan in a

room which can receive direct skylight is reduced to less than 0.8 times its former value.'

This deals with the design of new development in relation to sunlight. The document makes recommendations concerning the preservation of sunlight to existing buildings. Diagrams and calculation methods are contained in the appendix.

13.30 The DoE Publication sets out guidelines[1] (which are stated not to be mandatory) on appropriate standards of sunlight and daylight for new developments. The most important chapters are 3 to 7. Various methods are put forward to measure the impact of new development on the daylight and sunlight received by existing buildings.

13.31 These documents can be of considerable importance in determining whether planning permission is granted for new development. As regards the design of new development, the LPA will tend to require at least proposed housing developments to conform with the Code of Practice, BRE Document or DoE Publication, depending on which of these it has adopted for development control purposes. National Planning Policy[2] also requires LPAs to have recourse to supplementary design guidances outside the UDP framework, which, it is observed, 'can usefully elucidate and exemplify Plan policies'.[3]

13.32 Most UDPs, in practice, are likely to adopt plan policies supporting design criteria which are devoted to achieving developments enjoying good natural light. Supplementary guidance issued by the LPA to supplement the UDP will often rely heavily on the Code of Practice or the DoE Publication. Close attention must therefore be paid to the relevant parts of the UDP, also the supplementary guidance issued by the LPA, the latter of which will often lay down extremely detailed design parameters. The task is not usually simplified by the presentation of UDPs, which tend to treat lighting matters as relatively incidental, as examination of individual UDPs shows.

13.33 Since the planning system is 'plan led', conformity with whatever daylight standards the local planning authority has adopted will usually be a precondition to the grant of permission, although some flexibility is likely to be found to exist either where policies conflict or where slavish insistence on a particular standard would prevent an otherwise desirable development proceeding.

13.34 The designer of new development must take into account its impact on the daylight received by existing nearby buildings. UDP policies and supplementary guidance issued by the LPA invariably seek to protect the privacy, sunlight and daylight of existing residents where new development is concerned. These policies typically are framed by reference to the DoE Guidance, insofar as

---

1 See, especially, PPGI: General Policy and Principles (February 1997).
2 PPGI (February 1997).
3 Ibid, Annex A at para A2. See more generally at paras 13–20 and 42.

daylight and sunlight are concerned, but frequently seek additionally to prevent any material worsening of the position of existing residents, to safeguard privacy and to prevent the new development giving an unacceptable sense of enclosure.

13.35 Many of these concerns, of course, go beyond issues of light. It should be emphasised that they are entirely independent of the questions as to the extent of private rights to light enjoyed by adjoining owners. Designers sometimes mistakenly assume either that if no rights to light issues arise from a proposed development the LPA will not itself raise questions as to whether the development will harm the light of nearby residents, or that if the LPA's criteria are satisfied, no rights to light issues will be capable of being raised by such residents.

Chapter 14

Conveyancing Issues which affect Rights to Light

RIGHTS OF LIGHT AND REGISTERED LAND

The dominant land

14.1 The easement of light is treated in the same way as any other easement by HM Land Registry. On first registration, benefit of an easement will pass as a right which appertains or is reputed to appertain to the land which is to be registered and no mention of the benefit is required to be made on the property register of the dominant land.[1] This principle applies whatever the class of title registered. Following registration, under LRR 1925, r 252 the dominant owner can apply to have the benefit of the easement expressly noted on his title. If such an application is made, the district land registry will notify those affected by the easement, being the registered proprietors and others interested in the potentially servient land where it is registered.[2] If the servient land is unregistered, the dominant owner will serve notice on the person who is in possession. In practice, not many registered proprietors of dominant land apply for the benefit of the easement of light to be placed on their title.

14.2 Thus, *on first registration*, it is not necessary to make an express application for the benefit of the easement of light to be noted on the title for that easement to be effective post-registration. The right, if appearing from the document of title to exist as a legal easement, will be entered on the property register. In practice, it is only where there is an express grant of a right to light that the Registry will make such an entry. On the subsequent transfer of the title to the dominant land, the right will pass whether or not noted on the register.[3]

14.3 But where the title to the dominant land is already registered, an easement of light granted by deed, or in a transfer of land, will take effect as a legal easement *only* if it is registered as appurtenant to the registered title of the dominant land.[4] This will also require the registry to serve notice on the servient land owner and for the burden of the easement to be noted on the register of that title.[5] In the case of a grant by deed (without any transfer), this requires the servient owner to produce his Land Certificate for this to be done. If unregistered, the owner of the servient land must deduce his title to show the ability to make the grant.

1 Sections 5 and 72 of the Land Registration Act 1925 ('LRA 1925'); r 251 of the Land Registration Rules 1925 ('LRR 1925').
2 LRR 1925, rr 252 and 253.
3 LRA 1925, ss 20, 23 and 72.
4 Ibid, s 19.
5 Ibid.

The servient land

14.4 As regards the burden of an easement, the position is as follows.

(1) Where an easement has been expressly granted, is shown on the title deeds, and on first registration appears adversely to affect the servient land which is to be registered, an entry on the charges register of the title to that land of that easement will be made.[1] In practice, the Registry will always make such an entry notwithstanding their status as overriding interests as described at (2) below.[2]

(2) Legal easements (which includes a right to light) are within the class of overriding interests defined by s 70(1)(a) of LRA 1925. Therefore, they can take effect and bind the servient land even if they are not noted on the charges register of the title to that land.[3] In practice, because of the way in which the Registry makes the entry under its practice set out in (1) above, there are few titles where express grants are not on the face of the register.

Both dominant and servient land; no express grant

14.5 What, however, is the position in registered land where a right to light is not the subject of an express grant by deed? In such cases, the status of easement as overriding interests leads to confusion. This is because in the case of non-apparent easements – of which light is a prime example – there is no evidence on the ground, and no evidence on the register to indicate whether any right to light exists for or against any particular title. The next three paragraphs deal with this problem.

1. Both dominant and servient titles – express agreements relating to rights to light not completed by deed, creating equitable easements

14.6 These are minor interests, unless they qualify as overriding interests. As regards the protection of the interest of the parties under equitable easements created by agreements regulating light or restricting it,[4] the sensible course in all cases is to ensure that all parties apply to have the benefit or burden of any such agreement noted on the register of titles of the land affected. In the case of restrictive agreements which amount to covenants, this must be done as regards the land burdened, for otherwise the successor to the covenantor will take free from such interests which are not protected by registration.[5]

14.7 In the case of equitable easements which may be enforceable as overriding

---

1 LRA 1925, s 70(2).

2 See Ruoff and Roper, *Registered Conveyancing* (Sweet & Maxwell), 6-28; citing *Re Dances Way Hayling Island* [1962] Ch 490.

3 LRR 1925, r 258.

4 See Chapter 9.

5 LRA 1925, ss 20 and 50.

interests, no entry need be made of them on the register. There are two instances where such equitable easements rank as overriding interests. First, where they fall within s 70(1)(g) of LRA 1925, being the rights of persons in actual occupation of the land (or in receipt of the rents and profits thereof) save where inquiry is made of such persons and the rights are not disclosed.[1] In the case of a right to light created by an agreement not made under seal, it is easy to see how the benefit of the right under the agreement can be part and parcel of the rights of the person in actual occupation of the dominant land, but less easy to see how that right extends to protect the servient owner. However, it can be said that as the right to light is a right which can extend over other land, there is no reason why the servient owner should not be bound, just as the rights of the occupying tenant-in-common may bind third parties.[2] Secondly, equitable easements which are an adverse right, privilege or appurtenance occupied or enjoyed with land may be overriding interests under LRA 1925, s 70(1)(a) by virtue of LRR 1925, r 278 and the decision in *Celsteel Steel v Alton House Holdings Ltd.*[3] However, in that authority the court's finding on the extent of overriding interests related only to a right of way, and it may be open to question whether the easement of light should fall within this category of interests.

14.8 The Law Commission[4] has recommended that equitable easements should not rank as overriding interests. They recommend that they should always be protected as minor interests.

14.9 Where protection as a minor interest against the servient owner's title is not possible (because he will not produce his Land Certificate for the noting of the entry of the agreement), the agreement may be protected by a caution against dealings against that title.[5]

2. Both dominant and servient titles – easements of light created by implication

14.10 Where the title of land is registered, an easement of light may be acquired by virtue of the doctrine of non-derogation from grant and LPA 1925, s 62, as if the title to the land was not registered.[6] Section 19(3) of LRA 1925 applies the 'general words' implied in conveyances to transfers of registered land.[7] No express entry on the register of either the dominant or the servient title is, therefore, necessary. Under LPR 1925, r 258, these rights will take effect as overriding interests. This can cause uncertainty in practice as it is necessary to

1 For a full discussion of s 70(1)(g), see Barnsley's *Conveyancing Law and Practice*, 4th edn, pp 55–63.
2 *Williams & Glyn's Bank v Boland* [1981] AC 487; *Ferrishurst Ltd v Wallcite Ltd and Another* [1999] 2 WLR 667.
3 [1985] 2 All ER 562.
4 Report No 158, para 2.33.
5 Sections 54 and 59(2) of LRA 1925.
6 Section 20(1) of LRA 1925.
7 For grants of rights to light by implication, see Chapter 5 at **5.8** *et seq*.

look behind the register at the history of the two titles to ascertain: (a) when the titles were sold off; and (b) what apertures or other means of enjoyment of light were in existence at that time. In addition, where an easement of light can arise by estoppel or by common intention of the parties,[1] some individual 'digging' will be needed to establish the right. Only where the dominant owner makes application for a right to light created by implication and only where the servient owner is duly notified and where the Registrar is satisfied as to the legal origin and existence of the right, will it be noted as appurtenant to the dominant title and as a burden on the servient title.[2]

3. Both dominant and servient titles – prescriptive rights

14.11 In cases where rights to light are not the subject of an express or implied grant, but rely for their existence upon enjoyment under the various ways in which such rights can be acquired by prescription, such rights may be enjoyed as overriding interests, just as if they were expressly or impliedly granted.[3] But as regards the servient land, because the prescriptive right claimed is inchoate until declared by a court, HM Land Registry will, subject to what is said below, decline to make an entry of the right claimed on the servient title unless there is an order declaring the right to light to be appurtenant to the dominant title and against the servient title.[4] In such cases, the Registry will enter the terms of the right declared against the servient title and may, if application is made, note the benefit of the right on the dominant title. In cases where no court order has been obtained, it is open to claimants to seek the entry of the right against the servient title under LRR 1925, r 250.[5] This requires proof of the existence and acquisition of the right and, in practice, may be difficult to achieve. In any such application, the Registry will serve notice of the application on the servient registered proprietor and other interested parties (under LRR 1925, r 253) and, if no objection is received, the entry of the right will be made on the charges register of the servient title. If objection is received, the Registry may decline to make the entry, or may enter the right as a claimed one only.[6] As a matter of experience, it is difficult in many claims to rights to light to establish the right (other than in clear cases) to the satisfaction of the Registry without an order of the court.[7] This is an instance where if an entry is to be made, the servient owner is obliged to produce his land, or charge certificate.[8]

1 See Chapter 5 at **5.3** and **5.9**.
2 See LRR 1925 rr 252 and 253 and Ruoff and Roper (above), 6-07.
3 Ibid, r 258 and Ruoff and Roper, 6-07.
4 See Ruoff and Roper, 6-07 and LRR 1925, r 302.
5 Pursuant to s 75(5) of LRA 1925.
6 The latter is made under s 70(3) of LRA 1925.
7 See Ruoff and Roper, 6-07 and 29-10.
8 LRA 1925, s 64(1); and see Ruoff and Roper, 3-30.

RIGHTS TO LIGHT AND UNREGISTERED TITLES

14.12 These titles are becoming rarer. No specific conveyancing issues arise, save that it is customary to draw a counterpart or copy of any agreement granting an easement of light so that all parties have counterparts or copies to keep with their documents of title. As regards agreements restricting the use of light or building which may be seen as restrictive covenants, these must be registered as Class D(ii) Land Charges, in the name of the estate owner of the land burdened, in order to bind a successor owner of that land.[1] An equitable (as opposed to a legal) easement must be registered as a Class D(iii) Land Charge to be valid.[2] In either case, if unregistered, they will not bind a purchaser of the legal estate for money or money's worth.[3]

14.13 In view of the practice of the registry on first registration (see above), the evidence of grants and agreements must be kept in such a way that the appropriate entries can be made on the new title on first registration.

LANDLORD AND TENANT

14.14 Attention is drawn to Chapter 6 at **6.13** as to the ability of tenants to prescribe both for and against their landlords and third parties. In summary, a well-drawn lease should:

(1) reserve all light to the landlord;
(2) give the landlord the right to build on any adjoining land as he pleases;
(3) prohibit the tenant from enjoying any light other than by consent of the landlord;
(4) prohibit the tenant from making any agreement regarding light without the consent of the landlord;
(5) oblige the tenant to inform the landlord of all notices (eg light obstruction notices) and of any attempted infringement of light coming to the demised premises;
(6) prohibit the tenant from stopping up any windows.

SEARCHES AND INQUIRIES

14.15 The following searches are material in the context of conveying land where the right to light may be material.

(1) Searches of adjoining registered titles for any easements, the benefit of which is claimed or to which that title may be subject. This is useful if there is doubt over one's own title and the rights for and against it.

---

1 Land Charges Act 1972, s 2(5); and see Chapter 9 at **9.30**.
2 Ibid, s 2(5).
3 Ibid, s 4(6).

(2) Searches of the land charges register against the names of successive estate owners to establish whether any entries reveal adverse Class D(ii) entries protecting restrictive deeds or agreements.
(3) Searches of the local land charges register to reveal whether any light obstruction notices have been registered.[1] Both the property being acquired and adjoining properties should be within this search. Note that properties may be located within different boroughs and more than one register may, therefore, have to be searched.

14.16 The importance of disclosing any documents relating to light and the results of any searches cannot be over-emphasised, and that requires careful management of such documents within unregistered titles in particular.[2]

14.17 Although not strictly a matter of conveyancing, management surveyors and others concerned with large buildings should maintain records of all elevations and plans and ideally photographic records of the dominant building and servient buildings, with views from windows which may be considered vulnerable if adjoining buildings are developed. In the context of abandonment,[3] where the position of apertures is altered in both the horizontal and vertical plane, such evidence may be vital. Photographic evidence taken to show adjoining buildings can also be vital when assessing interference after such buildings have been demolished and a 'before' and 'after' assessment of loss of light is required.

GENERAL CONVEYANCING POINTS IN BOTH REGISTERED AND UNREGISTERED TITLES

14.18 Consideration must always be given in any title where agreements relating to the use and enjoyment of light appear to affect the title whether the agreements are restrictive or permissive.[4]

14.19 As to general words,[5] it is usual to exclude any implied grant of rights to light under either s 62 of the Law of Property Act 1925, or ss 19(3) and 22(3) of LRA 1925. Likewise, exclusion of any implied grant of rights (former quasi-easements) arising under the principle of non-derogation from grant is customary by reserving rights to light to the vendor, or lessor.

---

1 See Chapter 7 at **7.10–7.14** and Chapter 8 at **8.31–8.37**.

2 See *Cemp Properties (UK) Ltd v Dentsply Research and Development Corporation (No 1)* [1989] 2 EGLR 192 for the consequences of the failure to observe these rules.

3 See Chapter 8.

4 See Chapter 9.

5 See Chapter 5.

PROPOSALS FOR REFORM

14.20 The Law Commission and the Land Registry have published a paper[1] which sets out proposals for reforming the existing system of land registration. The broad effect of the proposals would be to preserve the position of *legal* easements as overriding interests, whilst removing that status for equitable easements and various other matters currently classified as overriding interests. It is also proposed to render registration of easements simpler and make their protection more secure.

14.21 Legislation to implement these proposals is likely to be some way off; the principal interest of the report lies in its analysis of some of the pitfalls of the existing land registration system.

1 *Land Registration for the 21st Century* (Law Commission No 254, 1998).

Chapter 15

The Effect of the Human Rights Act 1998 on Rights to Light

SUMMARY

15.1 The Human Rights Act 1998 ('the 1998 Act') comes into force on 2 October 2000. The likely impact of the Act on property rights is, at the time of writing, a matter for speculation. This chapter seeks to examine the potential difference which the Act could make to rights to light.

15.2 The 1998 Act has a potential significance in two areas. First, s 6 of the 1998 Act makes it unlawful for a public authority to act in a way which is incompatible with Convention rights. It is therefore possible that an action for breach of the public authorities' duty under s 6 of the 1998 Act could arise where the authority interferes with the light of another. Secondly, the 1998 Act may have a significant impact on the construction of s 3 of the Prescription Act 1832.

15.3 The first question is whether rights to light fall within the scope of the 1998 Act.[1] Rights to light potentially raise issues under Article 1 of the First Protocol (protection of property) and under Article 8 of the Convention (right to respect for private and family life, his home and his correspondence).[2]

PROTECTION OF PROPERTY RIGHTS

15.4 Article 1 of the First Protocol states:

> 'Every natural or legal person is entitled to the peaceful enjoyment of his possessions. No one shall be deprived of his possessions except in the public interest and subject to conditions provided for by law and by the general principles of international law.
>
> The preceding provisions shall not, however, in any way impair the right of a State to enforce such laws as it deems necessary to control the use of property in accordance with the general interest or to secure the payment of taxes or other contributions or penalties.'

---

1 By s 1 of the 1998 Act, 'Convention rights' are defined as the rights and fundamental freedoms set out in Articles 2 to 12 and 14 of the Convention for the Protection of Human Rights and Fundamental Freedoms ('the Convention'), Articles 1 to 3 of the First Protocol (dated 20 March 1952) and Articles 1 and 2 of the Sixth Protocol (dated 28 April 1983). These Articles are set out in Sch 1 to the Act.

2 It is conceivable that Article 6 issues (right to a fair trial) could also arise because the determination of property rights is the determination of civil rights and that Article 14 rights (prohibition of discrimination) is the enjoyment of a Convention right. However, these issues are beyond the scope of this chapter.

15.5 It is well established under the case-law of the European Court of Human Rights ('ECHR') and the European Commission of Human Rights ('the Commission'),[1] that serious interference with the enjoyment of property[2] can potentially fall within the scope of Article 1 of the First Protocol. The ECHR and the Commission have tended to require an adverse impact on the economic value of possessions before accepting that there has been interference. Where serious interferences with rights to light occur, this should not be difficult to establish.

15.6 There is no specific authority on interference with the rights to light. An analogous type of case, where the ECHR and the Commission have found that there has been interference within Article 1 of the First Protocol, is noise nuisance. In *Baggs v UK*,[3] the Commission held that noise nuisance which was severe and frequent and which had a potential impact on the economic value of the property could amount to an interference with possessions within the scope of Article 1 of the First Protocol. It is therefore anticipated that serious interference with the amount of light that reaches another's property is likely to satisfy the requirement of interference with possessions within Article 1 of the First Protocol where an adverse impact on the economic value of property can be established.

15.7 It should be noted that Article 1 does not affect the ascription and identification of property rights which the ECHR and the Commission have considered being a matter for national courts.[4] However, it is submitted that this limitation is unlikely to affect the application of Article 1 of the First Protocol to rights to light. The courts are likely to focus on the interference with the enjoyment of the dominant tenement; not the process of acquisition of rights to light by prescription. It follows from this that Article 1 of the First Protocol may well be relevant in circumstances where no right to light has crystallised by the expiry of the 20-year prescription period.

15.8 Interference with enjoyment of property is simply the starting point for establishing a breach of Article 1 of the First Protocol. A claim will fail if it can be established that the interference can be justified because the law strikes a fair balance between the rights of the State and the individual. The text of Article 1 and the general approach adopted by the ECHR gives a wide ambit to States to justify interference. The extent of the interference is highly relevant. Generally speaking, interference with rights to light are at the lower end of the scale of interferences with property under Article 1, which is more commonly associated with the confiscation or total appropriation of an individual's property.

---

1 This body of case-law must be taken into account by the UK courts in determining a human rights question (1998 Act, s 2).

2 The Convention concept of 'possessions' is a broad one. It includes land and leases but is much wider, including contractual rights, shares, patents and debts (see, eg, *Tre Traktörer AB v Sweden* (1989) 13 EHRR 309).

3 (1987) 52 DR 29.

4 See Harris, O'Boyle and Warbrick *Law of the European Convention of Human Rights* at p 517 and *S v UK* 47 DR 274 at 279 and *Marckx v Belgium* (1979) Series A No 31 at para 50.

15.9 In considering whether or not an interference with property can be justified, the ECHR has considered it a highly material factor whether or not compensation has been awarded (see, eg, *Holy Monasteries v Greece*[1]). Therefore, the availability of compensation for the appropriation of rights to light under s 237 of the Town and Country Planning Act 1990 may well be a sufficient justification for any interference by the local authority within the scope of that section.[2]

15.10 Where the 20-year prescription period has not elapsed, there may well be a strong foundation for arguing that there is no breach of Article 1. This is because any interference with property rights may be justified on the basis that a fair balance is struck between the rights of the individual and the State by a rule requiring the enjoyment of light for 20 years before any right can be asserted.

15.11 However, it is easy to conceive a hypothetical situation where there has been a serious interference with the light enjoyed by a property owner by the Crown, where light has been enjoyed for a period exceeding 20 years. Under current domestic law, the Crown could rely on its immunity under s 3 of the Prescription Act 1832.[3] However, where there is no objective justification for the interference and no compensation, there may well be a breach of Article 1.

PROTECTION OF PRIVATE AND FAMILY LIFE AND THE HOME

15.12 Article 8 of the Convention states:

> '1. Everyone has the right to respect for his private and family life, his home and correspondence.
> 2. The shall be no interference by a public authority with the exercise of this right except such as is in accordance with the law and is necessary in a democratic society in the interests of national security, public safety or the economic well being of the country, for the prevention of disorder or crime, for the protection of health or morals, or for the protection of the rights and freedoms of others.'

15.13 Recent case-law of the ECHR has confirmed the potentially wide scope of Article 8 in relation to interference with a person's home. In *Powell and Rayner v UK*,[4] the court held that the quality of the applicant's private life and the scope for enjoying the amenities of his home have been adversely affected by the noise generated by aircraft using Heathrow Airport. In that case, the Court held that the interference was justified because noise abatements measures had been taken by the government. The case is important nevertheless because it

---

1 (1994) 20 EHRR 1. However, there is no guarantee of full compensation (see *James v United Kingdom* (1986) 8 EHRR 123).
2 See Chapter 8 at **8.56–8.61**.
3 See Chapter 6 at **6.29–6.31**.
4 (1990) 12 EHRR 355.

establishes that a breach of Article 8 can flow from nuisance, such as excessive noise.

15.14 Similarly, in *Lopez Ostra v Spain*,[1] the applicants' right to respect for their home had been interfered with by substantial pollution from a waste treatment plant near their home.

15.15 It is submitted that interferences with rights to light may well raise issues as to whether or not an individual's home has been interfered with. Clearly, questions of whether any interference can be justified are as relevant under the Article 8 analysis as they are under Article 1 of the First Protocol.

CONSTRUCTION OF SECTION 3 OF THE PRESCRIPTION ACT 1832

15.16 Section 3 of the Human Rights Act 1998 states:

> 'So far as it is possible to do so, primary legislation and subordinate legislation must be read and given effect in a way which is compatible with the Convention rights.'

This paragraph has a potentially significant impact on the construction of s 3 of the Prescription Act 1832 because if the court considers that:

(a) construing s 3 of the Prescription Act 1832 as conferring immunity to the Crown in relation to the acquisition of rights to light against the Crown[2] (following *Wheaton v Maple & Co*[3]), may lead to a result which interferes with a Convention right (under Article 1 of the First Protocol or Article 8 of the Convention); and
(b) it is possible to construe s 3 in a manner which does not involve such an interference (ie as binding the Crown),

then the Court is obliged to interpret s 3 in the manner which does not infringe Convention rights. There is no qualification that the (non-infringing) construction must be reasonable; it simply needs to be possible.[4]

15.17 It is therefore quite possible that the court may reconsider the scope of s 3 of the Prescription Act 1832 and conclude that it does apply to the Crown (because to hold otherwise would involve the impermissible sanction of breaches of Article 8 and Article 1 of the First Protocol in certain circumstances).

---

1 (1994) 20 EHRR 277.

2 See Chapter 6 at **6.29**.

3 [1893] 3 Ch 48, CA.

4 A Conservative amendment, which proposed that s 3 of the then Human Rights Bill should require the courts to construe Acts of Parliament as consistent with the Human Rights Act 1998 so far as reasonably possible was rejected. The Home Secretary stated: 'we want the courts to strive to find an interpretation of legislation that is consistent with Convention rights, so far as the plain words of the legislation allow, and only in the last resort to conclude that the legislation is simply incompatible with them' (Hansard HC, 3 June 1998, cols 421–422).

15.18 There is potential for a counter-argument that it is not possible to construe s 3 of the Prescription Act 1832 as applying to the Crown because of s 4(2) of the Rights of Light Act 1959. If this argument succeeded, the courts may declare s 3 of the Prescription Act 1832 (and s 4(2) of the Rights of Light Act 1959) incompatible with Article 1 of the First Protocol and/or Article 8 of the Convention).[1] However, given the obligation of the courts to strive to find a construction of the potentially offending Act that is compatible with Convention rights and the fact that s 4(2) does not state in terms that s 3 does not apply to the Crown in any circumstances, it is submitted that a new construction of s 3 of the Prescription Act 1832 is a more likely outcome than a declaration of incompatibility.

CONCLUSION

15.19 It is not possible to do more than engage in informed speculation as to the likely impact of the 1998 Act on rights to light. However, the 1998 Act does have the potential to have a radical impact on certain firmly established principles of the law relating to rights to light.

1 By s 4(6) of the 1998 Act, a declaration of incompatibility: (a) does not affect the validity, continuing operation and enforcement of the provision in respect of which it is given; and (b) is not binding on the parties to the proceedings in which it is made.

Appendix 1
Statutes

CONTRACTS (RIGHTS OF THIRD PARTIES) ACT 1999

(1999 c 31)
sections 1–8

1 Right of third party to enforce contractual term

(1) Subject to the provisions of this Act, a person who is not a party to a contract (a 'third party') may in his own right enforce a term of the contract if—

(a) the contract expressly provides that he may, or
(b) subject to subsection (2), the term purports to confer a benefit on him.

(2) Subsection (1)(b) does not apply if on a proper construction of the contract it appears that the parties did not intend the term to be enforceable by the third party.

(3) The third party must be expressly identified in the contract by name, as a member of a class or as answering a particular description but need not be in existence when the contract is entered into.

(4) This section does not confer a right on a third party to enforce a term of a contract otherwise than subject to and in accordance with any other relevant terms of the contract.

(5) For the purpose of exercising his right to enforce a term of the contract, there shall be available to the third party any remedy that would have been available to him in an action for breach of contract if he had been a party to the contract (and the rules relating to damages, injunctions, specific performance and other relief shall apply accordingly).

(6) Where a term of a contract excludes or limits liability in relation to any matter references in this Act to the third party enforcing the term shall be construed as references to his availing himself of the exclusion or limitation.

(7) In this Act, in relation to a term of a contract which is enforceable by a third party—

'the promisor' means the party to the contract against whom the term is enforceable by the third party, and
'the promisee' means the party to the contract by whom the term is enforceable against the promisor.

2 Variation and rescission of contract

(1) Subject to the provisions of this section, where a third party has a right under section 1 to enforce a term of the contract, the parties to the contract may not, by agreement, rescind the contract, or vary it in such a way as to extinguish or alter his entitlement under that right, without his consent if—

(a) the third party has communicated his assent to the term to the promisor,
(b) the promisor is aware that the third party has relied on the term, or
(c) the promisor can reasonably be expected to have foreseen that the third party would rely on the term and the third party has in fact relied on it.

(2) The assent referred to in subsection (1)(a)—

(a) may be by words or conduct, and
(b) if sent to the promisor by post or other means, shall not be regarded as communicated to the promisor until received by him.

(3) Subsection (1) is subject to any express term of the contract under which—

(a) the parties to the contract may by agreement rescind or vary the contract without the consent of the third party, or
(b) the consent of the third party is required in circumstances specified in the contract instead of those set out in subsection (1)(a) to (c).

(4) Where the consent of a third party is required under subsection (1) or (3), the court or arbitral tribunal may, on the application of the parties to the contract, dispense with his consent if satisfied—

(a) that his consent cannot be obtained because his whereabouts cannot reasonably be ascertained, or
(b) that he is mentally incapable of giving his consent.

(5) The court or arbitral tribunal may, on the application of the parties to a contract, dispense with any consent that may be required under subsection (1)(c) if satisfied that it cannot reasonably be ascertained whether or not the third party has in fact relied on the term.

(6) If the court or arbitral tribunal dispenses with a third party's consent, it may impose such conditions as it thinks fit, including a condition requiring the payment of compensation to the third party.

(7) The jurisdiction conferred on the court by subsections (4) to (6) is exercisable by both the High Court and a county court.

3 Defences etc. available to promisor

(1) Subsections (2) to (5) apply where, in reliance on section 1, proceedings for the enforcement of a term of a contract are brought by a third party.

(2) The promisor shall have available to him by way of defence or set-off any matter that—

(a) arises from or in connection with the contract and is relevant to the term, and
(b) would have been available to him by way of defence or set-off if the proceedings had been brought by the promisee.

(3) The promisor shall also have available to him by way of defence or set-off any matter if—

(a) an express term of the contract provides for it to be available to him in proceedings brought by the third party, and
(b) it would have been available to him by way of defence or set-off if the proceedings had been brought by the promisee.

(4) The promisor shall also have available to him—

(a) by way of defence or set-off any matter, and
(b) by way of counterclaim any matter not arising from the contract,

that would have been available to him by way of defence or set-off or, as the case may be, by way of counterclaim against the third party if the third party had been a party to the contract.

(5) Subsections (2) and (4) are subject to any express term of the contract as to the matters that are not to be available to the promisor by way of defence, set-off or counterclaim.

(6) Where in any proceedings brought against him a third party seeks in reliance on section 1 to enforce a term of a contract (including, in particular, a term purporting to exclude or limit liability), he may not do so if he could not have done so (whether by reason of any particular circumstances relating to him or otherwise) had he been a party to the contract.

4 Enforcement of contract by promisee

Section 1 does not affect any right of the promisee to enforce any term of the contract.

5 Protection of promisor from double liability

Where under section 1 a term of a contract is enforceable by a third party, and the promisee has recovered from the promisor a sum in respect of—

(a) the third party's loss in respect of the term, or
(b) the expense to the promisee of making good to the third party the default of the promisor,

then, in any proceedings brought in reliance on that section by the third party, the court or arbitral tribunal shall reduce any award to the third party to such extent as it thinks appropriate to take account of the sum recovered by the promisee.

6 Exceptions

(1) Section 1 confers no rights on a third party in the case of a contract on a bill of exchange, promissory note or other negotiable instrument.

(2) Section 1 confers no rights on a third party in the case of any contract binding on a company and its members under section 14 of the Companies Act 1985.

(3) Section 1 confers no right on a third party to enforce—

(a) any term of a contract of employment against an employee,
(b) any term of a worker's contract against a worker (including a home worker), or
(c) any term of a relevant contract against an agency worker.

(4) In subsection (3)—

(a) 'contract of employment', 'employee', 'worker's contract', and 'worker' have the meaning given by section 54 of the National Minimum Wage Act 1998,
(b) 'home worker' has the meaning given by section 35(2) of that Act,
(c) 'agency worker' has the same meaning as in section 34(1) of that Act, and
(d) 'relevant contract' means a contract entered into, in a case where section 34 of that Act applies, by the agency worker as respects work falling within subsection (1)(a) of that section.

(5) Section 1 confers no rights on a third party in the case of—

(a) a contract for the carriage of goods by sea, or
(b) a contract for the carriage of goods by rail or road, or for the carriage of cargo by air, which is subject to the rules of the appropriate international transport convention,

except that a third party may in reliance on that section avail himself of an exclusion or limitation of liability in such a contract.

(6) In subsection (5) 'contract for the carriage of goods by sea' means a contract of carriage—

(a) contained in or evidenced by a bill of lading, sea waybill or a corresponding electronic transaction, or
(b) under or for the purposes of which there is given an undertaking which is contained in a ship's delivery order or a corresponding electronic transaction.

(7) For the purposes of subsection (6)—

(a) 'bill of lading', 'sea waybill' and 'ship's delivery order' have the same meaning as in the Carriage of Goods by Sea Act 1992, and
(b) a corresponding electronic transaction is a transaction within section 1(5) of that Act which corresponds to the issue, indorsement, delivery or transfer of a bill of lading, sea waybill or ship's delivery order.

(8) In subsection (5) 'the appropriate international transport convention' means—

(a) in relation to a contract for the carriage of goods by rail, the Convention which has the force of law in the United Kingdom under section 1 of the International Transport Conventions Act 1983,
(b) in relation to a contract for the carriage of goods by road, the Convention which has the force of law in the United Kingdom under section 1 of the Carriage of Goods by Road Act 1965, and
(c) in relation to a contract for the carriage of cargo by air—
    (i) the Convention which has the force of law in the United Kingdom under section 1 of the Carriage by Air Act 1961, or
    (ii) the Convention which has the force of law under section 1 of the Carriage by Air (Supplementary Provisions) Act 1962, or
    (iii) either of the amended Conventions set out in Part B of Schedule 2 or 3 to the Carriage by Air Acts (Application of Provisions) Order 1967.

7 Supplementary provisions relating to third party

(1) Section 1 does not affect any right or remedy of a third party that exists or is available apart from this Act.

(2) Section 2(2) of the Unfair Contract Terms Act 1977 (restriction on exclusion etc. of liability for negligence) shall not apply where the negligence consists of the breach of an obligation arising from a term of a contract and the person seeking to enforce it is a third party acting in reliance on section 1.

(3) In sections 5 and 8 of the Limitation Act 1980 the references to an action founded on a simple contract and an action upon a specialty shall respectively include references to an action brought in reliance on section 1 relating to a simple contract and an action brought in reliance on that section relating to a specialty.

(4) A third party shall not, by virtue of section 1(5) or 3(4) or (6), be treated as a party to the contract for the purposes of any other Act (or any instrument made under any other Act).

8 Arbitration provisions

(1) Where—

(a) a right under section 1 to enforce a term ('the substantive term') is subject to a term providing for the submission of disputes to arbitration ('the arbitration agreement'), and
(b) the arbitration agreement is an agreement in writing for the purposes of Part I of the Arbitration Act 1996,

the third party shall be treated for the purposes of that Act as a party to the arbitration agreement as regards disputes between himself and the promisor relating to the enforcement of the substantive term by the third party.

(2) Where—

(a) a third party has a right under section 1 to enforce a term providing for one or more descriptions of dispute between the third party and the promisor to be submitted to arbitration ('the arbitration agreement'),
(b) the arbitration agreement is an agreement in writing for the purposes of Part I of the Arbitration Act 1996, and
(c) the third party does not fall to be treated under subsection (1) as a party to the arbitration agreement,

the third party shall, if he exercises the right, be treated for the purposes of that Act as a party to the arbitration agreement in relation to the matter with respect to which the right is exercised, and be treated as having been so immediately before the exercise of the right.

[...]

LAND REGISTRATION ACT 1925

(1925 c 21)
sections 18, 20, 70

[...]

PART III
REGISTERED DEALINGS WITH REGISTERED LAND

Dispositions of Freehold Land

18 Powers of disposition of registered freeholds

(1) Where the registered land is a freehold estate the proprietor may, in the prescribed manner, transfer the registered estate in the land or any part thereof, and, subject to any entry in the register to the contrary, may in the prescribed manner—

(a) transfer the fee simple in possession of all or any mines or minerals apart from the surface; or of the surface without all or any part of the mines and minerals;

[...]

(c) grant in fee simple in possession any easement, right, or privilege in, over, or derived from the registered land or any part thereof, in any form which sufficiently refers, in the prescribed manner, to the registered servient tenement and to the dominant tenement, whether being registered land or not;

(d) transfer the fee simple in possession of the registered land or any part thereof, subject to the creation thereout, by way of reservation, in favour of any person of an annuity or a rentcharge in possession (either perpetual or for a term of years absolute), or of any easement, right, or privilege in possession (either in fee simple or for a term of years absolute);

(e) grant (subject or not to the reservation of an easement, right, or privilege) a lease of the registered land or any part thereof, or of all or any mines and minerals apart from the surface, or of the surface without all or any of the mines and minerals, or of an easement, right or privilege in or over the land, or any part thereof, for any term of years absolute for any purpose (but where by way of mortgage subject to the provisions of this Act and the Law of Property Act 1925 relating thereto), and in any form which sufficiently refers, in the prescribed manner, to the registered land.

[...]

20 Effect of registration and dispositions of freeholds

(1) In the case of a freehold estate registered with an absolute title, a disposition of the registered land or of a legal estate therein, including a lease thereof, for valuable consideration shall, when registered, confer on the transferee or grantee an estate in fee simple or the term of years absolute or other legal estate expressed to be created in the land dealt with, together with all rights, privileges, and appurtenances belonging or appurtenant thereto, including (subject to any entry to the contrary in the register) the appropriate rights and interests which would, under the Law of Property Act 1925, have been transferred if the land had not been registered, subject—

(a) to the incumbrances and other entries, if any, appearing on the register and any charge for inheritance tax subject to which the disposition takes effect under section 73 of this Act; and
(b) unless the contrary is expressed on the register, to the overriding interests, if any, affecting the estate transferred or created,

but free from all other estates and interests whatsoever, including estates and interests of His Majesty, and the disposition shall operate in like manner as if the registered transferor or grantor were (subject to any entry to the contrary in the register) entitled to the registered land in fee simple in possession for his own benefit.

(2) In the case of a freehold estate registered with a qualified title a disposition of the registered land or of a legal estate therein, including a lease thereof, for valuable consideration shall, when registered, have the same effect as it would have had if the land had been registered with an absolute title, save that such disposition shall not affect or prejudice the enforcement of any right or interest appearing by the register to be excepted.

[...]

NOTE
As amended by the Finance Act 1975, s 52(1), Sch 12, paras 2, 5(1), (2).

70 Liability of registered land to overriding interests

(1) All registered land shall, unless under the provisions of this Act the contrary is expressed on the register, be deemed to be subject to such of the following overriding interests as may be for the time being subsisting in reference thereto, and such interests shall not be treated as incumbrances within the meaning of this Act, (that is to say):—

(a) Rights of common, drainage rights, customary rights (until extinguished), public rights, profits à prendre, rights of sheepwalk, rights of way, watercourses, rights of water, and other easements not being equitable easements required to be protected by notice on the register;
[...]
(f) Subject to the provisions of this Act, rights acquired or in course of being acquired under the Limitation Acts;
(g) The rights of every person in actual occupation of the land or in receipt of the rents and profits thereof, save where enquiry is made of such person and the rights are not disclosed;
(h) In the case of a possessory, qualified, or good leasehold title, all estates, rights, interests, and powers excepted from the effect of registration;
(i) Rights under local land charges unless and until registered or protected on the register in the prescribed manner;
[...]

LAW OF PROPERTY ACT 1925

(1925 c 20)
sections 1, 12, 52–54, 62, 187

PART I
GENERAL PRINCIPLES AS TO LEGAL ESTATES, EQUITABLE INTERESTS AND POWERS

1 Legal estates and equitable interests

(1) The only estates in land which are capable of subsisting or of being conveyed or created at law are—

(a) An estate in fee simple absolute in possession;
(b) A term of years absolute.

(2) The only interests or charges in or over land which are capable of subsisting or of being conveyed or created at law are—

(a) An easement, right, or privilege in or over land for an interest equivalent to an estate in fee simple absolute in possession or a term of years absolute;

[. . .]

12 Limitation and Prescription Acts

Nothing in this Part of this Act affects the operation of any statute, or of the general law for the limitation of actions or proceedings relating to land or with reference to the acquisition of easements or rights over or in respect of land.

[. . .]

52 Conveyances to be by deed

(1) All conveyances of land or of any interest therein are void for the purpose of conveying or creating a legal estate unless made by deed.

(2) This section does not apply to—

(a) assents by a personal representative;
(b) disclaimers made in accordance with sections 178 to 180 or sections 315 to 319 of the Insolvency Act 1986, or not required to be evidenced in writing;
(c) surrenders by operation of law, including surrenders which may, by law, be effected without writing;
(d) leases or tenancies or other assurances not required by law to be made in writing;
(e) receipts other than those falling within section 115 below;
(f) vesting orders of the court or other competent authority;
(g) conveyances taking effect by operation of law.

NOTES
As amended by the Insolvency Act 1986, s 439(2), Sch 14; the Law of Property (Miscellaneous Provisions) Act 1989, s 1(8), Sch 1, para 2, except in relation to instruments delivered as deeds before 31 July 1990.

53 Instruments required to be in writing

(1) Subject to the provisions hereinafter contained with respect to the creation of interests in land by parol—

- (a) no interest in land can be created or disposed of except by writing signed by the person creating or conveying the same, or by his agent thereunto lawfully authorised in writing, or by will, or by operation of law;
- (b) a declaration of trust respecting any land or any interest therein must be manifested and proved by some writing signed by some person who is able to declare such trust or by his will;
- (c) a disposition of an equitable interest or trust subsisting at the time of the disposition, must be in writing signed by the person disposing of the same, or by his agent thereunto lawfully authorised in writing or by will.

(2) This section does not affect the creation or operation of resulting, implied or constructive trusts.

54 Creation of interests in land by parol

(1) All interests in land created by parol and not put in writing and signed by the persons so creating the same, or by their agents thereunto lawfully authorised in writing, have, notwithstanding any consideration having been given for the same, the force and effect of interests at will only.

(2) Nothing in the foregoing provisions of this Part of this Act shall affect the creation by parol of leases taking effect in possession for a term not exceeding three years (whether or not the lessee is given power to extend the term) at the best rent which can be reasonably obtained without taking a fine.

[...]

62 General words implied in conveyances

(1) A conveyance of land shall be deemed to include and shall by virtue of this Act operate to convey, with the land, all buildings, erections, fixtures, commons, hedges, ditches, fences, ways, waters, watercourses, liberties, privileges, easements, rights, and advantages whatsoever, appertaining or reputed to appertain to the land, or any part thereof, or, at the time of conveyance, demised, occupied, or enjoyed with or reputed or known as part or parcel of or appurtenant to the land or any part thereof.

(2) A conveyance of land, having houses or other buildings thereon, shall be deemed to include and shall by virtue of this Act operate to convey, with the land, houses, or other buildings, all outhouses, erections, fixtures, cellars, areas, courts, courtyards, cisterns, sewers, gutters, drains, ways, passages, lights, watercourses, liberties, privileges, easements, rights, and advantages whatsoever, appertaining or reputed to appertain to the land, houses, or other buildings conveyed, or any of them, or any part thereof, or, at the time of conveyance, demised, occupied, or enjoyed with, or reputed or known as part or parcel of or appurtenant to, the land, houses, other buildings conveyed, or any of them, or any part thereof.

[...]

(4) This section applies only if and as far as a contrary intention is not expressed in the conveyance, and has effect subject to the terms of the conveyance and to the provisions therein contained.

(5) This section shall not be construed as giving to any person a better title to any property, right, or thing in this section mentioned than the title which the conveyance gives to him to the land or manor expressed to be conveyed, or as conveying to him any property, right, or thing in this section mentioned, further or otherwise than as the same could have been conveyed to him by the conveying parties.

(6) This section applies to conveyances made after the thirty-first day of December, eighteen hundred and eighty-one.

[...]

187 Legal easements

(1) Where an easement, right or privilege for a legal estate is created, it shall enure for the benefit of the land to which it is intended to be annexed.

(2) Nothing in this Act affects the right of a person to acquire, hold or exercise an easement, right or privilege over or in relation to land for a legal estate in common with any other person, or the power of creating or conveying such an easement right or privilege.

[...]

LOCAL LAND CHARGES ACT 1975

(1975 c 76)
sections 1, 3–5, 8–11

Definition of local land charges

1 Local land charges

(1) A charge or other matter affecting land is a local land charge if it falls within any of the following descriptions and is not one of the matters set out in section 2 below:—

[...]

Local land charges registers, registration and related matters

3 Registering authorities, local land charges registers, and indexes

(1) Each of the following local authorities—

(a) the council of any district;
(aa) a Welsh county council;
(ab) a county borough council;
(b) the council of any London borough; and
(c) the Common Council of the City of London,

shall be a registered authority for the purposes of this Act.

(2) There shall continue to be kept for the area of each registering authority—

(a) a local land charges register, and
(b) an index whereby all entries made in that register can readily be traced,

and as from the commencement of this Act the register and index kept for the area of a registering authority shall be kept by that authority.

(3) Neither a local land charges register nor an index such as is mentioned in subsection (2)(b) above need be kept in documentary form.

(4) For the purposes of this Act the area of the Common Council of the City of London includes the Inner Temple and the Middle Temple.

NOTES
As amended by the Local Government (Wales) Act 1994, s 66(6), Sch 16, para 49; the Local Government (Miscellaneous Provisions) Act 1982, s 34(a).

4 The appropriate local land charges register

In this Act, unless the context otherwise requires, 'the appropriate local land charges register', in relation to any land or to a lcoal land charge, means the local land charges register for the area in which the land or, as the case may be, the land affected by the charge is situated or, if the land in question is situated in two or more areas for which local land charges registers are kept, each of the local land charges registers kept for those areas respectively.

NOTE

As amended by the Interpretation Act 1978, s 25(1), Sch 3.

5 Registration

(1) Subject to subsection (6) below, where the originating authority as respects a local land charge are the registering authority, it shall be their duty to register it in the appropriate local land charges register.

(2) Subject to subsection (6) below, where the originating authority as respects a local land charge are not the registering authority, it shall be the duty of the originating authority to apply to the registering authority for its registration in the appropriate local land charges register and upon any such application being made it shall be the duty of the registering authority to register the charge accordingly.

(3) The registration in a local land charges register of a local land charge, or of any matter which when registered becomes a local land charge, shall be carried out by reference to the land affected or such part of it as is situated in the area for which the register is kept.

(4) In this Act, 'the originating authority', as respects a local land charge, means the Minister of the Crown, government department, local authority or other person by whom the charge is brought into existence or by whom, on its coming into existence, the charge is enforceable; and for this purpose—

- (a) where a matter that is a local land charge consists of or is embodied in, or is otherwise given effect by, an order, scheme or other instrument made or confirmed by a Minister of the Crown or government department on the application of another authority the charge shall be treated as brought into existence by that other authority; and
- (b) a local land charge brought into existence by a Minister of the Crown or government department on an appeal from a decision or determination of another authority or in the exercise of powers ordinarily exercisable by another authority shall be treated as brought into existence by that other authority.

(5) The registration of a local land charge may be cancelled pursuant to an order of the court.

(6) Where a charge or other matter is registrable in a local land charges register and before the commencement of this Act was also registrable in a register kept under the Land Charges Act 1972, then, if before the commencement of this Act it was registered in a register kept under that Act, there shall be no duty to register it, or to apply for its registration, under this Act and section 10 below shall not apply in relation to it.

[...]

Searches

8 Personal searches

(1) Any person may search in any local land charges register on paying the prescribed fee.

(1A) If a local land charges register is kept otherwise than in documentary form, the entitlement of a person to search in it is satisfied if the registering authority makes the portion of it which he wishes to examine available for inspection in visible and legible form.

(2) Without prejudice to subsections (1) and (1A) above, a registering authority may provide facilities for enabling persons entitled to search in the authority's local land charges register to see photographic or other images of copies of any portion of the register which they may wish to examine.

NOTES

As amended by the Local Government (Miscellaneous Provisions) Act 1982, s 34(b); the Local Government (Miscellaneous Provisions) Act 1982, s 34(c).

9 Official searches

(1) Where any person requires an official search of the appropriate local land charges register to be made in respect of any land, he may make a requisition in that behalf to the registering authority.

(2) For the purposes of serving any such requisition on the Common Council of the City of London section 231(1) of the Local Government Act 1972 shall apply in relation to that Council as it applies in relation to a local authority within the meaning of that Act.

(3) The prescribed fee shall be payable in the prescribed manner in respect of every requisition made under this section.

(4) Where a requisition is made to a registering authority under this section and the fee payable in respect of it is paid in accordance with subsection (3) above, the registering authority shall thereupon make the search required and shall issue an official certificate setting out the result of the search.

NOTE

As amended by the Local Government and Housing Act 1989, ss 158, 194, Sch 12, Pt II.

Compensation for non-registration or defective official search certificate

10 Compensation for non-registration or defective official search certificate

(1) Failure to register a local land charge in the appropriate local land charges register shall not affect the enforceability of the charge but where a person has purchased any land affected by a local land charge, then—

- (a) in a case where a material personal search of the appropriate local land charges register was made in respect of the land in question before the relevant time, if at the time of the search the charge was in existence but not registered in that register; or
- (aa) in a case where the appropriate local land charges register is kept otherwise than in documentary form and a material personal search of that register was made in respect of the land in question before the relevant time, if the entitlement to search in that register conferred by section 8 above was not satisfied as mentioned in subsection (1A) of that section; or
- (b) in a case where a material official search of the appropriate local land charges register was made in respect of the land in question before the relevant time, if the charge was in existence at the time of the search but (whether registered or not) was not shown by the official search certificate as registered in that register,

the purchaser shall (subject to section 11(1) below) be entitled to compensation for any loss suffered by him in consequence.

(2) At any time when rules made under this Act make provision for local land charges registers to be divided into parts then, for the purposes subsection (1) above—

(a) a search (whether personal or official) of a part or parts only of any such register shall not constitute a search of that register in relation to any local land charge registrable in a part of the register not searched; and
(b) a charge shall not be taken to be registered in the appropriate local land charges register unless registered in the appropriate part of the register.

(3) For the purposes of this section—

(a) a person purchases land where, for valuable consideration, he acquires any interest in land or the proceeds of sale of land, and this includes cases where he acquires as lessee or mortgagee and shall be treated as including cases where an interest is conveyed or assigned at his direction to another person;
(b) the relevant time—
  (i) where the acquisition of the interest in question was preceded by a contract for its acquisition, other than a qualified liability contract, is the time when that contract was made;
  (ii) in any other case, is the time when the purchaser acquired the interest in question or, if he acquired it under a disposition which took effect only when registered under the Land Registration Act 1925, the time when that disposition was made; and for the purposes of sub-paragraph (i) above, a qualified liability contract is a contract containing a term the effect of which is to make the liability of the purchaser dependent upon, or avoidable by reference to, the outcome of a search for local land charges affecting the land to be purchased.
(c) a personal search is material if, but only if—
  (i) it is made after the commencement of this Act, and
  (ii) it is made by or on behalf of the purchaser or, before the relevant time, the purchaser or his agent has knowledge of the result of it;
(d) an official search is material if, but only if—
  (i) it is made after the commencement of this Act, and
  (ii) it is requisitioned by or on behalf of the purchaser or, before the relevant time, the purchaser or his agent has knowledge of the contents of the official search certificate.

(4) Any compensation for loss under this section shall be paid by the registering authority in whose area the land affected is situated; and where the purchaser has incurred expenditure for the purpose of obtaining compensation under this section, the amount of the compensation shall include the amount of the expenditure reasonably incurred by him for that purpose (so far as that expenditure would not otherwise fall to be treated as loss for which he is entitled to compensation under this section).

NOTE
As amended by the County Courts Act 1984, s 148(1), Sch 2, para 57; the High Court and County Courts Jurisdiction Order 1991, SI 1991/724, art 2(8), Sch, Pt I.

[. . .]

11 Mortgages, trusts for sale and settled land

(1) Where there appear to be grounds for a claim under section 10 above in respect of an interest that is subject to a mortgage—

(a) the claim may be made by any mortgagee of the interest as if he were the person entitled to that interest but without prejudice to the making of a claim by that person;
(b) no compensation shall be payable under that section in respect of the interest of the mortgagee (as distinct from the interest which is subject to the mortgage);
(c) any compensation payable under that section in respect of the interest that is subject to the mortgage shall be paid to the mortgagee or, if there is more than one mortgagee, to the first mortgagee and shall in either case be applied by him as if it were proceeds of sale.

(2) Where an interest is subject to a trust of land any compensation payable in respect of it under section 10 above shall be dealt with as if it were proceeds of sale arising under the trust.

(3) Where an interest is settled land for the purposes of the Settled Land Act 1925 any compensation payable in respect of it under section 10 above shall be treated as capital money arising under that Act.

NOTE
As amended by the Trusts of Land and Appointment of Trustees Act 1996, s 25(1), Sch 3, para 14.

[...]

PARTY WALL ETC ACT 1996

(1996 c 40)
section 9

[...]

9 Easements

Nothing in this Act shall—

(a) authorise any interference with an easement of light or other easements in or relating to a party wall; or
(b) prejudicially affect any right of any person to preserve or restore any right or other thing in or connected with a party wall in case of the party wall being pulled down or rebuilt.

[...]

PRESCRIPTION ACT 1832

(2 & 3 Will 4 c 71)
sections 2–9

[...]

2 In claims of rights of way or other easement the periods to be twenty years and forty years

No claim which may be lawfully made at the common law, by custom, prescription, or grant, to any way or other easement, or to any watercourse, or the use of any water, to be enjoyed or derived upon, over, or from any land or water of our said lord the King ... or being parcel of the duchy of Lancaster or of the duchy of Cornwall, or being the property of any ecclesiastical or lay person, or body corporate, when such way or other matter as herein last before mentioned shall have been actually enjoyed by any person claiming right thereto without interruption for the full period of twenty years, shall be defeated or destroyed by showing only that such way or other matter was first enjoyed at any time prior to such period of twenty years, but nevertheless such claim may be defeated in any other way by which the same is now liable to be defeated; and where such way or other matter as herein last before mentioned shall have been so enjoyed as aforesaid for the full period of forty years, the right thereto shall be deemed absolute and indefeasible, unless it shall appear that the same was enjoyed by some consent or agreement expressly given or made for that purpose by deed or writing.

NOTE
As amended by the Statute Law Revision (No 2) Act 1888; the Statute Law Revision Act 1890.

3 Right to the use of light enjoyed for twenty years indefeasible, unless shown to have been by consent

When the access and use of light to and for any dwelling house, workshop, or other building shall have been actually enjoyed therewith for the full period of twenty years without interruption, the right thereto shall be deemed absolute and indefeasible, any local usage or custom to the contrary notwithstanding, unless it shall appear that the same was enjoyed by some consent or agreement expressly made or given for that purpose by deed or writing.

NOTE
As amended by the Statute Law Revision (No 2) Act 1888.

4 Before mentioned periods to be deemed those next before suits for claiming to which such periods relate – What shall constitute an interruption

Each of the respective periods of years herein-before mentioned shall be deemed and taken to be the period next before some suit or action wherein the claim or matter to which such period may relate shall have been or shall be brought into question; and no act or other matter shall be deemed to be an interruption, within the meaning of this statute, unless the same shall have been or shall be submitted to or acquiesced in for one year after the period interrupted shall have had or shall have notice therefore, and of the person making or authorizing the same to be made.

NOTE
As amended by the Statute Law Revision (No 2) Act 1888.

5 In actions on the case the claimant may allege his right generally, as at present. In pleas to trespass and other pleadings, etc, the period mentioned in this Act may be alleged; and exceptions, etc, to be replied to specially

In all actions upon the case and other pleadings, wherein the party claiming may now by law allege his right generally, without averring the existence of such right from time immemorial, such general allegation shall still be deemed sufficient, and if the same shall be denied, all and every the matters in this Act mentioned and provided, which shall be applicable to the case, shall be admissible in evidence to sustain or rebut such allegation; and in all pleadings to actions of trespass, and in all other pleadings wherein before the passing of this Act it would have been necessary to allege the right to have existed from time immemorial, it shall be sufficient to allege the enjoyment thereof as of right by the occupiers of the tenement in respect whereof the same is claimed for and during such of the periods mentioned in this Act as may be applicable to the case, and without claiming in the name or right of the owner of the fee, as is now usually done; and if the other party shall intend to rely on any proviso, exception, incapacity, disability, contract, agreement, or other matter herein-before mentioned, or on any cause or matter of fact or of law not inconsistent with the simple fact of enjoyment, the same shall be specially alleged and set forth in answer to the allegation of the party claiming, and shall not be received in evidence on any general traverse or denial of such allegation.

NOTE
As amended by the Statute Law Revision (No 2) Act 1888.

6 Restricting the presumption to be allowed in support of claims herein provided for

In the several cases mentioned in and provided for by this Act, no presumption shall be allowed or made in favour or support of any claim, upon proof of the exercise or enjoyment of the right or matter claimed for any less period of time or number of years than for such period or number mentioned in this Act as may be applicable to the case and to the nature of the claim.

NOTE
As amended by the Statute Law Revision (No 2) Act 1888.

7 Proviso for infants, etc

Provided also, that the time during which any person otherwise capable of resisting any claim to any of the matters before mentioned shall have been or shall be infant, idiot, non compos mentis, feme covert, or tenant for life, or during which any action or suit shall have been pending, and which shall have been diligently prosecuted, until abated by the death of any party or parties thereto, shall be excluded in the computation of the periods herein-before mentioned, except only in cases where the right or claim is hereby declared to be absolute and indefeasible.

8 What time to be excluded in computing the term of forty years appointed by this Act

Provided always, that when any land or water upon, over or from which any such way or other convenient watercourse or use of water shall have been or shall be enjoyed or derived hath been or shall be held under or by virtue of any term of life, or any term of years exceeding three years from the granting thereof, the time of the enjoyment of any such way or other matter as herein last before mentioned, during the continuance of such term, shall be excluded in the computation of the said period of forty years, in case the claim shall within three years next after the end or sooner determination of such term be resisted by any period entitled to any reversion expectant on the determination thereof.

NOTE
As amended by the Statute Law Revision (No 2) Act 1888.

9 Extent of Act

This Act shall not extend to Scotland.

NOTE
As amended by the Statute Law Revision (No 2) Act 1888.

[...]

RIGHTS OF LIGHT ACT 1959

(1959 c 56)

1 (*Repealed by the SL(R) Act 1974.*)

2 Registration of notice in lieu of obstruction of access of light

(1) For the purpose of preventing the access and use of light from being taken to be enjoyed without interruption, any person who is an owner of land (in this and the next following section referred to as the 'servient land') over which light passes to a dwelling-house, workshop or other building (in this and the next following section referred to as the 'the dominant building') may apply to the local authority in whose area the dominant building is situated for the registration of a notice under this section.

(2) An application for the registration of a notice under this section shall be in the prescribed form and shall—

- (a) identify the servient land and the dominant building in the prescribed manner, and
- (b) state that the registration of a notice in pursuance of the application is intended to be equivalent to the obstruction of the access of light to the dominant building across the servient land which would be caused by the erection, in such position on the servient land as may be specified in the application, of an opaque structure of such dimensions (including, if the application so states, unlimited height) as may be so specified.

(3) Any such application shall be accompanied by one or other of the following certificates issued by the Lands Tribunal, that is to say—

- (a) a certificate certifying that adequate notice of the proposed application has been given to all persons who, in the circumstances existing at the time when the certificate is issued, appear to the Lands Tribunal to be persons likely to be affected by the registration of a notice in pursuance of the application;
- (b) a certificate certifying that, in the opinion of the Lands Tribunal, the case is one of exceptional urgency, and that accordingly a notice should be registered forthwith as a temporary notice for such period as may be specified in the certificate.

(4) Where application is duly made to a local authority for the registration of a notice under this section, it shall be the duty of that authority to register the notice in the appropriate local land charges register, and—

- (a) any notice so registered under this section shall be a local land charge; but
- (b) section 5(1) and (2) and section 10 of the Local Land Charges Act 1975 shall not apply in relation thereto.

(5) Provision shall be made by rules under section three of the Lands Tribunal Act 1949 for regulating proceedings before the Lands Tribunal with respect to the issue of certificates for the purposes of this section, and, subject to the approval of the Treasury, the fees chargeable in respect of those proceedings; and, without prejudice to the generality of subsection (6) of that section, any such rules made for the purposes of this section shall include provision—

- (a) for requiring applicants for certificates under paragraph (a) of subsection (3) of this section to give such notices, whether by way of advertisement or otherwise, and to produce such documents and provide such information, as may be determined by or under the rules;

(b) for determining the period to be specified in a certificate issued under paragraph (b) of subsection (3) of this section; and
(c) in connection with any certificate issued under the said paragraph (b), for enabling a further certificate to be issued in accordance (subject to the necessary modifications) with paragraph (a) of subsection (3) of this section.

NOTE
As amended by the Local Land Charges Act 1975, s 17(2), Sch 1.

3 Effect of registered notice and proceedings relating thereto

(1) Where, in pursuance of an application made in accordance with the last preceding section, a notice is registered thereunder, then, for the purpose of determining whether any person is entitled (by virtue of the Prescription Act 1832, or otherwise) to a right to the access of light to the dominant building across the servient land, the access of light to that building across that land shall be treated as obstructed to the same extent, and with the like consequences, as if an opaque structure, of the dimensions specified in the application,—

(a) had, on the date of registration of the notice, been erected in the position on the servient land specified in the application, and had been so erected by the person who made the application, and
(b) had remained in that position during the period for which the notice has effect and had been removed at the end of that period.

(2) For the purposes of this section a notice registered under the last preceding section shall be taken to have effect until either—

(a) the registration is cancelled, or
(b) the period of one year beginning with the date of registration of the notice expires, or
(c) in the case of a notice registered in pursuance of an application accompanied by a certificate issued under paragraph (b) of subsection (3) of the last preceding section, the period specified in the certificate expires without such a further certificate as is mentioned in paragraph (c) of subsection (5) of that section having before the end of that period been lodged with the local authority,

and shall cease to have effect on the occurrence of any one of those events.

(3) Subject to the following provisions of this section, any person who, if such a structure as is mentioned in subsection (1) of this section had been erected as therein mentioned, would have had a right of action in any court in respect of that structure, on the grounds that he was entitled to a right to the access of light to the dominant building across the servient land, and that the said right was infringed by that structure, shall have the like right of action in that court in respect of the registration of a notice under the last preceding section:

Provided that an action shall not be begun by virtue of this subsection after the notice in question has ceased to have effect.

(4) Where, at any time during the period for which a notice registered under the last preceding section has effect, the circumstances are such that, if the access of light to the dominant building had been enjoyed continuously from a date one year earlier than the date on which the enjoyment thereof in fact began, a person would have had a right of

action in any court by virtue of the last preceding subsection in respect of the registration of the notice, that person shall have the like right of action in that court by virtue of this subsection in respect of the registration of the notice.

(5) The remedies available to the plaintiff in an action brought by virtue of subsection (3) or subsection (4) of this section (apart from any order as to costs) shall be such declaration as the court may consider appropriate in the circumstances, and an order directing the registration of the notice to be cancelled or varied, as the court may determine.

(6) For the purposes of section four of the Prescription Act 1832 (under which a period of enjoyment of any of the rights to which that Act applies is not to be treated as interrupted except by a matter submitted to or acquiesced in for one year after notice thereof)—

- (a) as from the date of registration of a notice under the last preceding section, all persons interested in the dominant building or any part thereof shall be deemed to have notice of the registration thereof and of the person on whose application it was registered;
- (b) until such time as an action is brought by virtue of subsection (3) or subsection (4) of this section in respect of the registration of a notice under the last preceding section, all persons interested in the dominant building or any part thereof shall be deemed to acquiesce in the obstruction which, in accordance with subsection (1) of this section, is to be treated as resulting from the registration of the notice;
- (c) as from the date on which such action is brought, no person shall be treated as submitting to or acquiescing in that obstruction;

Provided that, if in any such action, the court decides against the claim of the plaintiff, the court may direct that the preceding provisions of this subsection shall apply in relation to the notice as if that action had not been brought.

4 Application to Crown land

(1) Subject to the next following subsection, this Act shall apply in relation to land in which there is a Crown or Duchy interest as it applies in relation to land in which there is no such interest.

(2) Section three of the Prescription Act 1832, as modified by the preceding provisions of this Act, shall not by virtue of this section be construed as applying to any land to which (by reason that there is a Crown or Duchy interest therein) that section would not apply apart from this Act.

(3) In this section 'Crown or Duchy interest' means an interest belonging to Her Majesty in right of the Crown or of the Duchy of Lancaster, or belonging to the Duchy of Cornwall, or belonging to a government department, or held in trust for Her Majesty for the purposes of a government department.

5 Power to make rules

(1) (*Repealed*).

(2) Any rules made under section 14 of the Local Land Charges Act 1975 for the purposes of section 2 of this Act shall (without prejudice to the inclusion therein of other provisions as to cancelling or varying the registration of notices or agreements) include provision for giving effect to any order of the court under subsection (5) of section three of this Act.

NOTE
As amended by the Local Land Charges Act 1975, ss 17(2), 19(1), Schs 1, 2.

6 (*Repealed by the Northern Ireland Constitution Act 1973, s 41(1), Sch 6, Pt I.*)

7 Interpretation

(1) In this Act, except in so far as the context otherwise requires, the following expressions have the meanings hereby assigned to them respectively, that is to say:—

'action' includes a counterclaim, and any reference to the plaintiff in an action shall be construed accordingly;

'local authority', in relation to land in a district or a London borough, means the council of the district or borough, and, in relation to land in the City of London, means the Common Council of the City;

'owner', in relation to any land, means a person who is the estate owner in respect of the fee simple thereof, or is entitled to a tenancy thereof (within the meaning of the Landlord and Tenant Act 1954) for a term of years certain of which, at the time in question, not less than seven years remain unexpired, or is a mortgagee in possession (within the meaning of the Law of Property Act 1925) where the interest mortgaged is either the fee simple of the land or such a tenancy thereof;

'prescribed' means prescribed by rules made by virtue of subsection (6) of section fifteen of the Land Charges Act 1925 as applied by section five of this Act.

(2) References in this Act to any enactment shall, except where the context otherwise requires, be construed as references to that enactment as amended by or under any other enactment.

NOTE
As amended by the Local Land Charges Act 1975, s 17(2), Sch 1.

8 Short title, commencement and extent

(1) This Act may be cited as the Rights of Light Act 1959.

(2) This Act, except sections one and six thereof, shall come into operation at the end of the period of three months beginning with the day on which it is passed.

(3) This Act shall not extend to Scotland.

(4) This Act shall not extend to Northern Ireland.

NOTE
As amended by the Northern Ireland Constitution Act 1973, s 41(1), Sch 6, Pt I.

[...]

Appendix 2

Statutory Instruments

LAND REGISTRATION RULES 1925

SI 1925/1093
rules 257, 258

[...]

257 Positive registration

The benefit of an easement, right, or privilege shall not be entered on the register except as appurtenant to a registered estate, and then only if capable of subsisting as a legal estate.

258 Adverse easements treated as overriding interests

Rights, privileges, and appurtenances appertaining or reputed to appertain to land or demised, occupied, or enjoyed therewith or reputed or known as part or parcel of or appurtenant thereto, which adversely affect registered land, are overriding interests within Section 70 of the Act, and shall not be deemed incumbrances for the purposes of the Act.

[...]

LANDS TRIBUNAL RULES 1996

SI 1996/1022

rules 1, 2, 21–24, 30, 34, 35, 38, Sch 1

PART I

PRELIMINARY

1 Citation and commencement

These Rules may be cited as the Lands Tribunal Rules 1996 and shall come into force on May 1, 1996.

2 Interpretation

(1) In these Rules—

'the Act' means the Lands Tribunal Act 1949;
'the 1961 Act' means the Lands Compensation Act 1961;
'appeal' means an appeal against a determination of any question by an authority in respect of whose decision an appeal lies to the Lands Tribunal;
'authority' means the person or body in respect of whose decision an appeal is brought;
'the office' means the office for the time being of the Lands Tribunal;
'party' in relation to an appeal, means the appellant, the authority and any person who has served notice of intention to respond in accordance with rule 7;
'the President' means the President of the Lands Tribunal, or the member appointed under section 2(3) of the Act to act for the time being as deputy for the President;
'proceedings' means proceedings before the Lands Tribunal;
'rating appeal' means an appeal from the decision of a valuation tribunal in relation to non-domestic rating;
'the registrar' means the registrar of the Lands Tribunal or, as respects any powers or functions of the registrar, an officer of the Lands Tribunal authorised by the Lord Chancellor to exercise those powers or functions;
'the Tribunal' means the member or members of the Lands Tribunal selected under section 3(2) of the Act to deal with a case;
'valuation officer' means a valuation officer appointed under section 61 of the Local Government Finance Act 1988 or any officer authorised by him in writing to act on his behalf.

(2) In these Rules, a form referred to by number alone means the form so numbered in Schedule 1 to these Rules.

NOTE
As amended by SI 1997/1965.

[...]

PART VI

APPLICATIONS UNDER SECTION 2 OF THE RIGHTS OF LIGHT ACT 1959

21 Form of application

(1) An application for a certificate of the Lands Tribunal under section 2 of the Rights of Light Act 1959 shall be in Form 1.

(2) An application under paragraph (1) shall be accompanied by two copies of the application which the applicant proposes to make to the local authority in whose area the dominant building is situated.

22 Publicity

(1) Upon receipt of an application the registrar shall determine what notices are to be given, whether by advertisement or otherwise, to persons who appear to have an interest in the dominant building referred to in rule 21(2).

(2) For the purpose of paragraph (1), the registrar shall require the applicant to provide any documents or information which it is within his power to provide.

(3) The notices that the registrar determines shall be given under this rule shall be given by the applicant who shall notify the registrar in writing once this has been done setting out full particulars of the steps he has taken.

23 Issue of temporary certificate

(1) Where the Tribunal is satisfied that exceptional urgency requires the immediate registration of a temporary notice in the register of local land charges, it shall issue a temporary certificate in Form 2.

(2) A temporary certificate shall not last longer than six months.

24 Issue of definitive certificates

The Tribunal shall issue a certificate in Form 3 or, where a temporary certificate has been issued under rule 23, in Form 4, once it is satisfied that the notices which the registrar has determined shall be given under rule 22 have been duly given.

[...]

30 Consolidation of proceedings

(1) Where two or more notices of appeal, references or applications have been made which—

- (a) are in respect of the same land or buildings; or
- (b) relate to different interests in the same land or buildings; or
- (c) raise the same issues;

the President or the Tribunal may, on his or its own motion or on the application of a party to the proceedings, order that the appeals, references or applications be consolidated or heard together.

(2) An order may be made with respect to some only of the matters to which the appeals, references or applications relate.

[...]

34 Powers to order discovery, etc.

(1) The Tribunal, or subject to any directions given by the Tribunal, the registrar may, on the application of any party to the proceedings or of its or his own motion, order any party—

- (a) to deliver to the registrar any document or information which the Tribunal may require and which it is in the power of the party to deliver;
- (b) to afford to every other party to the proceedings an opportunity to inspect those documents (or copies of them) and to take copies;
- (c) to deliver to the registrar an affidavit or make a list stating whether any document or class of document specified or described in the order or application is, or has at any time been in his possession, custody or power and stating when he parted with it;
- (d) to deliver to the registrar a statement in the form of a pleading setting out further and better particulars of the grounds on which he intends to rely and any relevant facts or contentions;
- (e) to answer interrogatories on affidavit relating to any matter at issue between the applicant and the other party;
- (f) to deliver to the registrar a statement of agreed facts, facts in dispute and the issue or issues to be tried by the Tribunal; or
- (g) to deliver to the registrar witness statements or proofs of evidence.

(2) Where an order is made under paragraph (1) the Tribunal or registrar may give directions as to the time within which any document is to be sent to the registrar (being at least 14 days from the date of the direction) and the parties to whom copies of the document are to be sent.

(3) Rule 38 shall apply to this rule as appropriate both in relation to applications and where the registrar acts of his own motion.

35 Extension of time

(1) The time appointed by or under these Rules for doing any act or taking any steps in connection with any proceedings may be extended on application to the registrar under rule 38.

(2) The registrar may extend the time limit on such terms as he thinks fit and may order an extension even if the application is not made until after the time limit has expired.

[...]

38 Interlocutory applications

(1) Except where these Rules make other provision or the President otherwise orders, an application for directions of an interlocutory nature in connection with any proceedings shall be made to the registrar.

(2) The application shall be made in writing and shall state the title of the proceedings, and the grounds upon which the application is made.

(3) If the application is made with the consent of all parties, it shall be accompanied by consents signed by or on behalf of the parties.

(4) If the application is not made with the consent of every party the applicant shall serve a copy of the proposed application on every other party before it is made and the application shall state that this has been done.

(5) A party who objects to an application may, within 7 days of service of a copy on him, send written notice of his objection to the registrar.

(6) Before making an order on an application the registrar shall consider all the objections that he has received and may allow any party who wishes to appear before him the opportunity to do so.

(7) In dealing with an application the registrar shall have regard to the convenience of all the parties and the desirability of limiting so far as practicable the costs of the proceedings and shall inform the parties in writing of his decision.

(8) The registrar may refer the application to the President for a decision and he shall do so if requested by the applicant or a party objecting to the application.

(9) A party may appeal to the President from a decision of the registrar under this rule by giving written notice to the registrar within 7 days of service of the notice of decision or such further time as the registrar may allow.

(10) An appeal under paragraph (9) shall not act as a stay of proceedings unless the President so orders.

(11) Where an application under this rule is made—

- (a) with respect to a case that has been included by the President in a class or group of cases under section 3(2) of the Act, or
- (b) with respect to a case for which a member or members of the Lands Tribunal has or have been selected,

the powers and duties of the President under this rule may be exercised and discharged in relation to the application by any member or members of the Lands Tribunal authorised by the President for that purpose.

[...]

SCHEDULE 1

FORM 1

Application for Certificate under section 2 of the Rights of Light Act 1959

To:—The Registrar,
Lands Tribunal.

I/We ....
of ....
being [owner(s)] [tenant(s) for a term of years certain expiring in 19]

[mortgagee(s) in possession] of (*here describe the servient land*) ....
.... apply to the Lands Tribunal for the issue of a certificate that adequate publicity has been given to my/our proposed application for the registration in the register of local land charges of the ....
Council of a notice under section 2 of the Rights of Light Act 1959.

I/We attach two copies of the proposed application.

[I/We also apply for the issue of a certificate authorising the registration forthwith of the proposed notice as a temporary notice. The case is one of exceptional urgency because (*here insert reasons*) ....
....].

To the best of my/our knowledge persons likely to be affected by the registration of the notice are (*here insert names and addresses of all persons in occupation of the dominant building or having a proprietary interest in it*) ....
....
....

All communications regarding this application should be addressed to me/us at the address shown above [*or* to my/our solicitor/agent ....
of ....].

Dated .... Signed ....

FORM 2

Temporary Certificate for Registration of a Notice under section 2 of the Rights of Light Act 1959

I hereby certify that for reasons of exceptional urgency a temporary notice may be registered by (*name of applicant*) ....
forthwith against the building specified in the attached Form of Application for the registration of a notice under section 2 of the Rights of Light Act 1959.

A notice registered under the said application shall not have effect after the effluxion of .... months from the date of registration unless before the expiration of that period a further certificate of this Tribunal has been lodged with the registering authority stating that due publicity has been given to the proposed registration.

Dated .... Signed ....
Registrar
Lands Tribunal

FORM 3

Certificate for Registration of a Notice under section 2 of the Rights of Light Act 1959

I certify that adequate notice of the proposed application by (*name of applicant*)
....
a copy of which is attached to this certificate, to register a notice under section 2 of the Rights of Light Act 1959 against (*description of dominant building as specified in the application*) ....
has been given to all persons who, in the circumstances existing at the present time, appear to the Lands Tribunal to be persons likely to be affected by the registration of such a notice.

Dated .... Signed ....
Registrar
Lands Tribunal

FORM 4

Certificate for Registration of a Notice under section 2 of the Rights of Light Act 1959 following Registration of a Temporary Notice

I certify that adequate notice of the proposed application by (*name of applicant*)
....
to register a notice under section 2 of the Rights of Light Act 1959 against (*description of dominant building as specified in the application*) ....
....
has been given to all person who, in the circumstances existing at the present time, appear to the Lands Tribunal to be persons likely to be affected by the registration of such a notice.

A temporary certificate authorising the registration of a temporary notice was issued by the Lands Tribunal on .... 19 ....

Dated .... Signed ....

Registrar
Lands Tribunal

LOCAL LAND CHARGES RULES 1977

SI 1977/985
rules 1–16, Sch 1

(as amended by the Local Land Charges (Amendment) Rules 1995, SI 1995/260)

[*These rules are reproduced here only insofar as they affect applications under the Rights of Light Act 1959, s 2.*]

1 Title and commencement

These Rules may be cited as the Local Land Charges Rules 1977 and shall come into operation on 1st August 1977.

2 Interpretation

(1) The Interpretation Act 1889 shall apply to the interpretation of these Rules as it applies to the interpretation of an Act of Parliament.

(2) In these Rules, unless the context otherwise requires—

'the Act' means the Local Land Charges Act 1975;
'charge' means a local land charge or a matter which is registrable in a local land charges register;
'description' in relation to a charge means a description which is sufficient to indicate—

(a) the nature of any agreement, certificate, notice, order, resolution, scheme or other instrument or document (not being a statute or an instrument embodying statutory provisions) which comprises the charge or in connection with which the charge came into existence;
(b) where apparent from the instrument or document, the date on which the charge came into existence;
(c) any statutory provision (other than section 1(1)(e) of the Act or a provision specified in the part of Schedule 2 appropriate for the charge) under or by virtue of which the charge is a local land charge or registrable, or which comprises the charge;

[...]

'register' means local land charges register;

[...]

(3) In these Rules, unless the context otherwise requires, a rule or schedule referred to by number means the rule or schedule so numbered in these Rules and a form designated by letter means the form so designated in Schedule 1.

(4) In these Rules, unless the context otherwise requires, a reference to an enactment is a reference to that enactment as amended, extended or applied by or under any other enactment.

3 Parts of the Register

The register shall continue to be divided into parts, for the registration of different types of charge, as follows—

[...]

Part 11, for charges falling within section 2(4) of the Rights of Light Act 1959 ('light obstruction notices');

[...]

4 Application for registration

(1) Without prejudice to rule 10(1) below, an application to a registering authority for registration of a charge shall be in writing and shall contain a description of the charge and any other particulars necessary to enable the registering authority to register the charge in accordance with these Rules.

(2) An application for registration may be sent by post to, or left at the office of, the registering authority.

5 Delivery of applications

(1) For the purposes of section 10(5) of the Act, it shall be regarded as practicable for a registering authority to register a charge on the day on which the application for registration is delivered or treated in accordance with paragraph (2) below as having been delivered.

(2) An application for registration delivered between the time when the office of the registering authority closes and the time when it next opens shall be treated as having been delivered immediately after that interval.

6 Registration

(1) Every charge shall be registered by reference to the land in the area of the registering authority affected by the charge, in such a manner as to show the situation and extent of that land.

(2) Subject to rule 7, the registration of a charge shall be effected by entering in the part of the register appropriate for that charge the particulars specified in Schedule 2 in relation to that part.

7 Use of existing registers

Where the particulars of a planning charge or other charge which are required by these Rules to be entered in the register have been entered in another record maintained and kept open for public inspection in pursuance of a statutory obligation, it shall be a sufficient compliance with that requirement to enter in the register a reference whereby the particulars in that other record can readily be traced.

8 Amendment and cancellation of registrations

(1) Without prejudice to any other provisions of these Rules ...

(a) where a registered charge has been varied or modified or any registration is incorrect, the registering authority shall amend the registration accordingly;

(b) where a registered charge has been disclosed, ceased to have effect or ceased to be a charge, the registering authority shall cancel the registration.

[...]

10 Light obstruction notices

(1) An application under section 2(2) of the Rights of Light Act 1959 for registration of a light obstruction notice shall be in Form A and shall be accompanied by the certificate of the Lands Tribunal relating to the notice.

(2) On receiving the application and the certificate the registering authority shall file them and register the notice in accordance with rule 6.

(3) Where, after a temporary certificate has been filed and before the period for which it operates has expired a definitive certificate is lodged with the registering authority, they shall file the definitive certificate with the application and amend the registration accordingly.

(4) On receiving an office copy of a judgment or order directing the registration of a light obstruction notice to be varied or cancelled, the registering authority shall file the office copy with the application for that registration and shall amend or cancel the registration accordingly.

(5) The person on whose application the notice was registered, or any owner of the servient land or part of it who is a successor in title to that person, may within a year from the date of registration apply in Form B for—

(a) amendment of the registered particulars of the position or dimensions of the structure to which registration is intended to be equivalent, so as to reduce its height or length or to increase its distance from the dominant building; or
(b) cancellation of the registration;

and on receiving any such application the registering authority shall file it and amend or cancel the registration accordingly.

(6) Without prejudice to the preceding paragraphs of this rule, the registering authority shall cancel the registration of a notice—

(a) where in relation to the notice a temporary certificate has been filed and no definitive certificate has been filed, on the expiration of the period of operation specified in the temporary certificate;
(b) in any other case, on the expiration of 21 years from the date of registration;

and thereupon any document relating to the notice and filed pursuant to these Rules shall be taken off the file.

(7) In this rule 'definitive certificate' means a certificate issued by the Lands Tribunal under section 2(3)(a) of the Rights of Light Act 1959 and 'temporary certificate' means a certificate so issued under section 2(3)(b) of that Act; 'dominant building' and 'servient land' have the meanings assigned to them by section 2(1) of that Act; and 'owner' has the meaning assigned to it by section 7(1) of that Act.

11 Searches

(1) A person who wishes to make a personal search shall, if so requested by the registering authority, state his name and address and indicate the parcel of land in respect of which he wishes to search.

(2) Subject to Rule 16 (requisition and issue of official search certificates by electronic means) a requisition for an official search of the register and the official search certificate shall be in Form C.

(3) A separate personal search or (as the case may be) a separate requisition for an official search shall be made in respect of each parcel of land against which a search is required, except where for the purpose of a single transaction the search is required in respect of two or more parcels of land which have a common boundary or are separated only by a road, railway, river, stream or canal.

(4) Subject to Rule 16 (requisition and issue of official search certificates by electronic means) an official search certificate shall, where there are subsisting registrations, be accompanied by a schedule substantially in accordance with Schedule 2 (or such numbered parts of it as may be appropriate) showing the particulars of the registrations.

12 Office copies

On the written request of any person, and on payment of the prescribed fee, the registering authority shall supply an office copy of any registration or any document, map or plan deposited with or filed by that authority in connection with a registration.

13 Use of forms

Subject to Rule 16 (requisition and issue of official search certificates by electronic means) except for the purposes of schedules accompanying official search certificates in accordance with rule 11(4) above, no forms other than those supplied by Her Majesty's Stationery Office or, until the Lord Chancellor otherwise directs, clear and legible facsimiles of such forms may be used for the purposes of these Rules.

NOTE
As amended by Local Land Charges (Amendment) Rules 1978, SI 1978/1638 and 1995, SI 1995/260.

14 Fees

The fees specified in Schedule 3 shall be payable under the Act and every fee shall be paid in advance.

15 Transitional provisions

(1) Any application or requisition which—

(a) was sent to the registering authority before 1st August 1977;
(b) was not dealt with by the registering authority before that date;
(c) could have been made under these Rules if they had been in force;

shall be treated as an application or requisition under these Rules and shall be dealt with by the registering authority accordingly.

(2) As respects registrations subsisting on 31st July 1977, registering authorities shall not be bound to register or to disclose by an official certificate of search or otherwise any particulars the registration or disclosure of which could not be required by or under the Rules applicable on that date to such registrations.

(3) Notwithstanding the provisions of these Rules, the forms prescribed by the rules applicable on 31st July 1977 to charges may, until the Lord Chancellor otherwise directs, be used, with such adaptations as may be appropriate, for the purposes of these Rules.

16 Requisition and issue of office search certificates by electronic means

(1) A requisition for an official search of the register may be made by electronic means, notwithstanding section 231(1) of the Local Government Act 1972 (service of documents on local authorities), where the local authority to whom it is made consents to the use of those means.

(2) An official search certificate may be issued by electronic means where the person requiring the search consents to the use of those means.

(3) Where a requisition is made under paragraph (1), or a certificate issued under paragraph (2), all the information that would otherwise be required by these Rules to be set out in Form C shall be transmitted electronically together with—

- (a) in the case of a requisition, the name of the person making the requisition or his solicitor; or
- (b) in the case of a certificate, the name and office of the person certifying the search and the name of the registering authority.

(4) The signatures otherwise required by these Rules shall not be transmitted.

[...]

SCHEDULE 1

FORMS

Form A

APPLICATION FOR REGISTRATION OF
A LIGHT OBSTRUCTION NOTICE

[1]Delete inapplicable words.

[2]Insert description of servient land.

[3]Insert description of dominant building (wherever practicable, a map or plan of the building should be attached).

I, ... of ...., being the freehold owner *or* the tenant of a term of years of which over 7 years remain unexpired *or* the mortgagee in possession[1] of ....
....
....
....[2],
which is shown on the plan attached hereto, hereby apply to the ....Council for registration of this notice under section 2 of the Rights of Light Act 1959 against the building known as ....
....
....
....[3]

[4]Delete inappropriate words.

[5]Delete "of unlimited height" if inappropriate and insert description of height and other dimensions.

Registration of this notice is intended to be equivalent to the obstruction of the access of light to the said building across my land which would be caused by the erection of an opaque structure on all the boundaries of my land *or* in the position on my land marked on the attached plan[4] and of unlimited height
or ....
....
....
....
....[5]

Signed ....
Date ....

Form B

APPLICATION TO AMEND OR CANCEL A LIGHT OBSTRUCTION NOTICE WITH STATUTORY DECLARATION

Application

[1]Delete inapplicable words.

[2]Delete and insert as appropriate.

[3]If an amendment is required, give particulars; if a cancellation, delete sentence.

[4]Give names and addresses of persons indicated; if there are no such persons, delete sentence.

I, ... of ...., being the owner of the interest described below in the land known as ....
....
hereby apply for the amendment *or* the cancellation[1] of the light obstruction notice registered on my application *or* on the application of ....
of ....[2]
The amendment[3] which I require is ....
....
....
The consent to this application by the following persons, being persons who would be entitled to apply for the registration of a light obstruction notice, is attached: ....
....
....[4]

Signed ....
Date ....

Statutory Declaration

[1]Delete inapplicable words.

[2]Insert description of servient land.

[3]Delete and insert as appropriate.

[4]Insert if appropriate "apart from the persons named above."

I, ... of ...., solemnly and sincerely declare that:—

(*a*) I am the freehold owner *or* the tenant for a term of years of which over 7 years remain unexpired *or* the mortgagee in possession[1] of ....
....
....[2];

(*b*) the light obstruction notice referred to above was registered on my application *or* on the application of ....
....
of ....[3];

(*c*) there are no other persons who would be entitled to apply for the registration of a light obstruction notice ....
....[4]

And I make this solemn declaration, conscientiously believing the same to be true, by virtue of the Statutory Declarations Act 1835.

Declared by the said ....
at .... this day of
.... before me ....

A Commissioner for Oaths *or*
a practising solicitor.

Form C

REQUISITION FOR SEARCH AND OFFICIAL CERTIFICATE OF SEARCH

Requisition for Search

Official number ....

Name of registering authority ....

[1]Delete if inappropriate.

[2]Delete if inappropriate.

An official search is required in [[Part of][1] the register of local land charges kept by the above-named registering authority for subsisting registration against the land [defined in the attached plan and][2] described below:

....

....

....

....

Signature of applicant or his solicitor ....

Date ....

Official Certificate of Search

[3]Delete inappropriate words.

[4]Insert name of registering authority.

It is hereby certified that the search requested above reveals no subsisting registration *or* the registrations described in the Schedule hereto[3] up to and including the date of this certificate.

Signed ....

On behalf of ....[4]

Date ....

Part 11 of local land charges register: light obstruction notices
Rights of Light Act 1959, section 2(4)

Description of charge	Description of dominant building	Name and address of applicant and short description of his interest in servient land	Position and dimension of structure to which registration equivalent	Date of temporary Lands Tribunal certificate (if any) and of its expiration	Date of definitive Lands Tribunal certificate	List of documents filed	Date of registration
1	2	3	4	5	6	7	8

[**Author's note:** see rule 3]

SCHEDULE 3 – FEES

[Not reproduced.]

Appendix 3
Other Materials

MATERIALS ON THE CUSTOM OF LONDON

Hilary Term 30 Geo. 2.

Plummer versus Bentham.

Saturday, 12th February 1757.
If a custom of the city of London be put in issue,
it is triable by the mayor and aldermen,
certified at the bar of the court, *ore temùs,*
by the mouth of their recorder.

THE recorder of *London (Sir William Moreton)* came to the bar, and CERTIFIED TWO *customs* of that city ORE TENUS.

Mr. *Williams* moved (when Sir *William Moreton* was down at the bar,) that the *recorder of London* might return two writs of *certiorari* directed to the lord mayor and aldermen of *London,* to certify two of the customs of their city.

And then Mr. *Williams* opened the case, *viz.* That it was an action of trespass on the case brought by the plaintiff against the defendant, for *obstructing his ancient lights,* by a *new erection or building* which the defendant had raised against them: to which the defendant had (by leave) pleaded two justifications, both of them under the custom of the city of *London.* One of them was, that there is an ancient custom in the city of *London,* 'That if any person has a messusage or house in the city of *London,* adjoining or contiguous to another MESSUAGE OR HOUSE, or to the ancient *foundations of one* in the said city, which former house has *ancient lights or windows* fronting, opposite to, or over such other adjoining or contiguous MESSUAGE OR HOUSE, or ancient *foundation of one*; such *other* person, *owner of the* LATTER *message or house or ancient* foundation of one, may well and lawfully *exalt* such his *messuage or house,* or *rebuild upon the ancient foundations* of such his adjacent or contiguous MESSUAGE OR HOUSE any *new messuage or house,* to ANY HEIGHT *that he shall please, against and opposite to the said ancient lights and windows* of such first mentioned neighbouring messuage or house to which his *messuage or house* or ancient foundations of a *messuage or house* are so contiguous or adjoining; and *thereby darken and obscure* such ancient lights and windows of such first-mentioned neighbouring house, having such ancient lights and windows: unless there has been some writing, instrument, or record of an agreement or restriction to the contrary.'

On this plea issue was joined: and a *certiorari* issued, directed to the mayor and aldermen of the city of *London,* to certify 'whether they have or have not such a custom.'

The second plea, issue, and *certiorari,* were the same with the first, only with this difference or rather *extension* of the custom pleaded; *viz.*

'That the owner of any ERECTION OR BUILDING, or the ancient foundation of any ERECTION OR BUILDING, might well and lawfully exalt such ERECTION OR BUILDING, or erect and build thereon a new ERECTION OR BUILDING to any height that he pleases, &c.' and so on as in the former plea: only that the former plea confined the claim of the privilege to *messuages* or *houses*; which this latter plea extends to *all erections or buildings*.'

Sir *William Moreton* Knt. recorder of *London*, accordingly *certified* ORE TENUS, by command of the lord mayor and aldermen, (after having recited the pleadings and *certiorari*), 'That there *is* such a custom as is alleged in the *former* plea: but that there is NO such custom as is alleged in the latter plea.'

See the first case in Sir H. Calthrop's Reports (prettily reported and worth reading;) where the question was very like the present, and the determination agreeable to the certificate as to this first plea.

The recorder then delivered in both the writs of *certiorari*, with *written copies* of the respective returns annexed; though he had delivered them *ore tenùs* at the bar: (which, he told me, was usual.) The returns were worded as follows: *viz*. The execution of this writ appears in a certain certificte by us the mayor and aldermen of the said city of *London*, made by the recorder of the said city at the day and place within contained, according to the custom of the said city, by word of mouth, as is within commanded.

The Answer of Marshe Dickinson *Esq. the mayor, and of the aldermen of the said city.*

We the said mayor and aldermen of the said city, by Sir *William Morteon* Knt. Recorder of the said city, by word of mouth of the said recorder, according to the said custom of the said city, do, in obedience to the said annexed writ, humbly certify, that there is now had, and from the time whereof the memory of man is not to the contrary there hath been had and received such ancient and laudable custom in the said city used and approved; to wit, 'That if any one hath a messuage or house in the said city, near or contiguous and adjoining to *another ancient* MESSUAGE OR HOUSE, or to the ancient *foundation or another ancient* MESSUAGE OR HOUSE in the said city, *of another person his neighbour* there: and the windows or lights of *such messuage or house* are looking fronting or situate towards, upon, over, or against the said *other* ancient MESSUAGE OR HOUSE, or ancient *foundation* of such other ancient MESSUAGE OR HOUSE of such *other person his neighbour*, so being near, adjacent, contiguous, or adjoining, *although* such messuage or house, and the lights and windows thereof be or were *ancient*, YET such *other person his neighbour*, being the owner of such other MESSUAGE OR HOUSE or ancient *foundations* so being near, adjacent or adjoining, by and according to the custom of the said city in the same city for all the time aforesaid used and approved, *well and lawfully may*, might and hath used, at his will and pleasure, his *said other* MESSUAGE OR HOUSE so being near, adjacent or adjoining, by building *to exalt or erect*; or, of new, upon the ancient *foundations* of such *other* MESSUAGE OR HOUSE so being near, adjacent or adjoining, *to build and erect a new messuage or house* to SUCH HEIGHT AS THE SAID OWNER SHALL PLEASE, *against* and *opposite* to the said *lights and windows* near or contiguous to such OTHER MESSUAGE OR HOUSE, and by means thereof TO OBSCURE AND DARKEN such windows or lights: unless there be or hath been some writing, instrument or record of an agreement or restriction to the contrary thereof in that behalf.'

The return to the other writ of *certiorari* was in the same form, and to the very same effect as to the custom certified by the former; and repeated the return to the former *certiorari in totidem verbis*, very nearly: but it went on further, with a *negation* of the existence of any such custom as the defendant had alledged in his *second* justification. The additional part was as follows.

And that in the said city of *London* there is not now or ever was any *such* custom, 'That if any one hath a messuage or house in the said city, near or contiguous and adjoining to an ERECTION *or* BUILDING, or to the ancient foundations of an ERECTION *or* BUILDING in the said city, of another person his neighbour there; and the windows or lights of such messuage or house are looking fronting or situate towards, upon, over, or against such ERECTION *or* BUILDING, or the ancient foundations of such ERECTION *or* BUILDING of such other person his neighbour so being near, adjacent, contiguous or adjoining; although such messuage or house and the lights and windows thereof be or were ancient, yet such other person his neighbour, being the owner of such ERECTION *or* BUILDING, *or ancient* foundations of such ERECTION *or* BUILDING so being near, adjacent or adjoining, by and according to the custom of the said city in the same city for all the time aforesaid used and approved, well and lawfully may, might, and hath used, at his will and pleasure, his said ERECTION *or* BUILDING so being adjacent or adjoining, by building to *exalt and erect*; or, of new, upon the ancient foundations of the said ERECTION OR BUILDING so being near, adjacent or adjoining to build and erect a *new erection or building* to SUCH HEIGHT *as the owner shall please* against and opposite to the said lights and windows of such messuage or house, and by means thereof to obscure and darken such windows or lights.'

The Court ordered the certiorari to be filed, and the *return* RECORDED.

Note—Nothing of this kind has actually happened for many years past (not even since *H*. the sixth's reign,) in *this* Court; (though it has in the Court of Chancery.) And a consultation was had in the city concerning the sort of gown which it was proper for the recorder to put on, to make his *ore tenùs* return: in which consultation it was determined that it ought to be the purple cloth robe, faced with black velvet: and not his scarlet gown, his black silk one, nor the common bar-gown.

REPORT OF THE COMMITTEE ON THE LAW RELATING TO RIGHTS OF LIGHT

(extract)

To the Right Honourable the Viscount KILMUIR,
Lord High Chancellor of Great Britain.

MY LORD,

We were appointed on the 29th March, 1957, to advise you whether legislation is desirable—

(1) to amend the law relating to rights of light in relation to war-damaged sites or sites whose development was prevented or impeded by reason of restrictions or controls imposed during or after the late war; and
(2) to preserve rights of light acquired or in process of acquisition by buildings which subsequently suffered war damage.

2. At an early stage in our deliberations we became aware that planning legislation of recent decades has altered to a very significant degree the position of owners of land or buildings over which rights of light may be acquired. The impact of these changes in the law of light, which does not hitherto appear to have been widely appreciated, is universal and not confined to war-damaged sites or sites prejudiced in their development as a result of the war. We therefore sought an extension of our terms of reference which would enable us to consider the wider problems which arise, and were invited by you in December, 1957, to consider also—

> 'Whether any alterations are desirable in the law and practice relating to the means whereby the acquisition of rights of light over any land may be prevented.'

3. We held seven meetings and were assisted by written and oral evidence from the various persons and bodies whose names are set out in the Appendix to this Report. We express our thanks and appreciation to all of them.

The practical extent of the problem

4. It is evident that the value of a site can be greatly reduced if, by lapse of time, neighbouring buildings acquire rights of light over it. If the opportunities of acquiring such rights are afforded by circumstances outside the control of the owner, as in war, or if factors not of his choosing prevent him from protecting himself against the acquisition of such rights, the owner has *prima facie* a moral claim to relief. Owners of sites of the classes defined in our terms of reference fall within this category. But legislation for hard cases may easily make bad law. Hence, before examining possible forms of relief, we have thought it necessary to satisfy ourselves that the need for a remedy in the cases to which our enquiry relates is a real one. Not only has a decade now passed since the end of the war, during which much destroyed property has been rebuilt, but it has also been suggested to us that present day planning legislation leaves so little room for the operation of the old established law on rights of light that the need for measures in support of such rights has disappeared.

5. The evidence we have received, particularly from the Royal Institution of Chartered Surveyors and the Law Society, convinces us that there remain to this day numbers of sites, empty since before the war or damaged in the war, on which the erection of buildings will before long be seriously hampered by adverse rights of light. Indeed in some cases which were brought to our notice adverse rights have already accrued. Difficulties are

likely to be experienced primarily in densely built-up areas, amongst which the City of London and such towns as Bristol and Manchester may prove to be particularly affected. It is impossible to estimate the number of properties involved, but we are satisfied on the evidence before us that the potential loss in individual cases is so substantial that it would call for a remedy even if the total numbers proved to be few.

6. It is true that planning legislation has had a considerable impact on rights of light, but it has not superseded the ordinary law. We have been given examples where legal rights to light over a site could prevent the erection of buildings for which planning permission would be readily granted. The standards of daylighting applied by local planning authorities, whether evolved by the authorities themselves or based on the guidance about daylighting given in the advisory handbook on the Redevelopment of Central Areas issued by the Ministry of Town and Country Planning in 1946, may not in all circumstances recommend a flow of light equal to that which the owner of a building can claim at law; and there may well be instances where even the complete obstruction of light would not conflict with high standards of town planning.

We have accordingly reached the conclusion that there is a real practical problem calling for a remedy.

The right to light

7. In order to ascertain the exact nature of the problems facing owners and occupiers of war-damaged and vacant sites, it may perhaps be useful briefly to summarize the present law in relation to the right of light. This right is not a natural right of property, but an easement; it cannot appertain to open land, nor even to buildings as such, but only to apertures in buildings, and it exists only in those cases in which it has been acquired by one or other of the means which the law recognises for the acquisition of easements.

8. An easement must be an advantage to a dominant tenement and a burden on a servient tenement. It may be acquired either by express or implied grant or by long enjoyment. There are three ways in which long enjoyment can create an easement, *viz.*, by prescription at common law, under the doctrine of lost grant, and by prescription under the Prescription Act, 1832. We are not concerned with cases of express or implied grant, and prescription at common law is in this sphere of no practical significance. Rights of light can be acquired under the doctrine of lost grant, but such cases are rare. In practice, the normal mode of acquiring an easement of light is under the Prescription Act, 1832.

Prescription Act, 1832, section 3

9. The easement of light is treated separately from all other easements by section 3 of the Act, which is as follows:

> 'When the access and use of light to and for any dwelling house, workshop, or other building shall have been actually enjoyed therewith for the full period of twenty years without interruption, the right thereto shall be deemed absolute and indefeasible, any local usage or custom to the contrary notwithstanding, unless it shall appear that the same was enjoyed by some consent or agreement expressly made or given for that purpose by deed or writing'.

10. Section 3 must be read with section 4, which provides that any period specified in the Act is to be the period 'next before some suit or action wherein the claim or matter to which such period may relate shall . . . be brought into question.' and that nothing 'should be deemed to be an interruption . . . unless the same shall . . . be submitted to or acquiesced

in for one year after the party interrupted shall . . . have notice thereof . . .'. It follows that, since an interruption lasting less than a year does not stop the running of time, an easement of light can be acquired under the Act by actual enjoyment (not under a written consent) for nineteen years and one day. But since this period must immediately precede action brought, the right under the Act may still be lost by one year's interruption occurring at any time later than the original period of nineteen years and a day. Hence the statutory right is, strictly speaking, inchoate in every case in which it has not been brought in issue in an action. On the other hand, where there has been enjoyment for upwards of nineteen years, followed by an interruption for more than one year but not for long enough to lead to the inference that the right has been abandoned, the court would be inclined to uphold the right under the doctrine of lost grant. This, we think, is the only practical relevance of that doctrine to the subject of our inquiry.

The right to light is a negative easement

11. An easement may be either positive or negative. A positive easement entitles the dominant owner to do something upon the land of the servient owner; in terms of pleading, a positive easement affords to the dominant owner a defence to the servient owner's action for trespass. A negative easement merely entitles the dominant owner to restrain the servient owner from doing on the servient land something which interferes with the enjoyment of the easement; in terms of pleading, a negative easement gives the dominant owner an action for nuisance against a servient owner who fails to observe it.

12. This distinction has important practical consequences. A person who is in process of acquiring a positive easement (eg a right of way) by long enjoyment must throughout the prescriptive period go on the servient tenement as a trespasser. It is only when time has fully run that he acquires the positive easement and so is protected by the defence which it affords. At all earlier times the servient owner can sue successfully for trespass; he will normally obtain an injunction which will effectively interrupt the running of time. But a period who is in process of acquiring a negative easement (eg a right to light) by long enjoyment never trespasses on the servient tenement at all; he merely enjoys the access of light to his holding across the servient tenement. There is no process of law by which the owner of the prospective servient tenement can compel the prospective dominant owner to interrupt his enjoyment, and so protect the prospective servient tenement against the acquisition of a negative easement. In some cases, no doubt, the prospective dominant owner can be persuaded to accept a deed or written agreement granting him consent for the passage of light over the grantor's premises; if so, time will not run at all, because of the concluding words of section 3 of the Prescription Act. But the prospective servient owner's only weapon in negotiation for such an agreement is to threaten physically to interrupt the access of light to his neighbour's building; and, if the threat does not succeed, his only remedy is actually to bring about such an interruption.

Interruption of the access of light: planning legislation

13. Of course, if the owner of the servient tenement can erect buildings on his land before the dominant owner's right to light has accrued, he does not need to take prior preventive action. But, for various reasons it is not always practicable or desirable to do so at the time when it becomes necessary or expedient to interrupt the flow of light to the dominant tenement. The conventional remedy has therefore been to erect a screen on the prospective servient tenement. The cost of doing so has been some check upon frivolous interruptions; nevertheless the remedy is a crude one and its results are unsightly.

14. The conventional remedy has, however, ceased to exist as of right. Early in the war which started on 3rd September, 1939, controls were imposed on building operations and on the use of timber and other materials, which in practice made it impossible to erect a screen. Those difficulties were, no doubt, of a transient kind. But from 1st July, 1948, there has been a permanent change, in that it has been necessary, under the Town and Country Planning Act, 1947, to obtain planning permission for all development, a term which is so defined as to include the erection of a screen. We have been informed of cases in which a planning authority has refused permission for a screen. In some cases development of this kind has been allowed on appeal by the Minister of Housing and Local Government who, we are informed, in reaching his decision took account of the fact that the object of erecting the screen was to prevent the acquisition of a right of light. Nevertheless, the present position is unsatisfactory. On the one hand, we do not think that Parliament can have intended, in enacting the Town and Country Planning Act, 1947, to make precarious the time-honoured remedy of erecting a screen to interrupt the access of light and so prevent the acquisition of an easement. On the other hand, a screen erected for such a purpose is at best unsightly, uses up labour and materials which might with advantage be put to more productive purposes, and, since it is in no one's interest to spend money on its maintenance once it has stood for a year, it is calculated to deteriorate progressively. We do not think that in these days the planning authorities or the Minister should be expected to permit such an affront. It appears to us to be desirable to devise a scheme by which a statutory notice may be given having the like legal effect as the actual erection of a screen. That is to say, the giving of the notice should be treated as an interruption of the access of light both for the purposes of the Prescription Act, 1832, and at common law.

[...]

War damage to the dominant tenement

19. So far in this Report we have been concerned mainly with the position of servient owners needing protection against adverse rights of light. But we were also invited to consider whether a dominant owner, namely the owner of a building which had acquired rights of light or was in process of doing so, should be protected against any loss of his rights which might otherwise result from its subsequent destruction. In our opinion no such protection is necessary. A subsisting right to light is lost only by express release or abandonment. Abandonment is a matter of inference and intention, and it is manifest that a person whose building is demolished by the enemy does not *ipso facto* abandon his right to light. He may have difficulty in proving exactly what his rights were, if there are no plans or drawings of the old building; but no change in the law could supply that deficiency. The time will, no doubt, come when the owner's prolonged failure to rebuild could induce the court to infer that he has abandoned his right; but in considering the question of abandonment we do not think that the court would hold it against him that he failed to rebuild while building restrictions were in force.

20. Different considerations apply to buildings which have been demolished while they were in the process of acquiring rights of light, for destruction of the building will have put an end to the running of time. In our opinion it would not be right now to revive such embryonic rights; they might never have matured even if the building had survived. Furthermore as rights of light must be claimed in respect of specific apertures in buildings, legislation to revive such rights would probably be neither useful nor effective. For it is improbable that the exact extent of the former rights could now be established, or, if it could, that the old building would be replaced by one whose windows and dimensions would enable the former rights to be reclaimed.

General conclusions

21. Our general conclusions therefore are—

(i) that the present system, by which a prospective servient owner can protect his land only by the erection of a screen, is unsatisfactory, and that he should be enabled instead to serve a statutory notice having the like effect (paragraphs 13 and 14);
(ii) that in computing the period of prescription under section 3 of the Act of 1832, and in applying the doctrine of lost grant in cases of light, some allowance ought to be made, in favour of the prospective servient owner, for the period during which there were serious restrictions on building operations (paragraphs 15 to 17);
(iii) that it is not desirable to legislate for the preservation of rights of light acquired by buildings which later suffered war damage or of rights in process of acquisition by such buildings (paragraphs 19 and 20).

We now turn to consider the best means to give effect to our general conclusions.

Statutory notice in lieu of screen

22. The erection of a screen was a troublesome and expensive matter, but once it was erected there was little doubt that all those concerned to know of the interruption did know of it. Any system of registration in lieu of physical obstruction must not, in our view, be so easy or cheap as to encourage notices that are frivolous or worse, and it must contain full safeguards that all interested parties do in fact know of the notice.

23. We recommend that, by registering a statutory notice against a prospective dominant building, the prospective servient owner should be able to bring about the like legal consequences as at present flow from the erection of a screen. The consequences of a registration which remains on the register for the requisite period (as suggested in the next paragraph) should be that there will be a break in the runnning of time for the purposes of acquiring an easement of light under the Prescription Act, 1832, and that in proceedings at common law the fact that the notice has been registered and has not been removed from the register is to be taken into account by the court in considering whether an easement of light has been acquired by prescription at common law or under the doctrine of lost grant, or whether an easement already existing has been abandoned. The notice should adequately identify the servient owner's site, reference being made in appropriate cases to a plan attached to the notice; and registration should be treated as a notional obstruction of the light of the dominant building by a screen, erected on the boundaries of that site, either of unlimited height or of such limited height as the notice may specify.

Registration of notice

24. The notice should be registered, provisionally in the first place, in the register of local land charges and should take effect (subject as mentioned below) as if the access of light from the neighbouring property had been interrupted on the date of the registration. Unless the notice is taken off the register, as explained in paragraph 31 below, the notional obstruction should be treated as having begun at the date of registration. After the notice has been registered for one year, the obstruction should be treated as having been submitted to or acquiesced in for one year after registration by all persons interested in the property against which the registration is made.

25. We suggest one year as an appropriate period of notional obstruction, because that is the minimum period required under section 4 of the Prescription Act to effect a break in the running of the period of prescription. No building in fact exists on the servient

owner's site and the fiction of its existence should not be maintained for longer than is necessary. If the notional obstruction endures for one year, the servient owner will have twenty years before the period of prescription has run against him once more, which should be ample time to carry out his building projects. It follows, of course, that the notice should remain on the register for twenty years from the date of registration.

26. The registration should, in our opinion, be in a local land charges register and not in one of the central registers, because it is essential that the charge should be registered against potentially dominant premises identified by their site and that the register should be open to inspection by all interested parties. These requirements are partially satisfied in the case of the Land Registry where charges on registered land are entered, but not in the case of the central Land Charges Register which deals with unregistered land and operates by reference to names of owners and not by reference to a map. On the other hand the system of registration in local land charges registers fulfils all the requirements.

Notification of registration

27. As the notional interruption of the access of light will start on the date of provisional registration, it is necessary that notice should in fact be given to all interested persons who are likely to be affected by it and that it should be given within so short a time after that registration as to give them plenty of time in which to challenge the notional interruption before it has subsisted for a year. For a notice acquiesced in for a year will be fatal to any claims under the Prescription act, 1832, by persons interested in the property against which the notice is registered.

28. The giving of notice should be too widespread rather than too chary and cannot, in our opinion, be left without judicial supervision to the person serving the statutory notice. A somewhat similar need has for a generation existed in respect of notice of proceedings under subsection (1) of section 84 of the Law of Property Act, 1925, for the modification or removal by the Lands Tribunal of a covenant restrictive of the use of land. In the Lands Tribunal the procedure, governed by Rule 21 of the Lands Tribunal Rules, 1956, is that the Registrar arranges before the hearing for the necessary notices to be given, subject to reference to the President in cases of difficulty. This is, we understand, a simple and informal procedure and is in most cases carried through by correspondence. The notices are given to any neighbours who are near enough to be likely to be affected, and public notices are given in the local newspapers and by being posted on the site affected by the restrictions which it is sought to modify or remove. We suggest that a similar procedure should be adopted and that the judicial supervision of the notices should be vested in the Lands Tribunal. It will be a matter of internal organisation how far these cases are dealt with by a member of the Tribunal or by the Registrar; but we should expect them normally to be in the hands of the Registrar, at least when the system is fully under way.

29. Having provisionally registered his notice, the prospective servient owner would next apply to the Lands Tribunal for directions. He would attach a copy of his notice (including the identification of his own site) and a plan indicating clearly the property against which the notice has been registered. The Tribunal would then issue directions as to service, designed to ensure that all persons whose interests in the properties concerned are likely to be affected will receive due notice of the proposed notional obstruction. As soon as the tribunal has been satisfied that its directions as to service have been carried out, it would issue a certificate to that effect, and on the filing of this certificate in the register of local land charges the provisional notice would become definitive with effect from the date of original registration.

30. In order to ensure that all interested persons receive notice quickly, leaving them plenty of time to assert their rights before a year has expired, we also recommend that the provisional notice should cease to have any validity unless the Lands Tribunal's certificate is filed by the end of three months from the date of provisional registration. There should be provision for an extension of the time limit by order of the court, provided application for the order is made within the three months, but no power of extension should be conferred upon the Lands Tribunal.

Variation or cancellation of registration

31. A person who receives a notice given under the directions of the Lands Tribunal, or who otherwise learns of the registration, and who claims to be entitled to object to the notional obstruction, should be free to bring an action for a declaration that the obstruction infringes his rights and for an injunction against its continuance. The court should be given power in such an action to make any order that it sees fit for the variation or cancellation of the entries in the register of local land charges. It would be of assistance to the parties concerned if rules of court could also provide a more summary method of taking the court's opinion on the right of the person serving the statutory notice to interrupt the flow of light to his neighbour's premises. In a simple case application might, for instance, be made to the Chancery Division of the High Court by originating motion for a declaration as to the parties' rights, a simple and expeditious form of proceeding. We do not contemplate that the Lands Tribunal should receive or consider any objections that may be made to the notional obstructions: such objections will normally raise questions of title, which are a matter for the court. The Lands Tribunal's only functions would be to ensure that the notices receive all necessary publicity among persons likely to be interested and to issue its certificate within the prescribed time.

[...]

Summary of recommendations

37. Our recommendations may be summarised as follows—

- (i) A prospective servient owner should be able to bring about the consequences which at present flow from the erection of a screen by registering a statutory notice against a prospective dominant building (paras 14 and 23).
- (ii) The statutory notice should have the same effect as a screen erected on the boundary of the servient owner's land and maintained there for one year (paras 23 to 25).
- (iii) The statutory notice should be registered in a register of local land charges and the registration published under directions to be given by the Lands Tribunal. Registration should cease to have effect unless the Lands Tribunal certifies within three months (or such extended period as the court may allow) from the original date of registration that it has been duly publicised (paras 26 to 30).
- (iv) Objections to the notional obstruction should be raised by proceedings in the court, which should have power to make any order it sees fit for the variation or cancellation of the restriction (para 31).
- (v) The twenty year period for the prescriptive acquisition of rights of light under the Prescription Act, 1832, should be extended to 27 years for the purposes of any action either asserting a claim to rights of light and started after the date of publication of this Report and before the 31st December, 1962, or brought in respect of an actual or notional interruption effected between those dates (paras 33 and 34).

(vi) We do not recommend any legislation for the preservation of rights of light acquired by buildings which later suffered war damage or of rights in process of acquisition by such buildings (paras 19 and 20).

CHARLES HARMAN, *Chairman*,
GUY BISCOE,
PERCY V. BURNETT,
JOHN CATLOW,
J. C. CRAIG,
ARTHUR J. DRIVER,
G. H. NEWSOM.

K. M. NEWMAN, *Secretary*,
12th May, 1958.

Index

References are to paragraph numbers and Appendix numbers.